AF449171

FROM *THE RUSSIAN FUGITIVE* TO *THE BALLAD OF BULGARIE*

From *The Russian Fugitive* to *The Ballad of Bulgarie*

Episodes in English Literary Attitudes to Russia from Wordsworth to Swinburne

Patrick Waddington

BERG

Oxford/Providence, USA

First published in 1994 by

Berg Publishers Limited

Editorial offices:
150 Cowley Road, Oxford, OX4 1JJ, UK
221 Waterman Street, Providence, RI 02906, USA

Library of Congress Cataloging-in-Publication Data
A catalogue record for this book is available from the Library of Congress.

British Library Cataloguing in Publication Data
A catalogue record for this book is available from the British Library.

ISBN 0 85496 860 1

Printed and bound by WBC, Bridgend, Mid Glam.

CONTENTS

PREFACE

This book is not a systematic survey of the reception of things Russian by English writers in the period chosen. It restricts itself to poets. But even here it is selective, for to be complete it would need to include dozens of minor figures of contemporary importance as well as full coverage of great poets not here dealt with separately, such as Byron and Southey, not to speak of some who were not English at all, like Thomas Moore or Sir Walter Scott. One good reason for omitting most of these is that they have already been exceptionally well treated by the late doyen of the field, Mikhail Pavlovich Alekseev, in *Russko-angliiskie literaturnye sviazi (XVIII vek-pervaia polovina XIX veka)* (Russo-English Literary Connections in the 18th Century and First Half of the 19th Century). Published in Moscow in 1982, this incorporates among other things long essays on Byron, Moore and Scott in relation to Russian authors, scholars, travellers, statesmen and society generally. Its importance, readability and scholarly weight cannot be overestimated. It is, of course, inaccessible to those who have no Russian, but to match its treatment of the poets named would be impossible. The same holds for the general background to Anglo-Russian literary relations up to and during the early part of my chosen period, splendidly covered in the opening chapters of Alekseev's miscellany. Here, however, other books spring to mind, for example Dorothy Brewster's pioneering study *East-West Passage* (1954), and several works by Professor A.G. Cross including *The Russian Theme in English Literature from the Sixteenth Century to 1980: An Introductory Survey and a Bibliography* (1985). As far as actual poems on Russian subjects are concerned, there exists an excellent anthology entitled *Russia* (1878) in Henry Wadsworth Longfellow's serial publication *Poems of Places*; this contains pieces by Thomson, Cowper, Campbell, Wordsworth, Southey, Tennyson and many others, English and American, including Longfellow himself. I have not attempted to repeat the ground covered by these or any other relevant works, but rather to set in context the Russian themes in some of the finest and most characteristic English poets of the nineteenth century: Wordsworth, Tennyson, Robert Browning and Swinburne. I had hoped also to include the Rossettis, but considerations of space precluded this; it must, besides, be admitted that in relation to Russia only the least famous of them, William Michael, contributed a significant body of poetry. I now intend to treat the Rossettis in a separate short study.

My task has naturally entailed more than a modicum of politics and international affairs, since a large part of the appeal of Russia to these chosen poets had to do with grand historical events or Anglo-Russian rivalry. Here again, I have been greatly indebted to numerous historical studies and to contemporary newspaper reports, as well, of course, as to the letters and other personal writings of the authors in question. Among the better general accounts of Britain's relations with Russia over the centuries are Edward Crankshaw's *Russia and Britain* (1943) and K.W.B. Middleton's *Britain and Russia: An Historical Essay* (1947). Neither is very original and neither, of course, is recent, but both were written at a period when the two countries were close and their relations could be described with some sincerity and warmth. A little later John Howes Gleason produced a fine monograph which retains great force today: *The Genesis of Russophobia in Great Britain* (1950). Subtitled *A Study of the Interaction of Policy and Opinion*, this well-researched telescopic work conducted from the distance of America shows how and why Russia and England so often and so nearly came to blows — and just occasionally did.

The nineteenth century saw a great quickening of British interest in things Russian. Before it lay spasmodic curiosity about Muscovy and Muscovites; after it would come a flood of knowledge, often frightening or contradictory, about the land of revolution and the Soviets. Russia emerged dramatically as a full European partner during the Napoleonic Wars, was felt increasingly by England as a rival, had become the enemy by the time of the Crimean War, and during the late 1870s and beyond appeared to threaten British interests at every point of natural conflict from Greece and Turkey to India, Afghanistan, and the Far East. There was a 'Russian scare' even in remote New Zealand. The changing British attitudes to Russia could be approached from many different angles: historical, political, cultural, sociological, axetogrindical. They might perhaps be traced most simply through the popular and learned press. But the impact of Russia on English writers, especially on the more sensitive poets, is particularly striking and intriguing. These eminent Victorians were makers of public or critical opinion. Though not all actually laureates (two were), they perceived a need to make comment on national and international morality. France was one obvious recurring subject for their musings, but Russia was increasingly another. In their various ways they showed curiosity, detachment, anger and contempt in relation to Imperial Russian motives and ambitions.

My presentation of the poets is both separate and chronological. This procedure obviates distortion of each author's life and work in relation to the historical background, but I am painfully aware that it can also imply repetition: key events like the Crimean War need to come up time and again. But to have linked all the writers in a single historical chain would at best have been confusing and at worst chaotic. There seemed no sense in integrating, say, late Wordsworth with early Tennyson or late Tennyson with Swinburne. Contrasts and comparisons could and did present themselves from time to time, but for the most part the poets worked too much in isolation for these to be of importance. More interesting was the manner in which each writer in turn drew from, or rejected, the common stock of English attitudes to Russia. This book is therefore an analysis of some individual poets' reactions to political, social and cultural events in Russia: it comprises significant episodes, not a consecutive chronicle. I must point out finally that although my subject is obviously not the reception of English poets in Russia, this can sometimes impinge upon their contemporary importance — as also of course upon their own understanding of Russian civilisation. Information on it is therefore discussed from time to time.

I offer here the fruit of research which has extended over two decades. Parts of it, the chapters on Tennyson and Browning, are adapted but considerably expanded from earlier short monographs published respectively by the Tennyson Research Centre at Lincoln and the Armstrong Browning Library at Waco, Texas. I acknowledge the generous help of these institutions, as also of the Wordsworth Trust at Dove Cottage, the British Library, the Public Record Office, Cambridge University Library, Trinity College Library, the Rothschild Archives, the National Library of Scotland, the Bibliothèque Nationale, the Russian Academy of Sciences, the Library of Congress, the Huntington Library, the Harry Ransom Humanities Research Center of the University of Texas at Austin, and *Punch* and the *Spectator* of London through their respective archivists Amanda Doran and Charles Seaton. I have received invaluable practical help and encouragement from a host of librarians in three continents, but especially from Cambridge's Nicholas Smith and Nicola Thwaite, and from Victoria University's Dorothy Freed, Celia Dunlop, Diane Hadley, Barbro Harris and others. In common with my former colleagues in the Department of Russian at Victoria University of Wellington, New Zealand (transmogrified now, alas, into a mere section of a 'School'), I benefited beyond measure from a sequence of efficient, ever cheerful and constantly informative secretaries — Joanna Pohl, Irene Hughes and Veronika Romankin-Arndt.

My thanks are due to many other people who have helped me with this book, of whom I shall now single out some at peril of forgetting others. I must mention first a number of research students or assistants, some generously financed by Victoria University's Internal Grants Committee or by the Provisional Employment Programme of a once remarkably enlightened New Zealand government. These included Colin Bevan, Michelle Donovan, Peter Simpson, Milan Melnichenko, Ian James, Anthony Ahkit, and especially the following: Wayne Nelson, Susan Wauchop, Chin Wen, Barbara Mills and Hilary Chapman. But my research has been most helped and inspired by the wisdom of various colleagues, scholars and friends in language and literature including Don McKenzie, Ian Gordon, Harry Orsman, Geraldine Atkinson, John Davidson, Peter Norrish, André Le Cesne, Michèle Beaulieu, Georges Lubin, Stuart Young, Stephen Marder, Roger Bartlett, John Goodliffe, Nicholas Žekulin, Paul Dukes, April Fitz-Lyon, Ian Campbell, Scott Lewis, and in particular: Jack Herring, Betty Coley, Cecil Lang, Dick Fredeman, Philip Kelley, John Simmons, Richard Freeborn, Marcus Wheeler, the late Barry Hollingsworth and the late M.P. Alekseev. Especial gratitude is due to my life-long associate and friend Tony Cross, the series editor, for commissioning, encouraging, and helping to guide this project through the press. I warmly thank Kim Gutchlag for her caring support in the last stages of its very long gestation. And finally I must record a quarter-century's debt to Madeleine Waddington-Le Jeune, whose fearless mind and sharp wit may have helped to make my writing less dull than it would surely otherwise have been. I dedicate the book to our daughters, Marian, Emma and Claire.

Patrick Waddington
Wellington, New Zealand
28 June 1994

INTRODUCTION

In September 1849, at Rydal Mount near Grasmere, a ginger-headed Eton schoolboy talked of poetry with England's laureate and wept when leaving him.[1] The one was born in 1770; the other died in 1909. The entire nineteenth century — and more — is spanned by the careers of William Wordsworth and Algernon Charles Swinburne. During this time Britain came to be Europe's leading power, but only at the cost of increased insularity and imperialism. Rival nations were not easily tolerated and were looked at with growing suspicion. The Russian empire in particular was achieving a parallel but different rise from that of Britain and in some respects had already outstripped it in the later stages of the period. An increasing interest in, involvement with, and detestation and fear of Russia was apparent among the British. They can be seen hinted at in many novels of the time, as well of course as in travel books and other works of non-fiction, but it was the great poets whose Russian or related subjects perhaps best reflected changing national moods. Between the unpolitical curiosity of Wordsworth in his *Russian Fugitive* and Swinburne's blatant anti-Russian stand in *The Ballad of Bulgarie* and beyond lies a graduated development that matches fluctuating policy and attitudes in Britain.

Anglo-Russian cultural and political ties have become significant only in relatively recent times. Relations between Anglo-Saxon England and the early Russian principalities, strong as they undoubtedly were, are difficult to document with accuracy. Medieval historians indulged in much wishful fantasy. The legendary King Arthur's 'Easterly bounds' were supposedly set 'even unto Russia'.[2] The sons of Eadmund Ironside, Eadmund and Eadward, are said to have sought refuge in Kiev after their father's defeat by Canute in 1016, but other sources maintain they went to Hungary. Similarly, the Harold who fell to William the Conqueror in 1066 was once thought to have married Elizaveta, daughter of Iaroslav the Wise of Kiev, and his daughter Gytha to have fled to Russia to become the wife of Vladimir Monomakh and have offspring by him who, after his death, ruled over Kiev for a while before it went into terminal decline. 'Wherefore' (one reads in a chronicle) 'the English blood on the one side and the Russian on the other side concurring to the joyfull birth of our prince, caused that mutual kinred to be an ornament unto both nations.'[3] However, the dates of all this information, when examined closely, do not match: Harold cannot have espoused Elizaveta, and the person here called Gytha would have needed to be his granddaughter. More probable accounts assert, for example, that the Harold who married Elizaveta was a Nordic prince and minstrel, killed indeed at Hastings but beside and not inside his famous counterpart, or else that she was the wife of Harold Hardrada, king of Norway.[4]

Certainly some English people did find their way to Russia from a very early period, whether for military or commercial purposes. References to Russia and things Russian start to appear in literature from at least the fourteenth century. In the Prologue to the *Canterbury Tales* (begun about 1386), Chaucer introduced his very first character as a Knight who had fought and travelled more widely than any other Christian man:

> In Lettow hadde he reysed and in Ruce

— where 'Ruce' represents the old name of Russia (that is, *Rus'*) and 'Lettow' is an antecedent of Lithuania and Latvia.[5] Similarly, the Squire's Tale opens 'in the land of Tartarye', where once[6]

> Ther dwelte a kyng that werryed Russye.

Clearly there was already much curiosity in England about this variously-named land. But although trade links had become quite important by the fourteenth and fifteenth centuries, especially between London and Novgorod via the Hanseatic ports, Anglo-Russian relations did not really burgeon until the middle of the sixteenth century.

The date most often cited in this regard is 1553. In that year Richard Chancellor discovered by chance a route into Russia through the White Sea and the Northern Dvina, near modern Arkhangelsk. He pushed on by land and river as far as Moscow, where Ivan the Terrible received him cordially. In 1555 he went back to Russia on a more formal mission, and brought out with him Russia's first ambassador to Britain, Osip Grigor'evich Nepeia (customarily known in English as Napea or Nepea). On the way home Chancellor was shipwrecked in Scotland and perished, but Nepeia escaped and established himself in London.[7] In 1557 he was conveyed back to Russia by Anthony Jenkinson, who himself undertook a voyage of discovery there. His own and his colleagues' observations on the life and customs of the Muscovites were not exactly complimentary. Among the things objected to were certain matrimonial arrangements. 'When there is loue betweene the parties', the travellers recorded, 'the man sendeth vnto the woman a small chest or boxe, wherein is a whippe, needles, thred, silke, linnen cloth, sheres, & such necessaries as she shall occupy when she is a wife'. The Englishmen did not demur at the implied domestic thraldom, but explained that the Russian bride was also meant 'to vnderstand that if she doe offend she must be beaten with the whippe'. It was, however, further noted that 'if the woman be not beaten with the whippe once a weeke, she will not be good, and therefore they looke for it orderly'.[8]

Contacts between England and Russia now multiplied, in a great flurry of activity. The Muscovy Company was formed, introducing fashionable London society not only to fine Siberian furs but also to 'Muscovy glass' (actually sliced transparent rock), which remained in vogue for some years.[9] Keen interest was shown in the cold and cruel country of the bears, and even the Russian language became a subject of curiosity. Queen Elizabeth I herself is reported to have encouraged its circulation at her court, claiming she 'could quickly learn it' to show how.[10] One who rapidly did so was the merchant Jerome Horsey who, together with Her Majesty's ambassador Giles Fletcher, was successful in negotiating rights for the safety and satisfaction of English traders in Russia in defiance of the most improbable, horrific inconveniences to himself. As one historian has remarked, Horsey may well have survived all the would-be poisonings and plagues thanks to his self-professed mastery of the Muscovites' 'vulgar speach, the Sclavonian tonge, the most copius and elegent language in the world'.[11] Giles Fletcher's own authoritative work on his experiences in Russia, *Of the Russe Common Wealth* (1591), is less sensational no doubt but also more varied and rewarding. It is the earliest of a long line of distinguished studies of that country undertaken by Englishmen, being followed most closely by *Sir Thomas Smithes Voiage and Entertainment in Rushia* (1605).

English travellers were now taking in Russia almost as a matter of routine (though usually for expected profit), and already by the end of the sixteenth century Richard Hakluyt had recorded their adventures in two editions of his book *The Principall Nauigations, Voiages, and Discoueries of the English Nation, made by Sea or ouer Land, to the most remote and farthest distant Quarters of the Earth, at any time within the compasse of these 1500 yeeres...* (one volume, 1589, and three volumes with slightly altered title, 1598-1600). Hakluyt's great endeavour was later continued by Samuel Purchas in *Hakluytus Posthumus; or, Purchase his Pilgrimes, contayning a History of the World in Sea Voyages and Lande Trauells by Englishmen and Others...* (4 volumes, 1625), which extracted among many other things the accounts of Russian life and customs by Richard Chancellor, Anthony

Jenkinson, Jerome Horsey, Giles Fletcher and Thomas Smith.

All this was meanwhile finding abundant echoes in contemporary English literature. Most authors were able by now to draw upon a pool of familiar information, though a few gained knowledge of Russia through family or friends. References to things Russian became common, even casual. Writers of non-fiction were able to exploit the findings of the travellers. Robert Burton, for example, mentioned Russia many times in his *Anatomy of Melancholy* (1620), chiefly to point out the tyranny, boredom, gluttony and introspection of that country's inhabitants. Speaking of the jealousy of husbands among more southern peoples, he averred that Muscovites were 'not so troubled with this feral malady', but he elsewhere noted that they were 'no whit inferior' even to the ancients in their multiplicity of concubines.[12] Poets, too, made prosaic allusions to Russia. In his verse letter 'To E.G.' (written perhaps around 1600) John Donne is bored with life in London and plans to retire for a season to the country. He bids his correspondent do the same, yet warns:[13]

> fill not like a Bee
> Thy thighs with hony, but as plenteously
> As Russian Marchants, thy selfes whole vessel load.

Similarly, trade with Russia seemed so natural by the time of Michael Drayton's poem *The Battle of Agincourt* (about 1605) that the author was able, no doubt anachronistically, to place among the ships of Henry V's makeshift fleet which sailed to France[14]

> The Cow of Harwich, never put to flight,
> For hides and furs late to Muscovia bound.

Many poets were also drawing freely upon contemporary travel accounts to evoke British contacts with Russian life and culture.[15] Drayton himself was one of the earliest. 'Song the Nineteenth' of his *Poly-Olbion* (1613), an interminable celebration of England's geography and history, alludes to the Russian journeys of Chancellor and Jenkinson who each inaugurated his 'eternal fame' by measuring Muscovia.[16] In the meantime William Warner discussed the Russian adventures of the early voyagers in the definitive version of his long historical and descriptive poem *Albions England* (1602). His attitude to Russia, and the need for trade with it, was both practical and friendly, as is seen in these lines from chapter LXVI:[17]

> Nor little is their Amitie of vs to be respected:
> For, though the *Moscouites* from vs be People farre remote,
> Yeat, if how *Danes* and *Norses* haue inuaded vs we note,

> And how the *Russies*, in the like Attempts, might hold them backe,
> For onely it, were thence no Trade, ill might their Friendship lacke.

An early drama devoted to a specifically Russian theme was John Fletcher's tragicomedy *The Loyal Subject* (1618). Inspired by the stirring political events in Moscow of a few years earlier under Tsar Boris Godunov (here called Burris), this contained colourful and exciting scenes whose relative authenticity benefited, in part, from the dramatist's own uncle Giles Fletcher's heterogeneous experiences as ambassador in Russia in 1588 and his subsequent book *Of the Russe Commonwealth*.[18]

One or two English poets even ventured into Russia in person. Already in 1568 the luckless George Turbervile accompanied Thomas Randolph on a mission to the court of Ivan the Terrible and experienced the worst features of diplomatic ostracism. He recounted his miserable existence in three rhymed epistles. According to these *Certaine letters in verse, written by Master George Turbervile out of Moscovia ...to certeine friends of his in London, describing the maners of the Countrey and people*, the icy weather was unbearable, the monarch lawless and tyrannical, the Russians scruffy, greasy, vulgar, hypocritical, drunken, beastly, lecherous and crude: they allowed their women to put on paint, yet themselves wore neither ruffs nor codpieces. Think of it:[19]

> The common game is chesse, almost the simplest will
> Both giue a checke and eke a mate, by practise comes theyre skill.

It is interesting to compare Turbervile's problems with those of Richard James, who served in Russia as chaplain to Dudley Diggs half a century later, in 1618-20. On the whole James had a more profitable time in that country, learning the language, compiling a grammar and vocabulary of it, transcribing some Russian songs, and turning his hand to little poems in both English and Latin including one on the comet of 1618 and one inscribed *To Mr Daniel Clutterbooke vppon Occasion keepinge himself a Ship Boarde in the Haven of Archangell in Russia in a Hamborow Ship*.[20] But still, as the modern editor of James's works notes of this trip, 'It was like disappearing underground then to set off for Russia; and as the years (apparently) elapsed, rumours of the Traveller's death reached England.'[21] As a result, James was obliged to address a poem *To Mr. Anthonye White, whoe had made an Elegye on my supposed Death in Rusland*.[22] His circumstances must certainly have been difficult. However, by contrast with Turbervile, James seems to have derived enjoyment from his verse at least, as is evident in the energetic piece called *An Execration on*

Marie of Colmogorod in whose House I should haue binne lodged if my Man had not tould me ye Condicion of ye Place. As if his title did not tell all, James describes to us in exuberant detail this 'jailours wife and bawd and witch and hoare' who, in order to secure a client,[23]

> makes his bags of luste enflame as bigg
> As futbals, and againe with champing of a figg
> Return vnto their measure.

In view of experiences like these, it is not surprising that the initial enthusiasm for Russia soon cooled, even among those who knew little about it. Side by side with the waning excitement of discovery grew up an ever increasing corpus of purely casual references to Muscovy and its relations with England. Shakespeare incorporated some details about Russia in his all-encompassing purview, always with the casualness of common knowledge. Angelo in *Measure for Measure*, made impatient by the endless telling of a tale, cries:[24]

> This will last out a night in Russia,
> When nights are longest there.

In *The Winter's Tale* Hermione perhaps implausibly announces that the Emperor of Russia was her father.[25] In *Henry V* the French lords, waiting confidently to do unequal battle with the English at Agincourt, agree that their opponents are like valiant but stupid dogs 'that run winking into the mouth of a Russian bear and have their heads crushed like rotten apples'.[26] Macbeth entreats Banquo's ghost to come back in another shape, less fearful because physical: the 'horrible shadow' is more frightening even than 'the rugged Russian bear'.[27] And then there is the famous masque of the 'frozen Muscovits' in *Love's Labour's Lost*, thought by some to relate to the first arrival of Osip Nepeia, and by others to have been inspired by F.A. Pisemskii's farcical mission to find a noble English spouse for Ivan IV ('the Terrible') in 1582. Ivan did indeed at one point have designs on marrying England's Elizabeth or, failing that, a noble lady of rank, but this scene of Shakespeare's probably has no specific reference at all, beyond the common curiosity about Russia so widespread in England by the late sixteenth century.[28]

Shakespeare's contemporaries and successors were inspired by knowledge of Russia in a variety of ways. An already common view of the country is used to clever effect in Act IV, Scene I, of William Davenant's tragedy *The Cruel Brother* (written in 1630 but not produced for several decades thereafter). In a dialogue full of sexual innuendo, the courtier Castruchio tells the maidservant Duarte that women are like wax: some soft, some hard. There are workmen who can make impression on even the hardest wax, but[29]

> 'tis hardest of all
> To find these workmen; unless by Russia
> Where the people freeze till they spit snow.

Similarly, Thomas Heywood's comedy *A Challenge for Beautie* (1636) is rich in allusions to Russia. In the first scene of Act II Lord Bonavida asks the Clowne, his servant, what women are like in various countries. They resemble their climates, comes the answer. In Portugal, for instance, they are 'like their Orindges, the fayrer the outside the rottenner within.' 'What of *Russian* then?' Bonavida enquires, to which the Clowne responds: 'As of a Country too cold, and in cold countries I know we should have but cold comfort, besides the women goe wrapt in so much fur, that of necessity they must have more haire than wit, besides they cannot be wise they have so much adoo to keep themselves warme....'[30] Later, there is mention of the whip presented to one's future spouse as a sign of things that may come, and in Scene I of Act V Manhurst is made to sing a jolly song about the different races, in which 'the Rush' appears as a drinker of 'quasse' (that is, rye beer, or kvas) crowned with a sable cap. It is further slyly added: 'And some like breech-lesse women go.'[31]

Most contemporary allusions to Russia were of this negative kind, whether they related to the coldness and remoteness of the country or to its people's alleged slavery. Such echoes of the mysterious north were naturally at second hand — or third or fourth, — and all the modern clichés about Russia derive from this early period. Muscovy quickly became for the Elizabethans a metaphor for individual suffering, even for the tyranny of love. Already in 1582, in the second sonnet of his *Astrophil and Stella*, Sir Philip Sidney adverted to this when speaking of the power of love to overcome the will entirely, leaving the victim to celebrate enslavement as if it were the natural state of man:[32]

> Now even that footstep of lost libertie
> Is gone, and now like slave-borne *Muscovite*,
> I call it praise to suffer Tyrannie.

Meanwhile Thomas Nashe, who in 1591 wrote a preface for the unauthorised first quarto edition of *Syr P.S. His Astrophel and Stella*, himself alluded to Russia several times in the satirical and uproariously bawdy pamphlet *Have with You to Saffron Walden* (1596). He imagined, for example, a person called 'the grand commander of silence (which is a chiefe Office in the Emperour of *Russiaes* Court)', and described a body being 'sent with a paire of new shooes on his feete, and a scrowle in his hand to saint *Peter*, like a *Russian* when he is buried'.[33] Above all, Nashe made a curious Anglo-Russian pun on his own name in some famous lines about his enemies, real or suspected: 'how-euer they curse and raile vpon mee in the beginning, I will compell them to fall downe and worship mee ere I cease or make an end, crying vpon their knees *Pomiloi nashe*, which is in the *Russian* tongue, Haue mercie vpon us....'[34]

Russia at this time, in poetry as in travelogues, was thus most often presented as a land of brutal manners and strange superstitions, a nation whose humanity seemed as ambiguous as its boundaries. It was confused, moreover, with the vast and ill-defined Tartary, conceived now as a swelling canker overwhelming Russia, now as a territory incorporated by it. Around 1589 Edmund Spenser used the perennial conflict between the two as a striking image in his *Faerie Queene*. Recounting Prince Arthur's combat with Maleger (the personification of lechery and venereal disease) and his attendant hags Impotence and Impatience, he wrote:[35]

> And in his flight the villein turn'd his face
> (As wonts the Tartar by the Caspian lake,
> Whenas the Russian him in fight does chace).

Numerous other purely geographical references to the Russian empire, of little interest in themselves, were beginning to be found in contemporary English literature. In Christopher Marlowe's *Tamburlaine the Great* (1590), for example, the erstwhile 'Scythian Shephearde' of the title who, 'by his rare and wonderfull Conquests, became a most puissant and mightye Monarque', is portrayed as God's scourge upon vast Asiatic and European regions including all of Tartary and 'the fiftie headed *Vuolgas* waues'.[36] In Marlowe's *The Famous Tragedy of the Rich Jew of Malta* (performed from about 1590, but not published until 1633), Barabas has money in the banks, and grand debts owing, in a string of capitals including '*Mosco*, and where not'.[37]

Some specific details of Russia's unique geography became literary stereotypes. Novaia Zemlia, for instance, was taken as a synonym for icy wastes. There is an allusion to it in Dabridgcourt Belchier's curious play *Hans Beer-Pot his invisible Comedie, of See me, and See me not* (1618), stated to have been 'acted in the Low Countries by an honest company of health-drinkers':[38]

> But *Hans* my nose is quicke and sharpe of sent,
> Like those great Beares in *noua Zembla* found,
> Whose smelling sence was better than their sight.

The tradition continued into the eighteenth century and beyond, both in verse and prose. Alexander Pope has in his *Temple of Fame* (1711):[39]

> So Zembla's rocks (the beauteous work of frost)
> Rise white in air, and glitter o'er the coast.

Laurence Sterne, in *Tristram Shandy*, suggests a journey down from Nova Zembla to St Petersburg and beyond in search of 'some small glimmerings (as it were) of wit'.[40]

Although by the mid-seventeenth century Anglo-Russian understanding had already suffered numerous reverses, there are grounds for believing that the seeds for later Russophobia in England were sown during Oliver Cromwell's rule. Tsar Aleksei Mikhailovich broke off relations with Britain in 1649, at the time of the execution of Charles I. English merchants residing in Russia were expelled, and the diplomatic benefits of a hundred years were nullified. London turned its back on Moscow and started to ignore its existence. Despite a few odd references here and there, interest in Russia among English writers of the mid-seventeenth century remained sparse, even following the Restoration. A notable exception is Samuel Butler's *Hudibras* (1663-78), where one reads of 'the Gallant *Bruin*' who[41]

> was by birth, some Authors write,
> A *Russian*, some a *Muscovite*,
> And 'mong the *Cossacks* had been bred.

Like his cousin '*Scrimansky*', his manners were rude, for

> though his Country-men, the *Huns*,
> Did use to stew between their Bums
> And their warm Horses backs, their meat
> And every man his saddle eat:
> He was not half so nice as they,
> But eat it raw, when't came in's way.

Towards the end of the century, something of a renaissance occurred in English curiosity about Russia. It was best typified, perhaps, by the publication in Oxford in 1696 of the first printed Russian grammar for the use of foreigners, *Grammatica Russica*, by the German-born English linguist Heinrich Wilhelm Ludolf. What was specially interesting about this pioneering book was that it gave, for practically the first time in England, useful and reasonably accurate information about Russian writers, as well as precise details of the country's flora and fauna.[42] The revived curiosity in Russia had, however, been inaugurated in 1682 from a rather unlikely quarter — a prose work by John Milton called *A Brief History of Moscovia and of other less-*

known Countries lying Eastward of Russia as far as Cathay. Actually written earlier and 'gathered', as its author stated on the title-page, 'from the writings of several eye-witnesses', this skilful compilation sought to digest what was most reliably reported in Hakluyt, Purchas, and elsewhere about the geography, history, and present political state of Muscovy. Despite its faults, some grave, it presented a vigorous and credible picture of a land as yet dimly understood by most English readers. Milton's interest in Russia was evident, besides, in *Paradise Lost* itself, mentioning as that poem does Russian rivers, seas and mountains, and depicting Adam led to a height by the archangel Michael to behold the earth below, where — among other dignitaries in other cities of 'old or modern fame' — 'the *Russian Ksar*/In *Mosco*' would in due time reign.[43] As M.P. Alekseev rightly pointed out, the context here clearly shows that, for English people at least, Moscow was still on the confines of the eastern, not the western, world.[44] At another point in *Paradise Lost*, indeed, Milton reverted to Spenser's image of the seemingly eternal conflict between Russia and Tartary:[45]

> As when the *Tartar* from his *Russian* Foe
> By *Astracan* over the Snowie Plaines
> Retires...

But the view of Russia as an Eastern nation was not to last much longer. Peter the Great was soon to create a new capital, St Petersburg, not quite yet as a door, but at least as a window between his country and the West. One contributory factor in the process which led up to this was his visit to England with a so-called Great Embassy in 1698. He arrived on 21 January that year and remained for more than twelve weeks. The tales of his activities in London and at the Thames dockyards in Deptford are both legion and legendary. He dressed in English clothes, whether figuring as a gentleman or as a sailor or navvy, but whereas in the West End he was grand, in the docklands he went as far as possible incognito. Among many leading sights that Peter visited were the Tower of London, the Mint, and Wren's new Royal Observatory at Greenwich. He went to clubs, was received at the Royal Society, and observed Quakers and other dissenters at their worship. He showed little taste for the theatre, though he went there on a couple of occasions and (according to an early commentator) 'it was whisper'd about, that one of the Actresses, Miss *Cross*, had found the way to please him, and had been once admitted into his Company'.[46] Peter was also taken to a debate in the House of Lords, which quickly persuaded him that British parliamentary government was not the best thing for Russia: a monarch with a vision could be frustrated by the asking of too many questions. One is inevitably reminded here of Joseph Stalin's alleged remark that the trouble with democracy was that people might not vote for you.

In the Thames dockyards Peter laboured with his hands, actively studied shipbuilding and joinery, and became fascinated by all English woodturning artefacts including coffins, one of which he ordered for himself. Some perhaps thought that he would need it sooner than he did, for tales of his drinking and debauchery shocked polite London society. He quaffed gallons of hot pepper and brandy with the aristocracy, hogsheads of less concentrated liquors with the plebs. It was reliably reported that he could take a bottle of sherry and a pint of brandy before noon, and eight bottles of sack before bedtime.[47] Not surprisingly, he behaved like a hog in a sty. Hints of this even found their way into English letters, in the diary of John Evelyn in whose house at Deptford Peter set up 'court and palace' from 30 January to 21 April. The absent master was warned by his servant that there was 'a house full of people, and right nasty', but when the Russian guests had gone, Evelyn was greatly distressed to find his locks all broken, the furniture smashed, and the lawns trampled over from Peter's drunken games and dancing. Too busy to walk round, the Tsar had even wheeled his labourer's barrow straight through Evelyn's special pride, a lovely holly hedge.[48] Evelyn kept quiet at the time, but not everyone publicly respected Peter. Once when he complained to a porter who knocked into him in the Strand he was shocked to receive the retort: 'Tsar? What's that? We are all tsars in this country.'[49]

Despite all this, Peter's stay in England proved a remarkable success. His courtly image was fixed by the portrait-painter Godfrey Kneller, who represented the young Tsar in full armour and imperial gown, a dashing and handsome figure with a galleon resplendent behind.[50] His fame in south-east London was perhaps of a different kind, but nevertheless so great that enterprising taverners put up pictures of him to advertise the establishments where he had loved to repair. One such was a public house in Great Tower Street, near Tower Hill, another Edward Wild's 'Czar of Muscovy' in Gravesend. The painted signboards with Peter's head remained in the area until well into the nineteenth century,[51] and indeed the folk memory of his stay in Britain lived on to be enshrined, for example, in John O'Keeffe's comic opera *The Czar Peter* (1790) and, much later still, in Daniel Maclise's painting *Peter the Great Working as a Shipwright in Deptford Dockyard*, first exhibited in 1857.[52]

The reception in English literature of Peter and his rule was mixed but very widespread. He was mentioned already in a famous work of 1701, Congreve's *The Way of the World*, where Fainall in Act V gives a catalogue of conditions for his marriage which is then described as 'most inhumanly savage, exceeding the barbarity of a Muscovite husband'. But he instantly retorts: 'I learned it from his Czarish Majesty's retinue in a winter evening's conference over brandy and pepper, amongst other secrets of matrimony and policy, as they are at present practised in the northern hemisphere.'[53] One finds Peter in Addison and Steele, in Swift, and especially in Defoe, whose ironic and vicious attack on the Russian monarchy in his essay *On the Clemency of the Tsar* (1718) was followed up by the strangely lightweight and improbable episode which concludes *The Farther Adventures of Robinson Crusoe* (1719), where the hero travels across Russia from the Amur to Tobolsk and finally to Archangel, criticising local manners as he goes. As the century progressed, the memory of Peter's exploits led many more prose-writers than before to take an interest in Russia. Goldsmith, Fielding, Smollett and David Hume all made reference from time to time to that country's history and politics. The general tone, though, remained on the whole uncomplimentary.

However, some leading poets of the period adopted a quite different attitude. A tenuous line of English Russophiles is headed by Aaron Hill, whose ode *The Northern Star* (originally 1718, later revised) was a veritable paean of praise for Peter and his achievements. Mindful of the derivation of the Russian word *tsar'*, Hill wrote:[54]

> Thy *line*, great CZAR! shall stretch that shorten'd name,
> To more than CAESAR's pow'r, and all his fame.

There was scarcely any limit to what Peter might do, in fact: his beneficent reign would bring harmony to all the many peoples of the Russian empire. This was taking the Enlightenment quite far, but there was more. According to Hill, Athens and Constantinople themselves would one day be liberated from the infidel yoke by an Orthodox Christian Tsar. Indeed, Russia would shake the Porte, restore the soul of Greece, unite Europe and Asia, even breach the great wall of China.[55] And, lest his own readers should become suspicious or offended, Hill sought to reconcile Britain and Russia in a concord of universal friendship:[56]

> PERISH the pride, in *poor* distinction shewn,
> That makes man blind, to blessings *not his own!*
> *Briton* and *Russian* differ, but in *name*:
> In *nature's* sense, all nations are the *same*.
> One world, divided, *distant brothers* share,
> And man is *reason's* subject — *every where*.

Later editions of *The Northern Star* carried subtitles like *A Poem on the Great and Glorious Actions of the Present Czar of Russia* and (when this monarch was dead) *Sacred to the Name and Memory of the Immortal Czar of Russia.* Hill was equally enthusiastic about the Empress Catherine I, devoting to her his poem *The Northern Heroine* (1727). Much to his own (but nobody else's) surprise, she granted him on her late husband's behalf an Imperial Russian gold medal.[57] Towards the end of his life Hill did, it is true, have doubts, and viewed more recent developments in Russia with not a little distress. But he never lost faith in Peter. In *On the March of the Russian Auxiliaries, in 1748*, he asked the late Tsar's soul to arise and watch over his much-changed country.[58]

James Thomson, celebrated author of *The Seasons* (1726), also reacted positively. He seized upon the illustrious reign of Peter as an illustration of the everlasting strife between humanity and Nature. References to Russia, some perhaps incongruous, abound in the division 'Winter'. First, the poet speaks of how, 'with highly blooming charms',[59]

> Scandinavia's dames,
> Or Russia's buxom daughters, glow around.

But then he notes how, further north and east,[60]

> through the prison of unbounded wilds,
> Barr'd by the hand of Nature from escape,
> Wide roams the Russian exile. Naught around
> Strikes his sad eye, but deserts lost in snow;
> And heavy-loaded groves; and solid floods,
> That stretch, athwart the solitary vast,
> Their icy horrors to the Frozen Main...

Yet Nature's horrors can be transformed! As Thomson continues, ebulliently,[61]

> Immortal Peter! first of monarchs! He
> His stubborn country tam'd, — her rocks, her fens,
> Her floods, her seas, her ill-submitting sons;
> And while the fierce barbarian he subdu'd,
> To more exalted soul he rais'd the man.

There is, however, a problem here for the cynic. The nagging question arises: was the 'Russian exile' of the earlier passage a 'barbarian', or a newly 'exalted soul'? One only wonders whether Thomson knew, like Peter, which was which.

The visit to England by the new and vigorous young Russian monarch, soon to open up his country to full European influence, nevertheless had a chiefly positive effect on Anglo-Russian relations. It was, first, of long-term economic benefit. Peter signed up, for instance, a most lucrative contract with British merchants for the importation of tobacco into Russia, flaunting the ban on it by Orthodox clergy.[62] He engaged many British engineers, bankers and industrialists. Notwithstanding the earlier English fashion for so-called 'Muscovy glass', he even started to import glass from England, and set up manufactories for it under English supervision.[63] He needed it in fact to build St Petersburg, his window into Europe...[64] Bilateral contacts of all kinds multiplied, travel rapidly increased, an English community was established at the Tsar's new capital. English books began to flood into Russia. Above all, many valiant or impecunious English — or more especially, Scottish — soldiers were recruited for the Russian Imperial army. One of these, by the name of Learmonth, was the ancestor of the great Romantic poet Lermontov. Another who went to serve with Peter in various guises and wrote mainly favourable reports of his reforming reign was the distinguished engineer Captain John Perry, subsequently author of *The State of Russia, under the Present Czar, in relation to the several Great and Remarkable Things he has done, ...particularly those Works on which the Author was employ'd, with the Reasons of his quitting the Czar's Service after having been Fourteen Yeares in that Countrey...* (1716). As can be supposed from this title, Perry was unhappy at the end and indeed had great difficulty in leaving Russia in 1712 — an experience suffered also a little later by Peter Henry Bruce.

These dates have their significance. The foundation of St Petersburg in 1703 and the removal of the Tsar's capital there nine years afterwards were matched by Peter's triumphs over Sweden. The battle of Poltava in 1709 saw the defeat of the powerful Charles XII, presaging the end of Scandinavian power and the full appearance of Russia on the European scene. As Robert Southey would much later recount, in his poem *The Battle of Pultowa* (1798), this was the 'death-day' of the glory of the 'iron-hearted King', forced now to 'fly before the Muscovite'.[65] England for a time took fright for the balance of power in Europe, halfheartedly joined in with the Swedes against Russia in 1714 and again in 1720, but its fleet achieved nothing and luckily no lasting enmity was occasioned. Although later the two countries nearly came into conflict more than once, particularly over the Ochakov affair in 1791, where British diplomacy received a serious rebuff with Russia's retention of this captured Black Sea port, they managed to keep their distance until the overweening ambitions of Napoleon finally brought them together as allies. In 1812 as again in 1941, it seemed to be in Britain's interest to maintain the state of Russia against an invader who threatened to bring universal tyranny much less desirable than any supposed Russian barbarity.

As the eighteenth century had progressed, the British came to know the Russians more intimately than before. Already about the time of Peter's visit, letters from Moscow had begun to appear in the London press, particularly in the *Gentleman's Journal,* a monthly miscellany of news, history and the arts, and by 1714 it was possible to establish a serious (though short-lived) periodical devoted chiefly to Anglo-Russian relations, *The Muscovite.*[66] A rapidly increasing number of travel books about Russia, and public or private reports on its history, life and manners, now started to appear and have continued without interruption to the present day. Russia became one of those distinctive countries, more written about than visited. Leading commentators in the mid- and late eighteenth century were Jonas Hanway, George Macartney, Nathaniel Wraxall, William Richardson, William Coxe and Andrew Swinton, and at the beginning of the nineteenth, John Carr, Edward Clarke, and John Atkinson and James Walker.[67] Moreover, the interest in Russia was not confined to Anglo-Russian relations only. In 1744 there appeared for instance *A Consolatory Ode, inscrib'd to the Marquis de la Chetardie, on his Disgrace, and Return from the Russian Court.*

A new and important development was that Russians, after Peter, began to visit Britain much more frequently. The satirist Prince A. D. Kantemir was Imperial ambassador in London in the 1730s, and came to know English literature well, but little is known about his personal acquaintanceships. Some of his poetry was translated and published in London in 1749 — only into French prose. Later in the century, many young Russians came to study at the universities of Oxford, Glasgow and Edinburgh. In Edinburgh also for a time was Princess E.R. Dashkova, whose musical talent was praised by the great actor David Garrick. In a curious letter to her of 30 May 1778, he wrote: 'in Short I fear what one of our Poets once prophesy'd will most certainly come to pass — *Russia shall teach the Arts to Britain's Isle.*'[68] However this might be, there were as yet few direct contacts between British and Russian writers, and Russian literature took a very long time to establish itself in the public consciousness of English readers. The interest was still in politics, history and travel, rather than in such creative productions as were starting to be published in the Russia of the Enlightenment. As an example of the general curiosity about Russia one may cite John Glen King's *A Letter to the Right Reverend the Lord Bishop of Durham ...on the Climate of Russia....* (1778), which contained a detailed description and magnificent illustration of 'the Flying Mountains at Zarsko Sello' (that is, Tsarskoe Selo, now called Pushkin, the Empress's country residence near St Petersburg). Likewise, the English were most impressed by another Russian wonder, the Empress Anne's palace of ice on the Neva at St Petersburg in

1740, later touchingly described in William Cowper's poem *The Task* (1785) as[69]

once a stream,
And soon to slide into a stream again.

Only towards the end of the eighteenth century did Russian literature begin to penetrate into English society through translations, and even here the interest was chiefly political. An early exception was George Macartney who, on returning from two years' diplomatic service in Russia, printed for private circulation in 1768 a largely friendly account of that country which included, surprisingly, a warm appraisal of its language and its poetry. In addition to Kantemir, he singled out for special commendation Lomonosov and Sumarokov.[70] This was confirmed two decades later in Rev. William Coxe's popular and often reprinted *Travels into Poland, Russia, Sweden and Denmark* (1784-90). Though much of what he said was culled from French or German authorities, Coxe provided considerable detail for the English reading public and gave an interesting though feebly rendered specimen of verse by the poet, tragedian and critic A.P. Sumarokov.[71] As for the poet, scientist and historian M.V. Lomonosov, his *Russkaia istoriia* (Russian History) was published in London in 1767 in a 'chronological abridgment', 'continued to the present time by the translator'; it is significant that he was described on the title-page as 'Counsellor of State' and 'Professor of Chymistry [sic] at the Academy of Sciences at Petersburg'. The concept of Russian life and literature was still a very tenuous one in England. Similarly, when S.I. Pleshcheev's seminal *Obozrenie Rossiiskoi imperii v nyneshnem ee sostoianii* appeared in English in 1792 as *Survey of the Russian Empire, according to its present newly regulated state, divided into different governments, etc.*, its author was designated only as a naval captain.[72]

One of the earliest would-be critical articles to be published in England was James Harris's 'Some Account of Literature in Russia, and of its Progress towards being Civilized'. The title of this piece, published as an appendix to the author's *Philological Inquiries* (1781), has of course a sting in its tail: few in England believed that civilisation in Russia had yet been achieved, despite the already long process of Europeanisation initiated by Peter and actively pursued at present by Catherine II, also known as the Great. Harris himself, besides, did not say much to disabuse them. He obtained his very sketchy information on the progress of Russian letters through his son, who was British Minister at St Petersburg. In a superficial and rather trivial essay of only ten pages he managed to repeat himself, concentrated on works originally composed in Latin or Greek, and became enthusiastic only in the by now customary praise for the Great Peter, under whom civilisation (as he opined) 'burst forth with all the splendour of a Rising Sun, and ...has continued ever since to ascend towards its Meridian'.[73]

But many reviews and translations of individual Russian works did start to appear in British periodicals, and not only Lomonosov and Sumarokov but, especially, the journalist, historian and story-writer N.M. Karamzin became familiar enough names with more discerning members of the British reading public. Two collections of Karamzin's translated tales appeared in volume form in 1803-4.[74] One has to emphasise that almost everything translated from the Russian still came to English via German or French, and this would remain largely true for a long time yet to come. Anglo-Russian literary relations had nevertheless now shifted to a higher and more influential plane. Although the flow was still chiefly in the opposite direction, with wild enthusiasm in Russia for Ossian, Sterne, Gray, Thomson, Young and all the rest, Russian writers were at last receiving serious if still spasmodic attention in Britain. What is more, English poems on Russian subjects started to increase in number, ranging from the obscurity of Peter Cunningham's anonymously and privately printed *The Russian Prophecy: A Poem* (Sheffield, 1787) to more or less significant works by Southey, Campbell and Coleridge. English novels on Russian subjects also started to appear, including a spoof by Mary Ann Radcliffe (not the Gothic novelist) entitled *Radzivil: A Romance* (1790), which claimed to have been taken from the original Russian of 'the celebrated M. Wocklow'.[75]

It should not be thought that the new trend meant necessarily that British writers would be amicably disposed towards Russia. Imbued as they were with the ideals of national and personal liberty, English poets of the Romantic period tended to view with suspicion the dubiously enlightened empire of Catherine the Great. Everything for them depended upon how it would fit into the new Europe of revolutionary change. In so far as it impinged upon their consciousness, as a rival to the older countries — Italy, Germany, Spain, and of course now especially France, — it tended to constitute a threat to the progress of social reform and national self-determination. Poland here emerged as a symbol of Russian reaction and repression, and its rebel leader Tadeusz Kościuszko as a potentially tragic hero. In the autumn of 1794 the ragged remnants of his loyal army were finally crushed by Imperial Russian might and he himself was badly wounded and captured. No nation lifted a finger to save the gallant Poles. The young Samuel Taylor Coleridge reacted quickly with a moving sonnet called simply (and sic) *Koskiusko*. What is interesting about this forceful piece is that he first celebrated in English verse the legendary concerted shout of the Polish warriors when their general was perceived to fall. As Coleridge put it, this epitomised their 'murdered hope'.[76]

> Oh what a loud and fearful shriek was there,
> As though a thousand souls one death-groan poured!

In 1799, after the Polish struggle for independence had finally been thwarted by partition of the country, recent events there were reviewed by Thomas Campbell in his long poem *The Pleasures of Hope*. Borrowing from but outdramatising even Coleridge, Campbell fixed the former Polish leader in the English imagination with heroic lines concluding[77]

> Hope, for a season, bade the world farewell,
> And Freedom shrieked — as Kosciusko fell!

By contrast, other English poets were content to celebrate this great man's courage, pride and patriotism, holding them up as models to be followed. Such is the import of *An Ode to General Kosciusko* written in 1797 by Rev. Henry Francis Cary, better known now as a translator of Dante.[78] But Kościuszko was soon released from prison, and began his wanderings in search of political friends. These took him to England, America and France. He consistently refused to enter into any international arrangement which would not put Polish freedom high on its agenda. There is no doubt that Napoleon, in 1812, would have been well advised to have Kościuszko as an ally in his fateful Russian campaign, but the opportunity was missed. The Polish veteran's independent stand was applauded by Leigh Hunt in his sonnet *To Kosciusko, who never fought either for Buonaparte or the Allies* (1815).[79] Hunt also liked to tell anecdotes of Kościuszko's adoration by simple Poles (as well, incidentally, as of the fat and furious Empress Catherine the Second and of the brutal Russianness of Imperial horn bands, in which each player was 'converted into a crotchet').[80] Even John Keats, the least political of the English Romantics, referred twice to Kościuszko in poems of 1817, associating him on both occasions with England's own King Alfred. In *Sleep and Poetry* he described Kościuszko's uncrowned Polish head as 'worn by horrid suffrance — mightily forlorn',[81] but in his fine sonnet *To Kosciusko*, published actually some months before the patriot's death, he placed him in the company of immortals gathered in the spheres of God's eternity.[82]

A completely new phase in Anglo-Russian (and indeed in international) relations was inaugurated by the unexpected outcome of the Napoleonic Wars. At the beginning of the nineteenth century, no serious observer could maintain that Russia, economically speaking, was a great world power. Culturally, too, it was still considered backward and — by many — barbarous. But the politics of Europe at the time depended more on military strength and territorial extensiveness than on national or popular wealth; and it had for long been evident that Russia could and would grow as powerful as its European partners would allow. Napoleon took upon himself to subjugate it, but instead was humiliated. In view of the prominence later given to this by English commentators, it is worth considering the scale of Napoleon's defeat. He boldly entered Russia with his Grande Armée of over 400,000 men; he came ignominiously out with barely 20,000 survivors. Incompetent command structures, inadequate provisions, underfed horses, and severe losses in the pyrrhic victory at Borodino required that the French should winter in Moscow. Napoleon planned to move on St Petersburg in the spring. But the greater part of Moscow was burnt down, partly by accident, partly by arsonists in the pay of the Governor, Count Rostopchin. No alternative quarters could be found for such a large army, so a massive retreat began. Skilful Russian raids and ambushes combined with illness, hunger, snowstorms and appalling physical conditions to destroy the Frenchmen as they trudged along, hundred upon hundred at a time.[83]

In the long term, the amazing rout of Napoleon in Russia sent a wave of dread through Europe. The concept of a Russian Empire from the North Sea to the Pacific and from the Arctic to the Black Sea and the Mediterranean was as familiar a bogy for the British after 1812 as it would be for the Americans after 1945. Rightly or wrongly, it was thought that the Russians considered themselves destined to rule the globe; and their crushing rout of the overweening French was seen as the beginning of a new era as well as the end of an old. Russophobia became the cornerstone of international alignments: the Tsar was henceforth an enemy to be feared or an ally to be prized. And yet in the short term, as also in 1945, a wave of sympathy for Russia swept through British life and literature. Reflections of Napoleon's defeat included, at the simplest level, cartoons by George Cruikshank and others with titles like 'Jack Frost Attacking Boney in Russia' (published in November 1812) and 'General Frost Shaving Little Boney' (1 December 1812). These were sometimes accompanied by poems such as the intriguingly titled *The Valley of the Shadow of Death* (18 December 1812). A vigorous broadside of April 1813 called 'Boney and the Gay Lads of Paris Calculating for the Next Triumphal Entry into Moscow' was paired with a cartoon showing dilapidated French generals and a poem about the earlier disaster which concludes:[84]

Then ye nations whose voice through fear, not from choice,
    To this tyrant its homage has paid,

> Join the brave Russian throng, that your miseries ere long
>> May with Nap in Oblivion be laid.

To judge by perhaps exaggerated (or at least selective) accounts, Russomania hit the streets and salons of London in the winter of 1812-13, put down some shallow roots, and lingered on tenaciously for several years. Russian *lubki* (luboks, cheap prints) went on sale, and collections of 'favourite Russian songs' did the rounds of drawing-rooms and concert-halls. Prominent among them was a series of pieces translated by Rev. Benjamin Beresford, brought together anonymously in 1816 as *The Russian Troubadour*. The illustrated title-page for this, by Hopwood, would have led English readers to figure Russia as a bearded peasant with a balalaika, relaxing in the country with colourful pig-tailed dancing girls.[85] London also saw a number of so-called Russian operas, of greater or lesser authenticity. Already in 1813, audiences were able to admire spectacular scenes of fire and snowstorm in Henry Brereton Code's 'historical and musical drama' *The Russian Sacrifice; or, The Burning of Moscow*. A little later the Russian traveller P.P. Svin'in was perplexed and amused by the incongruities of Charles Armitage Brown's three-act 'serio-comic opera' *Narensky; or, The Road to Yaroslaf* (premièred at Drury Lane on 11 January 1814), which depicted for example a Russian peasant hut shaded by both a pine-tree and a palm, but he was both pleased and moved by the grace of English dancers and by the obvious fervour and sincerity of spectator reaction to this pseudo-Russian entertainment. More obviously genuine were some ballets staged with great success in London in the spring of 1813 by the celebrated Charles-Louis Didelot, choreographer in the theatres of St Petersburg, as were also the exotic manners and vigorous dancing of a cossack brought to London that year by the Emperor Alexander I — an event later celebrated in the Russian capital itself in the popular ballet 'Kozak v Londone' (A Cossack in London), complete with a Scottish dance and the English national anthem. Such spontaneous Anglo-Russian cultural exchanges went on for some time. Among the many dramas produced in London during this period of reawakened interest in Russia one notes: *The Brave Cossack; or, The Secret Enemy* (1812); Charles Armitage Brown's *The Russian Village* (1813); *The Russian Festival* (1817); *Moscow* (1819); *The Russian Daughter; or, Female Heroism* (1820); *The Czar of Muscovy; or, The Three Ambassadors* (1822); and *Napoleon Bonaparte's Invasion of Russia; or, The Conflagration of Moscow: A Military and Equestrian Spectacle* (1825). Later examples include *The Russian Captive* (1831) and *The Emperor of Russia; or, The Deserter of Moscow* (1844).[86]

Some of these plays were in verse. Countless echoes of 1812 are found also in contemporary English poetry,[87] prominent examples from 1813 alone being George Hardinge's anonymous ode *The Russian Chiefs*, Peter L. Courtier's *Russia; or, The Crisis of Europe*, and J. Hamilton Roche's *Russia: A Heroic Poem*, whose Romantic extravagance is seen in a verse printed on the title-page:

> How beautiful in death
> The Warrior's Corse appears;
> Entwin'd by fond affection's breath,
> And bath'd in female tears.

Among the most striking English celebrations of Napoleon's punishment at Russian hands was the hilarious poem *Bonaparte's Journey to Moscow*. Attributed in the British Library copy to James Winton, this parody of John Gilpin's ride has Boney tempted by his Dad the Devil to take a look at Russia and shows 'how he succeeded worse than he intended, but came home safe at last!'[88] On his way to Moscow and back, he experiences all the classic elements of the legendary disaster: the fires, the Cossacks with their famous leader Platov, the catastrophic skirmishes, the bitter cold and darkness. The piece has true lyric touches like 'Their winding-sheet is snow' and ends, significantly for British readers: 'Long live the King! long live the Czar!' More serious but less enduring treatments of Napoleon's ride were commonplace. One was J. Brookes's *A Poem on the Wars of Portugal and Spain ...; to which is added, The Russian Campaign, or, The Invasion of Russia and Moscow by France and her numerous Allies* (privately printed, Shrewsbury, 1814). Another was Charles Caleb Colton's *Lines on the Conflagration of Moscow* (1816). A publication which had considerable success at the time was *Moscow: A Poem* (1816) by Mrs Henry Rolls, self-styled 'authoress of sacred sketches from Scripture history', who inscribed and sent a copy of her latest work to Tsar Alexander I as a 'faint tribute of the British Muse' to that 'brightest act of patriotism and self-devotion' by the Russians which had astonished all Europe and turned the tide of modern history.[89] The fashion for writing poems about the events of 1812 long outlived probability or usefulness, in fact: R.C. Chater's *The Burning of Moscow* appeared as late as 1838, and in 1841-42 Lady Emmeline Stuart Wortley gave public birth to her long-gestated epic on this subject — *The Maiden of Moscow*, a saga in twenty-one cantos and more than eight hundred pages.[90] Numerous also were non-fictional narratives of Napoleon's Russian adventure, including those by Robert Ker Porter, Evan Rees, John Philippart and James McQueen.

Anglo-Russian amity, short-lived in the event, was sealed by the Tsar's visit to London in the summer of 1814 together with Hetman

Matvei Ivanovich Platov. Alexander I at this period was reputedly an ardent Anglophile and is said to have declared that, were he not the Emperor of All the Russias, he would have been glad to settle as a farmer on Richmond Hill.[91] No doubt he expected to find a lass there. As for Platov, his reputation as a leader of fearless Cossacks against France's finest troops had preceded him to England. Engravings of him were seen everywhere, and there was even one of his daughter, 'Miss Platov', whom the dear man had been offering to anyone who brought in Bonaparte, dead or alive, — with a dowry of 50,000 crowns as an additional attraction. This Russian state visit proved enormously successful. Oxford University awarded Alexander the degree of DCL (as also no fewer than nine members of his entourage); he was invested with the Order of the Garter; crowds swarmed round him everywhere. He discussed the slave trade with William Wilberforce, promising his devoted assistance. Platov was still more popular: at Ascot, elegant ladies plucked hairs from the tail of the horse he sat on, and men held his fingers, taking turns to present him to their parties.[92] Many poems were written in honour of the Tsar, including Horatio Smith's *The Triumph of Russia — A Song* (1814).[93] At the same time a retired Russia merchant, Michael Hoy, erected on St Catherine's Down near Ventnor in the Isle of Wight the impressive Alexandrian Pillar which still stands. In 1857 other hands would add to this a tablet commemorating the Crimean War, and three years later still the Russian novelist Ivan Turgenev conceived at eerie Blackgang Chine below it his great novel *Ottsy i deti* (Fathers and Sons).[94]

The quickening British interest in Russia also engendered imitation travelogues like *Letters from London: Observations of a Russian, During a Residence in England of Ten Months; of its Laws, Manners, Customs, Virtues, Vices, Commercial and Civil Polity, Legislation, etc.; Translated from the Original Manuscripts*, published by J. Badcock in 1816 under the pseudonym 'Oloff Napea'.[95] Similarly, Shelley's friend and biographer Thomas Jefferson Hogg published anonymously in 1813 a novel called *Memoirs of Prince Alexy Haimatoff*, purporting to have been 'translated from the original Latin MSS'. Publicly reviewed by Percy Bysshe himself, this found considerable favour in the Shelley circle and had some influence on Thomas Love Peacock's *Nightmare Abbey*.[96] Mary Shelley's *Frankenstein; or, A Modern Prometheus* (1818) has an intriguing framework in which the monster disappears for ever into Russia's icy Arctic wastes and — who knows? — may be ultimately responsible for the Revolution of 1917... Certainly a *Punch* cartoon of July 1854 called 'The Russian Frankenstein and his Monster' showed Tsar Nicholas I no longer able to control his terrifying war machine.[97]

Discounting Percy Bysshe Shelley's well-known fascination with the 'icy summits' of Caucasus, still thought of at the time as mythological, he himself has some references to Russia in a number of the longer works as well as in the early Esdaile poem *To the Emperors of Russia and Austria who eyed the Battle of Austerlitz from the Heights whilst Buonaparte was active in the thickest of the Fight.* In canto IV of *Queen Mab: A Philosophical Poem* (1813) there is a graphic evocation of Moscow burning and burnt, though the place is not specifically located. In *Hellas* (1822) the scene switches eastward to the perennial struggle of Greek with Turk and Turk with Russian. Shelley here depicts Turkey defending its control over Greece against the Western powers, eyeing also Russia which threatens to take pickings from the conflict and no more desires liberty for Christian Greece than peace for Mohammedan Turkey. Hassan says sagely to Mahmud:[98]

> Russia still hovers, as an eagle might
> Within a cloud, near which a kite and crane
> Hang tangled in inextricable fight,
> To stoop upon the victor; — for she fears
> The name of Freedom, even as she hates thine.

We are firmly in the age of Romantic literature, which creates a natural point of departure for a study of English poets and Russia. Every great writer of the period has references to it somewhere. Even the aesthetic young Keats alludes to Russia, in his posthumous poem *The Castle-Builder.* Following the French débâcle of 1812, he claims that he might meet among the varied and colourful personalities of Covent Garden market[99]

> one of few of that imperial host
> Who came unmaimèd from the Russian frost.

As is evident both here and in the case of Shelley, the new interest in Russia was still chiefly political, not the stuff of great Romantic poetry. This was also true, for instance, of Coleridge. Poets varied, however, in the way they dealt with the material. Some showed objectivity and reserve, even hostility to Russia and its aims, while others reacted with sympathy and at times even enthusiasm.

One poet who on the whole viewed Russia positively was Robert Southey. He read quite widely about the country and its history, jotting things down in his commonplace-books. On one occasion he copied from Clarke's *Travels* a horrifying practice in the bandit borderland with Tartary involving 'red boots' torture — scalping the skin from the legs. Elsewhere he noted, from Prudhomme's *Miroir de Paris*, 'When the Czar Peter was at Paris, he said he would burn it if he were king of France.'[100] Southey's view of more recent political events in

Russia was a natural and typical reaction, on a factual plane: 'Never in civilised Europe had there been so great an army brought together as Bonaparte had there collected, and never was there so total and tremendous a destruction.'[101] He went further than this, however, in an almost mystical interpretation of Russian wisdom and strategy. 'The destruction of Moscow with all its consequences is one of the grandest events that have ever taken place', he wrote. Never had sacrifice been made with such a great effect: 'the certain deliverance of Russia, — the probable deliverance of Europe.'[102]

Southey had in fact foreseen the rapid rise of Russia in his poem *The Battle of Pultowa* (1798), and later celebrated it in *The March to Moscow* (1813), written after the manner of a contemporary broadsheet. In some ways he was as much concerned with the shame done to the Romantics' beloved France as he was with the Russian victory. In his *Ode, written during the Negotiations with Bonaparte, in January, 1814*, he implored that country's people to redeem itself for all the evil ends of Napoleon's monstrous policies and referred, among other things, to the mounds of flesh which 'stiffen'd on the snowy plain/Of frozen Muscovy'.[103] Southey nevertheless developed a great feeling of affection for Russia, a country which he never properly knew. He believed acquaintances who had lived there and assured him that, while the nobles were certainly corrupt, the common people were natural, good, and brave.[104] Nor did he see them as a menace to Britain; as early as 1800 he had opined to a friend: 'those bears, you know, do not eat English folk.'[105] Although Southey's underlying view of Russia remained somewhat flippant, perhaps, — witness *The March to Moscow* where Napoleon and his men find the place too warm for them and are, as it were, finished offsky by 'Oscharoffsky and Rostoffsky/And all the others that end in -offsky',[106] — his praise for its present leader was genuine and warm. It is true that by 1813 he was England's poet laureate, but he did not see this function as an order to grovel. In celebration of the Tsar's visit to England in 1814 he published a remarkable *Ode to His Imperial Majesty, Alexander the First, Emperor of All the Russias* which opens

> Conqueror, Deliverer, Friend of human-kind!
> The free, the happy Island welcomes thee.

And there is much more. Entirely without sycophancy (though in the later view incredibly), Southey set Alexander in a glorious line from Peter and proclaimed him 'the Great, the Good, the Glorious, the Beneficent, the Just'![107] Southey's interest in Russia, and also its literature, persisted for the rest of his life. As late as 1831 he would read and recommend to a correspondent as a lively portrayal of contemporary manners in Russia and Poland the curious (as he described it) 'Ivan Vejeeghan, a *Russian* Gil Blas'; this was actually F.V. Bulgarin's novel *Ivan Vyzhigin* (1829), which enjoyed a considerable vogue both in Russia and outside.[108]

Wordsworth, as will be seen, was also honourable enough to take a deeply serious view of what Russia had achieved, but Southey's flippant side was perhaps more typical of English literature at the time. The age-old attitude of 'we know best' and 'foreigners talk funny' was evident in Byron's *Don Juan*, the Russian episodes of which (cantos VI-X, 1823) would later greatly appeal to Swinburne.[109] As is well known, Byron's hero wins the favours of an Empress Catherine beyond her prime but still very much within means. For the English bard, her 'lust' and 'other *extras*, which we need not mention' undoubtedly proved attractive to Don Juan,[110]

> But in such matters Russia's mighty Empress
> Behaved no better than a common sempstress.

Byron's facetious approach is certainly clever and amusing. He also introduced sharp political comment when noting how Catherine derived 'great joy' from the 'thirty thousand slain' in the massacre at the fortress of Izmail, captured by the Russians from the Turks in 1790.[111] Yet the overall tone is somewhat cheap: prejudice and English parochialism are evident in unremitting lines like[112]

> And Tschitsshakoff, and Roguenoff, and Chokenoff,
> And others of twelve consonants apiece.

In Byron's defence it may, however, be said that a genuine fascination with Russia is seen in his poem *Mazeppa* (1819), which manages to be fundamentally unpolitical while rendering the strangeness and excitement of Slavonic life and manners.[113]

Dislike and even contempt for Russia was also seen in the works of Thomas Campbell, owing largely to his ongoing sympathy for Poland. In 1804 the poet had been seriously interested in a chair at Wilna (now Vilnius) University, but withdrew from fear that rival candidates would quote awkward passages from *The Pleasures of Hope*. Even if he went to Poland, he said, he might be re-routed in the direction of Siberia.[114] In 1830 Campbell warmly welcomed the Warsaw uprising but in 1831, when it was being crushed, he wrote two furious and haunting poems about the plight of the Polish people. In *The Power of Russia* he deplored that country's militarism which, unlike Rome's, brought no compensatory new values to the nations that it conquered. The Russ was made of 'nature's basest clay'; his rule of law was 'sabre, knout, and dungeon'.[115] In *Lines on Poland* Campbell mourned the isolation in which Poland always found itself in grappling with 'the giant overgrown', and attacked in particular the policy of England who 'hates, but dares not chide, the Imperial Thief'.[116] The poet's sincerity was shown by his achievement in establishing an influential Association of the Friends of Poland.[117] However, there was widespread apathy about this in England as in most matters not strictly insular. The diarist Henry Crabb Robinson records a meeting with Campbell in the spring of 1832 in the following laconic terms: 'I did not like his face or the style or tone of his conversation. He has enlisted me to form one of a Society in favour of the Poles — about whom he talked with generous warmth but with no discrimination. I should not have suspected him of being in any way an eminent man.'[118] Campbell nevertheless remained until his death one of the most ardent opponents of Russia among English intellectuals. As late as 1843, he still saw every reason to dread the Tsar and his designs upon the world.[119]

Another bard who had little time for Russia, even for Alexander or his conquests, was the Irishman Thomas Moore. In 1819 he wrote a satirical poem called somewhat inconsequentially *Tom Crib's Memorial to the Congress* (1819), which represents the Tsar as a pugilist in a victorious prize-fight with the English George to win the Balance of Power. Henry Crabb Robinson found this piece amusing, but was primly surprised that 'a gentleman — for so Moore is, in station and connections — should so descend as to exhibit the Prince Regent and the Emperor of Russia at a boxing match under the names of Porpus and Long Sandy.'[120] Moore continued to satirise the Russians, against the common trend of the times. In his *Fables for the Holy Alliance* (1823) he not only attacked Catherine the Great for her treatment of the Poles; he laid into[121]

> her grandson, ALEXANDER,
> That mighty Northern salamander,
> Whose icy touch, felt all about,
> Puts every fire of Freedom out.

Moore in this poem also made wonderful play of the Empress Anne's famous palace of ice on the Neva. He dreamt that a new one had been built, to accommodate a grand ball for the holy European leaders; only while they were all dancing, it melted down and collapsed.[122]

A very significant link between Russia and British culture in the early nineteenth century was Sir Walter Scott. The news of Napoleon's catastrophes in Russia in 1812 greatly delighted him. 'Glorious news' of the débâcle came regularly to his study as the Grande Armée dwindled from half a million to a sick few thousand men.[128] Ever afterwards, he retained an interest in Bonaparte's defeat and acquainted himself as far as possible with the victors. In Paris in 1815 he was invited to a grand Russian dinner with Lord Cathcart, formerly Ambassador to St Petersburg, who introduced him to the Tsar. Alexander questioned Scott on his uniform and his limp, thinking him a military brave; Scott emerged from a potentially embarrassing situation with characteristic aplomb. At the same event he met the Cossack general, Platov, who thereafter gave him bear hugs in the streets of Paris. At the Jardin des Plantes he spied other Russians fraternally greeting genuine ursine quadrupeds.[129] Back in Scotland the following year, he welcomed the future Nicholas I with some extravagantly panegyric *Verses composed for the Occasion, adapted to Haydn's Air 'God save the Emperor Francis', and sung by a Select Band after the Dinner given by the Lord Provost of Edinburgh to the Grand Duke Nicholas of Russia and his Suite, 19 December, 1816.*[130]

During the mid-1820s Scott himself researched and wrote up the history of Napoleon's Moscow campaign, for his study *The Life of Napoleon Buonaparte* (1827). He compared various published accounts of it, including D.P. Buturlin's, received a great bundle of relevant notes made by the Duke of Wellington who had been to St Petersburg in 1826, and questioned knowledgeable Russian visitors about some of the local details. Prominent among these were General Aleksey Petrovich Ermolov, formerly second-in-command to the late Field Marshal Kutuzov, and Count Olenin, a captain of the Guards and son of the President of the Academy of Arts. Scott also entered into correspondence with the poet and partisan Denis Davydov, who had hounded Napoleon's troops as they retreated from Moscow.[131] Some of these links were made possible by a rather extraordinary Russian who first stayed at Scott's, together with his English tutor (a Mr Collyar), in the autumn of 1825. This was the sixteen-year-old Count Vladimir Petrovich Orlov-Davydov, a nephew of Denis. The young man afterwards lived in Edinburgh and studied at the University, but he called at Abbotsford as often as he could. Scott was most impressed by his maturity and modesty. They had serious debates on Peter the Great, the events of 1812, the Decembrists, and the present state of Russia. Orlov-Davydov also translated for Scott's benefit the *Slovo o polku Igoreve* (The Lay of Igor's Raid) and even helped him materially by purchasing the manuscript of *The Talisman*.[132] Thomas Moore, who met Orlov-Davydov at Abbotsford in November 1825, found him most intelligent; they talked much of Russian literature, especially of the fabulist Krylov.[133]

It is clear that Moore did not allow himself to be influenced by his own great popularity in Russia. In December 1819, in Paris, he met a

Prince Golitsyn who had his works by heart and kept sidling up to recite a line or two.[123] Not long afterwards, the Russian Empress was said to travel about with two copies of *Lalla Rookh* in bindings studded with precious stones.[124] On 3 January 1829, Moore dined at Lord Lansdowne's Bowood House with 'a Russian, whose name nobody could pronounce'. This was Aleksandr Ivanovich Turgenev, diarist, traveller, and 'ambassador-at-large of Russian culture in foreign parts'.[125] He greatly impressed Moore by his erudition and said that Moore's poetry was translated and widely read in Russia; particularly successful were the *Irish Melodies* and *The Peri*, part of which he read out for the poet's benefit in convincing-sounding Russian.[126] One likes to think that some of this did rub off on Moore. His poetic interest in Russia was certainly not all negative, as is seen in the charmingly Pushkinesque short piece *The Russian Lover*, where a young man speeds impetuously by sledge to be at his sweetheart's side.[127]

Scott's Russian connections continued on and off until his death. On a visit to Paris in the autumn of 1826 he was approached by Princess Praskov'ia Golitsyna (Galitzine), née Shuvalova, a granddaughter of Field Marshal Suvorov, who claimed she would have crossed the seas to meet him. He was often with her this winter, and through her became acquainted with a wider Russian society. At a *soirée* at her residence in the rue de Verneuil on 6 November he met 'a whole covey of Princesses of Russia arrayed in tartan! with music and singing to boot'. Princess Golitsyna had the artist Briullov do a portrait of him which she then had engraved for sale in the shops.[134] Another acquaintance was Baron Aleksandr Kazimirovich Meiendorf, who visited Scott in March 1829 and was remembered as a 'fine lively spirited young man'. The two talked of heraldry and literature, in both of which Meiendorf was well versed. Meiendorf later corresponded with Scott and maintained an enthusiastic admiration for his writings.[135] Also of some importance was the visit to Abbotsford in August 1828 by Alexander Turgenev. While there, this Turgenev noticed in Sir Walter's study a bust of 'Worthsworth', whom he claimed the Scottish bard described as 'the poet of the lacks'.[136] Finally, in Naples during the carnival season in 1832, Scott met a Countess Volkonskaia who questioned him about *Count Robert of Paris*. She shouldn't read it, he told her: it wasn't worth the trouble. She also earnestly entreated him for an autograph, and he promised to write a piece of verse; but although he began to do so and became quite worked up over it, he apparently abandoned the attempt. The extant manuscript includes the lines[137]

> Say, can fair Wolkonsky expect
> Fruit from a wither'd Scottish thorn?

By the time of the British Romantics, then, Russia and Russian life and culture had made a lasting mark. Translations from Russian literature were beginning to appear more frequently. The interpreter most often cited was John Bowring, whose two-part anthology *Specimens of the Russian Poets* appeared in London in 1821 and 1823 and included all the best-known writers of the late eighteenth and early nineteenth centuries. Bowring had spent some time in Russia in the winter of 1819-20, met in person the poet-historian Karamzin and the fabulist Krylov, and learnt enough of the Russian language to produce these pioneering translations.[138] His two volumes also contained lively versions of some typical folk poetry, as well as an introduction and notes which gave more discerning readers some useful background knowledge about Russian language and literature.[139] Meanwhile Russia's first great star was rising in the person of its national bard, A.S. Pushkin. Among his early English translators was George Borrow, whose rendering of *The Talisman* and other poems came out in book form in 1835, first in St Petersburg and then in London. Borrow's so-called *Targum*, published in both cities that same year, also contained a few Russian pieces among contributions from a boasted 'thirty languages and dialects'. A little later, Pushkin's poetry was given greater celebrity in Britain by the work of Thomas Budge Shaw, especially by his long and immensely informative article 'Púshkin, the Russian Poet', published by *Blackwood's Edinburgh Magazine* in the summer of 1845.

During all this time, however, Russian policy of the post-Napoleonic period had started to impinge upon the patriotic consciousness of the British people. Already in the early 1820s a new spirit of hostility to Russia was felt in the English cultural air, the praises of Alexander having given way to knowledge of his failure to establish better conditions for his people. The accession of Nicholas I after the abortive Decembrist uprising in 1825 made things markedly worse. Common British reactions to Russia at the time are seen in a series of *Imaginary Conversations* by Walter Savage Landor: *Kosciusko and Poniatowski* (1824), *The Emperor Alexander and Capo d'Istria* (1824), *Beniowski and Aphanasia* (1828), *Peter the Great and Alexis* (1828), *The Empress Catharine and Princess Dashkof* (1829), and *Nicolas and Michel* (1829).[140] These fundamentally anti-Russian pieces, often sarcastic and occasionally scurrilous, have scant regard for historical truth but show great dramatic force and typify some prevalent views of British liberals and intellectuals.

The fact is that Russia was considered to be overreaching itself. Just when its culture was beginning to be appreciated, its politics created new hostility. This ambiguity is well seen in a rather extraordinary unsigned article, almost certainly by John Bowring, in the opening number for 1824 of the influential *Westminster Review*. The author gave a most sympathetic treatment of Russian literature from the time of Peter the Great down to Derzhavin, Krylov, Zhukovskii and Pushkin, but also took upon himself to show how Russia had suddenly thrust forwards to the centre of the world stage. Bowring's remarks are worth quoting at some length, echoing as they do the new sense of threat which thinking English people experienced when reflecting upon the state of post-Napoleonic Europe.[141]

There was a country a century ago which excited neither interest, nor jealousy, nor anxiety; it was known and thought of only as the land of strange and distant barbarians, of whom some vague notions might indeed be gathered together by the curious, from the travels of a few adventurous wanderers.... He who should now prophesy that the Laplander or the Esquimaux will in the lapse of another hundred years domineer over the world, would be scarcely less adventurous than the man who formerly foretold the preponderance of the Muscovite power ...for what was *Muscovy* but a remote, and frozen, and barren region, — the chosen abode of inertness and ignorance?

But things are altered now; and Russia, barbarous still, has aspired to, and has obtained, a dictatorship over the states of Europe. She sits like a huge *incubus* upon the rest, disposing of kingdoms at her will, directing and controlling the fate of nations.... Russia, in the great struggle which is going on between improvement and barbarism, is the commanding champion as well as the efficient representative of the latter. And surely her governors are in the right, if they mean to preserve, if they hope to consolidate, the gigantic power they wield. It is impossible they can hold it long, if they consent to open the floodgates of knowledge upon the Russians, — for knowledge brings with it the want and the necessity of political amelioration, a necessity which must be satisfied.

'The art of good government is to foresee and to provide for this necessity', concluded the writer; but the last thing that the Russian rulers wanted was good government.

In 1827 a very similar statement about Russia was made by the authoritative General Register, though from a more mixed perspective. No nation could equal Russia 'in the rapidity of its advancement in culture and civilisation' since Peter the Great. The 'wise policy' of successive Emperors had brought their country to 'a state of tranquillity'. Though serfdom and ignorance remained, Russia was now a stable member of the fraternity of nations. However, the anonymous author warned that the fifty million inhabitants of the Russian Empire, 'united in one mass, and under the same government, form a powerful body, which, if not controlled, may prove the destruction of civilised Europe'. Britain must by all means retain friendly relations with Russia,[142]

But, amid the various changes in the political affairs of Europe, the colossal power of the North must be strictly watched, and every attempt to enlarge her territory, at the expense of any other country, carefully frustrated by a judicious policy. It is only by these means, that the danger arising from a country of such overwhelming magnitude, will be obviated, and the peace and prosperity of the European States secured.

Russia had finally arrived, and would not go away. The scene is set for a closer examination of British attitudes to it, through the medium of the works and sayings of our nineteenth-century poets.

CHAPTER 1: William Wordsworth (1770-1850)

In order to set our Anglo-Russian subject in context, it is worth first looking at its obverse. It is a commonplace of literary history to say that certain British writers of the Romantic period exercised a great and lasting influence upon Russian poets of the early nineteenth century. The examples of Ossian, Byron and Sir Walter Scott are particularly striking.[1] What is less generally realised is that certain other writers made scarcely any impact at all. William Wordsworth was relatively little known in Russia. His reception by newspapers and the literary journals was rare and unecstatic. They noted that he eschewed falsehood and rhetoric; that he championed the common man; that he was the 'head' of the Lake School. That said it all — or nothing.[2] Some commentators were more concerned to note the impossibility of rendering Wordsworth's name in Cyrillic letters than to discuss the substance of his poetry.[3] One of the few important early treatments of him in the Russian press was actually by a Frenchman, Amédée Pichot, in the context of an article published in St Petersburg in 1830 but originally part of the author's *Voyage historique et littéraire en Angleterre et en Ecosse* (Paris, 1825). Pichot — and most Russians who read him — viewed Wordsworth as an isolated relic of pure poetry at a time when active engagement in political and social questions had become the norm for writers.[4] A little later, the celebrated critic V.G. Belinskii made a few passing mentions of Wordsworth in his prolific writings, ranging him a little lower than Byron but extolling his 'powerful and sumptuous' lyric talent.[5] These judgments are found in articles of 1841.

Another leading critic, A.V. Druzhinin, knew Wordsworth's poetry well, read everything about it he could find, and in the early 1850s mentioned it from time to time in his monthly articles for *Sovremennik* (The Contemporary) or *Biblioteka dlia chteniia* (The Reading Library). At first he found it chiefly of historical interest, something to be venerated, a relic of the infamous controversy with Byron — who had triumphed among Russian readers, consigning the Lake Poets to obscurity. He readily acknowledged Wordsworth's great gifts, but thought him fussy and could not accept the extravagant English critical atmosphere that surrounded all his writings. Wordsworth would write a page describing a mossy stone, he said, and immediately the question would be seriously discussed as to whether an entire book could be devoted to it.[6] Elsewhere Druzhinin praised Sir Walter Scott for extolling the gaiety and variety of life, and claimed that Wordsworth, by contrast, 'could not understand life without books and solitude'. In order to appreciate the English poet, one had to struggle through endless pages of explanations and additions, childish passages and downright awful lines. It was like being at a long and tedious concert, with wrong notes to boot.[7] Druzhinin did, however, allow that Wordsworth had a certain greatness. If you were prepared to contemplate nature with him, and to listen to his voice, you would be struck by his extraordinarily penetrating analysis of human feelings for the commonest of things.[8] A much later echo of the Byron-Wordsworth confrontation is found in the notebook for December 1875 of the novelist and publicist F.M. Dostoevskii. He was reading Byron in a recent Russian edition by N.V. Gerbel', and in an admittedly ambiguous entry seemed to be amused by Byron who, in his 'dedication' of *Don Juan* to Robert Southey, railed at Wordsworth's conversion to political conformity in accepting a place in the Excise.[9] It must, however, be pointed out that Dostoevskii probably never read a single line of Wordsworth himself.

A few discerning Russian poets did show knowledge of Wordsworth. The voracious and omniscient Alexander Pushkin managed to discover him already in the 1820s, and read him on and off for several years. He particularly admired sonnets like *There is a pleasure in poetic pains* and *Scorn not the Sonnet; Critic, you have frowned*, and was inspired to write imitations of them. In a draft note of November 1828 concerning style in poetry, he cited Wordsworth and Coleridge as leading examples of a trend towards the people, towards a rich popular lore that had previously been spurned. A few years later he embarked ambitiously upon a prose translation of *The Excursion*, but apparently found it difficult to understand and wisely abandoned his attempt after the first twenty-five lines of Book First.[10] Others who appreciated 'Vortsvort' included the blind bard Ivan Kozlov, who made loose versions of *We are Seven* (*Nas semero*, 1832) and the sonnet *It is a beauteous evening, calm and free*,[11] and the minor poet Dmitrii Egorovich Min, a Professor of Legal Medicine at Moscow University, who turned the clever sonnet *Nuns fret not at their convent's narrow room* into a remarkable piece that might have been composed by Pushkin.[12]

More interesting still is a certain affinity between the poetry of Wordsworth and some purely original productions of his Russian contemporaries. Thematic and philosophical similarities between Wordsworth and Pushkin himself have been noted, sometimes to the detriment of the former; Prince P.A. Kropotkin thought that while both men derived their greatness from simplicity, Pushkin demonstrated this over a wider range of human experience.[13] Comparisons are perhaps more meaningful in the case of other poets of the Pushkin pleiad. D.S. Mirskii liked to associate Kiukhel'beker's elegy on the anniversary of the Lyceum at Tsarskoe Selo, *19 oktiabria* (19 October), with Wordsworth's *Extempore Effusion upon the Death of James Hogg*: the two were 'curiously near in time, if not in tone', he said.[14] Mirskii might also have pointed to similarities of mood and language elsewhere, notably as between an earlier anniversary piece by Kiukhel'beker, *19 oktiabria 1828 goda* (19 October 1828), and the opening of Wordsworth's ode *Intimations of Immortality from Recollections of Early Childhood*.[15] A little later, affinities with Wordsworth might be detected in I.S. Turgenev's poem *Razgovor* (1845), particularly in relation to its old man/young man theme.[16] All these are, of course, merely parallels. The ideas and feelings expressed were in the air, the age. But it was an age of shared experience, for Russian culture now existed as an equal partner with its ancient British counterpart.

Wordsworth's own interest in Russia was aroused at quite an early period, but did not find echoes in his work for some long time. He learned about the country, more or less tenuously, from the press of course but also perhaps through friends and associates who visited Russia or were authorities on it. Among these was the classical scholar John Tweddell, who spent some time in Odessa towards the end of his short life.[17] Others were the Wedgwood brothers, patrons of Samuel Taylor Coleridge and sons of Josiah Wedgwood whose famous pottery had proved extremely popular in Russia during the reign of Catherine the Great (though the Empress's own payments on dinner services specially commissioned for herself had barely covered their cost).[18] This would have intrigued Wordsworth, and (as will subsequently appear) we do know that he read some history books about the country. When, however, he began to mention Russia in his writings, he tended to do so casually — and not only in verse. As so much of Wordsworth's poetry is overtly autobiographical it would, besides, be idle to discriminate between it and his correspondence, so long as the meaning is clear and the dating unequivocal.

Wordsworth made passing reference to things Russian in *Peter Bell*, a poem much derided in its time but which he numbered among his best achievements.[19] First drafted in the spring of 1798, *Peter Bell* went through several revisions before its publication many years later, in 1819. Its appearance then was preceded and followed by parodies which effectively destroyed its critical acclaim, though they also helped promote it with the public. The poem is, besides, a strange work, describing as it does a man's salvation through natural rather than through spiritual influences. The whole has often been read as a reply to *The Ancient Mariner*; and the Prologue, in particular, is a friendly skit on Coleridge's fantasising.[20] The poet imagines himself borne aloft in a little crescent-shaped boat, from which he is shown all the wonders of the universe. Asking to return to earth, he stares a while at the Andes, the Pacific and the Alps before homing in to England (ll. 61-5):

> Yon tawny slip is Libya's sands;
> That silver thread the River Dnieper;
> And look, where clothed in brightest green
> Is a sweet Isle, of isles the Queen;
> Ye fairies, from all evil keep her!

An early version of this passage alluded also to 'little Tartary' and 'Caucasus so dear' (though neither of these, for Wordsworth, would have really signified 'Russia'). At last the poet determines to remain among the places that he knows and loves, forsaking all desire to visit more exotic climes. 'Burning Africa' is no more tempting to him than 'Siberian snows', and he opposes to each his own sweet Westmorland. 'Long have I loved what I behold' is his unadventurous philosophy (ll. 91-100, 131).

Although the Russian references in *Peter Bell* are in their context practically negligible, it is interesting, first, that Wordsworth should have taken Siberia, and not Lapland or the Arctic, as the abode of what he calls 'boreal morning' (l. 92), and, secondly, that he should have introduced the Dnepr as a world-impressive river. The fact that he designated it thus, rather than 'Borysthenes', shows that he gave it modern, rather than a classical significance; and he was not afraid to risk a comic effect in the rhyme 'Dnieper'/'keep her'. The cynic may suggest that the Dnepr was chosen simply for this reason; but the fact that Wordsworth allowed the rhyme to stand, in a context of such seriousness, is proof of his willingness to think of that river as a magnificent watercourse. That such a view had nothing to do with politics is obvious, but the poet's mind was clearly far from closed to phenomena beyond Western Europe's more comfortable confines.

A more fascinating but also very puzzling mention of Russia occurs in Wordsworth's *The Redbreast Chasing the Butterfly*, written in 1802 and first published in *Poems*, 1807.[21] The poet asks the bird (ll. 6-8):

> Art thou the Peter of Norway Boors?
> Their Thomas in Finland,
> And Russia far inland?

Whatever its meaning, this mysterious passage is an excellent illustration of the problem of sources in literary composition. It is virtually impossible to know everything that an author has been reading. Even if a complete list of books can be established, from a diary or other reliable records, there is no way of telling if all of them have been fully taken in, and one rarely knows with much certainty what newspapers and periodicals have been read. In our own time, the problem is made worse by radio and television broadcasts, not to speak yet of electronic news, but even in the relatively isolated life of the Lake Poets one cannot be sure of every written source, and not every conversation with every visitor or well-read acquaintance has been recorded. In Wordsworth's case, there is a relatively copious extant library, the catalogue of which is a precious store of information, but even here there must be uncertainty as to what was actually read and when. Speculation is essential, and it becomes near-certainty only in those cases where verbal or other textual similarities strongly suggest a specific debt or influence. However, neither the background to the composition of *The Redbreast Chasing the Butterfly* nor the context of its Russian allusion permits us to do *more* than speculate, and the problem must therefore be set aside. None of the sources that Wordsworth did clearly draw from with respect to the names Peter and Thomas, including what is commonly known as Bewick's *History of British Birds*,[22] would have allowed him to suppose that the robin is called Thomas in Russia, and he may have just invented this. Certainly Foma (the equivalent name) is not so used in Russian. In view of the poem's seriousness of purpose it is hard to accept that its onomastic complexity is merely a casual joke, but the line 'And Russia far inland' may actually have been introduced for purposes of rhyme and atmosphere.

There are a few glancing references to Russia in Book VII of *The Prelude*, not published until 1850 but first written in 1804 and revised two or three times during the 1830s. As a young man in 1791 Wordsworth had tried to settle in London, but was disconcerted by the noise and bustle. Formerly he had thought of England's capital as something utterly romantic, more wonderful by far than

> golden cities ten months' journey deep
> Among Tartarian wilds (ll. 83-4)

but now it seemed a

> monstrous ant-hill on the plain
> Of a too busy world! (ll. 149-50)

At first, however, he was much impressed by the variety of humankind that thronged the busy streets —

> the mighty concourse I surveyed
> With no unthinking mind, well pleased to note
> Among the crowd, all specimens of man,
> Through all the colours which the sun bestows,
> And every character of form and face;
> The Swede, the Russian; from the genial South,
> The Frenchman and the Spaniard; from remote
> America, the Hunter-Indian; Moors,
> Malays, Lascars, the Tartar, the Chinese,
> And Negro ladies in white muslin gowns. (ll. 219-28)

Whether London did indeed have Russians, Tatars and the rest in significant numbers at the time is immaterial: Wordsworth is deliberately fixing upon people from the four corners of the universe, of which the North, for him, was represented chiefly by the Russian and the Swede and the East in part by the Tatar.[23]

It is interesting that Wordsworth, like so many thinking people of his time (and indeed also before and since), was unable ever to reconcile the concept 'Russia' with the concepts 'Europe' and 'Asia'. Russia was now emerging on the European scene, as an equal partner with Austria, France and Britain, yet some sources of its power lay beyond the Urals. A similar problem exists again today, with regard to possible Russian membership of the European Community. On one level, Wordsworth certainly knew the facts of arbitrary geography: in a letter of as late as 1840, he casually referred to Moscow as being at one extremity of Europe, Cadiz at the other.[24] On another level, he rejected this as philosophically misleading. An excellent illustration of his more global approach to Russia is seen in *Lines Suggested by a Portrait from the Pencil of F. Stone*, a poem written in 1834 and published the following year. Speaking of the world's 'strange contrasts', he noted that there was yet a unity of attitude towards artistic greatness:[25]

> Is not then the Art
> Godlike, a humble branch of the divine,
> In visible quest of immortality,
> Stretched forth with trembling hope? — In every realm,
> From high Gibraltar to Siberian plains,
> Thousands, in each variety of tongue
> That Europe knows, would echo this appeal, etc. (ll. 88-94)

Although Russia as such is not actually mentioned here, Wordsworth clearly imagines 'Europe' as extending into Siberia, and thus as incorporating part of Asia thanks to Russian influence. Russia for him was a political entity on the world map, rather than a divided land of occidental political stature and oriental chaos and mystery.

The Russian allusions seen so far in Wordsworth's poetry are all indicative of important underlying attitudes, however incidental or insubstantial they may appear in themselves. Most others of this kind have to do ultimately with Napoleon. As is well known, Wordsworth as a young man had been greatly exhilarated by the French Revolution of 1789; he had even been tempted to participate in it himself. Gradually sickened, however, by its bloody outcome, he lost his faith in France as Napoleon's rule and conquests increasingly set that country on the road to war with Britain. In Book VII of *The Excursion* (first published in 1814) Wordsworth described how young men in the Welsh valleys had prepared to do service for their King against the French tyrant then threatening to invade their shores. The shepherd Oswald, with his band of volunteers, would lay out the map of Europe on the grass and show the places where the war was raging or might spread,[26]

> Now pointing this way, and now that. — 'Here flows,'
> Thus would he say, 'the Rhine, that famous stream!
> Eastward, the Danube toward this inland sea,
> A mightier river, winds from realm to realm;
> And, like a serpent, shows his glittering back
> Bespotted — with innumerable isles:
> Here reigns the Russian, there the Turk; observe
> His capital city!' (ll. 787-94)

Wordsworth doubtless wrote this a little before the conflict of 1812, and was certainly alluding to an earlier period. There is reason to suppose that he first had 1806 in mind, in view of a manuscript reference to the battles of Austerlitz and Jena having recently been fought. Shortly afterwards, Russia and Turkey were at war, and the poet may have felt that more local conflict of sufficient potential importance to be added in beside the general picture of Napoleonic oppression. However, he made nothing more of the allusion to Russia, still a cold and faraway place by contrast with brave Switzerland, of which he then went on to speak. The mention of Russia is therefore still hardly more significant, though at least it is more political, than a conventional (and classical) reference in Book VI of *The Excursion* to[27]

> That ancient story of Prometheus chained
> To the bare rock, on frozen Caucasus. (ll. 539-40)

Like any other English poet, Wordsworth here would be remembering Aeschylus, echoed in Shakespeare's *Titus Andronicus* (II, i) and taken up also by Shelley in *Prometheus Unbound*, and would probably scarcely know that the Caucasus, in his own time, was being steadily overrun by Russia.

Wordsworth, besides, knew relatively little yet about the political strength of Russia and its ever growing empire. While he felt that it would certainly gain importance in a post-Napoleonic era, and even allowed that it might then gobble up some of its lesser neighbours, as late as March 1811 he considered it no threat to France and no ally to be wooed by Britain. He exclaimed of Russia, Austria and Prussia: 'Military *Powers*! so these states have been called. A strange Misnomer! they are Weaknesses, a true though illsounding Title! — and not Powers!'[28] He was very soon disabused, however, and the French with him. In the summer of the following year Napoleon invaded Russia, and already six months afterwards nineteen out of every twenty men who had marched with him were dead or incapacitated. By the spring of 1814 Russians ruled in Paris, side by side with the English and the Prussians, banishing the great Napoleon to Elba and thrusting themselves upon a startled world's attention.[29] The swiftness of the Russians' ascendancy took all nations by surprise, and is matched in modern history only by the Soviet conquest of Berlin in 1945. After the Congress of Vienna and the final defeat of Napoleon in 1815, Russia was established as a full and equal European power.

It was now that Wordsworth made the first of his more substantial contributions to the history of English literary attitudes to Russia.[30] Definitive collections of his poetry contain a sequence of three linked items called *The French Army in Russia 1812-13*, *On the Same Occasion* and (to use its opening line — there is no title) *By Moscow self-devoted to a blaze*. The last two are irregularly (and differently) rhymed sonnets, the first a longer and more complex piece. The three together form part of what is now known as 'Poems Dedicated to National Independence and Liberty', which comprise chiefly sonnets and odes in praise of popular uprisings, individual valour and the like, the whole revealing Wordsworth's deeply democratic sensibility. The movement towards national self-determination was for him an 'unconquerable stream' — as he put it in the sonnet *The Germans on the Heights of Hochheim*, which customarily follows immediately after the Russian trilogy.

Although written in the order usually presented, these three poems belong actually to two different periods. *The French Army* was begun towards the end of February 1816, and *On the Same Occasion* very soon after it. Both were completed by mid-March that year and appeared almost immediately in Wordsworth's volume entitled *Thanksgiving Ode, January 18, 1816. With Other Short Pieces, Chiefly Referring to Recent Public Events*.[31] The *Thanksgiving Ode* itself was composed in response to the national victory celebrations following the final termination of the Napoleonic Wars, and Wordsworth subsequently added to it other, related poems written in February and March; hence the inclusion of specific dates in the original texts of *The French Army* and *On the Same Occasion*, whose titles at that time were respectively *In Recollection of the Expedition of the French into Russia. February 1816* and *Sonnet, on the Same Occasion. February 1816*. By contrast, the third poem in the present sequence, *By Moscow self-devoted to a blaze*, was not written until November or December 1822, and did not appear in print until the five-volume collected edition of Wordsworth's poetry published in 1827, where it took a considerably reworked form.[32]

This helps to explain why the three pieces sit uneasily with each other. In the first two, Wordsworth imputes to natural forces, and to winter in particular, the amazing destruction of the Grande Armée. At the time that was the fashionable explanation, of course, and indeed in some part the true one, but the poet seems to be interested by the elements almost to the exclusion of historical events; it is as if he were using Napoleon's retreat as an excuse to celebrate the powers of the universe. He later acknowledged a striking resemblance between the personification of winter in these poems and the treatment of it in a sonnet by Southey written in 1799, even though his colleague's work had nothing to do with Russia or Napoleon.[33] Wordsworth at this time appears to have believed that Napoleon's rise was as historically inevitable as his fall, though he intermixed a large and patriotic measure of British responsibility for the tyrant's ultimate defeat, leaving one to assume that other nations — and even nature itself — had followed the British lead. His 'Advertisement' (or preface) to the *Thanksgiving Ode* volume freely praises England's greatness and might, even though his patriotic fervour is somewhat moderated in the poems themselves.[34] But other countries must at least take note of British moral supremacy. The *Thanksgiving Ode* itself contained an indirect reference to Russia in the lines:[35]

> Such glad assurance suddenly went forth —
> It pierced the caverns of the sluggish North... (ll. 179-80).

It is true that this relates to Waterloo, not earlier, but the Russian triumph of 1812 is conveniently ignored; when Wordsworth turned to it in the separate shorter poems, it was relegated to a mechanistic act of nature. In so far as a divinity was involved, it must be responsible for both the victory and the carnage, being the God of pestilence as well as of peace and love, the God of the earthquake and volcano.[36] The mood of these pieces is correspondingly bleak, since God appears to leave the wind and the frost to get on with their eternal functions.

It is possible that, in 1816, Wordsworth could not bring himself to believe that the Russians and the French had ever been truly enemies. Just a few days before he wrote the first two poems in the trilogy, he agreed with a correspondent that captured art treasures had been retained by France after Napoleon's first defeat thanks to the intervention of Alexander I, and proceeded to assert of the Emperor of Russia that 'his is a Frenchified intellect'.[37] Regardless of such truth as this statement may contain, Wordsworth would perhaps have incorrectly subsumed the rude Russian people under their Europeanised Tsar, and considered them also to be reluctant participants in Napoleon's defeat. Later, he would have seen the Russian people as God's chosen agents. Maybe in part for this reason the third and last poem in the sequence places a different interpretation, or rather a different emphasis, upon the events of 1812: a personal God is back in control of natural and human forces, directing them to conspire for mortal good. Certainly Dorothy Wordsworth, in a letter to Henry Crabb Robinson of 21 December 1822, claimed that William had 'felt himself called upon' to write this new sonnet 'in justification of the Russians whom he felt he had injured; by not having given them *their* share in the overthrow of Buonaparte in conjunction with the elements'.[38] This explanation does not, however, seem completely candid, since the impression of suffering and fortitude in the sonnet is soon set aside as God gathers the created forces for yet another divine massacre. It is noteworthy, besides, that even in *The French Army* punishment clearly proceeds from disobedience of God. Here are the three poems; readers can judge for themselves Wordsworth's overall interpretation of Napoleon's Russian débâcle.[39]

[1.] COMPOSED IN RECOLLECTION OF
THE EXPEDITION OF THE FRENCH INTO RUSSIA.
February 1816.

<pre>
Humanity, delighting to behold
A fond reflexion of her own decay,
Hath painted Winter like a shrunken, old,
And close-wrapt Traveller — through the weary day —
Propped on a staff, and limping o'er the Plain,   5
As though his weakness were disturbed by pain;
Or, if a juster fancy should allow
An undisputed symbol of command,
The chosen sceptre is a withered bough,
Infirmly grasped within a palsied hand.   10
These emblems suit the helpless and forlorn;
But mighty Winter the device shall scorn.
For he it was — dread Winter! — who beset,
Flinging round van and rear his ghastly net,
That host, — when from the regions of the Pole   15
They shrunk, insane ambition's barren goal,
</pre>

That host, — as huge and strong as e'er defied
Their God, and placed their trust in human pride!
As Fathers persecute rebellious sons,
He smote the blossoms of their warrior youth;   20
He called on Frost's inexorable tooth
Life to consume in manhood's firmest hold;
Nor spared the reverend blood that feebly runs, —
For why, unless for liberty enrolled
And sacred home, ah! why should hoary age be bold?   25
Fleet the Tartar's reinless steed, —
But fleeter far the pinions of the Wind,
Which from Siberian caves the monarch freed,
And sent him forth, with squadrons of his kind,
And bade the Snow their ample backs bestride,   30
And to the battle ride; —
No pitying voice commands a halt —
No courage can repel the dire assault, —
Distracted, spiritless, benumbed and blind,
Whole legions sink — and, in one instant, find   35
Burial and death: look for them — and descry,
When morn returns, beneath the clear blue sky,
A soundless waste, a trackless vacancy!

[2.] SONNET,
ON THE SAME OCCASION.
February 1816.

Ye Storms, resound the praises of your King!
And ye mild Seasons — in a sunny clime,
Midway on some high hill, while Father Time
Looks on delighted — meet in festal ring,
And loud and long of Winter's triumph sing!   5
Sing ye, with blossoms crowned, and fruits, and flowers,
Of Winter's breath surcharged with sleety showers,
And the dire flapping of his hoary wing!
Knit the blithe dance upon the soft green grass;
With feet, hands, eyes, looks, lips, report your gain;   10
Whisper it to the billows of the main,
And to the aerial zephyrs as they pass,
That old decrepit Winter — *He* hath slain
That Host, which rendered all your bounties vain!

[3.]

By Moscow self-devoted to a blaze
Of dreadful sacrifice; by Russian blood
Lavished in fight with desperate hardihood;
The unfeeling Elements no claim shall raise
To rob our Human-nature of just praise   5
For what she did and suffered. Pledges sure
Of a deliverance absolute and pure
She gave, if Faith might tread the beaten ways
Of Providence. But now did the Most High

Exalt his still small voice; — to quell that Host   10
Gathered his power, a manifest ally;
He, whose heaped waves confounded the proud boast
Of Pharaoh, said to Famine, Snow, and Frost,
'Finish the strife by deadliest victory!'

As was perhaps inevitable in the British intellectual climate of that period, Wordsworth's interest in Russia continued to be dominated by what one might call a detached observer's knowledge of 1812. He came a little closer to historical sources during a European excursion with his sister in the summer of 1820. In an entry for 18 July that year in her *Journal of a Tour on the Continent*, Dorothy Wordsworth recounted a conversation with a French surgeon who had served with the Grande Armée in Russia: 'He told W. many dismal stories of the horrors of that time, but spoke more feelingly of the sufferings from cold than from any other cause.'[40] While this perhaps confirmed the poet in his view of nature's role in the destiny of humankind, it is evident that the Wordsworths' curiosity about Russia extended to its broader contribution to the European struggle with Napoleon. Despite spasmodic accords with the French, especially that of Tilsit in 1807 which in some respects foreshadowed the Nazi-Soviet pact of 1939, Russia had fought long and bitterly against the Corsican tyrant on various fields including Austerlitz where, on 2 December 1805, they lost over twenty thousand men. The Wordsworths' tour in Germany and Switzerland took in sites of other Franco-Russian battles, of which they heard graphic accounts from local people. They even condescended to historical trivia, visiting for example a hotel in Frankfurt where Tsar Alexander I had once resided and which now bore his name.[41]

Wordsworth did not, of course, live long enough to observe the confrontation between Britain and Russia that led, first, to the Crimean War and later to grave tension in the near and far east and in India. He did, however, witness an important foretaste of it in a now relatively forgotten chapter of Anglo-Russian diplomacy. During the 1820s Greece was struggling to consolidate its independence from Turkey, formally proclaimed on 27 January 1822. Several European powers were in sympathy with its cause, and it looked to them to repel reprisals by the Porte. But none intervened, despite passionate Greek appeals, and by the summer of 1827 the Turks had regained Athens. The Sultan rejected a joint truce Note from Russia, France and Britain and they started to take action. But while Britain and France pursued military and diplomatic policies aimed at liberating Greece, Russia worked for its own more complex ends involving progress on land against both Turkey and Persia. It formally declared war on Turkey on 26 April 1828 and swept to a speedy victory. Chiefly owing to this the Sultan, by the Treaty of Adrianople signed on 14 September 1829, guaranteed not only the independence of Greece but also that of Serbia and the Danubian Provinces (Moldavia and Wallachia), and also formally recognised Russian sovereignty in Transcaucasia. Furthermore, Russian forces occupied a large area of European Turkey pending reparations. The progress of this Russo-Turkish War had been so swift, after a long earlier period of diplomatic deadlock, that Britain and France had scarcely had time to notice what was going on. The Porte had asked for help, assuming that the other allies would wish to block Russian gains, but they had dithered and demanded politically impossible terms. At the end of 1829, however, they had cause to wonder what had happened. In a candid letter to his son Willy, Wordsworth neatly caught his country's mood and showed himself to be as patriotically anti-Russian as Tennyson and Swinburne would be one and two quarter-centuries afterwards. 'I assure you I never was so puzzled in my life', he wrote; 'nor can at all understand how the Powers of Europe could permit Russia to advance to Constantinople. Every body seems to be equally ignorant.'[42]

It was during the progress of this latest European conflict that Wordsworth conceived and wrote his longest and most memorable poem on a Russian subject, *The Russian Fugitive*. It is necessary to go back and consider how he came to it. For a number of years now, he had been gaining knowledge of Russia and the Russians from the point of view of social history and culture as well as of international politics. He was a voracious reader and acquired information on anything topical or curious. Already in the winter of 1805-6, for example, he seems to have opened his horizons further to world history and geography by studying a number of encyclopedic books like *Purchas his Pilgrimage; or, Relations of the World*. Some of these may have given him a taste for Russian customs.[43] In the summer of 1814, after discussions with Coleridge, Southey and others, he included in an ideal list of older English poetry George Turbervile's famous *Letters in Verse* of 1568. He pointed out that these were in Hakluyt and could be taken from there in any future republication, showing too thereby his knowledge of the latter's *Principall Nauigations, Voiages, and Discoueries of the English Nation* which contained, of course, a great wealth of facts about Russia.[44] There is also evidence that, a few years afterwards, Wordsworth read John Bowring's two-volume *Rossiiskaia antologiia: Specimens of the Russian Poets* (1821-23), which incorporated translations from the best writers of the Russian late eighteenth and early nineteenth century — Lomonosov, Derzhavin, Karamzin, Krylov and Zhukovskii. One may surmise this from the fact that when, in December 1827, Bowring sent Wordsworth another work of his the poet responded: 'It gives me pleasure to see that you continue transplanting the flowers of foreign Poetry into our tongue.'[45]

Around this time, Wordsworth's interest was definitely quickening in Russia's social structures and historical distinctiveness, which seemed backward and yet oddly comforting in the context of the post-Napoleonic world. In a letter of 27 November 1828 he commented on the special status of Russia and those few countries that — in his view — resembled it. 'The great monarchies of Russia, Prussia, and Austria,' he wrote, 'having not yet been subject to popular Revolutions, are still able to maintain themselves, through the old Feudal *Forms* and qualities, with something, not much, of the feudal *virtues*.'[46] Although Wordsworth's chief source for *The Russian Fugitive* was Peter Henry Bruce, as will be seen, it is worth speculating what other authors may have introduced him to such 'feudal virtues' as he supposed that Russia still exhibited. A work that he definitely knew and read which could have had some bearing on *The Russian Fugitive* was *A Relation of the Embassies from his Sacred Majestie Charles II to the Great Duke of Muscovie, the King of Sweden, and the King of Denmark, performed by the Right Hoble the Earle of Carlisle in the Years 1663 and 1664*.[47] Written by 'an Attendant on the Embassies', Guy Miege, and published in London in 1669, this very witty, racy book is most informative about Russia in the seventeenth century, though from a mainly parochial perspective: the natives, we are informed, 'stink very enormously all Lent long' — 'above all with Garlick and Onyons'.[48] Among the numerous more recent publications on Russia which could have come to Wordsworth's attention was Dr Augustus Bozzi Granville's splendid book of travels to and from St Petersburg, published precisely in this present year, 1828. The poet may also have been inspired to write *The Russian Fugitive* by more personal causes. One possible contact at the time was the artist and traveller Sir Robert Ker Porter, author of *Travelling Sketches in Russia and Sweden during the Years 1805-1808* (2 volumes, 1809) and *A Narrative of the Campaign in Russia, during the year 1812* (1813). Porter lived and worked for many years in Russia, married there a noblewoman called Mariia Fiodorovna Shcherbatova, and eventually died and was buried in St Petersburg. It is not clear when Wordsworth met him, but it was almost certainly before the composition of *The Russian Fugitive*.[49] Much more probable than Porter, however, was a personal influence of a very different kind, someone who himself never went to Russia but who had acquired an extensive knowledge of that country and its manners through the entourage of Sir Walter Scott. This was a diffident and unhappy man called George Huntly Gordon, whom Wordsworth among others had befriended, and whom the poet kept closely informed about the composition of *The Russian Fugitive*.

In August 1815 Sir Walter Scott had been conducted round the battlefield at Waterloo by Major Pryse Lockhart Gordon, a Scotsman from Macduff in Banffshire who had served with distinction under Wellington and now resided in Brussels. While dining at Gordon's, Scott had also met his eldest son, George Huntly. Then only nineteen, George Huntly Gordon had been intended for the Church of Scotland ministry, but premature deafness had thwarted (and would go on thwarting) this and other attempts to find a satisfying career. Scott subsequently corresponded with him, treated him with kindly conde-scension, gave him advice about unrequited love, engaged him as an amanuensis and librarian at Abbotsford, wrote sermons for him to use, and eventually helped find him employment in London, where he scraped a living as a junior official at the Treasury and later at Her Majesty's Stationery Office.[50] Gordon was devoted to Scott and kept extensive notes on his activities. Despite a now almost total deafness, a certain pathetic obstinacy in the man made him an excellent ob-server. Too shy and awkward to participate much in conversation, he carefully watched lip movements and gestures, missing little of what went on. He must thus have heard many anecdotes about Russia, for he was certainly at Abbotsford during visits by Orlov-Davydov, Er-molov and other Russian guests.

Wordsworth knew Scott well. He had been with him most recently in August 1825, at various venues in the Lake District including Sou-they's at Keswick and his own Rydal Mount.[51] In 1828 he hoped to go to Abbotsford, having previously visited it only at a time when the master was absent (in 1814), but his plans were frustrated and he did not get there for another three years.[52] In August 1828 he called in-stead on George Huntly Gordon in London, at the very time when Alexander Turgenev, at Abbotsford, was listening to Scott's daughter Anne play native airs on the harp, the old bard clicking his fingers or keeping time with his game leg.[53] Wordsworth and his young daugh-ter Dora introduced themselves to George Huntly with a letter from his father, Major Gordon, whom the poet had visited in Brussels ear-lier that summer together with Coleridge.[54] Why exactly Wordsworth wished to meet the son it would be hard to say, since George Huntly had little to offer England's future laureate. Gordon did, however, soon prove to be a most useful contact in London, where Wordsworth employed him as a forwarding agent for letters and even at times as an errand boy. Soon the entire Wordsworth circle was using him, in fact, and there is reason to believe some found him a figure of fun, aping his Scottish accent by referring to him as 'Gorrdon'.[55] But Words-worth himself was clearly impressed by Gordon's powers of friend-ship and loyalty, to the point where he promised to introduce him to the reticent Coleridge. This was in October 1828.[56] Despite a certain formality in their own correspondence, Wordsworth felt from the start so much at home with Gordon that he contemplated doing a tour of

Wales with him, sent him copies of his past and present works, and confided in him over the progress of his latest poetry. For instance, in November 1828 he described *The Egyptian Maid* in some detail for him.[57]

Most interestingly for us, it was to Gordon and Gordon alone (in his voluminous extant correspondence) that Wordsworth gave news of *The Russian Fugitive*. In a postscript to a letter to Gordon of 29 January 1829 he reported: 'I lately wrote a Tale (350) verses the Scene of which is laid in Russia, though it is not even tinged with Russian imagery. — It will give me great pleasure to shew it you — I think your Russian Friends would be pleased with it, in which number I include Mrs Oom and her brother though Germans.'[58] In a letter to Gordon of 20 March he reverted to 'the little Russian Poem' and assured his correspondent: 'You shall see it the first time I have the pleasure of seeing you.'[59] These remarks raise a puzzling problem. Who were Gordon's 'Russian friends', and why were Germans included among them?

The 'Germans' referred to were called Papendick; their name is sometimes found in Wordsworth's correspondence as Papendich, Papendiek, Pappendiek or Pappendike. A Herr G.E. Pappendick of Bremen was discovered by Huntly Gordon on Wordsworth's behalf as a tutor for his son Willy.[60] Unless he was perhaps originally a Baltic German, he could not be thought of as Russian. He had however a sister, a Mrs Oom, who took some responsibility for organising the little private school of which Papendick was head and at which Willy Wordsworth studied for a little over a year.[61] While it is true that there were Englishmen called Oom (in the 1840s a Mr Oom was a popular chief clerk in the Foreign Office; during one Parliamentary election his colleagues put up posters enquiring, 'For Oom shall we vote?'),[62] her husband was probably Russian: an F.A. Oom (died 1898), for instance, was secretary to Empress Mariia Aleksandrovna around 1865-68. It is nevertheless perfectly obvious from what Wordsworth had said that the Papendick family, whatever its origins, cannot have comprised the entire extent of Huntly Gordon's 'Russians'.

The explanation, I believe, is that Gordon was in correspondence, in part on Sir Walter Scott's behalf, with the guests that he had known at Abbotsford, and that Wordsworth was aware of this. Furthermore, A.I. Turgenev was in London in the spring and summer of 1828, and Gordon may have met him.[63] On 11 April Scott dined with Turgenev at the house of Mrs Elizabeth Alexander of Ballochmyle, 12 Hanover Terrace, and invited him to Scotland. Nearer the time for Turgenev to leave on his journey north, he consulted in London with Orlov-Davydov, whom Huntly Gordon may well also have seen at this period.[64] On his way up to Scotland, Turgenev stopped at Keswick to have a long talk with Southey about the impact of English poetry in Russia, telling him of Zhukovskii's translation of his fantastic ballad *The Old Woman of Berkeley* (1798), for long banned by the Russian censors.[65] Wordsworth must surely have had wind of this.

One of the greatest modern scholars in the field of Anglo-Russian relations has even asserted, without specific evidence but as a matter of fact, that A.I. Turgenev also made Wordsworth's acquaintance.[66] Certainly Turgenev followed with interest the English bard's publications, even though he probably did not understand them well. In the winter of 1828-9 he was present at a public debate in London as to whether Byron or Wordsworth was the greater poet. Byron won, Turgenev reported to some Russian friends, but only by a nose because Wordsworth was a very fine artist and a profound thinker: they would do well to read his 'Graveyard in Mountainous Scotland' and 'Two Brothers'. The works in question must actually have been *The Brothers* and 'The Churchyard among the Mountains', the latter comprising Books VI and VII of *The Excursion*.[67] Curiously enough, *The Brothers* opens with a sardonic attack on tourists who, like A.I. Turgenev perhaps,

> look and scribble, scribble on and look,
> Until a man might travel twelve stout miles,
> Or reap an acre of his neighbour's corn.

While such links as this must remain for the time being speculative, it is clear from his letters that Wordsworth considered *The Russian Fugitive* to be of potential interest for other than the likes of Mr Papendick and Mrs Oom. What is more, as soon as young Willy was settled more independently, away from any tutor's influence, Huntly Gordon's own usefulness significantly diminished and Wordsworth increasingly neglected him. Once in London in the spring of 1831 he even managed to be out at a time when he had specifically invited Gordon to call.[68] Although it is known that Gordon did visit Rydal Mount on at least one occasion, in May 1835,[69] he may not have come often — despite or perhaps because of invitations that may not have sounded fully persuasive.[70] During the 1830s the Wordsworth-Gordon correspondence gradually petered out, though it flickered again in 1845 when Gordon, forever the optimist, sent his old friend a subject for a poem which was not, however, acceptable.[71]

Whatever its immediate inspiration, it is unlikely that Wordsworth began to write *The Russian Fugitive* before November 1828. There is no hint of it of any kind, however remote, in his correspondence up to this date. But by Christmas that year he had produced in a great rush over seven hundred lines of poetry of varied character, not all of which has been positively identified. Mary Moorman believes that the corpus referred to included *The Russian Fugitive*, even though she has to admit that, with the inclusion also of several other pieces which can be named with more authority, the total tally of lines should then be much greater than it was.[72] Wordsworth may well, in fact, have composed the poem after Christmas and in the new year 1829, for the first certain mention of it is in the letter to George Huntly Gordon of 29 January. Although he did not name it then, he presumably had in mind to call it by the title which stands on the first extant manuscript: 'Ina; or, The Lodge in the Forest: A Russian Tale'.

This draft, dating from no earlier than December 1830, is actually a fair copy in Dora Wordsworth's hand; it follows versions of *The Somnambulist* and *The Poet and the Caged Turtledove*.[73] The poem next appears, now with its definitive title *The Russian Fugitive*, as a fair copy in a much longer manuscript volume made probably a little later by Dora Wordsworth and Sara Hutchinson with some additions in the poet's own hand; here it is placed between drafts of *On the Power of Sound* and the two pieces just mentioned.[74] Later still, when Wordsworth was preparing the collection *Yarrow Revisited, and Other Poems* (1835), *The Russian Fugitive* was included in two alternative manuscript volumes. The first and shorter one, apparently not used in the end, is again in Dora's hand with a few authorial changes; the poem here comes between *The Armenian Lady's Love* and *The Egyptian Maid*.[75] The second text, actually sent to and used by the printer, is a composite transcription in various hands which features some further alterations by the poet and some queries by the printer; *The Russian Fugitive* now stands between the sonnets *St. Catherine of Ledbury* and 'Why art thou silent! Is thy love a plant'.[76] There are also corrected proofs for this final text.[77]

Knowledge of the sequences of poems in which *The Russian Fugitive* was successively intended to appear is rather instructive. The pieces surrounding it were not all cognate, but some have definite relevance. Its theme of womanly constancy and virtue was explored also in *The Somnambulist*, though there with a tragic outcome. *St. Catherine of Ledbury* concerns 'a saintly Anchoress', a role which the heroine of *The Russian Fugitive* was starting to assume before her discovery by a knight (ll. 157-60). In *The Armenian Lady's Love*, Wordsworth treated the theme of a Christian captive, delivered by an admiring infidel. And in *The Poet and the Caged Turtledove* he asserted:

Love, blessed Love, is everywhere
The spirit of my song.

Another poem with which it is revealing to compare *The Russian Fu-*

gitive, though for different reasons, is the one which preceded it almost immediately in Wordsworth's poetic output: *The Egyptian Maid; or, The Romance of the Water Lily*. He described this as 'a kind of romance with as much magic in it as would serve for half a Dozen', adding that 'it rose from my brain, without let or hindrance, like a vapour'.[78] Perhaps by contrast, *The Russian Fugitive* was more realistic, and yet for English readers it was also still exotic. Wordsworth was not, of course, a stranger to such exotic subjects, which allowed his Romantic contemplation of loneliness to seem more fresh and poignant. Already in *The Complaint of a Forsaken Indian Woman*, for example, written and published as early as 1798, the alleged behaviour of some North American tribes had provided him with a novel excuse to underline the pathos of a mother, cut off from her child and left to perish in the snow. Beneath the external trappings of such strange narrative material lay universal feelings and ideas, captured at a particularly dramatic stage of their development in a given individual.

The complete text of *The Russian Fugitive* will be found in Appendix One.[79] Although a poem of impressive length and subject-matter, it has never been granted much serious critical acclaim. Mary Moorman, who in her detailed biography of Wordsworth pays little attention to the circumstances of its composition, is not alone in regarding it with patent condescension.[80] Alone among modern scholars and in an isolated article, Charles Norton Coe has ventured to give it the thorough treatment it deserves.[81] One must, however, agree at least in part with the poet's nephew Christopher, Bishop of Lincoln, who grouped *The Russian Fugitive* with *The Armenian Lady's Love* and *The Egyptian Maid* as 'beautiful specimens of the author's powers of blending the simplicity and tenderness of the old ballad with the exquisite graces of a most pure and finished diction'.[82]

Wordsworth himself acknowledged that the theme and story-line of *The Russian Fugitive* were taken from a book called *Memoirs of Peter Henry Bruce, Esq., a Military Officer, in the Services of Prussia, Russia, and Great Britain; Containing an Account of his Travels in Germany, Russia, Tartary, Turkey, the West Indies, &c., as also, Several very Interesting Private Anecdotes of the Czar, Peter I. of Russia*. This is the highly entertaining autobiography of a most remarkable man. Peter Henry Bruce was born in Germany in 1692 and brought up there and in his ancestral Scotland. Thanks to an influential Slavonicised uncle, the soldier, scientist and teacher Count Iakov (James) Vilimovich Brius, the young man was invited to enter the service of Peter the Great as a military engineer and captain of artillery.[83] He arrived in Russia in the spring of 1711 and remained there (with foreign excursions) for the next thirteen years. The account of his exploits was written up in the form of a journal, as they occurred at the time, and in

German, which was actually Bruce's native language. He himself translated it into English much later, in 1755, but it remained unpublished on his death two years afterwards and did not appear in print until 1782, at the instigation of his widow. The London edition of that year was reprinted in Dublin in 1783, and a German translation came out in Leipzig in 1784. Bruce's work achieved wide popularity with readers over the years, both in Britain and abroad. A copy found its way into the library of Alexander Pushkin, at a later date still than the composition of *The Russian Fugitive*.[84] Similarly, Henry Crabb Robinson noted in his diary for 27 May 1843: 'I rose early and looked over an entertaining book of Memoirs by Henry Bruce, from which Wordsworth has taken his Russian lady' (that is, the heroine of *The Russian Fugitive*).[85]

Wordsworth possessed the Dublin reprint of 1783.[86] He may have had it since it first came out, for he informs us that the story told in his poem had captured his imagination 'early in life'. He would thus have come across the Bruce book as a boy of thirteen, appreciating it primarily as a tale of adventure and missing, perhaps, its more adult and ambiguous particularities. On the other hand he probably reread it at a later stage, for he also tells us he had often thought that the fugitive theme would go well as an opera or music drama.[87] This was due to a belief in its historicity and grandeur, as is seen from his own brief notes on *The Russian Fugitive*: 'Peter Henry Bruce, having given in his entertaining Memoirs the substance of this Tale, affirms that, besides the concurring reports of others, he had the story from the lady's own mouth. The Lady Catherine, mentioned towards the close, is the famous Catherine, then bearing that name as the acknowledged Wife of Peter the Great.'[88]

Bruce did indeed insist on the truthfulness of his record, which he entitled 'A Virtuous Young Lady' and set in the year 1713. It is worth examining this in detail.[89] The Tsar was taken by a certain woman's beauty while dining one day at the house of her father, a foreign merchant in Moscow. He offered her any terms if she would live with him; but she refused and, fearing the consequences, quit the city without forewarning even her parents. To judge by Bruce's own account of murderous robberies, both on the Moscow streets and in the countryside,[90] the young woman was running a considerable risk by going out alone — the more so as she carried with her money enough to subsist for quite some time, and travelled several miles on foot to the village where her former nurse resided. Learning of her determination to hide in the woods near by, the nurse's husband and daughter set out at night with her to look for a suitable place. Fixing on a dry spot in the swampy forest, the man, a wood-cutter, built a little hut for her. There she stayed, attended each night by the womenfolk who purchased food for her with the money she had given them. Back in Moscow the Tsar, calling on the merchant and hearing of the young lady's flight, was angry at first, suspecting a plot, but seeing the parents' genuine grief he softened, and believed them when they said their child had taken nothing but what she stood up in. He ordered a search to be made, with a reward, but she was not to be found and her family, thinking her dead, went into mourning for her. A year and more passed before a colonel, on a hunting vacation with friends, chanced upon the hut and saw there 'a pretty young woman in a mean dress'. He learnt her story, listened kindly to her entreaties that he not betray her, but assured her that by now she might at least discover herself to her parents, the Tsar being 'otherways engaged'. He himself returned to Moscow, told the parents, and sought the advice of 'Madam Catherine' (Ekaterina Alekseevna, later Empress Catherine I, whom Peter had officially married in 1712). She procured him an audience with the Tsar, who repented of the suffering he had caused and promised to make amends. How better, urged Catherine, than to fix a 'handsome fortune' on the lady, 'and the colonel for a husband, who had the best right, having caught her in pursuit of his game'. The Tsar agreed, sent a favourite with the colonel to convey the lady back home, and personally arranged the wedding ceremony. In giving the bride to the groom he declared that he 'presented him with one of the most virtuous of women' — as well as with handsome gifts and a settlement of 3000 roubles a year upon herself and her heirs. The lady, Bruce assures us, lived 'highly esteemed' by the Tsar and by everyone who knew her. The story ends here, but Bruce later adds the coda that in 1715 the Order of St Catherine was founded, in honour of the Tsaritsa, with the motto 'For Love and Fidelity'.[91]

In view of certain differences between this anecdote and the story told by Wordsworth in *The Russian Fugitive*, the question arises as to whether the poet had access to any complementary sources. In the first place, he makes his heroine originally French. Bruce of course says that her father was foreign, but does not otherwise define her origins.[92] In various other histories of the reign of Peter the Great one reads of a French jeweller (or perhaps a wine merchant) called Monce or Munce de Lacroix, probably a Protestant, who lived first in Riga and then in Moscow and St Petersburg. He had two daughters and a son. The second daughter, Anne, was passionately loved by the Tsar but preferred the Prussian (or perhaps the Polish) ambassador. Peter found out this relationship only when her gallant drowned, leaving her letters on his body. He was at first very angry, but then broke down and wept, showing the woman unexpected clemency. A book which Wordsworth may have known, and which mentions some of this, was *Letters from a Lady, who resided some Years in Russia, to her Friend in England*, of which two editions appeared, in 1775 and 1777.[93] On the other hand, in a passage immediately preceding the story of the fugitive, Bruce himself does mention Tsar Peter's affection for 'one Miss Mons, a very beautiful young lady, born at Moscow, of foreign parents'.[94] Wordsworth may perhaps have simply made a connection between the two, assuming the name Mons to be French.

A second problem is to know why Wordsworth gave his heroine the name Ina, rather than something more obviously Russian which he might easily have found out from Huntly Gordon or others. Ina is not a common name in any language, in fact, and has not been used much in English literature save in relation to ancient British historical personages.[95] In Wordsworth's lifetime up to the period of *The Russian Fugitive*, the only literary model for the name was Barbarina, Lady Dacre's *Ina*, a five-act tragedy in verse first printed in London in 1815 and reissued in the author's *Dramas, Translations and Occasional Poems* (1821). In a short note on this play, Baroness Dacre explained why she had chosen to call her heroine Ina, even though she was aware there had been a king of that name; it had sounded feminine, she said, and reminded her of Inez de Castro on whose story the tragedy was in part based.[96] She did not point out that it happened to form the last three letters of her own given name. Lady Dacre's play is set in old Wessex, and its subject has no relation whatsoever with Wordsworth's, but he may of course have been aware of it, if only as a title.

If (as is probable) Wordsworth intended Ina as an abbreviated name, a suffix, he could have derived it from a work which may have had some influence upon him in his youth. This is Robert Merry's *Paulina; or, The Russian Daughter*.[97] Ostensibly based on a true-life story previously related by the author in a London newspaper four years earlier, this fascinating long poem was first published in 1787. A lovely maiden, her mother long since dead, lives in isolation in the country with her possessive, cruel father. A young swain appears; they woo, they embrace. Forced to hide in a chest when he hears the father approaching, he suffocates therein. Paulina asks the estate porter to dispose of the body, but he does so only on condition that she will be his. He repeatedly rapes and otherwise misuses her, and she ends by stabbing both him and his drunken, leering cronies. She then gets herself to a nunnery, with the connivance of Catherine the Great. While there can be no question of any specific influence, and while in any case there is no positive evidence that he ever read the work, it is possible that Wordsworth was inspired by Merry's poem in a general way. Though both the background and the outcome are very different from those of *The Russian Fugitive*, Paulina and the echoingly named Ina share the same attitude to nature, love and honour. In each case a

Lady Catherine helps the heroine to a solution of her predicament. Like Wordsworth himself, Merry also makes only a surface attempt to establish a specifically Russian setting, preferring to universalise his subject in a Romantic way.

This question of the Russianness or otherwise of Wordsworth's poem is something which did not concern him much but which in fact goes to the heart of its meaning and its importance. In his modest letter to Huntly Gordon of 29 January 1829 he noted that while the scene of *The Russian Fugitive* was laid in Russia it was 'not even tinged with Russian imagery'.[98] This remark has been generally misunderstood. Wordsworth was by no means ashamed of his poem and indeed was proud of its historical veracity. He was too modest to suppose that he, an Englishman who had never been to Russia and who knew far less about that country than his correspondent, could create convincing local colour, but that did not stop him from introducing a number of authentic references — to peasant huts, the Kremlin, and to icons, as well as to Peter the Great and Catherine I. All this was, however, part of the story, part of the truth, and not a vague concession to exoticism. His deviations from the original source are probably not, therefore, attempts to improve on and embellish the anecdote so much as to endow it with a greater psychological validity. In doing so, he makes it less specifically Russian, more universal.

Although perhaps too narrow in its scope, Charles Norton Coe's approach to this matter is illuminating. He claims that Wordsworth tried to give his poem 'the tone of a medieval narrative of injured innocence'.[99] Thus, the poet makes the heroine flee further into the 'wilderness' (ll. 165, 305) than Bruce does: seven nights' journey in Wordsworth (l. 18) as opposed to 'several miles' in Bruce. The place in the forest where she takes sanctuary is also gloomier and lonelier in Wordsworth than in Bruce: the noonday sunlight scarcely penetrates (ll. 99-100), and Ina is completely alone apart from occasional visits by her 'Guardians' (ll. 217-24). In her solitude the 'lone Recluse' occupies herself in tending flowers and taming birds (ll. 207-8, 221), and meditating on her parents and her distant home in France (ll. 241-56). The man who rescues her, a colonel in Bruce, becomes a 'Cavalier' in Wordsworth (l. 341), a knight-errant figure who has

> worn a sword,
> And will not hold in light esteem
> A suffering woman's word (ll. 282-4).

Whereas for Bruce's soldier the woman is an object of attraction, whom he is eventually given as a prize, Wordsworth's knight is at once romantically smitten by her and seeks high patronage in pursuit of his love. Whereas Bruce's final section about the heroine's return and triumph is relatively long, Wordsworth's is pared to a minimum so as not to detract from the overwhelming effect of her period of solitude. The poet wished above all to emphasise his heroine's feelings in relation to nature and to God and show, as so often elsewhere, 'the essential goodness of the common man'.[100]

Coe's conclusion here is doubtless valid, but he has come some way, of course, from the notion of medievalism. He is speaking in fact of the very essence of Wordsworth's Romanticism, as described in the celebrated preface to the *Lyrical Ballads* in which the poet stated that his aim was to present ordinary things in an unusual way and to examine the passions of the heart at a moment of crisis. Wordsworth's treatment of 'A Virtuous Young Lady' was thus no more medieval than Russian, but rather a dramatic and intensified study of Ina's moral fortitude. The repeated image of her as a fawn, deer, hind, or lamb (ll. 14, 61, 279, 311-12) may indeed be associated with medieval times, but equally may have classical, biblical or Romantic connotations. The poem's classical sense is, besides, reinforced by Ina's 'vestal purity' (l. 240) and by a lengthy reference to Ovid's *Metamorphoses* (ll. 177ff.), which Wordsworth himself even spelt out in a note.[101]

In some respects Wordsworth's poem is closer to Bruce than would appear from a simple comparison of the story-lines. For instance, it would not have escaped his notice that Bruce underlines the general freedom and promiscuity of Russian society women under Peter's rule, thus making the 'Virtuous Young Lady' seem more exceptional.[102] It is possible therefore that the anti-Romantic, almost prosaic opening lines 'Enough of rose-bud lips, etc.' contain an echo of Peter Henry Bruce's comment on what he considered the excessive use of make-up among society ladies: 'The Russian women are of a middling stature, generally well proportioned, and might pass for handsome in any part of Europe; their features far from despicable, were it not for that preposterous custom of painting their faces, which they lay on so abundantly, that it may truly be said they use it as a veil to hide their beauty.'[103] This is precisely it: beauty for Wordsworth, too, is not external, but rather one which scorns comparison with 'frail flowers' (ll. 5-6). His purpose is to demonstrate the commonality of such 'high beauty' (ll. 11, 193-200, 322-4) through the shining model of his Ina. Moreover, even this beauty cannot protect her, in the society of her time, from what Wordsworth primly calls 'meditated blight' (l. 12; read 'intended rape'): she needs to use her native wit and also — which is possibly unfortunate, though pathetic, too — bribery to get through the town gates (l. 9).

Another feature of *The Russian Fugitive* that may arise from references in Bruce other than in the 'Virtuous Young Lady' narrative itself is the poet's insistence on icons. The lines in question are 'To one mute Presence...' (ll. 209-16), where Wordsworth describes a picture of 'the Mother-maid' on Ina's cabin wall which helped to shorten her wearisome days and calm her troubled nights. This passage, interestingly enough, is not found in Wordsworth's earliest manuscript and must have been added in 1831 or later. One might therefore suppose that he put it in on the advice of Huntly Gordon or some other friend conversant with Russian practices. He could have discussed the poem with Scott, for instance, during his visit to Abbotsford from 19 to 22 September 1831.[104] On the other hand, Mrs Wordsworth noted in connection with *The Russian Fugitive*: 'Not a Russian house, Bruce tells us, was, at his time, without a picture of the Virgin.'[105]

Bruce in fact refers to Russian icons at two points in his memoirs. In one place he relates how a Western-educated Russian was burnt at the stake by the clergy for having thrown an icon into the fire.[106] Elsewhere he stresses the importance of icons in a Russian household, asserting that a message was once not delivered to him because he had no domestic icon and the messenger left in disgust.[107] It is striking anecdotes like this which have ensured the continuing relevance of Bruce and led to his being cited in more modern times.[108] However, Bruce consistently (and correctly) refers to images of saints in people's houses, not ones of the Virgin Mary. If Wordsworth went further, it was perhaps in the knowledge that cardinal importance in the Russian iconic tradition was accorded to the Bogoroditsa, Mother of God, in her manifestations of mother of compassion and mother enthroned. Her immaculate conception and her assumption, in the Orthodox faith as in the Catholic, endowed her with eternal purity and sinless femininity of the sort that Wordsworth wished readers to assume in his Ina.

On the other hand it is possible that Wordsworth here was following another source, namely the book by Guy Miege mentioned earlier — *A Relation of the Embassies from his Sacred Majestie Charles II to the Great Duke of Muscovie, ...in the Years 1663 and 1664*. This speaks much of icons and their veneration, right down to common people's houses where to pay respects to the holy picture is the first thing for any visitor to do, but is specific only in relation to the icon of the Virgin Mary over the city gates of Moscow.[109] Wordsworth could thus have assumed that icons were, essentially, the same as Catholic images. This would fit with other allusions in *The Russian Fugitive*, for instance to 'the Holy Virgin' and 'our Lady' (ll. 83, 85), to 'this fair Votaress' and 'anchoress' (ll. 158, 201), and of course to the fact that Ina's father (perhaps also her mother) came from France (ll. 241-56, 314). Interestingly enough, the longest passage added to the poem at a late stage (ll. 73-88) is precisely the most Catholic-sounding and makes comment, therefore, on the icon passage presumably introduced contemporaneously. One may note, finally, that two references to saints (ll. 169, 235) completely ignore the fact that a truly Orthodox heroine would have had a personal one of her own. It is therefore necessary to suggest, for the little that it is worth, that Wordsworth's thinking in relation to Ina's religion was at least muddled, if not actually wrong-headed. The fact that he could not really have studied the Russian milieu very closely is seen in an allusion to Moscow's supposed 'glittering spires' (l. 348) — a surprising concept for anyone at least mildly aware of those Orthodox onion domes.

Perhaps, therefore, Wordsworth was not being unduly modest when he said the poem was not very Russian. In some respects it is actually rather English, as witness the 'glimmering fire' (l. 34) and 'hearth' (l. 145). The fact is that the trappings were less crucial for Wordsworth than the truthfulness to life. That this proved a stumbling-block for some readers is seen in the way that John Masefield reworked Bruce's 'Virtuous Young Lady' theme in his interesting poem *Natalie Maisie* (1942). Here the daughter of an English merchant and a Russian mother in St Petersburg has earlier been reared by a 'wood-wife'. She falls in love with a sailor, Michael, who has to go off to sea. Tsar Peter dances with her, and is enamoured. Natalie Maisie flees to her foster-mother, who hides her, but in the end she returns to the city and is married to Michael. The whole is much more authentically Russian than Wordsworth, though of course it is also a tribute to him. For all its surface faults, *The Russian Fugitive* is a noble, tender and uplifting tale of virtue rewarded, a triumph of 'Faith, which doth all passions tame' (l. 173). Its Russianness may in the end be largely incidental, but without a Russian source and a historical Russian setting it has no raison d'être and would lose both its charm and its power.

Wordsworth devoted no further poems to Russian subjects, but retained to his death in 1850 a lively curiosity in Russia. This was, however, now primarily political. In 1839, for instance, he complained to an acquaintance that Russia (and also Prussia) secretly connived at the 'crushing despotism' of Austria in Italy.[110] He must have felt the same about Poland, for he started to take a considerable interest in that country through the works of opposition figures like the émigré Counts Krasiński.[111] There is even some evidence that he became personally involved with Polish exiles, because Henry Crabb Robinson noted in his diary for 8 August 1843: 'I forgot to mention yesterday that I had had a letter from John Wordsworth of Keswick enclosing a Russian letter which he wants me to translate, addressed to an impostor calling himself Count Osolinski. I took it to the Athenaeum, where Hall undertook to show it to Kohl, the Russian traveller.... This matter occupied my attention, though it was hardly right in Wordsworth to advise his nephew to send it to me; but this comes of having the character of a good-natured man....'[112]

Not long after this, Wordsworth had what might be termed his last brush with Russianness. In September 1843, while travelling by train from Darlington to York with his wife and their maid, he met and conversed with a woman whose identity it would be most intriguing to establish. She had lived for twenty years in St Petersburg, and was soon to return. All her ten children, of one of whom — a grown son — she had just taken leave, had been born to her in that city. Three or four years previous to the present time, however, she had visited the Lake District, entered the grounds of Rydal Mount, and caught a glimpse of Wordsworth. Though she was not handsome, her expression was animated and her conversation showed her to be 'a very interesting person, intelligent, wellread and informed'. Her voice had an attractive lilt associated with long residence abroad. As they parted, she declared that her meeting with Wordsworth would remain a memorable day for her.[113] For the poet, meanwhile, this authentic bicultural figure out of Russia must have provided a distant reminder of his own now long since matronly Fugitive.

During the last years of his life, Wordsworth also had dealings with some of the other chief subjects of this book. Elizabeth Barrett Barrett of course thrust herself upon his attention with her sonnet on Benjamin Haydon's painting *Wordsworth on Helvellyn*. He was not particularly enthusiastic about her work, and on learning she was to marry Browning drily remarked: 'Her choice is a very able man, and I trust that it will be a happy union, not doubting that they will speak more intelligibly to each other than, notwithstanding their abilities, they have yet done to the Public.'[114] A brief poetic association of a quite different kind occurred in the first week of September 1849, when Elizabeth Missing Sewell called at Rydal Mount with her Bonchurch friends and neighbours Captain and Lady Jane Swinburne. They had brought with them their twelve-year-old son Algernon, who knew Wordsworth's poetry well and greatly looked forward to meeting him. Learning of this from the boy's mother, their host said that 'he supposed Algernon might have read 'We are Seven' and some other little things', but that in any case 'there was nothing in his writings that would do the boy harm'; he agreed that young Swinburne would probably not forget his visit, implying by his tone of voice that he himself would not be of this world much longer.[115]

Wordsworth likewise had some desultory and often distant relations with Tennyson. He admired his work, but lukewarmly.[116] Tennyson, for his part, had mixed feelings about the laureate, and tended to avoid him through a mixture of shyness and doubt.[117] He found him insufficiently attentive to style, yet grudgingly considered him — at his best — to be 'the greatest English poet since Milton'.[118] The two bards met and dined together in London in the spring of 1845, and paid each other compliments.[119] Wordsworth afterwards wrote of Tennyson: 'He is decidedly the first of our living Poets, and I hope will live to give the world still better things.' What was more, Wordsworth added, 'he expressed in the strongest terms his gratitude to my writings. To this I was far from indifferent though persuaded that he is not much in sympathy with what I should myself most value in my attempts, viz the spirituality with which I have endeavoured to invest the material Universe, and the moral relation under which I have wished to exhibit its most ordinary appearances.'[120] While by no means true in all respects of Tennyson, this judgment doubtless has some validity for the younger laureate's outpourings on Russia.

CHAPTER 2: Alfred Tennyson (1809-92)

There is no doubting Tennyson's stance with respect to the land of the Tsars. In his late sixties he would declare: 'I've hated Russia ever since I was born, and I'll hate her till I die.'[1] In actual fact, the hatred started *before* he was born — in the very first year of the century.

George Clayton Tennyson, the poet's father, is often represented as something of a braggart and a ne'er-do-well. At Cambridge, certainly, his behaviour tended to be wild: he once put a pistol-shot through a window of Trinity chapel.[2] Perhaps as an ironic punishment, he was assigned for ordainment to the Church, but before taking a cure he made a continental trip. Wherever else he may have gone (the whole episode is mysterious), he went to Russia. The Emperor Paul had been murdered on the night of 11 March (old style), 1801, and was succeeded by his eldest son, Alexander. Paul's brief reign had been unpopular at home; and towards the end he concluded a pact with Napoleon which shocked and antagonised England. It is even said that he had plans for joining the French in a conquest of India. One can readily imagine the relief that his assassination brought in London and the consequent rejoicing there when, during the course of June, the new Emperor made formal reconciliation possible between the two nations. Some even believe that Sir Charles Whitworth, British Minister at St Petersburg from 1789 to 1800, who had as mistress Olga Zherebtsova, sister of the Zubov brothers at the centre of the plot, gave British secret service funds to bring Paul down. Whitworth hated the militarism and empty pomp of the reign, as well as fearing the Tsar's bouts of mad cruelty. How personal and how official an attitude this was is hard to say, but the British government did have a high regard for the most notable conspirator (though not technically a regicide), the military governor of St Petersburg Count Piotr Alekseevich Pahlen; and a more powerful man still whose name, rightly or wrongly, was also associated with the affair was one of Russia's leading anglophiles, General Aleksey Grigor'evich Orlov.[3] This background is important, crucial even, for a proper understanding of George Clayton Tennyson's supposed experiences in Russia.

The purpose of his visit was to attend Alexander's coronation in

Moscow on 15 September (old style). It is clear that he had some prior interest in the country, possessing as he did several books of travels in the Russian empire, a life of Catherine the Great, and the momentous *Secret Memoirs of the Court of Petersburg,* translated from the French and published in London in 1800.[4] Also, the man who was to represent England at the ceremony, Lord St Helens, was an alumnus of his own college, St John's, so an invitation would be easy to obtain. George duly set sail for Kronstadt, thinking to arrive in Moscow in good time, but on reaching St Petersburg saw that he had misjudged the distances and decided to stay on there in the hope of glimpsing the Emperor on his return to the capital. However, Alexander delayed in Moscow until quite late in October and George, meanwhile, left for the older city with some friends, intending to go back to England via Hamburg in the new year.[5] This is the external evidence, which seems reasonably reliable. The following anecdote, if at all true, must therefore begin in Moscow in the late autumn of 1801. It is given in Alfred Tennyson's own reported words:[6]

One night St. Helens had a grand dinner, at which were all the foreign ambassadors and many Russian notables, not one of whose names my father had caught. In some way it came about that a guarded allusion was made, during the dinner, to the death of the late czar. My father, who caught it, leaned over, almost across the breast of some Russian dignitary covered with decorations, who sat next to him, and cried out in his quick, impulsive way, 'Why, St. Helens, what's the use of speaking so gingerly about a matter so notorious? We know well enough in England that the Emperor Paul was murdered in the Mikhailovski Palace, and we know exactly who did it. Count Zoboff knocked him down, and Benningsen and Count Pahlen strangled him.'

An appalling hush fell for a moment upon the table, and then Lord St. Helens at once rushed into some subject discreetly foreign to the sixth commandment. 'It's the custom, as you know,' continued he, 'in Russia not to sit over the wine, as is usual in England, but to go into another room where the samovar is, and there have tea, or more wine or vodka, and a smoke.' As the company rose, Lord St. Helens, standing by the door as the guests filed out, gave my father a meaning look to drop behind the rest. As my father came up to him, he said in a hurried whisper: 'Don't go into the next room but fly for your life. No flag can protect you in such a country as this. The man next you across whose breast you leaned, was Count Pahlen, one of the most powerful nobles in Russia. Zoboff was at the table, too, and you have publicly charged both of them with being assassins. If you don't get away to-night, you'll be inside the dungeons of St. Peter and St. Paul within forty-eight hours. Go to a Scotch merchant's, whom I know, just outside of Odessa' (giving him the name), 'and he will conceal you until I can contrive to get you out of the country, if it be possible. Post to-night — the fastest horses you can get. I'll keep the company as late as I can. Don't even stop to change your clothes.'

My father rushed away to his hotel, called up his courier, and made him order a four-horse droshky, while he literally pitched his clothes into his portmanteau. He posted all night and the next day still in his evening clothes, weather bitterly cold; but he had a clever courier, and found his Scotchman, in whose house he lay perdue for weeks.

St. Helens managed to get a message to him to be on the alert, and when he heard the horn of the 'Queen's Messenger' blown three times to be ready to go with the man who gave the signal. At last, one stormy night, he heard the welcome sound, and, disguised as a servant of the messenger, who was being sent home with despatches (which, by the way, he lost, as he was very drunk, but which were found by my father), and for whom an English frigate was waiting at Odessa, got safe on board and so back to England.

Tennyson's account here recorded was first noted down in 1887 by W. G. McCabe and elaborated by him in an article written in 1899 and published in 1902. On discovering another version of the story in Hallam Tennyson's *Memoir* of his father, first printed publicly in 1897, McCabe acknowledged that there were differences but claimed: 'I set it down "as 'twas told to me".'[7] The fact that so much time had elapsed may explain some obvious errors, although Tennyson himself could be to blame for most. The fortress of Sts Peter and Paul is in St Petersburg, whereas the dinner is definitely stated in McCabe's introduction as taking place in Moscow. In 1801 the British government would have had a King's and not a Queen's Messenger; and a frigate would scarcely have met this man in Odessa to convey his despatches from St Petersburg and Moscow. A four-horse droshky would be an oddity. More seriously, not only is Zubov's name misspelt and his distinguishing Christian name (Platon) not given; Pahlen neither strangled Paul nor was likely to be at a banquet in Moscow in November, having been placed in internal exile by the Emperor Alexander.[8]

There is nevertheless a convincing similarity between McCabe's and Hallam's texts; and although the latter lacks some details provided by the other — notably the names of the conspirators — and differs slightly in the manner of St Helens's warning, it is actually more extravagant and less credible than McCabe's. It makes Tennyson's father ride through Russia on horseback 'for weeks and weeks' (presumably in part over snow); has him falling ill in the Crimea, tended by wild locals who dance round pronouncing magic formulae; has him sitting up in bed in his delirium each time he thinks he hears the horn; shows him sobering up the courier by threatening not to return the missing diplomatic papers; and has the intrepid pair rushing through a customs post at night crying out 'le duc de York!' This other version does, however, predate the McCabe — or so it seems. It was related by Tennyson to a couple of bishops in 1873 and recorded immediately by his wife; but the actual pages of Emily's diary used by Hallam for this account are missing from the manuscript at Lincoln and may, for all one knows, have been embroidered in the later retelling.[9]

What is to be made of all this? The first thing to stress is that Tennyson the poet did actually believe the story and told it on various occasions: there is at least one other extant version, noted by a lady in the 1880s.[10] On the other hand, he does appear to have altered it each time, depending on his audience. The lady, for example, was given the name of Orlov instead of those of Zubov and Pahlen, perhaps because it was better known to her; and although the McCabe text is long-winded, it has a certain factual restraint due, no doubt, to the circumstance that McCabe himself had just come back from Russia. The more lurid details, meanwhile, were included for the benefit of the Bishop of Winchester and the American Bishop of Albany (William Croswell Doane), probably in an attempt to show the originality of Tennyson's unorthodox clerical father. It is possible that the poet invented some things on the spur of the moment, whether to impress his visitors or to denigrate Russia. But even if many aspects of the tale were discounted, there would still be a centre which he found credible; he must have thought that escape there was, and that there had been cause for it. Outside evidence, besides, corroborates that the family had no direct news from George for many weeks, and perhaps not at all during his five-month journey, as also that he returned to England in early February 1802 in appallingly bad health. Sir Charles Tennyson and others have compared the incident to still more melodramatic adventures which were supposed to have befallen him in Italy in 1830, and which he almost certainly made up, but the difference is that by then he was already in poor mental health; his children did not repeat *these* tales, which were completely without political or historical significance.[11]

The whole truth will doubtless never be known, but the story demonstrates the importance, both for George Clayton and later for his son, of contemporary Anglo-Russian affairs. Politically speaking, Alfred Tennyson's early years were dominated by the complex European struggle with Napoleon. Anti-French epigrams and ditties, tales of British valour on land and sea, newspaper reports of interminable clashes, victories, defeats, speeches, treaties made and broken, great powers changing sides, Trafalgar, Waterloo, the Hundred Days: all this crowded pell-mell in the young child's consciousness and formed his patriotic love of England, contempt for France, belief in the righteous nature of his country's wars and — for our present purpose — a view of Russia which already showed the ambivalence of that which he displayed in middle and later life. As an apparently fickle power, intent on national aggrandisement and quick reward, Russia deserved chastisement by Napoleon as a latter-day Genghis Khan; yet as the nation who swallowed up the Grande Armée and spewed out the Beast of Revelation, it merited eternal praise. Treachery and heroism were thus closely intermingled in the popular British attitude to Russia — as they would be again in 1941. George Clayton Tennyson must have told his legendary tale innumerable times either to or in the presence of Frederick, Charles, Alfred, and the rest, in relation to events in 1812, 1815, 1825, and on any other occasion when there was the possibility of confrontation between England and Russia or when Russian behaviour seemed particularly barbarous. As a boy and youth, Alfred would have read into his father's strange adventures all the excitement, danger, and capriciousness of Russian life and experience.[12]

On the other hand, it is evident (and again this is typical) that our young poet had only a very hazy idea of Russia's actual appearance. In *King Charles's Vision*, published in *Poems by Two Brothers* in 1827, he spoke of Swedish dreams of advancing[13]

> 'Through narrow pass, over dark morass,
>> 'And the waste of the weary plain,
> 'Over ice and snow, where the dark streams flow,
>> 'Through the woods of the wild Ukraine...'

Here he was as confused over the geography of the Russian empire as he was elsewhere in the piece over the complexities of Ukrainian history: perhaps it is not surprising that he thought his father would have needed 'weeks and weeks' to ride from Moscow to the Crimea. Similarly, in the ode *On Sublimity*, also published in 1827, he added to a heterogeneous list of mountains with impressive peaks

> The dizzy cape of winds that cleaves the sky,
> Whence we look down into eternity,

— and explained in a note that the 'cape' in question was situated in the Ukraine.[14] Perhaps he was really thinking of the Caucasus; but then in *The Poet*, which appeared in 1830, he alluded to that region only as the eastern limit of the ancient world, and he elsewhere used the term 'Caucasian' in the early nineteenth- (and late twentieth-) century meaning of 'Indo-European'.[15] For the rest, Tennyson's conception of the Russian people (as opposed to the high nobility) was characteristically British and conventional. The boors who treated his sick father had been fierce and incantatory; and now in his play *The Devil and the Lady*, written probably in 1823-24, he made the necromancer tell a rosary of nationalistic clichés which include the 'bold brave Switzer', 'musical Italian', 'sleepy Turk' and 'thievish Russ'.[16]

Perhaps all this should not be taken seriously. It is no more meaningful to base arguments on such trivialities than to assume that Tennyson knew or cared anything about the Russian empire because he had in his garden at Somersby as a boy a fine Siberian crab-apple tree or at Farringford as a man some Russian violets.[17] When all is said, it is the philosophy and politics that count in life, not the history or geography; and if we follow the poet now to university, to Cambridge and to Trinity, in 1827, we shall see his first real effort to put into verse what he had long felt deeply about Russia. He wrote a poem on 'The Invasion of Russia by Napoleon Buonaparte', which was set as the subject for the Chancellor's Gold Medal for English Verse in 1828. This competition, first instituted in the academic year 1812-13, was open to anyone with at least one term's residence at the University of Cambridge. The Vice-Chancellor announced a topic, generally political or historical, at the end of the Michaelmas term. Entries, not exceeding 200 lines, had to be submitted by 31 March the following year; they were to be printed or lithographed, not written in the candidate's own hand. Secrecy was ensured by a complex system of envelopes, and all the material of unsuccessful candidates was theoretically destroyed as soon as the winner was announced. The medallist recited his poem in the Senate House on Commencement Day.[18] The annual roll of honour includes some famous names. The very first winner, in 1813, was George Waddington of Trinity for a poem on Columbus; subsequent medallists numbered William Whewell, Edward G. Lytton Bulwer and Thomas Babington Macaulay (twice).

The winner in 1828 was Christopher Wordsworth, afterwards Bishop of Lincoln, son of the then Master of Trinity and nephew of England's future laureate. Christopher had already secured the medal for Trinity in the previous year with a poem on 'The Druids'; he took it again this time with a forceful and melodious yet fundamentally unadventurous piece which, like his uncle's treatments of the same theme, emphasised the roles of nature and the Lord of Hosts in Napoleon's crushing defeat. Phrases like 'the artillery of heaven' and 'the white waste' of the snow, and the depiction of winter not as a conventional *'pale, palsied'* wanderer but as a 'dauntless Rider' echo or extend William Wordsworth's own metaphors. But although Christopher found space for a long apostrophe of the late Count Rostopchin, 'by whose advice' (as he said in a note) 'Moscow was set on fire by the Russians', and even introduced the pleasant but dubiously relevant remark 'And Granta bids her youthful bards relate/How bright in life thou wert, in death how great', he did not attempt to get into the mind of Napoleon and, again like his uncle, presented everything *sub specie aeternitatis*. As for the style of his poem, it is a continuous ode in couplets of iambic pentameters. It actually broke the rule of maximum length, consisting as it does of 250 lines and a Greek epigraph.[19] Another poem entered for the Chancellor's Medal in 1828, apparently by John Frere of Eton and Trinity, was printed in Cambridge that year and has survived. It is entitled *The Expedition of Napoleon Buonaparte into Russia* and bears the enigmatic Latin legend: 'Secundus, sed linus secundior'. We have here a measured, stately ode in twenty-eight nine-line stanzas, each comprising eight iambic pentameters and one iambic hexameter with a rhyme-scheme *ababbcbcc*. There is an excellent description of the Moscow fires, and striking (though perhaps already conventional) images like 'the corses in their winding sheet of snow'.[20]

Both Tennyson and his elder brother Charles wrote poems on Napoleon at the time which were probably submitted for the competition. Because the rules required that all entries but the winner's be destroyed, there is really no means of knowing this for sure.[21] What remains of Alfred's manuscript, almost a hundred lines of heroic couplets, is preserved in Notebook 19 at Trinity College under Hallam Tennyson's arbitrary title *Napoleon's Retreat from Moscow*. The text was first published by Christopher Ricks in 1969 and engendered correspondence and debate which have bearing on its proper interpretation.[22] Professor Ricks pointed out that the metre of the poem is Pope's, and one that had fascinated Tennyson since the age of ten or eleven. He also found linguistic affinities with other early pieces, including *The Vale of Bones*, published in 1827. Hallam's note 'written about 16', though vague, could therefore have sense in that there might well have been several youthful versions which have not come down to us. Perhaps, even, Tennyson was using material originally intended for a quite different purpose. 'It is quite likely', argued Professor Ricks, 'that he was revising some earlier verses, especially since much of the surviving fragment on Napoleon is not on Napoleon.' Readers of the poem as it stands may find this opinion controversial, since in the longer work that Tennyson would have needed to write for the Gold Medal the existing lines could have formed a perfectly relevant part. The poet, like Napoleon himself, was clearly obsessed by the strange and menacing oriental beauty of Moscow and by the almost incomprehensible suffering that the French were prepared to inflict upon themselves in order to possess and conquer it. There is something appropriately Romantic in this, and one might have expected the complete ode to add an artistic, mystical, and vaguely Pre-Raphaelite flavour to the historico-political dish.

A study of Tennyson's manuscript shows that we may in any case have here fragments rather than a fragment. Three leaves have been torn from the notebook just before the now published text starts, and two more after it finishes. In the former position there might have stood a passage that could make sense of the present opening, which is both inconsequential and probably misplaced. In the latter place, beginnings and ends of lines are just visible on what is left of the sheets: one notes, for example, the rhyme 'glares'/'squares' and the phrase 'ips' — presumably 'lips' — 'are dumb'. It is likely that these too had once formed part of the draft poem on Napoleon. What remains of the piece, moreover, is not entirely consecutive. There is a lacuna after 'sheeny gold'; after 'raptured eye' Tennyson deleted, and presumably intended partly to make up for, the couplet

> With all her domes of Copper richly dun,
> Her thirty steeples glittering in the Sun;

and the final passage from 'There stood' to 'shaken to its base' is completely crossed out. Probably the poet did not want it here at all, as in some ways it could seem to belong at or nearer to the beginning of the work. Its last two lines, besides, had been previously struck out by Tennyson and are given in the form re-established by Professor Ricks. It remains only to say that at 'sterner light' (1. 9) there was previously 'brighter sun', and that in this and the preceding line I have altered Ricks's 'fierce' and 'lie' to 'fiercer' and 'be'. In a letter to the *Times Literary Supplement* he cogently defended his readings against a critic, and the Librarian of Trinity came to his support, but my own study of the original persuades me that, however unsatisfactory in context, 'fiercer' and 'be' are correct.[23] Here then is all we have of *Napoleon's Retreat from Moscow*, alias *The Invasion of Russia by Napoleon Buonaparte*. If the poem was indeed entered for the Chancellor's Gold Medal, this draft may be dated between late December 1827 and mid-March the following year.

> Then when the snow-storm and the driving rain
> Mingle the white sky with the whiter plain
> And fast and far along the spangling snow
> In cloudy bands the vengeful Cossacks go,
> Hath not thy pride sought out and borne away
> Early and late the spoiling and the prey?
>
> The fiery glancing of thine eye shall quail
> Before a fiercer frown, thy star shall pale
> Before a sterner light, thy voice shall be
> Low from the dust and murmur noiselessly   10
> As one who summons from his silent clay
> The formless, shrouded Spirit past away
> And bending down above his narrow cell
> Whispers the name he loved so long and well.
>   Strange looked the City; no exulting smoke
> From her high halls in azure column broke,
> No note of crowded mart, or busy feet
> Or voice of man along the echoing street,
> No sound of high carouse or solemn wail
> Came down in mingled murmur on the gale;   20
> It seemed a city of the past, a land
> Of shadow and of silence, where the wand
> Of chill Enchantment over all had rolled
> Oblivion, as in Arab story told
> Where each unheard, unhearing, and alone

In his wide hall stood fixed to bloodless stone,
Or vision, such as that which dimly gleams
Through varied majesties of solemn dreams
Where terrace upon terrace and the height
Of Dome on Dome repose in placid light
Imperially beautiful, but wan
And pale and tenantless and void of Man.
Her princely Pagods of barbaric mould,
Her clustered Cupolas of sheeny gold [...]

'Hail to the Holy City' rung the cry
As Moscow burst upon the raptured eye,
Her proud Pavilions and her mingled trees
And Pomp of Oriental palaces,
The pillared front of many an airy Hall,
Crescent and gorgeous cross and golden Ball
Glistening and flashing with the restless play
Of rainbow hues beneath the waning day:
'Hail to the mighty town! the diadem
Of lordly Cities! the Jerusalem
Of Russia! Hail to Moscow!'
                    Far along
Rang the glad shouting through the haggard throng;
A deep, dark flush of momentary bloom
Lit up the warworn cheek's cadaverous gloom,
The hot tear trembled in each hollow eye,
There was a thought of former Victory,
A hope of future. All the trophied Past,
The days of glowing Conquest thick and fast
And brilliantly on the expanded brain
Came flashing through the Night of thought again,
Friends shook each other by the hand and wept
And some in ecstasy of transport leapt;
Some dashed them down upon their knees; some raised
Their tremulous eyes to where the Eagles blazed;
Some full of hope and glory fondly deemed
They were the Demi-Gods of Earth and dreamed
Of garlanded processions and the march
Of victor hosts beneath triumphal arch.
Where was the Glory ever equalled theirs,
Glory well purchased with uncounted cares,
Their freely-gushing blood the ample price,
Their martyred brethren the proud sacrifice?
All were forgotten now — the driving rains,
The lonely bivouack on the wintry plains,
The chill wild wind which murmured deep and harsh
O'er the lorn waste of many a putrid marsh,
Their nearest and their dearest whose wan forms
Lay mouldering whitely in the frequent storms,
The agony, the battle and the flood,
The houseless mountain fringed with horrent wood,
The humid couch upon the tentless mould,
Their watchings and their weariness, their cold,
Their hungers and their faintings and their tears,
Were but the glorious tale of coming years,

A tale of mighty deeds which would eclipse
All others, babbled forth by infant lips,   80
A tale which Age would dwell on, ever new,
A Paean of high Conquest thrilling through
Ages on Ages of undying Fame.
They were a name for ever, a great name,
A watchword to Posterity, a light
To future armies in the maddened fight.

    There stood a Monarch on the Sainted Hill,
A Monarch and a Despot whose high will
Well-nigh omnipotent on Earth had weighed
Strength against Strength and mightily essayed   90
To shadow with the compass of his Power
From East to West the grandeur and the flower
And Excellence and Pride of Earth — the Man
Of grasping Intellect and Giant Plan,
The man of many thoughts before whose face
The populous Earth was shaken to its base.

Brought up as he was in the age of Wilberforce and Byron, Tennyson soon learned to rail at tyranny and corruption... so long as they were safely ensconced on the other side of the Channel. In a poem *Written During the Convulsions in Spain*, composed in or before 1827, he exclaimed

Sweetly may Freedom's rays
Smile on thy future days,

and a similar sentiment was expressed about the same time in *Switzerland* (though this may be actually by Charles).[24] But it was the plight of the Poles under Russian domination which most concerned the young Cambridge undergraduate. By the terms of the Congress of Vienna of 1814-15, the ancient territories of Poland were divided between Prussia, Austria and Russia with the latter receiving the lion's share in the east. The so-called Kingdom of Poland thus formed, with Warsaw as its centre, had a relatively liberal constitution but its armed forces were under the command of Grand Duke Constantine, brother of the late Alexander I. Following the French revolution of July-August 1830, student unrest in Warsaw culminated on 29 November in an attempt to capture Constantine. Resisting the intention of Tsar Nicholas I both to crush such disaffection and to use Polish troops in a planned new invasion of France, the indigenous army joined with the students and the people, and it took the Russians many months to put down what became a fiercely-fought rebellion. Warsaw finally surrendered only on 8 September 1831; but on 26 February 1832 the separate constitution was revoked and the kingdom of Poland became, in effect, a province of the Russian empire.

English writers had consistently been attacking Russia over the Polish question. Walter Savage Landor had done so either openly or by implication in some of his earlier *Imaginary Conversations*, and would afterwards revert to the subject in various places including the brief poem *To Czartoryski, Attending on Foot the Funeral of the Poet Niemcewicz* (1841), which expressed the hope that Poland would one day be reunited and free.[25] During the new crisis of 1830-32, many poets rallied to the Polish cause. In 1831 Isaac Brandon published his anonymous *Poland: A Patriotic Ode*, and in the same year Henry Sewell Stokes included vigorous pro-Polish pieces in his collection *The Song of Albion, a Poem Commemorative of the Crisis; Lines on the Fall of Warsaw; and Other Poems*. Also this year one finds the Scottish weaver Charles Fleming's *Song of the Poles*, Richard Chenevix Trench's sonnet *Poland, 1831*, and the anonymous *Poland! Extracts from the Latest News from Poland, Describing the Gallant Conduct of the Poles, with an Order of the Day and a War Song for the Polish Soldiers, etc.* In 1832 there followed William Edmondstoune Aytoun's anonymous *Poland; Homer; and Other Poems*, in which the first title ode was inscribed to exiles of the recent uprising. Also in this period John Brent was working on his anti-Russian *Lays of Poland*, first collected in 1836, and Ebenezer Elliott in *The Polish Fugitives* (1835) and elsewhere would mourn the sad aftermath of the rebellion and, once again, criticise England for remaining idle at the time.[26]

Tennyson himself immediately celebrated the rising of 1830 with a sonnet, *Written on Hearing of the Outbreak of the Polish Insurrection*. It is obvious that he researched and constructed this carefully, since there were several drafts and the poem contains a number of historical details he could not have had by heart, going back to Bolesław the Great who around 1000 gained Pomerania and started driving Russia back towards Kiev. One version of the sonnet has a reference to the Jagiełło dynasty (as well as to the Piasts), rejected probably because of its barbaric sound in English; and all texts reach their climax in allusions, somewhat muddled in sense, to the chancellor Jan Zamoiski and the Herculean Jan Sobieski, later John III. Although deeply felt, the poem is somewhat conventional and ends in distinct bathos. Its form is intended as Petrarchan, but there is a faulty rhyme in the eighth line which rather throws the thing off balance: the last word makes a pair with that of the following line, the first of the sestet, and not with its ostensible partners in the octave. One therefore has an improbable abbaabbc cdcdcd instead of the expected abbaabba cdcdcd. (All this assumes, of course, that in Tennyson's Lincolnshire speech 'war' did not actually rhyme with 'afar'.) For reasons like these, perhaps, Tennyson never had the sonnet reprinted after it first appeared in

December 1832. Here it is:[27]

> Blow ye the trumpet, gather from afar
> The hosts to battle: be not bought and sold.
> Arise, brave Poles, the boldest of the bold;
> Break through your iron shackles — fling them far.
> O for those days of Piast, ere the Czar
> Grew to this strength among his deserts cold;
> When even to Moscow's cupolas were rolled
> The growing murmurs of the Polish war!
> Now must your noble anger blaze out more
> Than when from Sobieski, clan by clan,
> The Moslem myriads fell, and fled before —
> Than when Zamoysky smote the Tatar Khan;
> Than earlier, when on the Baltic shore
> Boleslas drove the Pomeranian.

In 1831 Tennyson wrote a second sonnet on Poland which he also published in his collected *Poems* of 1832 (dated 1833 on the title-page). Although there called *On the Result of the Late Russian Invasion of Poland*, it was probably composed originally in the summer of 1831 before the revolt was quite over. Tennyson reprinted this piece in 1872, and it is not hard to see why: not only had there by that time been another rebellion put down by the Russians — that of 1863-64, — the poem was also finer and suggested something rather daring for the age, namely that Britain should recognise a burden of responsibility for the partition of Poland after 1815. On the other hand it is interesting that Tennyson should still, at twenty-two, have considered Russians the 'last and least of men' and made a direct appeal to God to do something about them. The religious force of his poem is heightened by its being in Miltonic form and reminding one a little, in fact, of Milton's own *On the Late Massacre in Piedmont*; further, it begins and ends with allusions to Isaiah, the Psalms, Revelations, and St Luke. All this brings it great nobility. The only textual change of note made during the sonnet's composition was the substitution of 'icy-hearted' for the first manuscript reading 'iron-hearted'. Though a detail, this accords well with Tennyson's belief in the essential coldness of the Russian empire and its rule, seen already in the 'deserts cold' of the earlier poem. Pushkin's 'warm south' was unknown to him and he figured Russia as a kind of Arctic waste. Even the land of the midnight sun, for him, could only be Norway.[28] Here then is the second sonnet, called just *Poland* in its definitive edition:[29]

> How long, O God, shall men be ridden down,
> And trampled under by the last and least
> Of men? The heart of Poland hath not ceased
> To quiver, though her sacred blood doth drown

> The fields, and out of every smouldering town
> Cries to thee, lest brute Power be increased,
> Till that o'ergrown Barbarian in the East
> Transgress his ample bound to some new crown:—
> Cries to Thee, 'Lord, how long shall these things be?
> How long this icy-hearted Muscovite
> Oppress the region?' Us, O Just and Good,
> Forgive, who smiled when she was torn in three;
> Us, who stand now, when we should aid the right —
> A matter to be wept with tears of blood!

This was by no means the end of Tennyson's interest in Poland. He later claimed to have written, at about this same period, what he termed 'a beautiful poem' on the subject, 'hundreds of lines long', with which an inattentive housemaid lit the fire.[30] It is possible that *Hail Briton!* was connected with the same project, since it contains references to Poland and to Nicholas's reign and urges Britons to stand up for liberty. The history of this poem is complex, and it was not published in its entirety until modern times. It is in any case concerned chiefly with condemning party politics and selfish passions in the England of the Reform Bill, and preaches a conservative, or perhaps a gradualist, approach to change. But it does forge an unexpected yet powerful link between the British freedoms which — as Tennyson supposed — might be lost through civil strife, and the liberty for which Poles were being crushed. It is almost as though he were saying that the tyranny and bondage of contemporary Russian rule could be reserved for England, too, unless his country strove to conserve that intellectual equilibrium which — again as Tennyson understood it — had always been its strength. The argument, though unfashionable, is convincingly expressed. The lines of relevance to Russia are astonishingly mature for a man of twenty-three:[31]

> But he that or by deed or word,
>   And in an ancient land and free
>   Where none may plead necessity,
> Would make unsheathed the civil sword:
>
> For that he strove to kindle storm
>   From quiet, sought without respect
>   To soil the work of intellect,
> And forge confusion from reform —
>
> He will do well to hide his eyes,
>   Lest we should count him lower than
>   The Cossack curst of God and man
> To whom the Polish virgin cries.
>
> She cries unheard. So just a war,
>   So pure a hope is rendered vain

> Till God rise up and break in twain
> The iron sceptre of the Czar —
>
> Who rules a savage land where meet
> The coarse extremes of Power and Fear —
> A land where knowledge dreads to hear
> Her footsteps falling in the street —
>
> Who bides his time and quiet lies
> Though step by step his power grows
> And gathers like the silent snows
> And binds in fetters like the ice.

Tennyson has here created a prospect of Russia which, though in some respects simplistic, is of more general significance than that of his sonnets on Poland. There are still the eternal snows, still the conflation of Cossack and Russ, but the poet has well comprehended the gathering strength of Nicholas I in his post-Decembrist domain. It is impossible to know if Tennyson was aware that a Ryleev had been hanged, an Odoevskii thrown in chains; but his view of Russia around 1832 was doubtless less warped than our own, we seeing it rather through the triumphant resistance of the human spirit in Pushkin, Lermontov or Gogol than through the dark misdeeds of autocracy, serfdom, and repression. Certainly Tennyson's understanding of what he calls 'the coarse extremes of Power and Fear' contrasts markedly with Carlyle's infamous praise of that Russian talent of obeying for which Nicholas must be largely held responsible.[32] For Tennyson, true obedience lay in the mature use of freedom, not in the acceptance of an unjust yoke.

At the same time our poet was exhibiting in *Hail Briton!* a distastefully warlike mentality. History presents uncanny parallels: the England who had helped the Russians overthrow Napoleon, then set eyes of enmity upon them, was the same England who, after joining fronts in 1945, had a mind to press on further towards Moscow. The mutual tensions which existed between England and Russia have, however, been better echoed in our own time by the confrontation of the superpowers, and it is fairer to see them in these terms. In 1832, meanwhile, not even England appeared strong enough to 'break in twain the iron sceptre of the Czar', a task which Tennyson could only assign to God: but he thought already of his country as a possible agent of the Lord, and twenty years later we shall find him saying so loudly.

During the 1830s and 40s a great number of British travellers visited Russia, curious to know if there were human beings there. Keen as he must have been to test his father's tales, Tennyson would have read the reports of at least some of these tourists. One such was Rev. Richard Lister Venables, who in 1834 married the daughter of General Poltoratskii and five years later published *Domestic Scenes in Russia:*

in a Series of Letters Describing a Year's Residence in that Country, Chiefly in the Interior. Tennyson did not yet know Richard Lister, perhaps, but he was friendly with the brother, George Stovin Venables, who himself went to Russia in 1843, and it is likely that he came across this book early on; a second, later edition of the work is to be found in the Lincoln library, with an inscription by George Venables to Tennyson's wife. It is also possible (though for the moment purely speculative) that the Captain Richard Jesse who married Tennyson's sister Emily was related to the Captain William Jesse whose two-volume work on the Russian empire came out in 1841, precisely the year of the young couple's courtship. From such travel books, though maybe also from earlier sources in the family library, Tennyson learnt a number of strange things which doubtless mainly confirmed his jaundiced view of Russia. In his medley *The Princess*, for example, published in 1847 but meditated over a very long period, there is reference to what he called 'an old Russian custom'. The complaint is[33]

> Of lands in which at the altar the poor bride
> Gives her harsh groom for bridal gift a scourge.

Another piece of information turned out to be more equivocal. The Venables volume has several anecdotes about wolves, including one in which a sledge is pursued by a pack 'with their hard gallop' (in quotation marks in the text), frightening the horses and causing a traveller's servant to stab at them as they try to jump in.[34] Although Venables lacks the story now to be discussed, Tennyson could have heard it from the author's or his brother's own lips. It is the awful tale of a Russian couple who, while driving over snow-covered steppes, were obliged to offer one small child after another to stave off ravenous wolves. Around 1839 Tennyson is said to have 'wrung' his friend Mrs Harriet Allen's 'maternal heart' and 'visibly distressed' her by a dramatic rendering of this.[35] The importance of the thing for him is two-fold: first, he seems to have indulged (as with his father's tale) a certain licence in the retelling; none of the other extant versions has the woman's husband in the sledge, for example. Secondly, and more significantly, he liked to speak of it in order to pronounce his own heroic judgment. The next time we see him introducing a variant of the anecdote is at dinner with the T.H. Rawnsleys at Halton Holegate, Lincolnshire, on 18 November 1849. By good fortune a Colonel Weston Cracroft, who kept a diary, was there, and noted the following debate among guests:[36]

The Poet, Alfred Tennyson, started a hypothetical subject at dessert which divided opinion. It was borrowed from a Russian story. In the wilds of Russia and in the depth of winter a Lady was driving a sledge with 3 of her children towards a log hut where there were three younger ones all alone. She was banished there. She found herself pursued by a pack of wolves which were fast gaining on her. She sacrificed her 3 children successively in order to preserve the others who were alone and helpless in the hut, and so reached her home in safety. Was she right in what she did, or ought she to have died with her children and left the other 3 in the hut to the care of the Almighty? Mrs Rawnsley and Willie unhesitatingly declared that she should have died there and then. The Poet sided with them. Elmhirst and I maintained she did right, tho' we owned the struggle she must have undergone must have been intense. I think we had Sophy E. on my side.

Thus Tennyson in 1849, but more than three decades later, some time after the publication of Browning's dramatic idyl *Ivàn Ivànovitch* which made the story so famous, the laureate declared to William Allingham: 'I think the woman was right. The wolves would have eaten them all. She might have saved part by what she did.'[37] What could be the reason for the poet's change of mind? Maybe he was antagonised by Browning's version, in which the woman is killed in punishment for what she did; but Browning has no other children waiting in the hut, needing their mother to be saved, and the choice between morality and expediency thus seems starker. Nevertheless the crux is still that the woman, in dying to protect children who would in any case be devoured, could only be engaging in a hopeless act of heroism; to attempt to save even one child, while risking all, was an act of practical politics. By 1881, with the horror and pathos of the original tale already well behind him, Tennyson was able to see the mother's behaviour as both rational and natural, but in 1849 he could still pose the problem only in righteous, principled, and very British terms. The protagonist's actions seemed to him at that time selfish, immoral and — in a word — Russian. It is therefore reasonable to assume that, in spite of any reading he had done, his view of Russia and Britain was still fixed, as the difference between evil and good.

Perhaps it would be truer to say that Tennyson saw evil as lying generally abroad, and not just in Russia. For some time he had learnt to associate Russia in particular with France, in terms of political immorality; but with the accession of Louis Napoleon, his coup d'état, and his elevation to the rank of Napoleon III, the poet wrote many pieces on what he considered the new superior French menace. In one of these, *Hands All Round!*, of early 1852, he proposed a toast to universal freedom and suggested that England and (improbably) America should join to curse the upstart Bonaparte, not of course forgetting all the

> ...crimes of southern kings,
> The Russian whips and Austrian rods.

In another piece he went so far as to decree:[38]

> No little German state are we,
>   But the one voice in Europe: we *must* speak.

Although Tennyson signed both poems with a pseudonym, not wishing, as the laureate, to compromise the Queen who might some day wish, for all he knew, to enter into an alliance with Napoleon, he exhibited a blatant chauvinism which many saw as bordering on militarism. Emily Tennyson denied this: far from being a warmonger, there was really nothing that he hated more than war; but he also loved his country more than anything on earth. If he contended that every boy in every school should be drilled, it was as a means to defend British values. Whether these were so worthy of protection may now seem in doubt; but Tennyson's whole philosophy was founded on such a belief. It is too simplistic to claim, as Sir Leslie Stephen did, that war for Tennyson 'implied the moral generation of the country', but there was certainly an element of this in the bard's complex thinking.[39]

A characteristic prelude to the poet's intense involvement in the imminent war with Russia in the Crimea is seen in his effective piece *To the Rev. F.D. Maurice*, written in January 1854. Maurice, who was godfather to the Tennysons' baby son Hallam, had been obliged to resign his chair at King's College, London, for alleged heresy. Tennyson, who had recently moved to Farringford, above Freshwater on the south-west coast of the Isle of Wight, thought of publicly inviting him to come there and relax. But a shadow might fall across their pastoral conversations. Russia and Turkey had been locked in bitter conflict for some months, and news of the recent destruction of a Turkish fleet at Sinope had inflamed conservative opinion both in Britain and in France. Napoleon III appeared to be gunning for battle; the British government was under strong pressure to intervene; and the western powers' naval presence in the Mediterranean and Black Sea was being consolidated with a view to forcing Nicholas back into the Crimea. French and British warships were passing through the Channel in sight of Farringford. Tennyson, who by now hated Nicholas and Napoleon almost equally, scarcely minded if the two should go to war; but he also knew that England must join in, and displayed an already typical ambiguity of attitude. On the one hand, he realised that much unnecessary blood might be shed; on the other, he believed the crisis to have arisen from what he termed the 'Northern', that is, Russian 'sin', and felt that this could justly be condemned. For the time being, he put peace first, which is why his appeal to F.D. Maurice reads:[40]

> You'll have no scandal while you dine,
> But honest talk and wholesome wine,
>   And only hear the magpie gossip
> Garrulous under a roof of pine:

For groves of pine on either hand,
To break the blast of winter, stand;
    And further on, the hoary Channel
Tumbles a billow on chalk and sand;

Where, if below the milky steep
Some ship of battle slowly creep,
    And on through zones of light and shadow
Glimmer away to the lonely deep,

We might discuss the Northern sin
Which made a selfish war begin;
    Dispute the claims, arrange the chances;
Emperor, Ottoman, which shall win:

Or whether war's avenging rod
Shall lash all Europe into blood;
    Till you should turn to dearer matters,
Dear to the man that is dear to God;

How best to help the slender store,
How mend the dwellings, of the poor;
    How gain in life, as life advances,
Valour and charity more and more.

From the poetic point of view, these verses (about half the actual poem) do work rather splendidly. They are written in a metre of Tennyson's own invention, where the unrhyming and feminine third line makes a fine transition to the mainly dactylic last line of each stanza. The piece was clearly composed with discernment as well as with sincerity. It is thus a little disconcerting to find that the manuscript, which for the most part compares well with the published text of 1855, reads at lines 29-32:[41]

We would not scruple to discuss
The claims that shake the Bosporus,
    Nor Oltenitza, nor Sinope,
Ottoman, Emperor, Turk and Russ

A Trinity notebook has the further variant: 'Our fleet that keeps the Bosporus.'[42] All one can say, in considering these quaint lines, is that Tennyson always had the greatest difficulty in incorporating into his poetry anything that was strange and alien to him. He was no Byron, to do it jocularly; no Pushkin, to do it naturally. It is not surprising that he rejected these lines; what is surprising is that he could have penned them. Oltenitza, by the way, is in modern Rumania, on the border with Bulgaria. It was the scene of a Russian defeat at the hands of Omar Pasha in November 1853 (and again in July 1854).

When the Tennysons' second child was due, in the March of 1854, war between Russia and England was expected constantly. One night Tennyson, a keen amateur astronomer, observed Mars crossing the constellation Leo. Hearing that a son was born, he had him christened Lionel; superstitious as he was, he also saw the conjunction as a presage of England at war. Lionel arrived on the sixteenth, and twelve days later war was officially declared in London. For the next year or so, one finds the father pretty much obsessed by the conflict, and there are many references to it in his poetry and in Tennyson literature.[43] It is possible, indeed, that he published more on it than is at present known. In April he denied being the author of some newspaper verses on the British Baltic expedition, swearing that he had not even seen the ships depart, and categorically stating: 'Not a line have I written about it or the war.' That is as may be; but he did know something about Sir Charles Napier's comically ineffectual campaign in the Gulf of Finland, since his cousin Edwin Clayton Tennyson D'Eyncourt was now serving in it.[44] Moreover, by June 1854 Elizabeth Barrett Browning, at least, apparently believed that the laureate was 'cursing the Czar in Pindarics very prettily'.[45] A preliminary search for such poems in journals like the *Examiner* and the *Athenaeum* has produced nothing, but scrutiny of some of the daily papers may prove more successful. As a matter of fact, however, Tennyson's letters do not show that he was particularly obsessed by the war in its early stages, except in so far as it might affect his family. Sensitive of his relative poverty now that he had two sons, he was chiefly concerned that war with Russia could reduce his profits both from writing and from railway shares, 'for books are nearly as sensitive as the funds'. This was in March 1854; as late as October that year, he specifically asked his publishers whether sales had indeed been adversely affected.[46]

The work by Tennyson most impregnated by the war is *Maud*. Before considering it, some knowledge of the complex national mood is necessary. For months already, argument had raged on what came to be consecrated as the 'Peace and War' debate. Historians have found the origins of this in works by Tennyson's Trinity friend Franklin Lushington, published in May 1854, or in articles by George Carless Swayne in *Blackwood's Magazine* for November 1854 to January 1855. These were indeed important, as will be seen, but the debate goes back further. English political philosophy in the early Victorian period was profoundly affected by the insistent lobbying of the Society of Friends. Through the so-called 'Manchester School' of Richard Cobden and John Bright, Quakers enjoyed an influence in Britain beyond all proportion to their numerical importance, not just in the matter of free trade but also now, in the early 1850s, in the matter of war and peace. Bright in particular was a bitter and fanatical opponent of war, the moral leader of what came loosely to be known as the 'peace party'.[47] It was against this background that at the beginning of 1854 Professor William Whewell, Master of Trinity College, published his edition and abridged translation of *Hugonis Grotii De Jure Belli et Pacis Libri tres* (1625). Grotius (Huig de Groot), commonly thought of as the father of the science of international relations, established norms for keeping peace between the nations which, within the constraints of Christianity, sometimes implied the concept of just wars. One of the earliest reviewers of Whewell's edition, writing in *Fraser's Magazine* for April, made the obvious link with a situation in which Great Britain was 'about to take a leading part in the cause of right and justice'. Those activists who stood in the way of war had clearly not read Grotius. Most members of the Peace and Quaker parties were doubtless honourable and conscientious, though some were political adventurers, but their views were uniformly 'silly and mistaken'. 'If any war ever were justifiable this is the one', concluded the reviewer. Russia had for long behaved shamefully, contrary to the general Law of Nations, and the Queen was now compelled to take up arms in order (adapting a principle of Grotius) 'to save Europe from the preponderance of a power which has violated the faith of treaties and defies the opinion of the civilised world'.[48]

Most British intellectuals rallied to this point of view. William Archer Shee exhorted the 'peace at any price society' to 'shut up': 'we must punish the arrogance and check the encroachments of Russia'.[49] *Punch* was perhaps less restrained than most in dubbing the Quakers 'internal Russians'. A cartoon called 'Pet of the Manchester School' depicts these people giving a bad-tempered and violent young Nicholas a new and satisfying toy: 'a little Turk to pull to pieces'.[50] More than somewhat extravagantly, no doubt, Bright himself was taken by many of his opponents to have been the actual cause of the war, and his effigy, appropriately enough, was burnt by the citizens of Manchester on Guy Fawkes Day, and on New Year's Eve for good measure.[51] It is in this varied context that one needs to situate the theme of 'Peace and War', which became a commonplace of literature and journalism. John Westland Marston, for example, wrote a sonnet with this title arguing that, although we should never exult in war nor embark upon it 'for conquest, gain, or hate', we have a duty before God, the Lord of Hosts, to fight against oppression and injustice. 'Deem it then religion to bear the sword!' he cried.[52] The opening poem of Franklin Lushington's curious sequence *Points of War* pleaded for a genuine peace, not 'the peace of trembling', and argued that the 'giant evildoer' Nicholas must first be crushed, for

> Peace is no peace, if it lets the ill grow stronger,
> Merely cheating destiny a very little longer.

Lushington inscribed a copy of his book for Emily Tennyson on 15 May 1854, and it may well have reinforced her husband's view that war was often preferable to peace at any price.

A little later in the year, the same argument was dramatically rehearsed in *Blackwood's Magazine*. In September, in an article ostensibly on Harriet Beecher Stowe, the Maga deplored the activities of the official Peace Society (founded originally in 1816), whose ever-growing ladies' circles disseminated advertisements in the press of seven countries. The recent Quaker deputation to the Tsar of All the Russias, and its unctuous report of success, would be tragic were it not so farcical. Russia's naked aggression in the Danubian principalities had proved beyond doubt that there are circumstances where talk of peace and arbitration is not only misplaced but also dangerous.[53] This was followed up in the next few months by George Carless Swayne, an obscure schoolmaster and divine, who argued in the form of dialogues between himself as Tlepolemus and his disputant Irenaeus, a Quaker believing in peace at any price, that war in some circumstances was not only necessary but good. Only from it, and not from prevarication, could true peace ever come. The evils of war were patent, there for all to see, and the Peace Society was correct in pointing out that Russian soldiers also had wives and children. On the other hand, the good of war, less on the surface, was no less critical. The Tsar's power must be broken. His error (encouraged by the Peace Society) was that 'He mistook Manchester for Great Britain, and Messrs Pease, Sturge, and Co., for the United Services'. It was the men of peace, in effect, who had 'brought the Russian war upon us'. Thanks in great part to them, we had also been unprepared. But now at last we were disabusing Nicholas. The true peacemakers were the officer who led to victory and the private who followed him, even to an almost certain death.[54]

This, then, is the background to Tennyson's *Maud*, as also in some respects to his *Charge of the Light Brigade*. Whatever critics may have said of *Maud* as literature (it passes for some as trash, for others as its author's masterpiece), no one has denied its intense personal significance. The story of its composition is extremely complex and cannot concern us here, but leaving aside the more distant origins of some sections, the main body of the poem seems to have been sketched out from the early spring to late autumn of 1854, and added to and revised in the following six months. Tennyson family evidence suggests that what is now known as Part III was written first, at the time of the rumours and outbreak of war and the booming of British cannon practice in the Solent. Its opening lines even include a reference to Mars glowing red upon the Lion, as both a message of hope for the hero akin to the birth of Lionel and an emblem of the scourging power of battle. The solution whereby Tennyson's deranged protagonist is to drown his troubles in the service of Her Majesty must thus have relevance more to the theoretical, non-combatant stages of the Crimean War than to the horrors known to the public when *Maud* actually appeared, in the summer of 1855. The accusations of warmongering then levelled at Tennyson were therefore not much to the point, though he naturally (if at fault) could have changed the offensive passages before the final version came out. Here is the most celebrated section of Part III, with which the whole poem is brought to a disturbing, deeply fatalistic end:[55]

And I stood on a giant deck and mixed my breath
With a loyal people shouting a battle cry,
Till I saw the dreary phantom arise and fly
Far into the North, and battle, and seas of death.

IV

Let it go or stay, so I wake to the higher aims
Of a land that has lost for a little her lust of gold,
And love of a peace that was full of wrongs and shames,
Horrible, hateful, monstrous, not to be told;
And hail once more to the banner of battle unrolled!
Though many a light shall darken, and many shall weep
For those that are crushed in the clash of jarring claims
Yet God's just wrath shall be wreaked on a giant liar;
And many a darkness into the light shall leap,
And shine in the sudden making of splendid names,
And noble thought be freer under the sun,
And the heart of a people beat with one desire;
For the peace, that I deemed no peace, is over and done,
And now by the side of the Black and the Baltic deep,
And deathful-grinning mouths of the fortress, flames
The blood-red blossom of war with a heart of fire.

V

Let it flame or fade, and the war roll down like a wind,
We have proved we have hearts in a cause, we are noble still,
And myself have awaked, as it seems, to the better mind;
It is better to fight for the good than to rail at the ill;
I have felt with my native land, I am one with my kind,
I embrace the purpose of God, and the doom assigned.

Meanwhile, much earlier in *Maud* (in its definitive form, that is), the hero has likened some of England's own ills to the devilry of Nicholas I, showing also the 'couldn't-care-less' international attitude of much of British society. This is both an elucidation of the 'wrongs and shames' of Part III and a reversion by Tennyson to the mood shown in *Hail Briton!* twenty years before. Here are the two most relevant passages from Part I of *Maud* (section IV, stanzas ii and viii):

> Below me, there, is the village, and looks how quiet and small!
> And yet bubbles o'er like a city, with gossip, scandal, and spite;
> And Jack on his ale-house bench has as many lies as a Czar....
>
> Who knows the ways of the world, how God will bring them about?
> Our planet is one, the suns are many, the world is wide.
> Shall I weep if a Poland fall? shall I shriek if a Hungary fail?
> Or an infant civilisation be ruled with rod or with knout?
> *I* have not made the world, and He that made it will guide.

The so-called 'trial' or 'pre-natal' edition of the poem is supposed also to have contained the lines:

> Now are they serf-like, horribly bland,
> To this lord-captain up at the Hall.

A study of the Trinity manuscript suggests that some of the topical allusions to Russia were added at a fairly late stage, only the mentions of Poland and Hungary echoing the poet's earlier obsession with tsarist misrule. Tennyson thus seems to have been wanting to have it both ways: to strengthen and make public his continuing disgust at Russian repression, yet at the same time to use these images to increase the force of his attack on British moral decline. He apparently shared with his friends the Lushingtons a conviction that the present War could provide their country with a righteous escape from materialistic values.[56]

Much more could be said here of the contemporary importance of *Maud*, but Baum, Rader, Ricks and others have done it all too well. It is, however, necessary to emphasise how the poem reveals deep underlying doubts in Tennyson's mind about his own role in the war. He had originally wanted to call it *Maud; or, The Madness*, and he reverted to this idea for a time when he contemplated its effect on the public.[57] In making his hero insane, and patriotic from the wrong motives, he may have been attempting to hide from himself and others his uncertainty as to the wisdom of armed conflict. Could one seriously imagine his enlisting in support of Turkey against Christianity, or to bolster Napoleon III, even had he been younger and free? At the same time, there can be no doubt about his reverence for courage, self-denial, and the sacrifice of self for one's country and one's God. The ambivalence comes over well in Tennyson's own remarks about *Maud*. He later told one correspondent that, as well as many anonymous letters accusing him of warmongering or hypocrisy, he had received 'Peace Party papers' claiming the opposite on the ground that he had deliberately placed the cry for war in a madman's mouth. This, he thought, did make some sense, but he preferred artistic neutrality: 'Strictly speaking I do not see how from the poem I could be pronounced with certainty either peace man or war man.'[58] Later still, he attempted to play the whole thing down. Very near the end of his life, in August 1892, he recited parts of *Maud* for the visiting critic Henry Van Dyke and during their discussion of it said: 'It is dramatic, — the story of a man who has a touch of inherited insanity, morbid and selfish. The poem shows what love has done for him. The war is only an episode.'[59] Naturally enough, perhaps, Van Dyke was not completely persuaded by this explanation, fearing that the opinions expressed at the time of *Maud*'s composition had belonged as much to their author as to its tormented hero.[60] It is significant that *Maud* was widely construed as an attack upon Quakers, and on John Bright in particular. Tennyson vigorously denied this, it is true: in remarking much later how 'the passage about the Quaker preaching our poor little army down gave great offence to Bright', he said that at the time he had not even known that Bright was a Quaker and had in mind rather the peace-at-any-price merchants. The distinction, however, is fine, since Quakers had to be included in these; all one can really say is that the most offending phrase, 'broad-brimmed hawker of holy things', was not directed solely or personally at Bright but rather at the (for Tennyson) mindless pacifism that he represented.[61]

The fact that the equivocal *Maud* was elaborated in parallel with the progress of the war allows us to apply a certain caution in interpreting Tennyson's other Crimean offerings. As the conflict gathered momentum, he became increasingly uneasy. Though it would be absurd to say that he felt guilty he was not himself installed in the dust and the mud, he clearly believed that those who stayed comfortably at home had a duty, as it were, to play their own part in the fighting. In another age, there might have been a Home Guard for him to join, or an Isle of Wight Defence Committee; as it was, he had only the arm of patriotic poetry. It was easier for little Hallam, who revelled in the popular excitement. Though he was sad to be told that the British soldiers had no toast and butter for their breakfast, he could always take up his drum, strut along to do battle, and tumble over with a cry of 'This is the way the Russians fall when they're killed!' *He* had the vicarious satisfaction of make-believe. It was easier, too, for Emily, who desired to be 'some bird of fabulous size and power to carry warm clothing and nourishing food to the poor soldiers and death and destruction to the enemy'.[62] It was even simple enough for Tennyson himself when men that he admired were killed, like his neighbour Lieutenant-Colonel the Hon. Francis Grosvenor Hood of the Grenadier Guards, who died in the trenches before Sebastopol on 18 October; and he would probably not have demurred at his wife's definition of how nature itself can appear to strengthen an emotion: 'Looking from the Beacon', she wrote in November 1854, 'and seeing the white cliffs and the clear sea, their violet gray shading seemed to us tender and sad; perhaps the landscape seemed so sad because of the sorrowful news of the death roll in the Crimea...'[63] This was, however, to look at things romantically, pathetically, nostalgically, and not with the sterner realism of knowledge and practicality.

One sticky problem for the poet was that the French and English were fighting side by side. Like most Englishmen he had a very jaundiced view of the French and, as we have seen, entertained a vicious hatred of their current regime. When, therefore, he tossed off the lines

> Frenchman, a hand in thine!
> Our flags have waved together!
> Let us drink to the health of thine and mine
> At the battle of Alma River.

— it was ideological hesitation as much as good taste which prevented him from continuing the piece; nor, one thinks, can he have been inwardly too pleased when Emily added two stanzas of her own, set the doggerel to music, and could be heard declaiming a hypocritical British pledge to 'swear to be one for ever' with the French.[64] A second and more significant difficulty was British government policy and the British army's tactics. In October 1854 there was still little public controversy. W.H. Russell's brilliant reports to *The Times* had not yet started to bite, although his criticisms of the Alma battle were already rankling with some. But in mid-November reports of military mismanagement began to arouse nationwide anger and dismay. Tennyson himself was sent an anonymous account of the Heavy Brigade's charge of 25 October which, though evidently laudatory as far as the Scots and Enniskilleners were concerned, may well have been critical of some other aspects of the engagement: we know that it covered a period of several days, and presumably therefore brought in also the Light Brigade's charge and its aftermath.[65] It is important to note that these two charges, made on the same day, were thought of together from the start and contrasted as models respectively of controlled bravery and rash heroism. Tennyson could well have written of them both at the time, together or separately, but he was at first inspired only to celebrate the failure and the tragedy, not the too obvious triumph. Many years later he would revert to the Crimean War and sing the valour of the Heavy Brigade; but in November and December 1854 his head was obviously fuller of the poignancy and bloody poetry of the conflict, as well as of its double standards, than of its more directly historical and intellectual significance. Everyone expected him, as laureate, to commit himself to print: before *The Charge of the Light Brigade* appeared, it was being rumoured in the press that he was 'presently engaged in the task of commemorating the great campaign'.[66] But the question remained: in what way?

A study of *'The Charge'* is fraught with many complications — more even, relatively speaking, than with *Maud*. There is disagreement over the date on which it was first written, Hallam saying 2 December, 'in a few minutes', Emily agreeing with this in one source but in another suggesting rather the fifth; there is doubt whether the celebrated line 'some one had blundered' was really taken, as Hallam states, from *The Times* and whether it was indeed the origin of the poem's metre; the difference between the various printed texts cannot be accounted for by a study of the known manuscripts alone; and not all the reasons why Tennyson made certain quite important changes are yet perfectly explained despite extensive scholarship.[67] Here it will be possible only to summarise the poem's very complicated history; but it is essential first to establish what actually occurred at Balaklava.

After the bold dash by the Heavy Brigade had halted the advance of the Russian cavalry, the British horse regrouped to repulse any further attacks. The Light Cavalry Brigade was on the left flank, facing north-east in the direction of the Chernaia river and with high ground to the left, right and before it. Most of the heights were by now commanded by the Russians, the main body of whose forces were massed behind and above a battery of some thirty guns at the head of this socalled North Valley. The Light Brigade was made up of men from the 4th Light Dragoons, 8th Irish Hussars, 11th Prince Albert's Hussars, 13th Light Dragoons, and 17th Lancers; it is now most reliably calculated that there were rather more than 650 sabres in all, though at the time the number was reported variously as anything between 600 and 750. The brigade was under the command of Major-General the Earl of Cardigan, but his bitter rival Lord Lucan, lieutenant-general and chief of the Cavalry Division, was present with the Heavy Brigade near by. It has to be pointed out that these two men were of the old guard of British cavalry officers, who tended to view war as an exciting variant on fox-hunting. Lucan had already gained a reputation as 'Lord Look-on' and Cardigan, who often called the enemy 'the French', was known as 'the noble yachtsman' from the circumstance that he was quartered in his private boat at some distance from the brigade. A note was sent to Lucan indicating that Lord Raglan, British chief of staff, wished the cavalry to 'try to prevent the enemy carrying away the guns'; they were to act immediately. This message was conveyed by Captain Edward Nolan, a brave and brilliant but, it seems, somewhat arrogant young soldier who was something of an authority on modern cavalry warfare. What happened next is in dispute, but Lucan evidently did not understand the instructions, which he thought vague, and Nolan gave a summary explanation using gestures. Lucan, at least, supposed that his men must charge the Russian guns at the end of the plain, and maybe this is even what Nolan had appeared to indicate, but it is generally now thought that Raglan (as he himself suggested at the time) was referring to other allied guns on the Causeway Heights to the right which the frightened Turks had abandoned, retreating in confusion before the enemy. It is most charitably presumed that the British cavalry were unaware of this; certainly they could not actually see what was happening. Lucan passed on the order to Cardigan who, in spite of serious doubts, instructed the light horse to advance. What is perhaps not generally realised is that many of the men were far from fit or ready to do battle. Some were taking swigs of rum; cooks and invalids, and a butcher in his shirt-sleeves and a red nightcap, joined in on captured Russian horses; and Colonel Lord George Paget smoked a cigar as he issued orders and — it is said — lit another during the engagement. A dog is also supposed to have accompanied its master and returned. There is a lighter side to everything, of course: but the outcome was grisly enough.

The charge began at ten past eleven in the morning. Nolan, quite irregularly, rode out in front and was the first to be killed. According to official accounts, this was typical of his mettle, but a more likely explanation is that he had seen, too late, that the cavalry was pointed in the wrong direction.[68] Some detachments of the Heavy Brigade started following the Light, but Lucan ordered them back. Meanwhile, the Light Brigade reached the enemy guns, and did considerable damage; but on their way there and back they were attacked on three sides by cannon, musket and rifle fire and, while they were fighting with Russian lancers some way from the guns, it is said that some gunners came back to their positions and fired indiscriminately into the midst. Less than a third of the light horse rode to safety, although some eighty wounded later returned. Lucan was slightly injured in the leg, and Cardigan received a lance thrust through his clothes. One of the survivors considered the fact that anyone had escaped the foolish carnage was 'a perfect miracle'.[69] Everything was over in less than half an hour. During all the incident, the cavalry had practically no support from their British comrades: everyone watched open-mouthed. W.H. Russell compared the men to Don Quixote, who 'in his tilt against the windmill was not near so rash and reckless as the gallant fellows who prepared without a thought to rush on almost certain death'.[70] The same contemporary, Lieutenant-Colonel John Adye, who cited as a fine example of British discipline and bravery the '400 young soldiers standing quietly on parade on the deck of the Birkenhead steamer as she sank' off Capetown in February 1852, noted of the Light Brigade's charge: 'the steady advance of 500 men to almost certain death, is a perfect marvel of discipline and heroic courage'.[71] Of course, it was — once the men had been required to go — and the tragedy would be repeated again and again in World War I; but the overwhelming stupidity of the thing is less an argument against war in general than against bad planning, mismanagement, and a callous disregard for human life. During the British charge the French, at least, were not so gormless: General Bosquet saw to it that his Chasseurs d'Afrique, without excessive waste or fuss, silenced the guns on the Chernaia ridge. Those members of the Light Brigade who did return to safety probably owed their lives to these brave, efficient Frenchmen. It was Bosquet too, of course, who remarked of the charge at the time: 'C'est très magnifique, mais ce n'est pas la guerre.'[72]

The British nation's reaction to the disastrous news was nicely captured by a cartoon in *Punch* called 'Enthusiasm of Paterfamilias, on reading the Report of the Grand Charge of British Cavalry on the 25th'. While Father brandishes a poker in glee, his family look on with approval at best, and his married or nubile daughters weep or grieve.[73] Already in the following month, English poets were commemorating the events of 25 October. *Punch* was among the first to celebrate both charges in verse, praising the courage of each but regretting that the Light Brigade's had been so obviously wrongheaded.[74] As from the middle of November, Tennyson had ample time to read all about it in *The Times*. He would have seen explanations, more or less candid, by Raglan and Lucan; arguments for and against Nolan; letters from common soldiers; Russell's exciting but in some respects misleading report of the charge; and several leaders critical of authority but eulogistic of the men. The fine editorial of 13 November spoke of 'some misunderstanding', 'a mere mistake', 'an error'. It praised 'the progress of the cavalry through and through that valley of death, with a murderous fire, not only in front, but on both sides, above, and even in the rear'. Without intended irony in its own allusion to the *Birkenhead* débâcle, *The Times* said of the charge: 'Causeless and fruitless, it stands by itself as a grand heroic deed, surpassing even that spectacle of a shipwrecked regiment, settling down into the waves, each man still in his rank.' The paper did not, as has often been believed, introduce the expression 'some one had blundered', but the most striking sentence in this marvellously evocative leader of 13 November was: 'The British soldier will do his duty, even to certain death, and is not paralysed by feeling that he is the victim of some hideous blunder.'[75]

Here, then, ready made for Tennyson, was the scenario for a poem on the fortitude but also the chaos of war, with much of the vocabulary supplied. He needed only to versify it. Why he waited until December is not clear. His attitude was not in doubt: he had already plainly stated his concept of valour in lines of the *Ode on the Death of the Duke of Wellington* (1852, revised 1853) which read:[76]

> Not once or twice in our rough island-story,
> The path of duty was the way to glory.

Maybe Tennyson was held back by doubts as to whether he, as laureate, could criticise the management of the war as well as the courage of the Brigade; in the event, he signed the first edition of *The Charge* only as 'A.T.' Perhaps he would have held back entirely, but found himself impelled to write his own contribution to a poetic debate in which so many lesser figures were already taking part. Possibly his inspiration did indeed require the expression 'Some one had blundered', and he learnt it actually at the beginning of December from a Crimean informant or from the press: certainly the phrase, or variants on it, occurred in many soldiers' letters of the time.[77] This then would have set off in his mind memories of Michael Drayton's ballad *The Battle of Agincourt* in which 'wonder' and 'thunder' are used and which, in places, runs metrically in a very similar manner to the lines that he himself wrote down. (The fact that he strenuously denied this link need mean only that the echoes were not fully conscious, and — to be fair to him — one needs to add that the two poems are for the most part totally dissimilar.)[78]

Tennyson composed his poem, then, early in December 1854, more probably on the second than on the fifth. On the sixth, he sent it to his friend John Forster for publication in the *Examiner*. Emily explained that the poet had put 'six hundred' men remembering the figure from the first *Times* report. On checking, they found that later accounts claimed there were 700. 'Six hundred' was better for the metre, but Forster could change this if he wished.[79] Tennyson himself, meanwhile, feeling he had not polished the thing sufficiently, on the next day forwarded a revised text; but he reverted more or less to the first draft in time for the appearance of *The Charge* in the *Examiner* on 9 December. 'Six hundred' was allowed to stand, with a brief explanatory footnote supplied by Tennyson himself. It is perhaps important to note that this first published version of *The Charge of the Light Brigade*, otherwise similar to the text which everyone now knows, contained a specific reference to Nolan delivering 'an order which some one' (that is, not he at least) 'had blundered'.[80] In other respects it is evident that Tennyson wished to make his poem more universal, less specific to this particular incident. From the start he eschewed references to Raglan, Lucan or Cardigan, unlike some other poetic interpreters.

Many critics immediately took exception to the detail of the poem, even going so far as to point out that 'hundred' does not rhyme with 'blundered', 'thundered', 'wondered', or 'sundered' (or, as they might have added, 'onward'). Embarrassed by his Lincolnshire origins, where these words would commonly have rhymed, Tennyson determined to remove the non-standard pairings. He also had second thoughts about Nolan; and even the concept of a blunder began to raise doubts in his mind. Some London friends, as also the American poet Frederick Goddard Tuckerman who stayed at Farringford in January 1855, helped to reinforce his misgivings.[81] The whole thing started to break up and be spoiled: the version of *The Charge* which came out in *Maud; and Other Poems* in July (pp. 151-4) was a much adulterated and weakened one, revealing more than anything else the poet's self-questioning in that period. Most significantly, he altered the last stanza of the poem to read:

> Honour the brave and bold!
> Long shall the tale be told,
> Yea, when our babes are old —
>   How they rode onward.

This bathetic ending was in fact quite personal: Tennyson himself had 'babes' at the time, and doubtless wondered how they might come to view the charge in after years. It was also morally more comforting. But artistically, of course, it was really rather feeble.

Luckily, Tennyson soon had an opportunity to put things right. Early in August, he received from the Society for the Propagation of the Gospel a request to make *The Charge* more generally available to our men in the East; a good half of them were already singing the piece, and wanted their individual texts of it in black and white. In actual fact Rev. Charles Edward Hadow, the SPG chaplain at Scutari, had written on 5 July to say: 'Some of the soldiers who were in the Balaklava charge are delighted with Tennison's [sic] lines on "the Six Hundred" which I have copied out for them. I should like uncommonly to have some printed copies of them and also of Trench's verses on "Alma", to circulate among them.' Tennyson's own contact at the SPG had somewhat modified this, but no matter. In obliging the Society, he realised that the version known to at least some of the men was, of course, the *Examiner*'s; he therefore largely returned to it in the text that he now provided, affirming to his publisher John Forster: 'The soldiers are the best critics in what pleases them.' The separate four-page quarto copies of *The Charge* that he had printed for distribution at the scene of war, complete with a letter dated 8 August assuring the men that those who sat at home loved and honoured them, comprised in fact what was practically his last revision of the work.[82]

His decision at that time to restore in particular 'Some one had blundered' must certainly have been strengthened by the comment of John Ruskin, made to him in November, that this line was as essential to the tragic force of *The Charge* as it was to the history of the subject.[83] Such, then, in concise outline, was the genesis of Tennyson's poem, which is given here in its definitive form:[84]

I

Half a league, half a league,
　　Half a league onward,
All in the valley of Death
　　Rode the six hundred.
'Forward, the Light Brigade!
Charge for the guns!' he said:
Into the valley of Death
　　Rode the six hundred.

II

'Forward, the Light Brigade!'
Was there a man dismayed?
Not though the soldier knew
　　Some one had blundered:
Theirs not to make reply,
Theirs not to reason why,
Theirs but to do and die:
Into the valley of Death
　　Rode the six hundred.

III

Cannon to right of them,
Cannon to left of them,
Cannon in front of them
　　Volleyed and thundered;
Stormed at with shot and shell,
Boldly they rode and well,
Into the jaws of Death,
Into the mouth of Hell
　　Rode the six hundred.

IV

Flashed all their sabres bare,
Flashed as they turned in air
Sabring the gunners there,
Charging an army, while
　　All the world wondered:
Plunged in the battery-smoke
Right through the line they broke;
Cossack and Russian
Reeled from the sabre-stroke

        Shattered and sundered.
Then they rode back, but not
        Not the six hundred.

                    V

Cannon to right of them,
Cannon to left of them,
Cannon behind them
        Volleyed and thundered;
Stormed at with shot and shell,
While horse and hero fell,
They that had fought so well
Came through the jaws of Death,
Back from the mouth of Hell,
All that was left of them,
        Left of six hundred.

                    VI

When can their glory fade?
O the wild charge they made!
        All the world wondered.
Honour the charge they made!
Honour the Light Brigade,
        Noble six hundred!

Although Tennyson declared he did not 'pique' himself on these much-quoted verses, there is no doubt that they were very deeply felt. He is recorded as saying also to an unnamed correspondent, perhaps Sydney Dobell, on 29 January 1855: 'my heart almost bursts with indignation at the accursed mismanagement of our noble little army, that flower of men.'[85] This sense of waste was uncannily matched by an angry poem called *Balaklava*, published by *Punch* in February.[86] About the same time Emily Tennyson wrote: 'The one comfort we have is in the heroic endurance of our soldiers and I cannot rate this low, but how sad it is words cannot tell.'[87] By this period, their perspective of things was definitcly changing. Furthermore, other poems specifically about or touching upon the charge were being written from different political and moral standpoints by numerous authors.[88] It was nevertheless Tennyson's original view of what had happened on that 25 October that lived on. Thanks in great part to him, the Balaklava charges rapidly entered folk mythology and the Light Brigade, especially, was held up for its courage like Horatius at the bridge or — in more modern times — the evacuation of Dunkirk. Who else but the British would commemorate a disaster?[89] *The Charge of the Light Brigade* was set to music by Mrs W.H. Owen in 1855 and later by many others including J.J. Blockley, W.H. West and Mrs George Murray; Tennyson was usually glad to give his blessing to this practice.[90] The most popular arrangements made during his lifetime were perhaps the song by Gerard Francis Cobb (1865) and the version for chorus and orchestra by Richard Machill Garth (1889). There were also many pictorial representations of the charge, coloured for the most part by Tennyson's interpretation; the most famous one, painted by Richard Caton Woodville junior in 1894, has been used in recent and more cynical days as part of *The Times*'s advertising campaign with the slogan: *Have you ever wished you were better informed?*[91]

Back at the time of its appearance, however, Tennyson's stirring contribution to the British war effort had a surprisingly mixed reception. The minor poet Dicky Monckton Milnes thought *The Charge* (admittedly in the text of 1855) 'a real gallop in verse, and only good as such'.[92] Perhaps he had in mind the nominally dactylic metre of the piece, but of course no one, least of all Tennyson himself, has ever seriously wished to read it in that way. Meanwhile, for the general public, the fact that *The Charge* shared some of the apparent bellicosity of *Maud* did not help in the least. Farringford was bombarded with anonymous letters complaining of the poet's double standards in the question of valour, telling him to go and see what things were really like in the stinking disease-ridden Crimea. Perhaps they also pointed out to him the irony of the soldiers' first baptism of that land as 'the Isle of Wight of Russia'.[93] All this was, however, somewhat unfair, because the Tennysons themselves, despite their own little problems and the arduous English winter weather, were very conscious of their safety when compared with the men in the Crimea. 'One has no right to complain when one reflects on them in their thin tents', the poet declared to a friend.[94] But the vicious attacks persisted. The so-styled 'Poet of the People' who penned an *Anti-Maud* (not, as often thought implausibly, W.C. Bennett) remarked that it was easy for Tennyson to despatch his mad hero to the rump of the Light Brigade, but would he shift his own behind from Freshwater? Such, at least, was the implication of this clever and in places quite hilarious travesty, which made its mark with the public and went into a second edition in 1856.[95]

Tennyson was naturally hurt by all the abuse. As Cecil Lang has pithily observed, however, the critical reception of *Maud* 'brought him pain, but it bought him Farringford'.[96] The morbidity occasioned was also mitigated by his pride at being awarded an honorary DCL at Oxford on 20 June 1855. There were sixteen new doctors in all that year, including Monckton Milnes (as a statesman, not as a poet) and three soldiers — Colonel Edward Sabine, and Lieutenants-General Sir John Fox Burgoyne and Sir De Lacy Evans. Tennyson was able to have a long talk with Evans, whom he already knew slightly.[97] Before the presentations began, the students in the packed Sheldonian set the mood by shouting cheers for the Queen, Prince Albert, Napoleon III,

Lord Raglan, Florence Nightingale and — interestingly enough — Lord Cardigan. Three groans were proposed for Russia and for British politicians who, like Lords Aberdeen and Palmerston, were considered soft or lacking in patriotism. Mentions of the Alma, Balaklava, Inkerman, or any soldier associated with these allied victories, drew vociferous applause; at this stage Evans, who had retired ill and critical from the Crimea, was the obvious hero of the day.

Jackson's Oxford Journal assures us that most doctorands were greeted with relative calm. Some were in any case unknown: a Canadian judge called Robinson brought shouts of 'Where are Brown and Jones?' Burgoyne was loudly praised; but when De Lacy Evans was called 'there was a perfect tempest of cheers, clapping, and waving of hats, caps, and handkerchiefs'. However, we read further that: 'The presentation of the Poet Laureate was the signal for cheers almost as hearty and long..., and on taking his seat a crowning cheer was given to 'In Memoriam', a work which appeared to have left indelible impressions on its readers.' When the ceremony was done, all else was drowned by combined applause for Evans and Tennyson.[98] The *Examiner* and other friendly papers, as well as Mr Gladstone who was there, believed that the poet actually received *more* fervent cheers than Evans; but it is significant that his name had not been invoked before he came up for the degree, and that it was *In Memoriam* and not *The Charge of the Light Brigade* that was singled out for praise. (*Maud* was not yet published; if it had been, things could have been very different.) Some sardonicism, besides, did make itself apparent. When Tennyson came into view, his long hair hanging unkempt upon his neck and shoulders, a wag in the gallery cried out: 'Did your mother call you early, Alfred, dear?' — in the words of the bard's own song.[99] Tennyson afterwards denied this, but declared lamely: 'The only impertinence the young fellows uttered was *"Cut your hair!"'*[100]

Any such hints of ridicule were, of course, unthinkable in the crowd's reaction to the war heroes. Tennyson well realised this, declaring of the soldiers as he sent them copies of *The Charge*: 'No writing of mine can add to the glory they have acquired in the Crimea.' It was these same men, besides, who finally convinced him he had been right in publishing the poem and cured his despondency. Letters showed how sick or hopeless soldiers had been revived by having it read out to them; it was carried into battle as a talisman by an officer at Kars; one hero wrote of another engagement: 'I escaped with my life and my Tennyson'; and the chaplain who originally asked for copies assured the poet:[101]

If those who can speak and write well at home, and those who can pray and fight well abroad would only enter heart and soul into this war, under a strong sense of its justice, we should be more successful and victorious than we have hitherto been.... Your office, as you discharge it, can do more than comfort, it can encourage and inspire our soldiers. The poet can now make heroes, just as in days of yore, if he will.

This striking judgment prompts one to suggest that Tennyson, no doubt unconsciously, had in fact been trying less to turn others into heroes than to make one of himself. As Professor Ricks has subtly argued, 'In the heroic futility of the charge of the Light Brigade, he found a situation in which it was not merely condonable but actually honourable to commit suicide.'[102] With such a belief the poet would, of course, have harked back to his own Romantic roots; and in terms of Russian literature one is reminded of Lermontov's Pechorin who seeks, and Turgenev's Rudin who finds, an impersonal death in a military cause to which neither really subscribes.

If one discounts the references to it in *Maud*, Tennyson seems to have given up writing poems specifically on the Crimean War after the Balaklava episode. He did compose one line — 'Strong eight thousand of Inkermann' — on the battle which bore that name; but it is unlikely, as one authority has contended, that two sonnets on the death of Nicholas I, signed 'T' and published by the *Examiner* on 17 March 1855, were from our poet's pen.[103] On the other hand, his patriotic anti-Russian fervour persisted without abatement. At the Grand Review in the Solent on 23 April 1856, following the ambiguous resolution of the war, he hailed the men while Emily gazed and wondered at the ships.[104] In *Jack Tar*, a loyal ditty written in 1859, he called on the British navy to conserve his country's reputation in the face of a supposed new threat from Russia and France, joining in unholy alliance against her. 'Shall France and Russia brave us?' asked a manuscript variant, becoming in the final version: 'The whole world shall not brave us!'[105] Russia was still the lowest of the low: the Tennysons loved to play a game in which shocking messages were repeated from ear to ear, with comical elaboration; appropriately enough, it was called Russian Scandal.[106] (Nowadays, one learns, it has been converted into Chinese Whispers or Japanese Mixture.)

As the years progressed and peace endured, Tennyson paid less and less attention to things Russian in his poetry: he was too busy with researches into the past for works like *Idylls of the King*, as well as with various public responsibilities. He did not quite forget about Russia, however. How could he, with the Crimean War so close behind? For a start, through Colonel Hood's widow the Tennysons kept alive for many years their memories of heroes and the battles where they died.[107] The poet continued to be hostile towards Russia and its policies: we are told that in 1863, for instance, he felt 'boundless' indignation against its treatment of Poland. It is true that, in a more positive direction, he showed some interest in the Orthodox Church; and his spirit of scientific enquiry allowed him to become excited about reports of 'the Russian illumination of the body so that bullets may be seen and extracted afterwards, if they have any steel in them, by magnetism';[108] but his moral and religious ire was rekindled against Russia in November 1870 by the affair of the Gorchakov Note. This 'insolent' despatch repudiated those clauses of the Treaty of Paris, agreed at the end of the Crimean War, which guaranteed the neutrality of the Black Sea. Patriots in England envisaged another serious clash with Russia, abetted now, perhaps, by a unified Germany and by an upstart America. The Tennysons themselves foresaw — and countenanced — 'instant war' unless the note were retracted, and the laureate once more thought it time to drill all British schoolboys with that contingency in mind.[109] That this reaction was only relatively absurd is seen by comparison with Sydney Dobell, a famous singer of the Crimean campaign, who bounced back with *England's Day: A War-Saga, Commended to Gortschakoff, Grant, and Bismarck; and Dedicated to the British Navy* (1871), which opens preposterously:[110]

Russian, Yankee, and Prussian,
Wherever you be,
That stand by the shores of our sea
And shake your fists over,
This is the Castle of Dover,
You knaves!
And yon's the flag unfurl'd,
That shall flog you over the waves
Of the world.
Ay, by the shores of our sea,
You knaves!

In the event, the new Anglo-Russian confrontation was disarmed by diplomacy and by mutual preoccupation with the very conflict — the Franco-Prussian War — which the Russians had hoped might permit them to arrange their own best interests on the side.

At the height of the Gorchakov affair, the great Russian novelist Ivan Turgenev arrived in London for a winter's stay. He was scarcely an admirer of Tennyson: in 1852, perhaps with *The Princess* in mind, he had compared his poetry to Marino's and defined it as the product of trying to scratch one's nose with a hand passed round one's neck. Soon after reaching London he confirmed in conversation with Carlyle how disappointed he was, not only by Tennyson but by all of what he called Britain's *recentiores*. He must nevertheless have recognised the intellectual stature of the author of *In Memoriam*, and there is reason to suppose that he did approve of some other individual pieces. Certainly he was pleased when his friend the translator and folklorist William Ralston, who admired and knew the bard, took him down to spend a couple of days with the Tennysons at their new house on Blackdown, in Surrey, at the end of June 1871.[111] As a prelude to this visit one may note that, only two years earlier, Tennyson had replied to an offer by Ralston to show him Russian versions of his poems with the comment that it would be useless: he had yet to learn his ABC in the language. He had, however, been interested by Ralston's translations from the fables of Krylov, which he found uncommonly 'good and pithy'. Moreover, he was happy enough to receive information about the popularity of his own poetry in Russia.[112] Ralston's notes on this could not, one thinks, have been particularly extensive, since Tennyson did not enjoy a particularly good press in that country. There would certainly be a minor vogue for him in Russia at a later date. The poets Vladimir Solov'ev and Konstantin Bal'mont translated pieces by him, and by the beginning of the twentieth century, in the view of Prince Kropotkin, 'all that is worth knowing in Tennyson' (as also 'all that could be translated from Browning') was as familiar in Russia as it was in England.[113] That is as may be, but a few decades earlier the position was quite different. References to him were really rather hard to find. The radical publicist Mikhail Mikhailov translated a couple of poems by him, it is true, as did also the poet A.N. Pleshcheev; and the Anglophile critic A.V. Druzhinin knew his poetry already by the early 1850s. But although Druzhinin liked dipping into it from time to time, he never got much out of it. He considered it chiefly fashionable, fit (as he opined) for the education of young ladies. He did enjoy some individual pieces, notably the 'English Idyl' *Dora* and the ballad *The Lord of Burleigh* (the latter for its metric originality), but on the whole he found Tennyson rather strange and strangely unexciting. In an interesting comment in his diary for 2/14 August 1853 Druzhinin averred: 'Tennyson is a *clever* poet; every word of his has *parti pris*.'[114]

Given Tennyson's general attitude to Russia and Turgenev's own characteristically Russian attitude towards him, one might have thought that they were unlikely to gain much from a meeting. In the event, things went very well. For a start, the Tennysons were relieved to find Turgenev, diplomatic as he ever was with foreigners, 'very anxious' over the Gorchakov scare.[115] But they were also most impressed by him: 'a very interesting man', wrote Emily in her diary, 'who tells us stories of Russian life with great graphic power and vivacity'. As Turgenev was not given, while abroad, to speak much of Russian life (as opposed to politics) unless pressed to do so by his hosts, one may infer that Tennyson showed genuine curiosity as to the real nature of a people who had frightened his father, caused endless trouble for his country, and depressed and angered himself. Cossacks were especial bugbears: and he was probably not too surprised to hear Turgenev saying that the tradition with these warriors was to fight among themselves until they were in unanimous accord. Turgenev's most amusing and instructive tale was recorded by Emily in immense detail, some evidently incorrect, and added to at a later stage by Hallam according to his own and his father's memory of it. It is entitled 'The Origin of Legends' and concerns a visit to the Russian provinces by Alexander II to explain the terms of the emancipation of the serfs in 1861. He passed near Turgenev's estate at Spasskoe, but the novelist was ill and sent the headman of his village to watch. The observer returned with the following report:[116]

There came a chariot drawn by four horses, and inside the chariot was a beautiful man in glittering armour, but he was not the Czar. He passed by us and vanished in the wilderness. Then came another magnificent chariot with a still more beautiful man, in resplendent and bejewelled armour; and this was the White Czar of all the Russias! And he stood up in his chariot and spread his arms abroad! Then he beat upon his breast, and he said, 'Do you know who I am?' Then we all fell to the earth with our heads in the dust, and we saw nothing, but he beat upon his breast again three times, and cried aloud, 'Obey, obey, obey,' and then the chariot began to move and we watched him as far as eye could see and the chariot whirled him away, and he vanished into the wilderness.

The end of Turgenev's story is that, when he was better, he enquired the truth of neighbours and learned that the Tsar 'did not once get up in his carriage, that he was dressed in an ordinary frock-coat like an Englishman, and that he made ...[a] quiet little speech....'

There is some independent evidence that the core of this story was historical;[117] but it is likely that Turgenev embroidered the facts in the same way as Tennyson himself had elevated into a minor epic the sparse details of his father's trip to Russia. Surely he must have told Turgenev that anecdote, besides; but Emily did not note the fact. Nor, alas, did she note the conversation that they must have had on their respective countries' literatures, or on their own artistic values. The great critic Maurice Baring would later call them both typically 'mid-Victorian', in so far as they were idyllic 'landscape-lovers and lords of language'.[118] There are, besides, some interesting affinities in their works, notably of atmosphere and natural philosophy. The extraordinary twin poems from Tennyson's so-called 'Juvenilia', *Nothing Will Die* and *All Things Will Die*, neatly express the alternative truths about human life on earth to which Turgenev also subscribed. There are some striking similarities of mood in Tennyson's *Mariana* and Turgenev's *Dvorianskoe gnezdo* (A Nest of the Gentry). Tennyson is known to have liked that novel, doubtless because he often shared its sense of the poignancy and transience of human love and affections.[119] Another early poem by Tennyson, *A Dream of Fair Women*, seems to anticipate to a quite remarkable degree Turgenev's transcendental preoccupations in his sketch *Prizraki* (Phantoms). In this connection it is also pleasant to imagine the writers talking of the awesome shelf at Blackgang Chine, near Farringford. In *Maud* we observe the hero[120]

> Listening now to the tide in its broad-flung shipwrecking roar,
> Now to the scream of a maddened beach dragged down by the wave.

In Section IX of *Prizraki*, meditated by Turgenev during a stay at Ventnor in August 1860, we read of 'shaggy waves upraised' below Blackgang, and of 'the heart-rending screeching and grinding of pebbles on the shore'. Maybe this is pure coincidence of sensibility; but it is curious also that the 'dreary phantom' of *Maud*, like Turgenev's own English phantom, Ellis, is represented as a guide to destruction and doom. Another relevant factor is the writers' shared affection for De Quincey, who had a great influence on the Russian sketch. In the present year 1871, meanwhile, *Prizraki* was being mocked by the vicious Dostoevskii in his novel *Besy* (The Devils). A few years earlier, he had met Turgenev in Germany and borrowed money; now, in *Besy,* he was inventing all manner of slander and distortion. Tennyson liked to tell a comparable tale about an adventuress who once called on him and recited *The Charge of the Light Brigade*; afterwards, she declared she had seen the poet thrashing his wife and being carried blind drunk to his bed.[121]

In relation to Turgenev's visit to Aldworth, all this is speculative. Nor can it be said for sure what resulted from it. He was clearly pleased with his stay and appreciated the Tennysons' warm hospitality. He still did not understand the bard's enormous popularity, however, and could only assume it must be due to an absence in contemporary English poetry of more powerful or original minds. Doubtless he disliked the laureate's essential British insularity. As for Tennyson himself, although we are told that he loved *Ottsy i deti* (Fathers and Sons), as well as *Dvorianskoe gnezdo*, no book by Turgenev has been catalogued as belonging to his library. He was not, of course, especially keen on novels and did not start to read them systematically until much later in life. And by the time that he studied any other literature from Russia, neither Turgenev nor anyone else could have had any influence upon his writings. More positive is the fact that he did immediately show a curiosity in the ancient monuments of Russia and the steppes of Tartary, and a strong fascination with what Emily described as 'the strange sects among the Russians, and the character of the Russian peasant and the strong feeling of unity in the nation'. He studied books on the subject, including probably H.C. Romanoff's

Historical Narratives from the Russian. Other works that he may have been reading at this time include Robert Richardson-Gardner's *A Trip to St. Petersburg*, George Walter Thornbury's *Criss-cross Journeys*, and William Ralston's *Songs of the Russian People* and *Russian Folk Tales*. Although his new interest may have derived in part from Ralston, who always dedicated copies of his writings to the Tennysons, it must have been given great impetus by the recent meeting with Turgenev. One or two stories with a macabre twist that the poet liked to tell his sons very closely resemble Russian folk-tales, and some other of his future remarks sound like echoes of his enthralling talks with the novelist. Moreover, a couple of years later we find him recounting the sad tale of his father's trip to Russia, for the benefit of some visiting ecclesiastics, in an exciting but light-hearted way, not laying any emphasis upon Russian tyranny or treachery.[122]

The early 1870s witnessed in fact a certain lull in Anglo-Russian hostility. It is true that the Tsarist bogy was raised again in England from time to time: for instance, in the autumn of 1872 Alexander was preparing to invade Khiva, and the British government, yet once more, stood back in inactivity. A leader in *The Times* of 24 October even approved this reaction, on the grounds that Russia might do for Khiva what England was doing for India, and would then be 'an ally in the great war of enlightenment against barbarism'. But many of its readers were gravely disturbed by Russia's continuing advances towards India. Tennyson himself was 'much concerned and alarmed' by a letter in *The Times* of 28 October. Reading this out to a friend, he remarked how Russia had 'always been a bugbear to him'.[123] This was, however, a fairly isolated concern. At the highest level, things were going rather harmoniously. Even in July 1871, before the Gorchakov affair was quite forgotten, the Grand Duke Constantine had visited London, and in June 1873 the Queen received the Tsarevich (the future Alexander III), his Danish-born wife Mariia Fiodorovna (Dagmar), and their two small sons Nicholas and George. In May 1874 the Tsar himself came to Windsor, and was cheered by crowds on his visits to Westminster Abbey, the Houses of Parliament, the Crystal Palace and Woolwich Arsenal.[124] Before this last sequence of events, there occurred a circumstance of some import for Tennyson: Queen Victoria's second son Prince Alfred, Duke of Edinburgh, had fallen in love with and become engaged to the young Grand Duchess Mariia Aleksandrovna, daughter of Alexander II; they married in St Petersburg on 23 January 1874.

The Tennysons had been following the betrothal with great interest, and on the very day of the royal wedding Hallam read his mother an account of the annual blessing of the River Neva.[125] This could have come from anywhere, of course, but as it was not seasonal at the time it may have been taken from a travel book that the Tennysons had been studying rather than from a recent newspaper. The ducal pair were to arrive in England on 7 March and, at Queen Victoria's express request, Tennyson wrote for *The Times* of that day a poem called *A Welcome to Her Royal Highness Marie Alexandrovna, Duchess of Edinburgh*. He sent the Queen a copy of it early in the month.[126] Persuaded by Emily, and encouraged by flattering telegrams of congratulation from Windsor Castle, he went up to London on 12 March for the 'entry' of the Duke and Duchess in their state journey with the Queen. The enthusiasm of the many thousands of spectators who lined the route from Paddington to Buckingham Palace is said to have been 'unchecked by the chilling frost or drifting snow showers'. At night, London was brilliantly illuminated.[127] From his seat in Regent Street the poet had an excellent view, but despite the cheering crowds his fervour was dampened by the weather. A lack of fine military uniforms disappointed him, and the gloomy skies took the colour from the banners and the glint from soldiers' helmets. He was also somewhat snooty as to the Duchess's physique. She 'looked large and imperial', he opined, and (like the Queen herself) wagged her head continuously left and right, up and down, as if it were made of India rubber. Gladstone's daughter Mary said, 'They bowed until they were sick'; but whereas she found the Duchess quite attractive, with 'a delightful fresh young face', the general feeling was perhaps better conveyed by Tennyson's own remark that she was 'if not very pretty, not plain'. Curiously enough, this phrase is an exact description of the piece that he had written in her honour:[128]

I

The Son of him with whom we strove for power —
    Whose will is lord through all his world-domain —
    Who made the serf a man, and burst his chain —
Has given our Prince his own imperial Flower,
        Alexandrovna.
And welcome, Russian flower, a people's pride,
    To Britain, when her flowers begin to blow!
    From love to love, from home to home you go,
From mother unto mother, stately bride,
        Marie Alexandrovna!

II

The golden news along the steppes is blown,
    And at thy name the Tartar tents are stirred;
    Elburz and all the Caucasus have heard;
And all the sultry palms of India known
        Alexandrovna.
The voices of our universal sea

On capes of Afric as on cliffs of Kent,
    The Maoris and that Isle of Continent,
And loyal pines of Canada murmur thee,
        Marie Alexandrovna!

III

Fair empires branching, both, in lusty life! —
    Yet Harold's England fell to Norman swords;
    Yet thine own land has bowed to Tartar hordes
Since English Harold gave its throne a wife,
        Alexandrovna!
For thrones and peoples are as waifs that swing,
    And float or fall, in endless ebb and flow;
    But who love best have best the grace to know
That Love by right divine is deathless king,
        Marie Alexandrovna!

IV

And Love has led thee to the stranger land,
    Where men are bold and strongly say their say;—
    See, Empire upon Empire smiles today,
As thou with thy young lover hand in hand,
        Alexandrovna!
So now thy fuller life is in the west,
    Whose hand at home was gracious to thy poor:
    Thy name was blest within the narrow door;
Here also, Marie, shall thy name be blest,
        Marie Alexandrovna!

V

Shall fears and jealous hatreds flame again?
    Or at thy coming, Princess, everywhere,
    The blue heaven break, and some diviner air
Breathe through the world and change the hearts of men,
        Alexandrovna?
But hearts that change not, love that cannot cease,
    And peace be yours, the peace of soul in soul!
    And howsoever this wild world may roll,
Between your peoples truth and manful peace,
        Alfred — Alexandrovna!

Although Tennyson had clearly taken great pains with this iambic paean, he did get some details wrong. He confused the Iranian Elburz mountains with the Caucasian Elbrus; he introduced a chronological absurdity in the reference to Harold II and his daughter Gytha, reputed to have married Prince Vladimir of Novgorod when the latter was dead; and in insisting on the Grand Duchess's parentage by the use of her patronymic alone, he made her sound like a servant. None of this disconcerted him; he was worried only by something which scarcely mattered, namely that the stress in 'Aleksandrovna' falls on the third syllable and not, as he supposed, on the penultimate. 'I think [it] a little spoils the chorus', wrote Emily to Hallam, echoing her husband, 'but this thou wilt not feel so much not liking the chorus at all'.[129] Maybe Hallam was right. However, the poem does contain some felicities and has importance as a source for our knowledge of what its author was currently thinking about Russia. Notice especially Tennyson's gracious praise of Alexander for having freed the serfs. Admittedly, he needed this to counteract the poem's opening lines, with their allusions to oppression and war; nevertheless, by his juxtaposition of the Russian and British empires, 'both in lusty life' and smiling at each other, he implied that to have liberated the peasants from their masters might herald a general liberation of the human spirit in Russia. This sense is strengthened by the way that news of the wedding is made to pass from St Petersburg to India via the steppes, the Caucasus and Tartary. The route is somewhat circuitous, but no matter; while no one would suspect Tennyson of wishing Russia to have sway in India, there is a tacit acceptance that its power was on the land, while Britain ruled the seas. Provided that the Russian empire fell no more into barbarian hands, the poet now (despite his former scepticism) could see no reason why it should not complement Victoria's own and build a firm base for future peace and harmony throughout the world. The young couple's love figured universal love between peoples.

Unfortunately, Tennyson's welcome to the Grand Duchess, sincere though it undoubtedly was, and expressive of popular sentiment in Britain at that time, remained but a pious symbol: nations long at enmity do not make up their differences by a royal wedding alone. The British people had just elected a Tory government, with the clearest majority for over thirty years. The liberal Gladstone had been swept aside by Disraeli, who was to prove no friend of Russia's. Rivalry between Russia and England persisted, and Disraeli knew it: the Balkans, Turkey, Afghanistan, even India — all were centres of potential Anglo-Russian conflagration. Though unfair, it is hardly surprising that Tennyson's poem should have been treated in some quarters with irony and contempt. A very different piece devoted to the short-lived sunny phase in Anglo-Russian politics was Alfred Austin's *All Hail to the Czar!* Published in May 1874, this constituted a derisive attack on his countrymen's hypocrisy in welcoming Alexander II to British shores:[130]

> All hail to the Czar! Are ye then sunk so low,
> O ye sons of the once fearless masters of earth!
> That ye pour out the wine for an insolent foe,
> That in depths of dishonour ye simulate mirth?

But Tennyson's own attitude to Russia during the 1870s and 1880s was in fact vacillating and two-faced. In subjective terms, perhaps, he seemed logical enough: strong in his support of country and defence of Christianity, he showed more, or less, anti-Russian feeling in proportion to Russia's impingement upon each. His first significant new poem to touch remotely on things Russian was still neutral, and arose out of his friendship with Gladstone. In 1875 a cenotaph to Sir John Franklin was unveiled in Westminster Abbey. Tennyson wrote a four-line epitaph for it which he and Gladstone then undertook to have translated into various languages including Greek, Latin, Persian and (of relevance in view of Franklin's Arctic explorations) Russian.[131] Nothing seems to have come of this, but the Tennyson-Gladstone partnership was to continue. Already a year later, the Bulgarian crisis was at hand: Turkey was persecuting Slavonic peoples, and Russia was threatening to intervene. In September 1876 Gladstone committed himself to the Slavonic cause with his powerful pamphlet *The Bulgarian Horrors and the Question of the East*. Tennyson visited the Gladstones at Hawarden in late October and early November. He does not appear to have discussed the crisis much with his hosts, but it is of interest that Gladstone quoted some lines from Tennyson (of no relevance to the subject) in a subsequent article on the Eastern Question,[132] as also that *Punch*, on 4 November, should have published a cryptic note which reads: 'Mr. Tennyson on the Eastern Question. (*Dedicated, without express permission, to Servia.*)[133] —

> 'Tis better to have fought and lost,
> Than never to have fought at all.'

It is probable that Gladstone held off discussing the Eastern Question when Tennyson was present, knowing his guest's conservative, anti-Russian views. At a breakfast with him in April 1878, when jingoism was already rife, he did not start talking seriously about Russia until after the poet had gone.[134] It also seems that Tennyson, for his part, tended to avoid the subject in his commerce with Gladstone. He had the greatest admiration for Gladstone as a person, and the greatest contempt for Disraeli, but he was forced, however reluctantly, to incline to Disraeli's view in international politics. On several occasions during the 1880s he was reported as saying things like, 'Gladstone is personally my friend, but politically, I hate him like the devil.'[135] It is unlikely that Gladstone was within earshot at another party in the spring of 1878, when Tennyson made his infamous remark to the poet and diarist William Allingham: 'I've hated Russia ever since I was born, and I'll hate her till I die!' And he added at that time: 'I hate Dizzy, and I love Gladstone; still, I want Russia snubbed.'[136]

In relation to Tennyson's prejudices, it is instructive to consider here a rumour that he chiefly despised Russia because 'we English people cannot tolerate their knout system'. This, at least, is how it was reported by a mutual acquaintance to Olga Novikova, the Russian propagandist who signed herself 'O.K.' and came to be known jocularly as 'the M.P. for Russia'. In a pamphlet called *Is Russia Wrong?*, published at the time of greatest British jingoism in early 1878, she pointed out that the British navy, as far as she knew, still retained the cat-o'-nine-tails, whereas the use of the knout, actually a Tartar import, had been officially abolished soon after the Emancipation of the serfs in 1861. Surely Mr Tennyson should have learnt this fact by now?[137] Tennyson's abomination of the knout was of course long-standing: he had referred to it in *Maud*. English literary allusions to it were, besides, quite common. Not all were credulous, however: one thinks of Thackeray's Princess Scragamoffsky, in *The Book of Snobs*, unable to 'show' at Lady Palmerston's because, just a while before at the Russian Embassy in London, she had received 'thirteen dozen strokes of the knout' for stating 'that the Grand Duchess Olga's hair was red'.[138] But Tennyson may have been relying on George Walter Thornbury's *Criss-cross Journeys* (2 vols, 1873), which has a great deal on punishment by the knout. Thornbury, who had a long-standing interest in Russia and devoted impressive and moving poems to it such as *The Retreat from Moscow*, characterised the knout as a 'savage relic of a bygone cruelty'. Although he clearly stated that it had now been officially abolished, and praised the Emperor for this, his evocation of its effects was graphically realistic: when used by a skilled executioner, he said, it would kill its often innocent victim about the fifth blow at the latest.[139]

Ignorance and prejudice or not, the new Russian menace did not prevent Tennyson from publishing in 1877 his powerful poem *Montenegro*. It arose, in fact, from a talk that he had had with Gladstone and the reformer John Bright earlier in that year. Montenegro had declared war on Turkey in July 1876, in an effort to consolidate the territory which it had for centuries held inviolable from the empire of the Ottomans. Gladstone, who himself wrote an article on Montenegro, perhaps requested and certainly inspired Tennyson to devote a sonnet to this subject, maybe as a kind of concession to libertarian truths which the poet was otherwise ignoring. Tennyson now clearly supported Gladstone's stance on Slavonic minorities, and would have liked to hear him debate these in Parliament. He was also anxious for his approval of the sonnet, and the fact that he received this is seen by its appearance together with Gladstone's article at the head of the journal *Nineteenth Century* for May 1877.[140] In his poem, Tennyson lauded that brave little country for its resistance to the Turks and apostrophised it by its Slavonic name, Crna Gora (Black Mountain; 'Tsernogora' was a nineteenth-century variant). The poet was in effect now following Gladstone's lead, since to support Montenegro was to support Bulgaria and — by implication — Panslavism as well. The fact that Panslavism meant in practice Russian domination was, however, of little immediate consequence to Tennyson, who is said to have admired this fine Miltonic piece above all his other sonnets. Here it is:[141]

> They rose to where their sovran eagle sails,
> They kept their faith, their freedom, on the height,
> Chaste, frugal, savage, armed by day and night
> Against the Turk; whose inroad nowhere scales
> Their headlong passes, but his footstep fails,
> And red with blood the Crescent reels from fight
> Before their dauntless hundreds, in prone flight
> By thousands down the crags and through the vales.
> O smallest among peoples! rough rock-throne
> Of Freedom! warriors beating back the swarm
> Of Turkish Islam for five hundred years,
> Great Tsernogora! never since thine own
> Black ridges drew the cloud and brake the storm
> Has breathed a race of mightier mountaineers.

However, between the writing of this poem in March and its appearance in May, Russia itself had officially entered the Balkan war and in London, by late July, the British cabinet had decided to prevent it taking Constantinople. As the months passed, fear of Russian control in the Near East began to outweigh disgust at Turkish atrocities even in many liberal English minds. Tennyson became disenchanted with Gladstone's continuing stand against the Porte and moved towards (though by no means so far as) the extreme pro-Turkish position adopted by Swinburne in his *Ballad of Bulgarie*. In March 1878 Tennyson published his moving but fiercely patriotic poem *The Revenge: A Ballad of the Fleet*, in which he tacitly backed Disraeli's determination to stop Russia from closing off the Black Sea. In Tennyson's defence, one must remember that early 1878 in Britain was the time of greatest jingoism. Never before and perhaps never since was the spirit of Empire so strong. The mood was pathogenic. After the Congress of Berlin, however, tension considerably eased. Already in the June of 1879, Turgenev could be invited to take a DCL at Oxford and was actually applauded; this would have been unthinkable a year before. Tennyson himself had a relevant experience at this very same time. In the spring of 1879 he received an inscribed copy of Robert Browning's *Dramatic Idyls* and must have perused it thoroughly. That June he recited the remarkable little anti-vivisection piece *Tray* for the benefit of Mary Gladstone (later Drew) and Margaret Cowell-Stepney (née Warren), during their visit to Farringford. Although he said nothing now about *Ivàn Ivànovitch*, which immediately precedes *Tray* in the series, we know from a conversation that he later had with William Allingham how fascinated (though perhaps also repelled) he was by its treatment of the wolf story long since known to himself. It is interesting that after reading *Tray* to his guests he recited 'some Crimean War extracts'. What precisely is meant by this is unclear, but *Ivàn Ivànovitch* may have revived his curiosity about more general aspects of Russian life and culture as well as reminding him again of an empire which, for an Englishman, could only seem a bogy of repression. Just a few days before, in fact, he and Mary Gladstone had 'had a shindy about England and Politics and Russia, etc.,' which must certainly have reflected Tennyson's and Mary's father's conflicting views on Anglo-Russian rivalry in the Near and Middle East.[142]

Through William Ralston, meanwhile, Turgenev maintained some contact with Tennyson and in May 1880 sent a telegram inviting him to attend the great Pushkin celebrations to be held that summer in Moscow. Naturally, Tennyson did not go, but he wrote a courteous message of refusal (now lost) which was quoted at the opening ceremony.[143] In this connection, a strange coincidence may be noted. In the most famous speech of the festival, Dostoevskii urged that Pushkin was so great an international poet because he was first so national. Tennyson's *Hands All Round!*, originally of 1852 but soon to be revived for new patriotic purposes, contained the lines:[144]

> That man's the best cosmopolite,
>   Who loves his native country best.

Not long after the time of which we are speaking, Tennyson in effect cast doubt upon a Russian's right to be included in this definition, owing to the savagery of his manners, but he also showed that he was prepared to laugh now over Russia's continuing barbarity. In a further talk with Allingham he related an anecdote which, incidentally, may well have derived from Turgenev: 'A Russian noble, who spoke English well, said one morning to an English guest, "I've shot two peasants this morning." — "Pardon me, you mean pheasants." "No, indeed, two men — they were insolent and I shot them."'[145]

In October 1881, William Ralston threw a banquet in honour of Turgenev, again on a visit to London. A number of literary lions came, including Anthony Trollope and R.D. Blackmore. Tennyson was otherwise engaged, but sent a telegram which Ralston read to the assembled company and which 'gratified' and 'delighted' Turgenev 'immensely'. In it he demonstrated his good will by inviting Turgenev to drop in at Aldworth on the way back to France. This time it was Turgenev who did not manage to go.[146] The incident shows the respective priorities of these two great artists. Neither much esteemed the country of the other, yet both were prepared to keep up the lip-service of mutual regard. It was a microcosm of current Anglo-Russian relations. The writers would never meet again: Turgenev died in 1883.

Tennyson's last poem fully devoted to a Russian subject was *The Charge of the Heavy Brigade at Balaclava*, completed in February 1882 and first published the following month in *Macmillan's Magazine*.[147] In 1885 the poem would be reissued in a definitive form, preceded by the beautiful 'Prologue to General Hamley' and concluded by an intriguing 'Epilogue' which consists of a conversation between Irene (that is, Peace) and the Poet. This surrounding framework was composed actually in the autumn of 1883. Tennyson apparently started writing '*The Heavy Brigade*' as early as March 1881, in response to a suggestion by A.W. Kinglake, historian of the Crimean War. In Hallam Tennyson's privately printed *Materials* towards a life of his father there is a long and curious document by Kinglake, based upon a narration by a trooper of the Scots Greys, which amounts to a complete scenario in five acts — or 'instants' — describing the origin, purpose and progress of the Heavy Brigade's charge. From it, Tennyson took the men's adulation of their battle commander, Brigadier the Hon. James Yorke Scarlett of the 5th (Princess Charlotte of Wales's) Dragoon Guards; Scarlett's particular 'three hundred'; his order, 'Halt! Left wheel into line!'; the enemy's unexplained halt; the figure of 3,000 Russian sabres; the British trumpet sounding the advance; and Scarlett's special 'three' (explained in a note by Tennyson as his aide-de-camp, Lieutenant Alexander J.H. Elliot; an unnamed trumpeter; and Shegog the orderly who — as Kinglake elsewhere noted — was a skilled swordsman and valiant warrior, seemingly descended from some ancient Celtic giantess). Tennyson even borrowed, in adapted form, the expression 'drops of blood poured into the sea'. However, unlike Kinglake he chose to tell the story from the point of view of a non-combatant observer, probably intended as a member of the Light Brigade which was forced to stand idly by; and among the many striking details in Kinglake's account that he chose not to use, one may note the emergence of Scarlett 'with his helmet cloven, and bleeding from one or two wounds but not at all gravely hurt'.[148] In using the historian's text, Tennyson obviously checked it with Kinglake's published work, noting for instance the red wedge-like drive into a mass of grey.[149] He presumably also used the *Times* reports of November 1854, and an anonymous description of the Heavy Brigade's charge which he had received at the time.[150] Between 1882 and 1885 he may have reconsidered all the sources, since the poem in its final version lacks a geographical ambiguity in the original lines 14-15, and does not have Scarlett dashing on quite so far ahead. Maybe the Crimean veteran General Edward Hamley, who discussed the piece with its author during a visit to Aldworth in 1883, contributed in some way to these relatively minor revisions.[151]

As with the Light Cavalry's charge, it is hard to establish the precise truth of the engagement. According to Russell, it was Lord Lucan who commanded the Heavy Brigade to wheel and face the enemy. Again according to statistics noted by Russell, the Russian force may actually have outnumbered the British, not by ten to one but by little more than two to one. Russell also first established the historical facts as to the progress of the attack, which was made in two controlled waves: the initial charge by the Scots Greys and a squadron of Inniskillings was followed up by a second Enniskillener squadron together with the 4th Royal Irish Dragoon Guards and the 5th Dragoons. (There was actually a third, smaller wave — another 4th Dragoon squadron.)[152] Tennyson's view of the thing as a valorous charge by Scarlett's three hundred Scotsmen and Irishmen, backed up almost as an afterthought by the rest of the brigade, will therefore not bear scrutiny.[153] While there is no doubt as to the bravery of Scarlett or of individual soldiers — all applauded and cried 'Well done!' as the men cheered and slashed like demons and Russians 'went down like cut corn', — it is certain that Tennyson has at once simplified and exaggerated, in a word mythologised the incident. He evidently wanted to establish the superior, because less gratuitous, glory of the Heavy Brigade, having himself helped earlier to obscure it by his apotheosis of the Light. In one sense, he now saw that the Light Brigade's mad dash came in response to the 'chaff' of 'those damned heavies' for their colleagues' inactivity.[154] To compensate for the perhaps excessively romantic colouring of the earlier poem, he brought to his *Charge of the Heavy Brigade at Balaclava* a corresponding starkness of tone, the black and white of legend and of his own medieval romances. Whereas in *The Charge of the Light Brigade* all is nameless, leaderless, foredoomed (in the definitive version at least), in the later work Scarlett emerges as a hero-knight. The enemy, meanwhile, had to suffer in the process: whereas in the first poem they are treated rather neutrally, here they become 'Russian hordes' and a 'dark-muffled Russian crowd'. *The Charge of the Heavy Brigade* is given now in the text of 1885, but without its prologue or epilogue:[155]

I

The charge of the gallant three hundred, the Heavy Brigade!
Down the hill, down the hill, thousands of Russians,
Thousands of horsemen, drew to the valley — and stayed;

For Scarlett and Scarlett's three hundred were riding by
When the points of the Russian lances arose in the sky;
And he called 'Left wheel into line!' and they wheeled and obeyed.
Then he looked at the host that had halted he knew not why,
And he turned half round, and he bad his trumpeter sound
To the charge, and he rode on ahead, as he waved his blade
To the gallant three hundred whose glory will never die —
'Follow', and up the hill, up the hill, up the hill,
Followed the Heavy Brigade.

II

The trumpet, the gallop, the charge, and the might of the fight!
Thousands of horsemen had gathered there on the height,
With a wing pushed out to the left, and a wing to the right,
And who shall escape if they close? but he dashed up alone
Through the great gray slope of men,
Swayed his sabre, and held his own
Like an Englishman there and then;
All in a moment followed with force
Three that were next in their fiery course,
Wedged themselves in between horse and horse,
Fought for their lives in the narrow gap they had made —
Four amid thousands! and up the hill, up the hill,
Gallopt the gallant three hundred, the Heavy Brigade.

III

Fell like a cannonshot,
Burst like a thunderbolt,
Crashed like a hurricane,
Broke through the mass from below,
Drove through the midst of the foe,
Plunged up and down, to and fro,
Rode flashing blow upon blow,
Brave Inniskillens and Greys
Whirling their sabres in circles of light!
And some of us, all in amaze,
Who were held for a while from the fight,
And were only standing at gaze,
When the dark-muffled Russian crowd
Folded its wings from the left and the right,
And rolled them around like a cloud, —
O mad for the charge and the battle were we,
When our own good redcoats sank from sight,
Like drops of blood in a dark-gray sea,
And we turned to each other, whispering, all dismayed,
'Lost are the gallant three hundred of Scarlett's Brigade!'

IV

'Lost one and all' were the words
Muttered in our dismay;
But they rode like Victors and Lords
Through the forest of lances and swords

> In the heart of the Russian hordes,
> They rode, or they stood at bay —
> Struck with the sword-hand and slew,
> Down with the bridle-hand drew
> The foe from the saddle and threw
> Underfoot there in the fray —
> Ranged like a storm or stood like a rock
> In the wave of a stormy day;
> Till suddenly shock upon shock
> Staggered the mass from without,
> Drove it in wild disarray,
> For our men gallopt up with a cheer and a shout,
> And the foeman surged, and wavered, and reeled
> Up the hill, up the hill, up the hill, out of the field,
> And over the brow and away.

V

> Glory to each and to all, and the charge that they made!
> Glory to all the three hundred, and all the Brigade!

The stylistic irregularity of this poem, with its mixture of metres, different lengths of lines, and varied rhyme schemes, helps to make it more powerfully dramatic but at the same time less taut and artistically cyclical than *The Charge of the Light Brigade*. A contemporary critic spoke of its 'martial, sonorous, thrilling' verbal music which 'reproduces with extraordinary force the breathless, toiling, thunderous assault'.[156] If it was never so popular as the earlier piece, this was perhaps because the times — and poetry — had changed. Whereas in 1854-55 the accusation of warmongering was drowned by a chorus of patriotic praise, in 1882 the Crimean campaign in general seemed more blameworthy and Tennyson's new defence of it anachronistic. It is clear that he was greatly upset by the criticism: in the *Epilogue* he defended himself with the irritable lines:

> And who loves War for War's own sake
> Is fool, or crazed, or worse.

More disingenuously, he attached to the poem through this *Epilogue* a purpose of examining the existence of evil which it could not originally have had.[157] He nevertheless received much praise from quarters where it mattered. Colonel Elliot, one of 'the three', conveyed to him through Kinglake how proud it made him feel to be associated again with Scarlett, his 'dear old chief'. He had perused the ballad, he said, 'with a renewal of that blood-rising which I recognised on the day when we wheeled into line, and started to meet the big foe above us on the hillside...'[158] Doubtless this was ultimately enough justification for Tennyson, who at the end of his life was still citing with approval another officer's assertion that the charge was 'the finest excitement ever known, that drink, gambling, and horse-racing were nothing to it'.[159]

Although Tennyson scarcely referred again to Anglo-Russian matters in his poetry, it was perhaps only in this last phase of his long career that he came to recognise the deep divisions that existed in Russian society — whether of class, religion, philosophy, or political persuasion. The understanding developed too late to have any effect upon his published work, but one sees it increasingly in his private utterances. Several of his former assumptions were seriously tested, and even the lighter aspects of his encounters with things Russian carried some measure of ambiguity. In the first place, as he remained a monarchist and gradualist he could not bear to think that socialism or revolution might supplant the 'legitimate' order, even in Russia.[160] Although he gave no outward sign of it, he may therefore have been deeply shocked by the murder of the Tsar-Liberator, Alexander II, in 1881, and inclined to hope that his successor would escape the same fate. Indeed, he took a practical interest in Alexander III, chiefly but not only on account of his being the brother-in law of the Duke of Edinburgh. A cutting in the Lincoln archives shows that he read of the Imperial coronation in *The Times*; and later in the same year — 1883 — he actually met the new Tsar and his lady.

Tennyson was on a North Sea pleasure cruise with a party that included Gladstone, now prime minister again. During the trip he chatted, among others, with a sea captain who had transported British soldiers to the Crimea three decades before. On 16 September Tennyson's ship, the *Pembroke Castle,* put in at Copenhagen and a couple of days later a luncheon-party was given on board for the Danish King and Queen, the King and Queen of Greece, various British royal personages, and the Imperial Russian pair and their son and heir Nicholas, reportedly a jolly Tatar-looking boy. Several toasts were drunk, including one by the magnificently-uniformed Tsar for the absent Victoria, one by Gladstone for the Imperial Russian personages, and one for Tennyson by the Queen of Denmark. At one point the Russian Empress talked with the poet, remarking, 'What a kind and sympathetic man Mr Gladstone is! how he stood by little Montenegro!' To understand what happened next, it is necessary to assume either that Tennyson did not realise that this was the Tsaritsa, or that he was too excited, overawed, or drunk, to look at her. After lunch, the senior regal figures crowded into the ship's smoking-room, while the younger branches clustered round the doors. Inside, the wideawake-crowned laureate was pressed by the Princess of Wales to recite a little of his poetry. When a volume had been fetched, he read out the bugle song from *The Princess* ('The splendour falls on castle walls'), and then

The Grandmother. As he did so, he sat squeezed on a sofa between the Princess and the Empress, with the Tsar standing just in front of him. His task fulfilled, he was complimented by the Tsaritsa and patted her on the shoulder affectionately, saying, 'My dear girl, that's very kind of you, very kind.'

As with all anecdotes of this sort, elaborations and accretions are not lacking. In one version of the story, Tennyson takes the Tsaritsa for a maid of honour; in another, for the daughter of his doctor, Sir Andrew Clark. The Tsar is alternately offended and beguiled, the Tsaritsa 'immensely amused and delighted'. A third account has the laureate keeping metrical time on the Empress's back all through his quarter-hour's reading; in a fourth, he slaps her on the arm and says 'certainly' when she invites him to come and stay with her in St Petersburg. At one point, the Danish court jester is said to have looked in at the window and declared: 'He ought to be taught court manners!' In most texts, Tennyson's excuse is given as short-sightedness or the fact that he was wearing reading-spectacles. How ironic, then, that at the end of *The Grandmother* he should have the line, 'Get me my glasses, Annie: thank God that I keep my eyes.' Meanwhile, as a proof that the Tsar cannot really have been annoyed by the bard, he is reported to have afterwards spoken with him and exclaimed, 'I should like to be King of Denmark!' This seemingly inconsequential comment must relate to the high danger of Russian politics in comparison with those of Scandinavia, but one does wonder if Alexander had ever heard of King Claudius.[161]

In every variant of this anecdote, Tennyson emerges as a superior mind. European royalty itself is somehow subject to him, and he has poetic licence, as one might say, to behave boorishly. Had he not shown he ought be considered as grand as a Russian Emperor? However, there exists a second anecdote according to which the Tsaritsa had with her her small son Michael; perhaps this should be situated on board the Imperial yacht. Tennyson, we are told, 'had not been reading two minutes before the child said, in a loud voice: "Now I have heard him, Mamma, may I go?"'[162] Not all the cheering of Russian sailors on the following day, with their band playing 'God save the Queen', could obliterate a reprimand like that. Was it true? Who can tell? At all events, Tennyson appears actually to have formed an excellent impression of the Tsar, if not of the Imperial ménage. He promised to send a volume of his poetry, and himself seems to have been given, either now or as a prize for his elevation to the peerage shortly afterwards, the granddaughter of a Siberian wolf-hound belonging to Alexander III. This bitch is described as 'a beautiful, picturesque creature', 'the constant companion of her master in his last walks over the Freshwater downs'. Tennyson called her... Karenina.[163]

Why this name? Can it be that Tennyson had read the novel by Tolstoi? Certainly he knew the article on it by Matthew Arnold — 'Count Leo Tolstoi', published first in the *Fortnightly Review* in 1887 but reprinted the following year in the second series of *Essays in Criticism*. A copy of this was received at Aldworth on 13 November 1888, at a time when the poet was seriously ill and Hallam was doing his best to distract him by reading out things of current interest. He chose the Arnold piece for the very next day, and after it his father declared himself to be feeling much better.[164] The poet was chiefly interested by Tolstoi's views on Christianity, which is noteworthy since the essay itself is in some respects critical of these and deals mainly with the fiction. Arnold was deeply impressed by *Anna Karenina*, condoning what he saw as its excessive complexity and superfluous scenes on the ground that it should not be looked at as a work of art but rather as 'a piece of life'. Despite its apparently sensational subject, it showed none of the 'fine sentiment' or 'lubricity' of the French tradition, and was superior even to Flaubert's obviously comparable *Madame Bovary* in that Tolstoi supplied much greater 'compassion, tenderness, insight'. Arnold's article was one of the earliest in England to deal seriously with Tolstoi, at least among critics of such distinction as he. He even went so far as to say: 'If fresh literary productions maintain this vogue and enhance it, we shall all be learning Russian.'[165] Though not completely plausible, it is worth adducing here also Tolstoi's own frequently repeated statement, on hearing of the demise of Matthew Arnold, that his greatest friend had died. What he had in mind in revering him, undoubtedly, was the Englishman's own vision of the place of Christian education and culture at the heart of a nation's morality.[166]

It is, however, important to realise that Tolstoi's writings on Christianity were flooding into England during the 1880s and 1890s: there was a veritable craze for him in certain quarters, with several of his pamphlets coming out in translation each year. Not everyone, therefore, would have agreed with Arnold's conclusion that these were narrower and more dogmatic than the religious views expressed in relation to Levin at the end of *Anna Karenina*. On the contrary, Tolstoi's latest writings seemed like tracts for the time, especially for those who had faith, and must have been given impetus in England by the knowledge that their author was in serious conflict with his country's authorities. One such booklet, *Work While Ye Have the Light* (in the version by E.J. Dillon), was given as a present to Hallam Tennyson by his wife Audrey in 1890 and must have come also to the poet's attention.[167] Many of Tolstoi's religious ideas found a ready echo in his entourage, and Tennyson himself was probably impressed by them. Although in his late seventies he took more to novels than hitherto, it is therefore likely that his interest in Tolstoi was for what he had to say on religion rather than on human character. But the Russian novelist's earlier, creative writing did ride back into popularity on the tide of his spiritual eccentricity, and through *Anna Karenina* (always assuming that he also read it) Tennyson could have been made aware of Russia's literary maturity. 'It is the authors, more than the diplomats, who make nations love one another', he said. Tolstoi, of course, had just the same purpose in mind.[168]

In the intervening years since making the acquaintance of the Tsar, Tennyson had more than once had occasion to note the Russians' sharpness in the matter of international relations. In September 1884 he assured a visitor that they were 'the greatest diplomats in the world ...but the most unscrupulous people in the matter of annexation'. The two things went together, in fact, for he found the Russians good at exploiting other nations' gullibility — notably that of England which (as he himself had seen not long before) could naively show off to them its latest monster gun at Woolwich Arsenal.[169] For a number of years now, there had been warnings in the press and elsewhere of the possibility that Russia might even take India. As early as 1876, on his celebrated *Ride to Khiva*, Captain Fred Burnaby had met Russian officers and indigenous Afghan dignitaries who warned that India was a mine of wealth, that many roads led to it, and that the natives hated the English and would look upon the Russians as deliverers when war finally came.[170] The autumn and winter of 1884 was a period of increasing confrontation between Britain and Russia over Afghanistan and, potentially, India to which Imperial troops were indeed moving ever closer. By February 1885 they were not far from Herat. International negotiations were begun on the question of Afghan borders, but even while these were taking place the Russians captured the important strategic settlement of Penjdeh. News of this reached London on 8 April, causing panic on the Stock Exchange. Further arbitration was proposed, but many leading public figures were now publicly saying the same as Tennyson, if with a different emphasis, namely that Russia had for long been stealthily advancing while Britain's eyes were elsewhere.[171] Some desired to embark on yet another war, hoping this time that foreign intervention might be assisted by forces of revolution from within. Disabuse yourselves, however, came the message of perennial wiseacres claiming inside knowledge: the Russian Nihilists were making little headway now, being forced to use the wiles of monstrous women, their minds aflame with the fire of fanaticism.[172] Other public figures preferred simply to rearm, and wait.

It was in this context that Tennyson wrote his short piece *The Fleet*, published in *The Times* and the *Pall Mall Gazette* on 23 April under titles expressing his alarm at the insufficiencies of the Royal

Navy, which he considered ought to match in strength the combined French and Russian forces on the seas.[173] However, unlike Swinburne, who in his poem *A Word for the Navy* would specifically refer to the alleged threat from various countries including Russia, Tennyson gave *The Fleet* a vaguer import. His concern about Russia was now subject to a more general fear that Britain was in perhaps terminal decline.[174] Russia nevertheless remained a natural subject of conversation for him throughout this period of tension. He saw it as a continuing threat to the British raj in India, as is evident from the admittedly ambiguous *Locksley Hall Sixty Years After*, written in 1886:[175]

> Russia bursts our Indian barrier, shall we fight her? shall we yield?
> Pause! before you sound the trumpet, hear the voices from the field.

All in all, Tennyson came to believe that the Alexander he had met at Copenhagen was a dishonourable man, a blur on the pages of true history.[176] While ill in bed in November 1888 he once suddenly woke and told Hallam: 'Wait till Russia makes a move, and we go to sleep.'[177] It is obvious that the matter could disturb him deeply. This scare was becoming widespread, in fact, to judge by the number of futuristic fictions which came off the British presses at the time, such as Robert Cromie's *For England's Sake* (1889) and the anonymous *Bombardment of Scarboro' by the Russian Fleet in 1891* (also 1889) and, a little later, William Le Queux's novel *The Great War in England in 1897* (1894).

But it should not be thought that Tennyson saw Russia exclusively from the outside. At about the same period as he was reading Arnold on Tolstoi, he showed evidence of keen interest in Russian political developments. While talking with the doctors who attended him for his 'rheumatic gout', he said that he believed in progress, he believed in patriotism, but he believed above all in what he termed 'gradation'. 'Nihilism in Russia will never be laid to rest', he argued, 'until an Emperor comes, bold enough to trust the people and chance the hatred of the nobles. He may be assassinated, but he will be the saviour of Russia. The Russians do not ask for much. Their men of thought, who are their men of action in domestic politics, ask for a graduated scale of liberty. Their moderation must have struck you.'[178] Here Tennyson would have been at one with the late Turgenev, who ten years earlier was proclaiming something very similar. Tennyson did still believe in the Tsar; but he recognised better now the problem of the *dvoryanstvo* or — as it might then already have been more aptly described — the Russian bourgeoisie. It was this class, however, which bore the chief responsibility for another and different repression, namely that of the

Jews. In 1890-91, after a relative lull, anti-Semitism in Russia was again assuming terrifying proportions.

Despite his undoubted chauvinism and disrespect for negroes, Tennyson had a reasonably good record in regard to Jews. Some years earlier, he had made a public protest when anti-Jewish pogroms were being whipped up in Russia in the wake of the assassination of Alexander II. According to *The Times* of 2 February 1882, he added his support by letter to the protest rally held on that day in the Mansion House.[179] Now in 1890, new measures were announced in Russia to restrict the freedom of Jews: they must reside only in certain defined areas, could not own land, and were expelled from industry and from certain professions like engineering and the law. These new Imperial edicts were reported in *The Times* of 30 July and excited complaints by British Jews and Gentiles alike. The Irish journalist E.J. Dillon published in the *Fortnightly Review* for October an overwhelming indictment of the Russian empire for the systematic repression of its six million Jews. In particular, he proposed ironically that the Tsar should 'commute' their present miseries to 'painless death by electricity or poison'.[180] Petitions were organised and signed by leading public figures including the Archbishop of Canterbury, the Dukes of Westminster and Argyll, Sir Frederic Leighton, Baroness Burdett-Coutts, and Alfred, now Lord, Tennyson himself. On 10 December the Lord Mayor of London hosted a grand public meeting in the Guildhall, in the presence of archbishops, dukes and peers, whom the indefatigable Mme Novikova did not hesitate to dismiss as 'twaddlers'.[181] The meeting nevertheless passed strong resolutions deploring the persecution of Russian Jews and pleading for religious liberty in Russia. It even sent an official protest to Alexander III, but this was returned to the Lord Mayor in February 1891 without perhaps ever coming to the personal attention of the Tsar.

Not all English intellectuals took the liberal line. The *Contemporary Review* for March 1891 permitted a so-styled 'Anglo-Russian' to state that, if the Jews in Russia were mistreated, they had only themselves to blame.[182] At all events, the persecution continued. Tennyson followed the debate on it in *The Times* and in the recently established organ of the Russo-Jewish Committee, *Darkest Russia: A Weekly Record of the Struggle for Freedom*. On 1 October 1891 he wrote to the committee's secretary, Julian Goldsmid: 'I have read what is reported of the Russian persecutions by your paper, and by the press generally; and if that be true, I can only say that Russia has disgraced her Church and her nationality. I once met the Czar. He seemed a kind and good-natured man. I can scarcely believe that he is fully aware of the barbarities perpetrated with his apparent sanction.'[183] Here Tennyson appears to have been contradicting what he had thought about the Tsar not long before. Maybe he was partly right not to blame him directly for the current troubles, but he was becoming rather gullible. He might, of course, have said something similar, had he lived, about comrades Lenin or Stalin.

Tennyson died the following year, at the age of 83. In considering the legacy of his inveterate hatred of Russia, one is reminded time and again of the Balaklava charges and his attitude towards them. He never tired of hearing tales of the heroes. In 1883, he had hardly quit the Tsar at Copenhagen when he was singing the praises of General Hamley and concluding his *Epilogue* of peace with the ambivalent words:[184]

> 'The song that nerves a nation's heart,
>   Is in itself a deed.'

That song for Tennyson, of course, was really *The Charge of the Light Brigade*. It became for him, as for his people, an article of faith. Indeed, it even saved souls: a New England pastor once wrote to say that he had recited it in church in lieu of a biblical text, much to the scandal of his congregation; but a Balaklava veteran chanced to be there, and was converted from a life of iniquity.[185] Much more than that, the poem was also a military act. As Hallam Tennyson once wrote, 'I need hardly remark how much of a soldier at heart the poet was who had written "The Charge of the Light Brigade"; ...or what true, admiring sympathy he felt always for the self-sacrificing lives to which those who command and serve in our army are often called.'[186]

However, Tennyson was sometimes hesitant in giving practical proofs of his commitment. In 1875 men of all ranks of the Light Brigade's charge of 25 October 1854, not just officers as in previous years, came together for a twenty-first anniversary banquet at Alexandra Palace. Their secretary, Edward Woodham, invited Tennyson to join them. In regretfully declining, the poet promised instead to raise his glass on the day, and enclosed £5 to be distributed 'among the most indigent of the survivors of that glorious charge'. 'A blunder it may have been', he wrote, 'but one for which England should be grateful, having learned thereby that her soldiers are the most honest and most obedient under the sun.' This letter was read out at the banquet and *The Charge of the Light Brigade* was recited twice — by an actress and by a Balaclava survivor.[187] Tennyson's refusal to attend in person may be excused, perhaps, in so far as his habit was never to participate in public gatherings, but his gift — even for that time — may not seem greatly philanthropic.

In 1877 a Balaclava Commemoration Society was set up which, after some alterations to its initial constitution, became exclusively an association of privates and non-commissioned officers who had actually participated in the Light Brigade charge. It arranged an annual dinner and circulated a booklet of rules which listed survivors and, at the end, printed poems honouring the charge. In order to meet the expenses of the dinner, members had to pay an annual fee of five shillings. Not all survivors would be in a position to afford this, but it was proudly agreed 'That the Public shall not be applied to for subscriptions'.[188] However, as the veterans dwindled in number and aged, some became increasingly impoverished. A Balaclava Committee was formed to investigate ways of assisting them. At a meeting on 8 April 1890, the secretary of this group revealed the miserable plight of the survivors of the charge and announced the creation of a Light Brigade Relief Fund, calling for subscriptions through the London evening paper the *St James's Gazette*. As he and others pointed out, Lord Cardigan had declared after the engagement that England would be proud of these heroes. If they lived to get home, they would surely be provided for. 'Not one of you fine fellows', he had promised, 'will ever have to seek refuge in the workhouse!' But now they were indeed faced with that, and worse: some were practically starving. Previous canvassing had not achieved much, yet only a few shillings a week each would be enough to keep these men from misery. Unhappily, the present appeal, like its predecessors, at first drew little practical response. In reaction to this *Punch*, in a mordant example of its best black humour, printed on 26 April a double-edged piece called *The Last Charge of the Light Brigade (brought by the Survivors against those — who might have looked after them)*. This includes the memorable stanza:[189]

> Workhouse to right of them,
> Workhouse to left of them,
> Workhouse in front of them!
> Has no one wondered
> That British blood should cry,
> 'Shame!' and exact reply,
> Asking the country why
> Thus it sees droop and die
> Those brave Six Hundred?

In so far as it mocks those who saw the charge as merely 'a theme for rhyme' sung in theatres and music halls, *Punch*'s piece was not only a terrible indictment of neglect; it perhaps also implied some criticism of Tennyson himself, who this time was stung into giving ten guineas to the Light Brigade Relief Fund and agreeing to serve on its committee.[190] According to Sir Sidney Low, then editor of the *St James's Gazette*, Tennyson even sent 'some fine verses' in support of the appeal.[191] I have not been able to locate these (if indeed they existed), but Low's assertion that young Rudyard Kipling reacted generously in his turn with £5 and a 'sequel or commentary' on them is a fact: on 28 April the *Gazette* published an extraordinary ballad by him called *The Last of the Light Brigade*.[192]

'When can their glory fade?' must have been sounding in Kipling's ears as he wrote this piece. Maybe he also recalled Tennyson's famous words to the soldiers in 1855: 'No writing of mine can add to the glory they have acquired in the Crimea.' In reading Kipling's poem it is hard to separate the fancy from the truth, but it is easy enough to understand why he should have brought in the laureate in such a personal way: he had already parodied his work, yet owed him a patent and outstanding debt.[193] The work opens with a stark and ironic contrast between twenty down-and-outs from the Light Brigade and thirty million English talking of their country's military might. As yet the poor men

> knew not Art was long,
> Or, though they were dying of famine, they lived in deathless song.

So they applied first for support through a national campaign which produced, however, a mere £24. It was then that an old sergeant recalled

> '...the man who writes
> The things on Balaclava the kiddies at school recites'

— and the twenty trooped off to see Tennyson. Containing themselves as best they could on empty stomachs, they clustered by the garden gate until a servant was pleased to admit them into the presence of 'the Master-singer who had crowned them all in his song'. What you wrote about the mouth of Hell was true, sir, said the sergeant, but we are close to the workhouse now, and we thought we should come and explain. Is it food you want? asked Tennyson. Oh no, Sir, we need your publicity.

> '...We think that some one has blundered, an' couldn't you tell 'em how?
> You wrote we were heroes once, Sir. Please write, we are starving now.'

The little army limped away,

> And the heart of the Master-Singer grew hot with 'the scorn of scorn';
> And he wrote for them wondrous verses that swept the land like a flame,
> Till the fatted souls of the English were scourged with the thing called Shame.

However, Kipling did not finish on this note. What were people about, he asked? They gladly sent bountiful cheques for dogs, and for felons from Irish bogs, and then reluctantly found just a few pence for these brave Balaklava heroes.[194] And this remarkable poem concludes:

> Our children's children are lisping to 'honour the charge they made',
> And we leave to the streets and the workhouse the charge of the Light Brigade.

Whether or not the biographical incident related in Kipling's poem is grounded in fact — which seems improbable, — this ambiguous (and punning) conclusion was not entirely complimentary to Tennyson. It appears to say that the laureate's reaction was grudging, and that, even if he did write such a piece as is here described, the heroes of Balaklava would still lack the necessary funds. Man does not live by bread alone — nor yet by poetry. Perhaps that is also why Kipling never included *The Last of the Light Brigade* in his collected works until nearly thirty years afterwards. Tennyson did, however, admire such works by Kipling that he knew. He is supposed to have said about now that, among younger writers, only this one had 'the divine fire', and he was pleased to receive Kipling at Aldworth in August 1890.[195] In April the following year Tennyson came across, or perhaps was even sent for his scrutiny, Kipling's furiously patriotic poem *The Flag of England* (alias *The English Flag*). He had Hallam write to praise its author and was much tickled by Kipling's reply: 'When the commander in chief notices a private of the line the man does not say "thank you", but he never forgets the honour and it makes him fight better.'[196] Perhaps, then, there was more to *The Last of the Light Brigade* than at present meets the eye.

At all events, there was a fascinating sequel. Very soon after the publication of Kipling's poem, Thomas Edison's London representative, Colonel George Edward Gouraud, sent his assistant Charles R.C. Steytler to Farringford with phonograph equipment to record Tennyson's voice on wax cylinders. The poet's very first effort, on 15 May, was to 'shout' into the machine three stanzas of *The Charge of the Light Brigade*, piercing Emily's brain as he did so and making their baby grandson roar with laughter. His recording, still extant, ends: '"...Into the mouth of Hell/Rode the six hundred." I thank you for showing me this miraculous invention. Tennyson.' *The Charge of the Light Brigade* had in fact been for many years now one of the poet's half-dozen favourite recitation pieces. As he intoned it in that chanting, swooping voice that George Eliot likened to recitative and another writer to a mystical incantation, he revived all the force of his love of country and detestation of the enemy.[197] While it would therefore have been perfectly natural for him to choose this poem (he went on later, incidentally, to record *The Charge of the Heavy Brigade*, and parts of *Maud*), it is clear that he was being asked to do so for a purpose. The text of Hallam Tennyson's letter of confirmation to Colonel Gouraud that the recordings had been successful was given to the Relief Committee, which published it in the press to accompany a further appeal for funds, and Gouraud himself proposed to play the cylinders at a special party in his house for the Light Brigade survivors; he would have their photograph taken and send it to Tennyson.[198] Whether or not he did this, he recorded and performed in public not only Tennyson's voice but also that of Florence Nightingale, as well as the bugle of Trumpeter Kenneth Landfrey, who had served with the 17th Lancers at Balaklava. These, too, were clearly part of the publicity campaign, but also excellent subjects for his own professional purposes.[199] However, live performances would always draw more people, and consequently a grand variety show was staged on 25 October, the anniversary day, at which Landfrey's battered bugle sounded and Tennyson's *Charge* was recited with much feeling by the distinguished actor Charles Warner.[200] Much was therefore attempted, with old Tennyson's distant support, to put right the wrongs sung by Kipling. A great deal more money was subscribed to the Balaclava Fund. But the English public, so long after the event, was unwilling to meet the ambitious expectations of the Committee, and the British government, more significantly, most certainly never did so. And the heroes just faded away, leaving only the myth behind. As for Tennyson, all else we know is that at Farringford late in May this year Hallam read out out to him and to G.F. Watts, who was painting his portrait, an intriguing 'Story of a Balaclava Hero'. At least, therefore, one can say that he was thinking of these men, even though they may never actually have ventured down to see him.[201]

Moreover, when Tennyson was buried in the Abbey on 12 October 1892, with the flag of England on his coffin, the nave was lined with survivors of the Balaklava Light Brigade.[202] In what has been described as a 'who's who of literature and the arts', Russia was not represented. Nor did its government send telegrams. Both *Poland* and *Montenegro*, however, went through many Slavonic translations.[203]

CHAPTER 3: Robert Browning (1812-89)

Tennyson is reported to have said of Browning that he had not the
'glory of words'.[1] Be that as it may, he had their magic and their ambiguity. The political comment in his works is correspondingly obscure; and indeed politics was not so satisfying a subject for him as
philosophy or mysticism. He was not, besides, a poet laureate, and did
not need to engage in public posturing. There is therefore not so much
of Russia in his writings as in Tennyson's — nor even so much of
England. The irony is that Browning wrote perhaps the most important
single English poem on a purely Russian subject, and he alone of our
authors actually visited Russia.

Browning's first published work, *Pauline: A Fragment of a Confession*, was written in 1832 and came out anonymously in the following year. It has been aptly labelled 'inchoate' and 'nebulous', but also
'embryonic' in so far as it contains in essence most of the traits that
were to characterise the poet's mature expression: psychology, drama,
and persona-narrative. It marks both Browning's early debt to Shelley
and his independence from him; his own calling to write poetry; and
his discovery of a kind of God after years spent in a spiritual wilderness.[2] Towards the end of *Pauline* there is a passage (ll. 951-7) which
could perhaps relate to Russia. Some state baldly that it does.[3]

> The land which gave me thee shall be our home,
> Where nature lies all wild amid her lakes
> And snow-swathed mountains and vast pines begirt
> With ropes of snow — where nature lies all bare,
> Suffering none to view her but a race
> Or stinted or deformed, like the mute dwarfs
> Which wait upon a naked Indian queen.

Some details of these lines, combined with their context in the poem,
suggest an Asiatic country, possibly Tibet;[4] but the fact that Pauline
responds to the protagonist in cultured French would seem to negate
this. On the other hand, France itself, French-speaking Italy, or Switzerland, though fitting the natural description, would make little sense
in relation to the race said to people Pauline's land. Maybe therefore
Browning did have a Russian gentlewoman in mind. As a gallicised

form of Pelageia, Pauline was a common enough name with the French-speaking nobility — it is worth recalling Robert Merry's *Paulina; or, The Russian Daughter* (1787), — and most foreign observers did still consider Russia (especially its remoter parts) to be the home of strange oriental, dumb, half-human slaves. Of course, Browning's own land may be purely imaginary, and in any case has little importance for an understanding of his 'confession'; but it is curious that he should write these lines so soon before his trip to Russia in 1834.

Apart from this, it would be impossible to say that he had much early interest in that country. He may well have come across a travel book or two, like Hakluyt's *Voyages* or his sister Sarianna's first school prize, *Polar Scenes, Exhibited in the Voyages of Heemskirk and Barenz to the Northern Regions, and in the Adventures of Four Russian Sailors at the Island of Spitzbergen*. Translated from the German of Joachim Heinrich Campe, *Polar Scenes* offers specially for children a rather extraordinary introduction to the possibilities of foreign travel. Though centred on the far north and not exclusively in Russia, it gives a good idea of the natural hazards and extremes of cold experienced by many in that country, as well as of the courage and perseverance of both the inhabitants and the voyagers who withstood and overcame these.[5] We do know for certain that Browning read one important volume which made a few references to Russia. This was Nathaniel Wanley's *The Wonders of the Little World; or, A General and Complete History of Man* (1677), given to young Robert by his father in November 1825 and perused and extensively annotated by him over the following years. Among its Russian allusions is a description of the Muscovite torture of letting water fall drop by drop upon the victim's bare head. Browning himself did not, however, highlight this and it would be unwise to say any more.[6]

Various reasons have been suggested for the Russian journey. Before looking at more orthodox explanations, it is tempting to consider one which has to do with *Pauline*. According to Vivienne Browning, her kinsman Robert was fleeing an unhappy first love for his beautiful half-aunt Jemima (only one year older than he). Jemima was Pauline; and in a sense she was also the heroine of *The Last Ride Together*, *Porphyria's Lover*, and several other poems expressive of frustrated hope. Browning sought to sublimate his uncanonical love in a kind of spiritual unity. He dreamt of freezing the relationship, as it were, in 'the instant made eternity'. At the same time it appeared his 'spirit flew,/Saw other regions, cities new'.[7] His journey to Russia was thus both a trial and an escape. With his Paracelsus he could say:[8]

> My own affections laid to rest awhile,
> Will waken purified....

However, it is probable that Browning's need for emancipation was more general than this. There is some reason to believe that he was considering a career in diplomacy, for which his early training in modern languages had equipped him, and wished to use the Russian visit as a test. After his return home, he did actually apply — unsuccessfully as it turned out — for a government appointment in Persia. It was perhaps also because of such personal interest that he would later have ambitions for his son to be a diplomat.[9] Certainly Browning went to Russia ostensibly for reasons that had to do with diplomacy, even if these were not exclusively on the British side. Alexandra Orr, who knew the poet quite well in his later life and had frequent conversations with Sarianna, assures us that: 'The Russian consul-general, Mr Benckhausen, had taken a great liking to him, and being sent to St Petersburg on some special mission, proposed that he should accompany him, nominally in the character of secretary'.[10]

It is not known for certain how Browning gained an introduction to the consul. Egor Karlovich Benkgauzen lived at 9 Argyll Street, at the 'right' end of Soho, and had his office at 29 Great Winchester Street, near the Stock Exchange. He had been in London for six years and was reputed to be very knowledgeable about England. He was also well acquainted with Russian literary circles, and at one period sent autographs by Scott, Wordsworth, Southey, Shelley and Thomas Moore to the poet and collector Prince Piotr Viazemskii. It is possible that he enjoyed high contacts in France also, since he had been granted the title of Chevalier de la Légion d'honneur. Like many Russian diplomats he was, besides, of Baltic German origin. Princess Dar'ia (Doroteia) Khristoforovna Liven,[11] the wife of the Imperial ambassador in London and an influential figure in contemporary European society, had a high opinion of Benkgauzen and considered him shrewd and intelligent. Altogether, he would have been a pleasant and useful contact for young Browning; but this still does not explain their connection.[12]

Given that Benkgauzen's mission to Russia turns out to have had as much to do with Messrs Rothschilds' bank as with any national interest, it seems likely that the young poet came to his attention through their mutual contacts in the city. Reuben Browning, Robert's half-uncle, was employed by Rothschild of London at St Swithin's Lane. Himself a popular writer on financial matters, he was friend and counsellor to his nephew; one family tradition goes further and asserts that he was a Rosicrucian, and instructed the poet in the mysteries of his faith.[13] The Brownings' association with the house of Rothschild did not end here. William Shergold Browning, another half-uncle, worked for the bank's Paris establishment and was later influential in introducing Robert to leading members of French society. Robert's own father, of course, and his grandfather before him, were employed by the Bank of England. The poet thus had an impeccable pedigree as far as money matters were concerned. He also frequently referred to finance in his works. As late as 1876 his poem *Shop* alluded to 'Rothschild on his throne'. Bankers could put their trust in Browning — and did so: not only the present tour, but also some of his later European trips, had to do with his Rothschild connections.[14] Meanwhile, the Russian government, too, could rely on Browning's practically professional discretion.

Rothschilds at this period were the bankers of Europe. It was largely owing to their support and initiative that the new map of the continent, drawn after the final defeat of Napoleon in 1815, was able to establish itself and survive. At the Congress of Verona late in 1822, Salomon Mayer Rothschild, head of the Vienna house, had contracted a 5% loan for the Russian government amounting to £3,500,000.[15] The arrangement was for twelve years in the first instance, and bondholders were given twenty-four coupons each with which to claim half-yearly dividend, presentable either in St Petersburg or in London. In 1833 the Russian government decided to renew the loan (and indeed began negotiations with Nathan Mayer Rothschild of London for a further one), but proposed to issue coupons payable in St Petersburg only. Most creditors, being in London, resisted this, and were also reluctant to send their original bonds to Russia for renewal, fearing loss or delays. It was an ominous period in the reign of Nicholas I, with stricter censorship and tighter control of travel, as well as external alliances that seemed to menace Britain. The newspaper *Moskovskii Telegraf* was closed down and its editor detained. Alexander Herzen and members of his intellectual circle were arrested. Jews were again ill-treated in the Russian empire, which had lately been effectively extended by the crushing of Poland. Many of the London merchants made bitter complaints, and Messrs Rothschild sought various solutions to the financial problem. Nathaniel Rothschild went to Russia in January 1834 to investigate it at first hand. However, Count E.F. Kankrin, the Minister of Finance, confirmed the Russian decision; the Emperor ratified it; and all that remained was a half-jocular proposal from a German confrère that the house of Rothschild should open a branch in St Petersburg, so that interest on the loan, if paid there only, might at least be handled by a Western bank.[16]

It was natural, then, that Messrs Rothschild should turn for help to the anglophile Livens and the cosmopolitan Benkgauzen. The Russian ambassador, we are told, was a visitor at Nathan Mayer's house.[17] From subsequent correspondence between the British Foreign Secretary, Lord Palmerston, and the Minister Plenipotentiary at St Petersburg, John Duncan Bligh, it is evident that the bankers did not scruple to approach the Russians direct. Nathan Mayer at this period was treated as an equal by the first Minister of the Crown.[18] Whether, as Bligh thought, Liven would have sent Benkgauzen principally on the Rothschilds' behalf seems doubtful, however. It is more likely that he had some important despatches to get through, and allowed Benkgauzen to combine with this his errand for the Rothschilds. Maybe, even, Benkgauzen took the initiative himself and requested furlough. At all events, the consul went with messages from Liven and with a warm recommendation from the Princess (herself unaware of the precise reasons for Benkgauzen's departure) to her powerful brother Count A.Kh. Benkendorf, head of the Tsar's secret police.[19]

So much for Benkgauzen. Browning's role was less clear. Sarianna's reported statement that her brother went to Russia on a 'diplomatic mission' must refer rather to the Imperial government than to the Rothschilds, even if in reality Benkgauzen had taken him along, as it were, for the ride. Browning probably was acting as a representative for Rothschilds, maybe as a messenger to the so-called 'English Factory' at St Petersburg, maybe even as a kind of watchdog; but he cannot have gone only for that. The unfortunate destruction of his letters home prevents us from affirming anything with certainty. Doubtless he had several concurrent motives for the trip: friendship, family loyalty, business, and sheer curiosity. He cannot have undertaken it for the money, since expenses only were paid; and indeed Elizabeth Barrett, before her marriage to him, told a friend he could not desire her for pecuniary reasons, having been able to travel so far as Russia during his young man's *Wanderjahr*.[20]

Benkgauzen and Browning left London on 28 February, 1834.[21] It was the poet's first tour abroad and a round trip of some 3,000 miles. Anyone would be impressed by it; but the Browning who went to Russia was very young, younger even than his nearly twenty-two years suggested. A stocky figure with a pale complexion, pointed nose set in an oval face, fine mouth and forehead, bright grey eyes, dark brows, rounded chin, and black curly hair and side whiskers, he may have looked more like a dandy than a man about to investigate a diplomatic career. Coddled as he was, besides, by his mother, it might have seemed unlikely that he would survive abroad without her in tow. Who else would pack his bag for him, or bestow the goodnight kiss? The Cambridge gold-leaf Bible which she bought and inscribed for him on the day of his departure was a poor substitute for herself.[22]

Browning purchased, signed, and took with him to Russia a splendid road map of Europe by J.M.F. Schmidt, W. H. Matthias and C. Klöden, published in Berlin in 1830.[23] Among other things, this showed in red the main coaching routes to St Petersburg and Moscow. Although some details of the one followed by Benkgauzen and Browning can be established with a high degree of certainty, others are rather a matter for speculation. In the first place, it is not clear if they disembarked at Ostend or at Rotterdam. It seems probable that they would have wished to call at Amsterdam to see the bankers there, who had objections to Russian policy similar to those of the British themselves. Rotterdam would therefore seem more likely, but they could also have reached Amsterdam by road from Ostend via Bruges, Ghent and Antwerp. If they did get off at Rotterdam, they would not of course have seen these other towns. As for Aachen (Aix-la-Chapelle), which Browning is commonly thought to have visited during this trip, it would not only have been a completely meaningless detour from Amsterdam; to take it in on the way from Ostend to Russia, even without calling at Amsterdam, would have been a most improbable thing to do — especially in winter — as it was not on a main trunk road at that time. Browning's memories of the road from Ghent to Aix, enshrined in galloping lines, could thus belong rather to his next visit to the Low Countries, in 1838, as could also his examination of Charlemagne's portrait at the Aachen guildhall, or his contemplation of the river-flowers at Castle Ravestein on the Meuse.[24] He may well, however, have passed through Hameln and Pied Piper territory. We do know that, after quitting their ferry, the two men travelled the whole way to Russia by land. As we also know that their return route was the same as the outward, and included Courland and Livonia (parts of modern Lithuania and Latvia), they cannot have gone to St Petersburg by the eastern road through Warsaw and Minsk; indeed, they may have wished to avoid the ill-fated Kingdom of Poland, scene of recent uprising and repression.[25] Rather must they have gone via Berlin, then probably through Stettin (modern Szczecin) and Dantzig (Gdansk) to Königsberg, Tilsit and Riga.

One reads in a relevant history of the period: 'The expresses and couriers of the Rothschilds tore along at break-neck speed, as if on a matter of life and death, whilst the Government couriers were content with journeying by comparatively short and easy stages'.[26] Whatever expenses Browning may have been receiving from the bankers — actual or only notional, — he seems by all accounts to have made more than normal posthaste: Alexandra Orr speaks of his 'rushing for days and nights at the speed of six post-horses, without seeming to move from one spot'.[27] This last remark has to do, of course, with the flatness and monotony of the landscapes, especially the Russian ones, which would hypnotise a less observant traveller; but Browning did have wit — and rest — enough to register some vivid impressions. In scene ii of *Pippa Passes*, for example, the 'English vagabond' Bluphocks talks of Königsberg in 'Prussia Improper', and of its 'bleak hungry sun'; one presumes that Browning himself must have experienced this and visited the local Grand Rabbi's house, with its Chaldee inscription on the porch and its strange lore within, to which every 'bearded passenger' is said to have 'turned in'. At Tilsit (afterwards Sovetsk), Browning admired the meadows full of snowdrops, as he would tell a correspondent four years afterwards.[28] However, he was silent on the — for Britain — treacherous agreement which had taken place there in 1807 between Napoleon, Frederick William III, and Alexander I.

Beyond the River Neman (Niemen, Nemunas), Browning and Benkgauzen were soon on Russian territory. At that time one crossed the border at Laugzargen, with Russian customs at Tauroggen (now Lithuanian Taurage). According to a biographer who had consulted witnesses that knew the poet, he was immediately impressed by the sight of Cossack customs men, sheepskin-coated peasants, gabled wooden houses, and 'the huge inns with their double-windowed, stove-heated dining rooms festooned with ivy and other climbing plants, which grew as if in a hot house'.[29] Presumably Browning, accompanied as he was by an Imperial diplomat, was spared the normal trials of a foreigner first experiencing a Russian customs inspection; they did not even impound his Bible.[30] Russia was of course still snowbound at this season, and the endless forests of the north-western provinces were at once sacrificial in their splendour and appalling in their monotony. Slipping across great frozen rivers like the Dvina (Daugava) was an extraordinary experience. Quaint old Riga, with its bustling throng, was a respite from the empty flatness, as were also the coastal hills and dunes. It cannot be said for certain if the two men then passed through Revel (now Tallinn) to the north, through Pskov to the south, or through Dorpat (Tartu) in the centre on the road which later skirted the northern shore of Lake Peipus (Chudskoe) to Narva and beyond. The last-named route was by far the most probable, being marked on Browning's map as the chief coaching road at that time. It would make sense, too, in relation to Benkgauzen, whose ancestral home was in Tartu, as also for Browning himself who would then have seen enough of Estonia to celebrate its scenery in a later poem.

For mile upon mile the horses dragged the travellers' sleigh over bouncing tracks of logs laid sideways, rotting in the snow. In the day-time, Browning could philosophise:[31]

> In far Esthonian solitudes
> The parent-firs of future woods
> Gracefully, airily spire at first
> Up to the sky, by the soft sand nurst.

He could also meditate upon the frailty and ephemerality of humankind as the verst-poles slipped by, marking off so many seemingly identical kilometres on the path of mortal life:[32]

> Through forestry right and left, black verst and verst of pine,
> From village to village runs the road's long wide bare line.
> Clearance and clearance break the else-unconquered growth
> Of pine and all that breeds and broods there, leaving loth
> Man's inch of masterdom, — spot of life, spirt of fire, —
> To star the dark and dread, lest right and rule expire
> Throughout the monstrous wild, a-hungered to resume
> Its ancient sway, suck back the world into its womb....

Or else, sometimes at night, out would come the moon, recreating eerie, unnatural day, —

> yes, daylight, bred between
> Moon-light and snow-light, lamped those grotto-depths which screen
> Such devils from God's eye. Ah, pines, how straight you grow
> Nor bend one pitying branch, true breed of brutal snow!

At last Browning and Benkgauzen slipped across the frozen marshy approaches of St Petersburg, until there rose before them, as in a snowy mirage, the steeples and domes and granite blocks of Peter's city. It was a fortnight since they left London, and they had barely stopped on the way. This we know from despatches by the British Minister, and from the fact that well into the middle of the nineteenth century even urgent letters could take two weeks and more to get from London to the Russian capital, let alone to the interior.[33] The men arrived, then, around 2 March, old style; it remains to show how long they stayed in St Petersburg. Alexandra Orr and at least one contemporary Russian commentator claimed that Browning's trip lasted about three months in all; but this seems unlikely in so far as Benkgauzen, at least, was back in London quite early in May.[34] William Allingham, on information given him by Sarianna, says that Browning spent six weeks in St Petersburg.[35] John Maynard reckons that 'the total stay in Russia could not have been much more than two weeks',[36] but may have been misled by the fact that Browning's exit passport from St Petersburg, presumably issued very near the day of his departure, is dated 31 March. This date, of course, is old and not new style, and one may thus suppose that Browning cannot have left earlier than 1/13 April. His passport shows that he crossed the Prussian frontier on 7/19 April.[37] In round terms, we can therefore say with some confidence that the poet was in Petersburg for a month — and of course in Russia as a whole, counting travel, for between five and six weeks.

The loss of Browning's letters home naturally restricts our knowl-

edge of his activities in Russia, but a surprising amount may be de-
duced from other sources. We learn, for instance, that while in St
Petersburg he suffered greatly from the biting wind and cold, which
brought on an almighty headache that he could still remember and talk
about half a century later.[38] But this by no means stopped him from
enjoying himself. He had reached the capital towards the end of Butterweek — the Orthodox Shrovetide, — which in 1834 ran from the
end of February to early March. This was the Russian equivalent of
carnival time, a period of great rejoicing before the onset of Lent. The
festival was generally referred to as the Kacheli. St Petersburg was
second to no city in Europe for the range and quality of entertainment
that it provided. As if by magic, an entire new township made of wood
sprang up on the ice of the Neva from opposite Peter's statue and the
Admiralty to the Winter Palace and the Hermitage. Neat shops and
stalls were ranged beside menageries, amusement booths, and theatres
holding many hundreds of spectators who could stare at pantomimes,
harlequinades, acrobatics, pageants of all kinds including of course
Petrushka, the native equivalent of a Punch and Judy show. (By a
strange coincidence — it seems it can be nothing more — Stravin-
skii's famous ballet *Petrushka* takes as its setting the St Petersburg
Butterweek Fair in the early 1830s.) Near by were Russian ice-hills
for tobogganing, merry-go-rounds, roundabouts, see-saws, and the
many swings (*kacheli*) which gave the popular name to the proceedings. Towards the end of the week came promenades of carriages of
all descriptions, culminating in a grand parade attended often by the
Emperor himself.[39]

While Browning cracked his nuts and ate his greasy *pirogi*, he
must have sauntered round the multitude of theatres. It was his first
experience of colourful Russian customs, and he was greatly impressed by the singing of the common people; as will later be seen, he unconsciously memorised national airs and folk-tunes which would stay
with him throughout his life. Here, too, he would have admired the
antics of the dancing bears, the young blades on the windmill-swings,
the German and Italian harlequins and buffoons, the bewildering
artistry of Jews and gypsies come up for the fair. Above all, he wondered at the performance of a particular young actress who was to give
a title to his abortive five-act drama 'Only a Player-girl'. Browning
wrote this some years after his Russian trip but apparently abandoned
it. In August 1845 he was reminded of the play and in a letter to Elizabeth Barrett described it as 'Russian, and about a fair on the Neva, and
booths and droshkies and fish-pies, and so forth, with the Palaces in
the background'. Nothing else is known about the piece (many,
though not all, commentators believe it to be lost), and it would be
unwise to speculate further on its subject; but by the fact that Brow-

ning speaks of 'the sayings and doings' of the player-girl and 'the others — such others!', we may assume that he found his own powers of characterisation insufficient for the purpose.[40] This speaks as much for the impact that the experience made upon him as for his own emotional immaturity. He would revert to the topic, in a very different context, in *Fifine at the Fair*.

Between this lively start to Browning's visit, and its end some four or five weeks later, lay all the dreary deprivations of a Russian Lent. He countered these by busying himself in public and private affairs. In the first place, he needed to fulfil his tasks as secretary and adviser to Benkgauzen. Doubtless he also carried messages of reassurance to English merchants and financiers in the Russian capital, concerned as they were lest any refusal by Rothschild to extend the Russian loan might depress their own professions and make it harder for them to walk the streets with pride; already there were signs that the English, who were not accustomed to salute even the Emperor in public, were fearful that their privileges could be withdrawn.[41] Browning must also have had an introduction to Baron Ludwig Ivanovich Stieglitz, the so-called 'Rothschild of Russia', with whom Nathan Mayer had direct and frequent contacts. This short, fat figure with a keen eye, dressed in a plain green coat, was as familiar a visitor in the new Exchange (now the Central Naval Museum) next to the customhouse at the tip of Vasilii Ostrov as was Nathan Mayer himself on Threadneedle Street in London. He was also the wealthiest and most powerful man in Russian commerce, without whose encouragement or help no great undertaking (it was said) could ever be set on foot .[42] Doubtless owing in part to the influence of Stieglitz, such support was rallied for the British cause within a period of two weeks that the Emperor was prevailed upon by Benkgauzen not only to reconsider the matter but to recommend a change in policy. Overriding Count Kankrin, who was not admitted to the deliberations, he proposed that the loan coupons should be renewed in London and Amsterdam as well as in St Petersburg.[43]

Browning clearly had two main centres of interest for his leisure time, one the higher Russian and cosmopolitan society to which Benkgauzen was able to introduce him, the other the English factory. The latter consisted of only a few hundred souls — bankers, stockbrokers, merchants, manufacturers, managerial staff, diplomats, teachers, trainers, jockeys, even Imperial civil servants, — but it enjoyed a wealth and esteem equivalent to that of any other group ten or twenty times its size. It had its own church on the 'English Quay' (Naberezhnaia Krasnogo Flota), not far from the statue of Peter the Great. It had its English Magazine — the most fashionable store in the city. There was an English Club, to which Russians also could belong. Locally produced English stationery was on every table; sugar refined by English methods was most in demand; clothes made on English machines were on every fashionable back. Although the height of anglomania had long since passed, respect and feeling for the English were still strong.[44] It is evident that Browning was introduced into this society. One might speculate on individual encounters. Young George Borrow, for example, was living in St Petersburg at the time, editing a translation of the scriptures into Manchu on behalf of the British and Foreign Bible Society, and as a hobby rendering into English Pushkin's *Talisman* and other contemporary Russian poems. Borrow loved the Russian capital, where East met West, and knew enough of the language to appreciate aspects of local life and manners which most tourists failed to comprehend.[45] More obviously, Browning must have encountered the British ambassador, the Hon. J.D. Bligh, whom Borrow called 'a person of superb talents, kind disposition, and of much piety'.[46] Bligh, however, unfortunately made no mention of Browning in his despatches to Lord Palmerston concerning Benkgauzen's mission to Russia.

More definite information is available on some other contacts. On at least two occasions Browning met Sir James Wylie, formerly Imperial court physician and for thirty years president of the Medical Academy of St Petersburg and Moscow. The old Scottish émigré had a distinguished reputation as a court and military surgeon and physician, and had endeared himself to the authorities by his diplomatic diagnoses of embarrassing fatal illnesses, such as that which killed the Emperor Paul and which he described as apoplexy. He had also performed a couple of hundred operations at Borodino field. Wylie appears to have talked French with Browning, and for some reason took him for an Italian — perhaps for his black hair, or because of a particular accent that he may have had when speaking French. The second time that Browning came into his presence, Wylie was playing cards. As he looked up he exclaimed: 'M. l'Italien!'[47] Wylie had been, but was no longer, a romantic figure of the sort that could appeal to the young author of *Pauline*. Another who better succeeded was John Edward Waring, a forty-year-old King's Foreign Service Messenger who spent half his life carrying despatches for or from the British government in various parts of the globe. There is some indication that he was a Welshman from Denbigh, educated at Clare College, Cambridge, but who left the university without taking a degree. If so, this could help explain why Browning, in *Waring* (written in 1842), later associated the messenger with his own friend the poet Alfred Domett, who also left Cambridge without a degree in 1834.[48]

This association is of some importance because of Browning's treatment of Russia in that poem. Alfred Domett himself never went there; but his departure in 1842 for New Zealand, where he cleared bush, wrote for the press, produced some rather appalling verse, and rose to high rank in government, was only the fulfilment of an urge to travel which had taken him already to the United States and Canada as well as to several European countries. For Browning, Domett in going to New Zealand was doing something still more remote and extravagant than his own trip to the confines of Europe. He seemed 'almost a personification of the wandering spirit'[49] which to a lesser extent informed the young Browning's own character, and which he had earlier observed in a maturer form in the 'real' Waring. The conflation of Domett and Waring was thus natural, as was also some rehearsal of the author's knowledge of Russia. Whether his treatment of Russia in the actual poem was persuasive is another matter. The distinguished critic and Russianist Maurice Baring was not at all convinced by it. Quoting the relevant passage, he would note: 'This is fine poetry, but as a picture of Russia it is as far from the truth as Jules Verne.'[50]

Waring is in a sense an investigation of creative inspiration. A trusted friend with a quiet face and proud bearing prefers to abandon his potential at the centre of the artistic universe in favour of travel overseas. The poet wonders where he may be, and where the two of them may meet again, and half hopes that the friend may return to London to revive old intellectual standards. The piece ends somewhat fantastically with the hero glimpsed and then lost sight of for ever, suggesting that Browning himself may have met the real Waring again very briefly and mysteriously before beginning his poem. One place where the friend might be thought likely to turn up again is Moscow. This possibility is then rejected in favour of Spain; but in I, vi, Browning has time to consider

> Waring in Moscow, to those rough
> Cold northern natures borne....

like a pigeon

> from the myrrhy lands
> Rapt by the whirlblast to fierce Scythian strands
> Where breed the swallows, ...

— or, like Iphigenia, exiled to her Crimean solitude. Browning's image of Waring in Russia is characteristically recherché and obscure, and not without a certain syntactic confusion. We are required to picture the man

> who in Moscow, toward the Czar,
> With the demurest of footfalls

> Over the Kremlin's pavement bright
> With serpentine and syenite
> Steps, with five other Generals
> That simultaneously take snuff,
> For each to have pretext enough
> And kerchiefwise unfold his sash
> Which, softness' self, is yet the stuff
> To hold fast where a steel chain snaps,
> And leave the grand white neck no gash....

Some references here can be explained, some not. The 'generals' are perhaps not military men but high-ranking state servants. The civilised Waring is presumably included in their number, given Browning's use of the word 'other', and it may be for this that the poet goes on to reject the Russian vision. Whether the men are actually about to assassinate the Tsar, or merely have such potential, is unclear in the context; but the imagined British contribution to such a crime is faintly reminiscent of the circumstances of the murder of Tsar Paul. More interesting, for us, is the cohabitation of smooth manners and barbarity. This must have been amply evident to Browning in St Petersburg in 1834. An allusion some lines later to 'barbarous twitter', though applied ostensibly to Russian swallows, appears to relate also to the language spoken by the people and compares unfavourably with Waring's own (the pigeon's) 'melodious cry'. Maybe therefore Browning, too, was unimpressed by Russian speech, as by Russian treachery.

The strangest feature of the description is that it concerns not St Petersburg but Moscow. Since the creation of Peter's city, Moscow had declined politically, and though tsars were still crowned there their chief residence was in the newer capital. On the face of things, a Browning who stayed in St Petersburg only and (as we are told) was shown the Tsar's crown jewels there, ought not to have instinctively imagined such an incident as taking place in Moscow. On the other hand, one asks oneself if it is really likely that Browning should have spent a month and more in Russia without visiting Moscow. Certainly, there is no record of his having done so; nor was the season a very pleasant one for travel. Nevertheless, one detail of *Waring* is so striking as to seem the result of personal observation. This is the character of building materials within the Kremlin. Though perhaps seen less in the actual pavement than in the structure of the more modern, Italianate edifices there, decorative green serpentine and polished syenite would in fact be evident to an observant tourist's eyes. Admittedly, Browning would have seen such minerals in the capital as well; but a purely second-hand description of the Kremlin, so different an ensemble from the buildings of St Petersburg, would be less likely to emphasise these features.

There are two other indications that Browning may have been to Moscow. The first concerns the crown jewels. The reference to his having seen them is contained in a letter to Elizabeth Barrett of January 1846. In a particularly strong expression of his love for the woman he was soon to marry, he compared his feeling and desire for her to 'what I thought of the Queen-diamond they showed me in the crown of the Czar'.[51] The annotator of this letter remarks that Browning probably had in mind the famous Orlov diamond, which weighed nearly 195 carats. The history of this yellowish gem, rose-cut in the form of half a pigeon's egg, is controversial — some say it was the eye of an idol, stolen by a Frenchman in India, — but it is known to have been purchased for the Empress Catherine by Count Grigorii Orlov, apparently from a man who had hidden it for some time in an open sore in his leg. The vendor was given 450,000 silver roubles for it, together with an annuity of 4,000 roubles and a hereditary title, estates, and serfs.[52] However, this magnificent diamond decorated the Tsar's sceptre, not his crown; and unless Browning, admittedly more than a decade later, was misremembering its location, he may actually have had in mind another diamond which did indeed form part of a Russian crown. Whereas the sceptre (and indeed the current Imperial crown) would have been in St Petersburg, at the Hermitage, during the residence of the Tsar, the chief collection of his jewels was to be found in the Palace of Armoury (Ruzheinaia palata) in the Moscow Kremlin.[53] Many crowns there had impressive diamonds, and Browning could have been recalling one of them, perhaps the diamond crown of Ivan Alekseevich.

The other curious fact is that the setting of *Ivàn Ivànovitch*, the well-known poem by Browning which will be discussed here in due place, is not, as one might have expected, in a Baltic village through which the poet himself would have passed on his outward or inward journey, but on the road from St Petersburg to Moscow. The passage earlier quoted which describes the journey through the forest goes on to speak of

> man's craft which clove from North to South
> This highway broad and straight e'en from the Neva's mouth
> To Moscow's gates of gold.

It is true that Browning has the events of the poem occur 'in such a village' as the ones referred to in the earlier lines; but this statement cannot mean that the settlement concerned was on any other road. The fact that he portrays the Moscow highway in great detail and with circumstantial accuracy suggests that he may have driven along it himself. If one reads the accounts of contemporary travellers, such as that of Rev. R. Lister Venables who passed that way in 1837, one is struck by similar evocations of the dense forest masses, punctuated now and then by bleak clearings dotted with villages. It is true that the trees would be most commonly birch and white fir, rather than red pine, but Browning may be allowed poetic licence here.[54] There are, moreover, other things in the poem which help confirm the supposition: the hero is building a model of the Moscow Kremlin, and the village houses Jews, and a 'Gipsy-troop', 'bound with horses for the Fair'. The reference here may be to the great horse fair at Nizhnii Novgorod, rather than to the Butterweek or Easter festivals in the capitals as some commentators have believed;[55] but it again shows knowledge of the road and of the travellers who peopled it. If Browning did go to Moscow, he may well have met there Thomas (Foma Iakovlevich) Evans, an English teacher who lived and died in that city. A witty and erudite man who unfortunately left no written trace of his gifts, Evans was admired by P.Ia. Chaadaev and had good relations with Griboedov. According to a Russian obituary of him published in 1849, he had known Robert Browning well and been in correspondence with him.[56]

At all events, whether or not Browning went to Moscow, most of his time was spent in St Petersburg. Later echoes show that he must have visited the sights assiduously. At the Hermitage he enjoyed the phenomenal collection of Western European paintings. It was the young art-lover's first acquaintance with one of the world's great galleries. The Rembrandts especially must have impressed him, although the only direct recollection concerns *The Rape of Europa* by the Bolognese Seicento painter Francesco Albani. Though not much appreciated today, exhibiting as he does much of the decadence and sentiment of his age, Albani was very popular in Browning's time and still considered the Anacreon of painting. Our poet must have admired the delicacy and charm of his technique. Much later, at the Uffizi in Florence, he was to see a replica of *The Rape of Europa* and would mention it in *The Ring and the Book* as 'florid old rogue Albano's masterpiece'.[57] Perhaps inspired by what he saw at the Hermitage, though also from a natural bent, Browning made some drawings of his own and sent them home to his family. Though their present whereabouts are unknown, one was a sketch of three men, presumed to be Russians, standing in front of a building in St Petersburg. There is some indication that the draughtsman may have made a playful attempt to give it apparent age by heating it over a candle.[58] Other drawings could well have been devoted to the many scenes which Browning observed and later used for his lost play. Of his creativity of a more poetic kind, there is nothing definite to say. It has been traditionally believed that he composed or planned while in Russia *Por-*

phyria's Lover and *Johannes Agricola in Meditation*; but these two God-tempting, somewhat vainglorious pieces have nothing to do with that country and may not actually have been written until 1835.[59]

The end of Browning's stay in the Russian capital was enlivened by an event more dramatic than any that he had observed at the Kacheli: the break-up of the ice on the Neva. Not long after the Butterweek fair, driving on the frozen river would be discontinued. In earlier years, even the famous Easter fair was sometimes held on the ice; but this practice had been abandoned owing to a serious accident, and in 1834 the Russian Easter was in any case quite late. Towards the end of March, the first signs of cracking could be seen and heard. People started to assemble in the streets. For the citizens of St Petersburg, who had no other reliable source of water, the Neva was a kind of goddess: a new supply of her pure liquid was about to be released, in honour of the spring. And then the cannon boomed from the Fortress of St Peter and St Paul; heavy-booted workmen clad in sheepskin tunics, their red beards shining in a mass, thronged toward the quays; and the military Governor of the city, Count P.K. Essen, could be seen advancing in his decorated barge. Dressed in full insignia and flanked by senior officers, he bore across to the Winter Palace for Tsar Nicholas I the year's first goblet of fresh water. Browning, we are told, was witness to all this before quitting the capital for the long journey back to England.[60]

The passport at the Armstrong Browning Library bears the Imperial seal and signature and the authorisation of Count Essen for a departure through Livonia and Courland. It describes the 'British subject Robert Browning' as a *pomeshchik* (landlord, or squire) and is dated 31 March (old style) 1834. The poet must have left soon after this, presumably in the company of Benkgauzen, and retraced the route by which he had come, only on wheels now and not sledges. The two men bore excellent news for the Rothschilds but bad tidings for the Livens. Thanks to their efforts in St Petersburg, good relations were restored between the British bankers and the Russian government, for which Baron Lionel, successor to Nathan Mayer, would be agent for over twenty years.[61] It is true that some alarm was caused for a short time by the recall of the Livens to St Petersburg following Benkgauzen's return, and this brought great distress to the Livens themselves, as also to their many friends in Britain.[62] However, the reason given — that they were to oversee the education of the Imperial Crown Prince, Alexander, — turned out to be correct, and close ties were established between Rothschilds and their successors. It was only Lionel's hesitation over a proposed new Russian loan at the time of the Polish crisis of 1863 that lost him the business and prevented the association from continuing to the end of the century.[63]

The Livens left London in July 1834, but Benkgauzen retained his position there until his death (which occurred actually at Marienbad) in 1844. One supposes that he and Browning would have kept up their acquaintance, but there is no documentary proof of this. Nor is there much hint of a Russian legacy in Browning's works, except in so far as his journey to St Petersburg had to some extent provided both the maturing and the escape which he was supposed to have sought. Although the mention in *Paracelsus* (written in 1834-35) of

> Einsiedeln, now, and Würzburg which the Mayne
> Forsakes her course to fold as with an arm

can presumably have nothing to do with this trip, the bold reference in the same work to 'mountains rough with pines' and 'dazzling wastes of frozen snow' may well have some historical basis in Browning's progress through the plains and hills of Livonia and Estonia. (See *Paracelsus*, II, ll. 127-8, 162-3).

Meanwhile *Sordello,* which occupied the poet for many years before its publication in 1840, and which rehearsed problems similar to those in *Pauline* but expressed them with somewhat greater clarity and less personal involvement, would seem to have as its only allusion to Russia ll. 27-9 in Book V:

> But here's our son excels
> At hurdle-weaving any Scythian, fells
> Oak and devises rafters....

However, this does present some interest since it evokes, several decades before its final expression, the image of the carpenter Ivàn Ivànovitch which Browning appears to have carried away with him from Russia. Similarly, the much later *Ring and the Book* (published in 1868-69) provides a link with the future *Ivàn Ivànovitch* in so far as it demonstrates time and again its author's fascination with wolves — and werewolves (see, for instance, the title-canto, ll. 611-30). *Aristophanes' Apology,* moreover, which appeared only four years before *Ivàn Ivànovitch*, in 1875, speaks of 'infamies the Scythian's whip should cure' (l. 431). But more of this subject anon.

For the rest, the Russian fur trade is mentioned near the end of *Bishop Blougram's Apology*, a poem of 1855 that Browning had begun some years earlier. The passage concerned (ll. 790-1) is used as an image of life's journey in which we often need to spurn what may seem useful at the time:

> As when a traveller, bound from North to South,
> Scouts fur in Russia: what's its use in France?

Similarly, pine-trees, black priests, bears, and gypsies akin to the Russian are to be found in *The Flight of the Duchess*, first published in 1845. Though set in a duchy of Moldavia, then a precariously independent principality on Russia's Bessarabian border, this piece has too much atmospheric kinship with the St Petersburg experience to have grown up quite independently. Peripheral perhaps yet a memento to the Russian trip is a reference in Browning's play *A Blot in the 'Scutcheon* (1843) to the alleged brightness of a Polish gaze: 'Why, Ralph, no falcon, Pole or Swede/Has got a starrier eye' (I. i, l. 60). But that is all, at least as far as the poet's creative art is concerned. Nevertheless he had come away from Russia, according to one indigenous contemporary commentator, with a better knowledge of it than was customarily shown by foreigners who had lived there for years.[64] This would have most significant repercussions for him in his later life.

Before remarking on Robert Browning's subsequent interest in Russia, it is necessary to look at the early life of Elizabeth Barrett, who would become his wife in 1846. One could not say that she knew or cared much about Russia, even though in one of her earliest extant letters, as a child of six, she had written gleefully to her mother of a Russian victory over Napoleon in 1812: 'tell dear Papa the Rusians has beat the french killd 18,000 men and taken 14,000 prisners.'[65] Later, she was proud to have a book bound in Russian leather; believed (but was not sure) that a ship of her father's had made a journey with a cargo of wool to Odessa; and was amused by some incidents connected with the visit to Malvern Wells in 1831 by the Grand Duchess Elena Pavlovna, sister-in-law of Nicholas I.[66] While in Sidmouth in December 1832, she and her father met and were greatly impressed by the Polish politician and historian Count Walerjan Skorobohaty Krasiński, who had been sent to London as an envoy by the 1830 revolutionary council and remained in exile in England after the Polish rebellion had been definitively crushed by the Russians. Elizabeth called him 'a very intelligent and interesting person', and was touched by the national pride which led him to prefer continued banishment to 'the Emperor of Russia's offer of golden chains'.[67]

For all her early learning classical and modern, Elizabeth Barrett had, however, little understanding of the geography or culture of the Russian empire. In a letter of 1845, she described a translation of hers as being 'cold as Caucasus, and flat as the neighbouring plain'.[68] Even allowing that the misleading concept of a 'frosty Caucasus' was Shakespeare's, it is unlikely that Elizabeth Barrett had any truer idea of other Russian scenery. The Caucasus, for her, was the end of the civilised world — or beyond; but so, too, was St Petersburg. As a warm admirer of France and its literature, she was quite startled to learn that the works of Balzac, Victor Hugo and George Sand were flooding into Russia and proved much more popular and successful there than they did with her friends in old England.[69] She did dip into Russian travel books, but she seems to have learnt nothing from her reading of Lady Eastlake's *Residence on the Shores of the Baltic* and when, in 1844, she recommended Custine's *Russia* to a friend, she surrounded it by miscellaneous other titles which suggested (as she in fact foresaw) that she herself could be thought of as 'running up and down the stairs of all sorts of subjects'.[70] It would be interesting to know if Miss Barrett approved of all the strictures contained in the Marquis's book. She seems to have had some respect for Russian authority: perhaps it was not for nothing that her doctor called her the 'Empress Catherine' when she disregarded his advice (although she herself at least jocularly considered that monarch to be a private murderess).[71] She compared unfavourably, for example, the British treatment of Napoleon with that of Russia. Unlike Robert Browning, she admired Napoleon — at least for his heroic figure and his gigantic place in modern history — and was indignant that England should have exiled him to St Helena and not granted him asylum. 'One fact pricks me... like a sword', she exclaimed to her friend the painter Benjamin Haydon (who himself had Russian connections), '..Alexander of Russia said, .. "If he had come to *me*...."'[72] Doubtless she was influenced in her sympathy for Napoleon in his disastrous campaign of 1812 by Haydon's belief that the Russian winter of that year set in unusually early and was the most severe ever known.[73] Her reverence for Napoleon led her to see even his rout in Russia as an example of his self-composure. 'He was always equal to his position', she told a friend in 1844.[74] Meanwhile her poem *Crowned and Buried*, written in 1840, is a votary offering to Napoleon's memory, in spite of its ifs and buts; the grand phrase 'from the Russias west to Spain' conceals some of the principal ignominies of a man whose fragile fame she had never properly examined.

It is clear, therefore, that Elizabeth Barrett did not entertain a very high regard for Russia generally. On the few occasions when she spoke to Browning of it in their courting correspondence, she did so disparagingly; and he himself was affected by her approach. When, in August 1845, he read some articles on Russia in the *Athenaeum*, he not only recalled with disdain his own play about the fair on the Neva; he was unnecessarily supercilious about the author of what he termed this 'very simple moony stuff', the Scottish obstetrician Dr Robert Lee. Lee, who had spent two years in Russia in 1824-26 and spoken with Alexander I shortly before the Tsar's death, had in fact much of interest to say about the Russians' anglophilia in the earlier part of the century.[75] Likewise, the lovers were extremely condescending with regard to the philanthropist Sir Moses Montefiore, who in February

1846 went to Russia to plead against the renewal of the Tsar's edict that Jews living in frontier districts should remove fifty versts into the interior.[76] Sir Moses was the uncle of Lionel Rothschild, and Browning, through William Shergold, was invited to accompany Montefiore in the capacity of adviser. He firmly refused. 'Grazie tante!' he sneeringly remarked to Elizabeth when reporting the 'mission of humanity' of this 'wandering Jew', and did not need her plea to recall her loathing of the cold: 'Dearest, do not go to St Petersburgh. Do not think of going, for fear it should come true and you should go: and while you were helping the Jews and teaching Nicholas, what (in that case) would become of your Ba?'[77]

After their marriage, the Brownings' — or rather Elizabeth's — attitude to the Russian emperor and his rule remained equivocal. In her two-part poem *Casa Guidi Windows* (written in 1847-51), she made plain her lack of sympathy for any repression of one nation by another.[78] 'Annihilated Poland' and 'Hungary fainting 'neath the thong' were two prime examples of downtrodden nations for which she had lifelong respect. She even wished that England might intervene; but instead, her country drew all nations in a mercenary peace to the gorgeous Crystal Palace. Each one cried his wares, his arts, his pride; but where were the gifts for Christ? where the cure for darkness?

> Hast thou found
> No remedy, my England, for such woes?
> No outlet, Austria, for the scourged and bound,
> No entrance for the exiled? no repose,
> Russia, for knouted Poles worked underground,
> And gentle ladies bleached among the snows?
> No mercy for the slave, America?

But was this deeply felt? Was it founded on knowledge, or on sentiment alone? In December 1848 Elizabeth had written to a friend: 'While Italy shows herself so politically demoralised, and the blood of poor Russia smokes from the ground, the ground seems to care no more for it than the newspapers or anybody else'.[79] What could she mean by this? Was she thinking of Poland? Meanwhile, in another more than usually obscure passage of *Casa Guidi Windows* (II, ll. 100ff.), she spoke of the 'dangerous shouting' of oppressed peoples who might change their 'Vivats' into cries for a constituent assembly, striking terror in the hearts of 'all these Czars, from Paul to Paulovitch'; but this latter meaningless phrase was unfortunately typical of the hollowness of it all. Mrs Browning remained at heart a monarchist, approved of royal patronage, was pleased that her son should play with a toddling Russian princess, frowned at revolutions, and declared: 'I love liberty so intensely that I hate Socialism. I hold it to be the most desecrating and dishonouring to humanity of all creeds. I would rather (for *me*) live under the absolutism of Nicholas of Russia than in a Fourier machine, with my individuality sucked out of me by a social air pump'.[80] This was in the summer of 1850. In February 1852, despite Louis-Napoleon's coup d'état and subsequent repression of all opposition, she would go still further. The French socialists were propagating 'ideas that kill, ideas which defile, ideas which, if carried out, would be the worst and most crushing kind of despotism. I would', she concluded, 'rather live under the feet of the Czar'.[81]

Much as one may sympathise with Mrs Browning's sentiment regarding Fourier, it is hard to believe that she had properly reflected on her comparison with Nicholas. There is also something rather obscene in her wilful preference for Napoleon III. No matter what she said about her high view of democracy, it is hard to condone her moral concern at whether it was proper for her to sleep on the night of the coup d'état, while what she termed 'a little popular scum' was 'cleared off' by the troops.[82] Equally depressing was her new-found passion for spirit-rapping and table-turning. Again her humour seemed misplaced when she complained to Henry Chorley of the disbelieving *Athenaeum*: 'now that your Czars ...have set your Faradays on us, ukase and knout, what Pole, in the deepest of the brain, would dare to have a thought on the subject?' As a matter of fact, she added, 'the opposition Czar of St Petersburg supports us, ...and Louis Napoleon comes to us for oracles'.[83] She repeated this assertion in a letter to another friend. Nicholas, though perhaps politically mad (she said), 'supported' her position by receiving oracles through the raps.[84] We are at the time of the outbreak of the Crimean War. Robert Browning, who much disapproved of his wife's fanaticism, doubtless felt easier when she joked: 'Louis Napoleon gets oracles from the spirits — and so does the Czar! (Pity he is not better advised)....'[85]

The war itself was another testing-time for the Brownings. Already in the autumn of 1853, they had been 'writhing with rage and inquietude' about the Russian threat. Many of the locals were crying for war, expecting it to bring them national good. Elizabeth felt that the British government under Lord Aberdeen had procrastinated for too long. Negotiations with Russia, Turkey and France were getting nowhere. 'If the allies had acted with decision from the first', she told her brother, 'the Czar would probably have retreated by this time, — but now his pride and obstinacy are deeply engaged and retreat is more difficult.' One had to be prepared for any eventuality, hoping only that it would be honourable.[86] When the bloody confrontation had begun, Robert was supposedly quite frantic about it all.[87] Elizabeth was on the whole less worried. Everything seemed simple to her.

The war was 'most righteous and necessary'.[88] It was the Tsar's fault: he was 'struck with madness — mad in good earnest'. Obviously the spirits had forsaken him. Britain must intervene with as much 'integrity and boldness' as Louis Napoleon.[89] In the spring of 1854, before Britain's pride had started to be humbled, she penned a patriotic ditty called *A Song for the Ragged Schools of London* which began:

I am listening here in Rome.
'England's strong', say many speakers,
'If she winks, the Czar must come,
Prow and topsail, to the breakers.'

But above all, Elizabeth's attitude to the war, and therefore to the Russians, was informed by her fervent francophilia. Her son Pen spoke her own mind when he bellowed Napoleonic huzzas in the streets and salons of Florence. 'The French are dood. — The Russians — oh, hollid!' he expostulated.[90] Secondarily, Elizabeth's love of Italy helped to keep things simple: Cavour's participation in the war and the victory of his troops at the Chernaia provided further cause for her rejoicing.[91]

Mrs Browning cannot, therefore, be said to have taken the war quite seriously. Indeed, she could joke about it, and not only grimly, either. From her cosy Florentine refuge she criticised Thackeray's *The Newcomes* for having a plot 'not strong enough to resist the Czar'.[92] She imagined what might have been were she, and not Tennyson, poet laureate, and how she might have 'cursed the Czar in Pindarics very prettily'.[93] Tennyson's own efforts she regarded flippantly, calling *The Charge of the Light Brigade* 'ragged and unartistic'.[94] Altogether, the war was just a kind of melodrama for her: things were coming to a tragic head, then 'down drops the Czar, by apoplexy or other strangulation'.[95] Elizabeth's somewhat casual attitude to the war is well represented in a letter to a friend, written from the comforting security of Casa Guidi in Florence on 16 December 1854. She was just as interested in the current English fashions as she was in the possible effects of the conflict, and could feel for less fortunate families only by the circumstance that Captain William Surtees Cook, husband of her sister Henrietta and father of her small nephews Altham and Edward, had not only come out of his half-pay retirement as a home guard but was seriously contemplating transfer to the Crimea. 'I hear it is very gloomy in England,' she wrote, 'through bereavements by war & bereavements by cholera, & fears & anxieties about the dearest. They say it has proven a sort of "fashion" to wear black or grey, apart from domestic losses. I suppose you think a great deal, as we all do, of the

Crimea, & of what is to come next, & of who is to go next.. though I hope you have no near relation or friend in the east, to be fearful about especially. My sister's husband is threatening to go out to the seat of war.. which will be sad for her and her two babies, both younger than my child is.'[96]

It is true that, as the war progressed, Elizabeth came to regret some of her smugness. At one low point she confessed to a friend how much she and her husband were preoccupied with the conflict. She foresaw sardonic laughter at her earlier belief in Russia's weakness.[97] When her family moved to less comfortable conditions in Paris, she sympathised with Pen who, sleeping on the floor, observed that it was 'just lite the soldiers at Sebastopol'.[98] Her own feeling for the suffering soldiers undoubtedly intensified. But even then she managed to fill her mind with peripheral attitudes. Far from rejoicing, with all England, that Florence Nightingale should go to the Crimea with a touch of quintessential femininity, Elizabeth found her action a disservice to the cause of women's emancipation: she should (like herself) have shown men how a woman could paint or versify![99] Needless to say, Robert found all this perverse, as also his wife's extravagant gallomania. What worried *him* was the disgrace, the needless loss, and he bowed his head for England and himself.[100] Yet he did nothing obvious to help, even when the occasion presented itself. His poem *Instans Tyrannus*, though written earlier, was first published during the Crimean War. Commenting on its significance, a Browning Society member noted in 1885: 'Any tyrant will do — inquisitor, autocrat, Czar — who is suppressing by high-handed terrorism forces which in his heart he knows to have truth and right upon their side.'[101] This is true; yet Browning, precisely, gave the piece no special relevance to Russia or to Nicholas I. Indeed, the impressive two-volume collection in which it appeared, *Men and Women*, came out in 1855 without a single allusion to the sad and savage war — unless one counts that brief apotheosis of peace which is *Love among the Ruins*.

But at last the Crimean War was over, and the Brownings could both return with a clearer conscience to their art. The peace had settled little: nothing would be done for Italy or Poland.[102] But no matter: Elizabeth was less concerned by this than by the question whether she should now replace by the hoop the crinoline dubbed 'the tower of Malakoff'.[103] She was also still engrossed in spiritualism and continued to frustrate her husband by her fascination with the table-turner Daniel Dunglas Home, denounced by Robert as a charlatan or perhaps a crook and taken off by him in *Mr. Sludge, 'The Medium'*. Home, besides, soon fell in Elizabeth's own esteem. In 1858, he was married to a Russian girl in St Petersburg. Disabused as Mrs Browning was now by the Russians, and by the Tsar who gave the couple his blessing, she could even joke about the spirits and pity Home's poor bride, her 'conjugal furniture floating about the room at night'.[104]

Elizabeth Barrett, who died in 1861, will soon disappear from our history; and there is little more to say, indeed, of Robert's interest in Russia or things Russian during the next ten years. However, a few matters are worth mentioning, in the light of certain developments which occurred in 1870-71. In the first place, an address book of Browning's dating probably from the 1850s contains, without mention of a town or street, the name 'Mdme Tourgeneff'.[105] This can only be Clara Viaris, the French Protestant wife of the émigré Decembrist Nikolay Ivanovich Turgenev. The Turgenevs' apartment at 97 rue de Lille in Paris and their country villa Vert-Bois, near Bougival, were fashionable resorts of leading Russian, French, British, and Italian political, artistic, and intellectual figures throughout the Second Empire and beyond. Although Clara herself spoke no Russian, any contact with her family, however slight, must have brought the Brownings some increased awareness of the importance of Russia, both in authority and in exile. Another curious detail is that the Brownings' last Rome address in the via Felice (now Sestina) in 1860 was the same as that of the novelist and playwright Nikolay Gogol, who had spent many years there two decades earlier.[106] One cannot, of course, be certain that the Brownings were aware of this. Similar caution is necessary about their frequent conversations at that period in Rome with old Sir John Bowring, whose two-volume *Specimens of the Russian Poets* had introduced Russian literature to the English-speaking world in the early 1820s. The only information that we have is that they talked together of international relations; however, Bowring is at least more likely to have known that Gogol had lived on the Pincio, and to have spoken of this with the Brownings.[107]

Three other associations are more certain to have kept alive in the now widowed Robert Browning's mind his memories of St Petersburg. One was with the ubiquitous William Ralston, the librarian, translator, and folklorist who made Russia his chief special field. Browning is known to have been in touch with Ralston as early as 1865, when Ralston had taken the liberty of supplying the poet with some useful information.[108] There was doubtless talk between them of things Russian, especially of writers whom Ralston was busy rendering into English. Later Browning would read a piece by Ralston on the lyricist Kol'tsov and the philanthropic poet Nikitin, published in the *Contemporary Review* for April 1874 under the intriguing title 'Russian Idylls'.[109] Although the echo might be purely verbal, one must remember that Browning's own Russian 'idyl', *Ivàn Ivànovitch*, was not too far away. The second circumstance is that in 1867 and 1868 Browning often heard the great Anton Rubinstein play in London salons. On at least one occasion, at a party at Mrs Julie Salis Schwabe's, he met and spoke with him.[110] Perhaps it was now that the two men had a most interesting discussion on sacred music dramas. Rubinstein was enthusiastic about these and felt that the English, with their love and knowledge of the Bible, would take to them immediately. Mendelssohn's *Elijah*, for example, was immensely popular; why not clothe its subject with costumes, scenery and dramatic action? But Browning vehemently disagreed. The English, by their very reverence for the Scriptures, could not accept their being elaborated further than by oratorio. 'No one in England' (he declared) 'would tolerate *Elijah* any more than Christ dressed up and strutting about on the operatic stage.'[111] Browning nevertheless thought the pianist's performances were 'marvellous', and was not disconcerted when he broke a friend's instrument 'in the rush of his inspiration'.[112] Finally, Browning must have had some talk of Russia with Rev. Moncure Daniel Conway, pastor of South Place Chapel, Finsbury, and a long-standing friend of the family. Conway visited Russia in the summer of 1869, with introductions from Ralston, but before he did so invited Browning to go with him. The fact that this greatly tempted the poet shows that he had not completely lost his former curiosity.[113]

Throughout all this period, there is no sign that Browning took much interest in the more political side of Anglo-Russian relations. He was far too busy with *The Ring and the Book*. Nor in late 1870, during the 'Gorchakov fever' caused by Russia's repudiation of certain naval restrictions imposed upon it following the Crimean War, did Browning make any known public or private comment showing his annoyance or concern. He had mentioned Gorchakov in his poem *Apparent Failure* (1864), with reference to the Treaty of Paris; but as usual any political connotation was far removed from the actual subject of the piece, in this case a meditation on dead men in the Paris Morgue. However, during the Franco-Prussian War of 1870-71 there developed a new link which not only directed Browning's thoughts more frequently to Russia but may well have had real influence upon his poem *Ivàn Ivànovitch*. This was his association with Ivan Turgenev.

Turgenev left his home in Baden-Baden not long after his friends the Viardots had decided to abandon hostile Germany for neutral London. He spent the best part of a year in Britain, interrupted by some visits abroad.[114] The Viardots resided at 30 Devonshire Place, a street where the Brownings themselves had lived for a time in 1856. Here Pauline practised her singing, taught, and looked after her children, while her husband, Louis, listened to news of French disasters. Turgenev occupied various dingy apartments in the immediate vicinity but was found most regularly in the Viardots' salon. Many London celebrities came there, too, Robert Browning included. The Brownings had met Pauline once or twice in the 1850s and knew many people closely associated with her: Ary Scheffer, Henry Chorley, the Paris Turgenevs, the Sartorises, the Benzons, Mary Mohl, Anna Jameson, Lady Monson, and in particular George Sand whom Elizabeth had greatly admired.[115] It was therefore most natural that Browning should gladly accept Pauline's invitation to attend 'all the Saturdays' at Devonshire Place and make flattering remarks about her musical appearances.[116] It was there that he first encountered Turgenev.

According to Sir Charles Hallé, Browning was an unfailingly good judge of music, and a genuine connoisseur of its literature;[117] whether the same was true of his appreciation of Russian culture seems doubtful. Of course, he could have spoken with Turgenev of the work of William Ralston, of his meeting with Rubinstein, perhaps of Bowring and of Gogol; but did he have any first-hand knowledge of Russian literature? British writers' lack of interest in his country's civilisation somewhat riled Turgenev, although in the much-travelled Browning's case he must at least have found a more sympathetic hearer than most. But Turgenev also disliked Browning's poetry, if we can believe what he told Carlyle not long before,[118] and therefore had little incentive to come close to him. Besides, the men had nothing in common politically in the divisive atmosphere of the war: whereas Turgenev sympathised more and more with the now downtrodden French, Browning took comfort from the Germans' having trounced them so utterly.[119] Altogether, therefore, it would not have been surprising if the writers found some antipathy in each other's company; and in fact in August 1871, when both were staying as guests of Ernest Benzon near Pitlochry (Turgenev for the grouse-shooting, Browning for peace to write), the Russian came to find the poet 'most vain', 'not very amusing', and 'boring'.[120] Clearly, this cannot only have had to do with the chase, which Browning (unlike Pen, his mighty hunter of a son) cordially detested.[121] Meanwhile, despite the two authors' obvious differences of vocation and temperament, more than one commentator at the time saw similarities between them. A casual but circumstantially interesting comparison was made by the poet Ernest Dowson, who said that if Turgenev had written his masterpieces in verse they would have been like Browning's.[122] Such vague statements may not seem too helpful, but they do have significance as contemporary interpretations.

Browning had no known reciprocal reaction to Turgenev; perhaps the novelist's feelings were concealed from him. Nor is there any definite proof that their conversations had a useful impact on himself. However, the writers may well have discussed the Russian story of the woman abandoning her children to the wolves, which Browning would enshrine in verse some seven years later. That this is not merely misplaced speculation is shown by the fact that on separate visits to Carlyle and Tennyson, made earlier in 1871, Turgenev had spoken much of Russian lore, even though neither of these others had any first-hand knowledge of his country.[123] It is therefore just possible that Turgenev was in part 'my friend the Russ', Browning's ostensible narrator in *I、vàn Ivànovitch*. It is important to say 'in part', for everything about that implausibly styled 'idyl' is complex, from its origins to its ultimate expression.

Another contributory factor in the long genesis of *Ivàn Ivànovitch* was Browning's involvement in the Eastern Question debate of 1876-78. He is often said to have actively supported Gladstone's line on Bulgaria, Russia and Turkey, but the facts have never been properly assembled. One leading authority on the period has called his position the polar opposite of Tennyson's, while admitting that 'there is little evidence of Browning's precise opinion on the Bulgarian affair' apart from a pro-Gladstone sonnet on the atrocities by his 'disciple' Domett.[124] We do know that, together with Charles Darwin, Anthony Trollope, W.T. Stead and others, Browning was an official convener of the National Conference held at the St James's Hall in London on 8 December 1876.[125] What this really meant to him, however, is an open question. He may have let his name go forward simply as a paper commitment, perhaps under pressure from a prime mover like William Morris or Edward Burne-Jones. Not surprisingly, he did not go so far as to sit on the platform at the meetings: such was never his habit. Nevertheless, to undertake even such a purely nominal role in support of the National Conference was something that Tennyson and of course Swinburne would never have done, nor yet Dante Gabriel Rossetti.[126]

Everyone knew that this conference could have no practical results and was really only a talking forum, but as a demonstration of current public opinion about Turkish atrocities in Bulgaria it was remarkably powerful and significant.[127] Browning was therefore less than candid when he wrote on 30 November to assure his uncle Reuben that, in the matter of the convenership, he had had greatness thrust upon him. A friend had entreated him to give his name to the proposed motion, he said, and as a result, 'I am figuring as a politician — which I never wish to do'.[128] But the fact is that people *expected* Browning not to want a war with Russia. On 17 July 1877 the political philosopher and publicist Auberon Herbert sent him a peace declaration in the hope that he would sign it, adding that it might be 'useful as a counterblast to our Cabinet's mutterings and threatenings'. Herbert was setting up a small committee to help circulate the petition, and wanted the poet to join; he promised there would be only one meeting and very little work.[129] One must assume that Browning complied, for on 2 April the following year Herbert wrote to him again to ask if he would serve in a similar capacity, this time to participate in a select band who would receive and send on names of protesters.[130] Herbert achieved some notoriety by organising a grand anti-Jingoist rally in Hyde Park in 1878, and for Browning to collaborate with such a person was politically significant.

One may, however, suppose that Browning was pro-Bulgarian and anti-Turk chiefly for philosophical reasons. In his sonnet *Why I am a Liberal*, written and first published in 1885, he would express a deep conviction that nothing mattered so much as personal liberty.

> Who, then, dares hold — emancipated thus —
> His fellow shall continue bound?

What he here called 'a brother's right to freedom' was naturally applicable to the Bulgarians in relation to their Turkish overlords.[131] It may be noted, though, that Browning's refreshingly humanitarian stance over the Eastern Question was perhaps easier for him than for most, having lived in Italy for so long and viewing his country and its chauvinism with expatriate eyes. Certainly he was not immune from prejudice: like many other intellectuals at the time, his support for Gladstone arose in part from a personal dislike for Disraeli. No one obliged him to make up in response to G.W. Hunt's famous lines

> We don't want to fight,
> But by Jingo if we do...

the cheaply anti-Semitic retort:[132]

> The head I'd like to punch
> Is Beaconsfield the Jew.

In Browning's weak defence here it may be said that the humanitarian socialist William Morris went still further, calling Lord Beaconsfield 'the Jew wretch' and 'that piece of dirt'.[133] Disraeli, besides, had little time for Browning: he found him and his works both noisy and conceited.[134]

During this period of Anglo-Russian confrontation over Turkey and the Balkans, the British press was full of travel accounts and anecdotes. Whatever the origin of the wolf story which Browning would use in *Ivàn Ivànovitch* (this will shortly be the subject for debate), he may very well have come across one version of it in a series of amusing articles by Mr Burnand in *Punch* in the spring and summer of 1877. These consisted of a drawn-out skit on Fred Burnaby's popular book *A Ride to Khiva*. Burnaby, a captain of the Royal Horse

Guards, had journeyed through Central Asia in the winter of 1875-76 and warned his readers about the menacing Russian troop movements that he had observed there. But he also recounted his daily doings, not all of which were exciting. *Punch* took this off hilariously, rendering trivial incidents in Burnaby melodramatic or ludicrous. Where, for instance, Burnaby simply notes that wolves are in the area and need watching,[135] *Punch* creates a mad chase in which the imaginary author, encountering a pack of wolves in Russia at the hour of their breakfastski, at first seeks to stave them off with buns. Their Wagnerian howls calling for weightier fodder, he throws down his mechanical piano and electric telegraph machine. But he finally needs to sacrifice either the sleigh-driver or the sleigh-driver's boy in order to save his own skin. Noting that the man has thicker clothes and a whip (and also that he is the one who needs to be paid), he chooses him and drives on to safety in the town of Gladitzova.[136]

Browning wrote *Ivàn Ivànovitch* in August-September 1878, at Splügen near the Swiss-Italian border. Seeking rest and relative cool, away from the European heat wave, he and his sister Sarianna had stopped a mile high in the Alps at the Hotel Bodenhaus. There they had an annexe almost to themselves for the five or six weeks that they spent in the mountain pass before proceeding down to Venice. On their many walks they enjoyed the glaciers, the panoramic vistas, and the almost spring-like greenery of it all. Despite such relaxation, Browning completed at least two, and perhaps as many as five, of what was to be his first series of *Dramatic Idyls,* published in 1879. In particular, he composed *Ivàn Ivànovitch* in a great rush, for fear of losing concentration. Sarianna even thought he worked too much, fearing for his health.[137] Several commentators have suggested that the Splügen scenery reminded Browning of his Russian journey, thus inspiring him to write *Ivàn Ivànovitch.*[138] If this was so, it could only be for the snow and possibly the conifers, as he would not have seen many mountains or alpine pastures on his ride through Courland and Livonia. In view of the poem's philosophical and religious content, one wonders if it was not rather that Browning had here a vision of man's triviality beside the grandeurs of nature, leading him to reflect upon relative and absolute moralities. The question has also been asked, however, whether his subject has an Italian source as well as a Russian one.[139] If there was such, he could have heard it during his stay in the Swiss-Italian Alps, been interested by it, but preferred the Russian setting owing to some personal knowledge of the particular incidents described. We are told that among the characteristically Russian features he needed to check only the names and their stresses. This he did while staying with Sarianna at the Albergo dell'Universo on the Grand Canal in Venice: a Russian lady turned up providentially in his aid and allowed him to ensure that all details were right.[140] Who the lady was cannot be said; nor can one be sure how much of her learning, opinions, or interpretation of the story may have been incorporated in the final version. To judge by some features to be considered in a moment, she cannot in fact have looked too carefully at the spelling of names. Moreover, she could scarcely be Browning's 'friend the Russ', a conversation with whom is the foundation of the piece and not a commentary upon it.

The opening of *Ivàn Ivànovitch* is surely indicative of Browning's own first-hand knowledge of Russia, even though he chooses to express it indirectly:

'They tell me, your carpenters,' quoth I to my friend the Russ,
'Make a simple hatchet serve as a tool-box serves with us.
Arm but each man with his axe, 'tis a hammer and saw and plane
And chisel. and — what know I else? We should imitate in vain
The mastery wherewithal, by a flourish of just the adze,
He cleaves, clamps, dovetails in, — no need of our nails and brads, —
The manageable pine: 'tis said he could shave himself
With the axe, — so all adroit, now a giant and now an elf,
Does he work and play at once!'

Here we see the Browning who has passed through forests of pine for days on end, stopped in villages to watch the work that he describes, perhaps seen shipbuilding at St Petersburg, heard of Peter the Great's own passion for the craft, contemplated the role of timber in Russian houses, roads, pavements, bridges, seen the wooden town of the Butterweek fair, and himself later cited, in *Sordello*, the Scythian's way with wood. Furthermore, the Russian terms and words (some anglicised) which he introduces in *Ivàn Ivànovitch* suggest a keen interest in the manners and institutions of the empire. The priest is correctly a 'pope' (Russian *pop*), the village elder 'stárosta' (although in the manuscript this is wrongly stressed as *staròsta*), the lord of the manor 'pomeshchik' (though Browning spells and mistakenly stresses this as *pomeschík*, rather than *poméshchik*). Browning also uses the modern spelling *Tsar* (1. 147), as opposed to the then still customary *Czar* which is found, for instance, in *Waring* (1. 109). Distances are rightly measured in versts (Russian singular *verstà*). Ivàn is making his children a 'kremlin' (Russian *kreml'*, 'citadel'), which is obviously a model of the famous Moscow Kremlin since it will have its great bell, *Tsar' kolokol*. Browning called this 'Kolokol the Big', maybe misremembering its more evocative name; and it is also odd, perhaps, that he should speak of 'Sacred Pictures' rather than more authentically of 'icons'. However, in general he clearly took extreme care to establish a true Russian atmosphere. The distinguished Russian critic Zinaida

Vengerova, writing some years after the first publication of *Ivàn Ivànovitch*, praised its author for his deep understanding of the Slavonic nature and for a remarkably truthful evocation of Russian life and manners.[141] She even congratulated him on the accuracy of his Russian names, but here she appears to be exaggerating somewhat.

Indeed, it is all the more surprising that things should have gone wrong with Browning's Russian names, given the advice that he is said to have been proffered in Venice. It would be unfair, of course, to expect him to employ a code of transliteration from Cyrillics that was either scientific or completely consistent. Also, the system of stressing with a grave stroke [`], rather than with an acute ['], was common enough at his time. Disregarding modern conventions, some names that he uses are in fact completely acceptable: Dmìtri, Kàtia, Stepàn and its diminutive Stiòpka. If one allows that he is transliterating after the French manner, then Ivànovitch (Ivanovich), Loukèria (Luker'ia), and the horse's name, Droug (*drug*, 'friend'), are all tolerable. Vàssili, too, can be explained in this way, even though it is mis-stressed (for Vasílii), as can also Kìrill (for Kiríll). However, Loùscha, Stèscha, and Teriòscha are more serious deviations from any sort of norm: one could only construe them as Franco-German. Lusha, Stesha, and Teriosha would be more natural English spellings for these names, which are diminutives respectively of Luker'ia, Stepanida, and Terentii. But Browning's strangest mistake (if one discounts the absurd hypercorrection Màrpha for Marfa) is his stress on Terentiì (for Teréntii) and Sergeì (for Sergéi). Clearly he must have recalled seeing the short sign [ˇ] over the Cyrillic [и] and imagined it meant that the letter was accentuated; in fact, of course, it shortens it. That he is not simply indulging in poetic licence is proved by his repetition of the name Terentiì; and in any case the Russian [й] can never under any circumstances be stressed. So much, then, for the Russian lady in Venice.

Alexandra Orr, our only source for knowledge of this person, notes: 'It would be interesting to know what suggestions or corrections she made, and how far they adapted themselves to the rhythm already established, or compelled changes in it; but the one alternative would as little have troubled him as the other ...[because] to the end of his life he could at any moment recast a line or passage for the sake of greater correctness, and leave all that was essential in it untouched.'[142] Maybe in this instance Browning's talent failed him. On the other hand, it seems probable that the Russian lady would have helped him with the sort of names that his characters might possess, rather than with the finer points of their stress or English spelling. He did not perhaps need to be told, only to have confirmed, that Ivan Ivanovich may denote a typical Russian — though not, it should be noted, one exclusively of peasant origins. Among other British commentators on

Russia, George Augustus Sala used the name for an average *muzhik*, Herbert Barry and Mackenzie Wallace for a *pomeshchik*.[143] Gogol employed it for a title character in his *Povest' o tom, kak possorilsia Ivan Ivanovich s Ivanom Nikiforovichem* (The Story of How Ivan Ivanovich Quarrelled with Ivan Nikiforovich). Turgenev at one time intended writing a sketch called 'Ivan Ivanovich' for his collection *Zapiski okhotnika* (Notes of a Hunter). It is doubtful that this would have had anything to do with wolves; but again it shows the universality of the name.[144] Much later, both Leonid Andreev and the Soviet author Antonina Koptiaeva would write prose works called *Ivan Ivanovich*, without reference, of course, to Browning. In England during the Second World War, to be precise in 1943, Henry de Vere Stacpoole published a poem called *Ivan Ivanovich* in aid of the Fund for Russian Horses. It is also relevant to note that in Louis Viardot's tragic *Histoire de Dmitri*, based in great part on information given to the author by Turgenev, the victim is Ivan Ivanovich, the master, and the assassin-hero is the peasant Dmitry.[145] Finally, as American commentators in Browning's day were quick to point out, the function of the name Ivan Ivanovich in Russian could be compared to usages like 'Uncle Sam'.[146] As for Browning's other names, they too are convincing enough, especially since they combine some of the commonest (Dmitrii, Sergei, Katia) with less common but still popular ones (Terentii, Stepanida). Luker'a (from Glikeriia) is of interest as the name of the heroine in Turgenev's story *Zhivye moshchi* (A Living Relic), which Browning could have read in French in 1874 or later.[147]

The most fascinating and problematical thing about *Ivàn Ivànovitch* is of course the poem's narrative. Whole articles have been written in an attempt to elucidate its origins.[148] Browning himself, through 'my friend the Russ', expressed his own perplexity as follows (ll. 10-16):

> '...It scarce may be
> You never heard tell a tale told children, time out of mind,
> By father and mother and nurse, for a moral that's behind,
> Which children quickly seize. If the incident happened at all,
> We place it in Peter's time when hearts were great not small,
> Germanised, Frenchified. I wager 'tis old to you
> As the story of Adam and Eve, and possibly quite as true.'

This last line is odd, to say the least: it is not at all clear if it makes the story more, or less, historical. However, it is evident that Browning himself was not sure if the adventure really happened or if it happened in this particular form. Some contemporary Russians stated that the story was a popular legend from the time of Peter the Great, but they may simply have been following what Browning himself says.[149] The problem is to know to which source or sources he had access, and how much if anything he added to them. In outline, his own version goes like this: A woman, her husband, and their three children have left their village to work for a short time in another. The period having expired, they are about to return, but the husband is delayed. The others travel alone in a one-horse sleigh on a cold moonlit night. A large pack of wolves pursues them, and either snatches or is allowed to take each child in turn. The woman reaches her village, more dead than alive, and is revived by friends including Ivàn Ivànovitch, a carpenter. She tells her story, and he fells her with his axe. A discussion takes place in the village, led by the squire, the peasant elder, and the priest. The priest's view of justice prevails, and the carpenter is informed he may go free.

According to the late M.P. Alekseev, Browning took this tale from *Les Mystères de la Russie* by Frédéric Lacroix.[150] W.C. DeVane, by contrast, says that it comes from a travel book called *The English-woman in Russia*.[151] William Allingham believed it had appeared earlier in a magazine called *The Mirror*.[152] Tennyson told the story twice, as we have seen, independently of Browning. There were several other published versions. Many critics have supposed that Browning heard the anecdote in Russia in 1834 and was remembering it. Edward Berdoe, writing at the beginning of this century, thought the same but declared it to be 'a variant of a Russian wolf story which, in one form or another, we all heard in our childhood'.[153] Alexandra Orr (who in general relied upon information from Sarianna Browning) said that it was based on a folk tale called 'The Judgment of God'.[154] Browning's early American interpreters Charlotte Porter and Helen A. Clarke called the poem 'a vivid re-picturing of a typical Russian folk tale'.[155] What is the truth of the matter?

The first thing to note is that if the story is a folk tale, it is foreign to any published collection or to Russian folklorists today. In the early 1930s Frances Bolton corresponded extensively with famous Russians including G.V. Vernadskii, Avram Iarmolinskii, M.P. Alekseev and even Lev Tolstoi's son Il'ia. All without exception told her that the wolf story was not a Russian legend or folk tale, and more than one strongly implied that it was made up by foreigners about Russia![156] Most independent nineteenth-century sources claim it to have been a true occurrence, though one or two admit it may be very old. On the other hand, the overwhelming evidence of experts is that wolves do not pack other than in family groups, and do not attack human beings under the circumstances described (though they might just eat defenceless babies).[157] Nevertheless, in the Russia which Browning knew, wolves did represent a menace and were considered a great nuisance. Both wolves and bears marauded freely on the edges of St

Petersburg and were even known to enter the grounds of palaces. One Russian lady, sitting in her garden about 1840, is said to have scared away a bear by flinging a novel by George Sand at him;[158] but that is beside the point. Wolves, at least, feature prominently in most travel books of the period. What is perhaps still more important, a young poet in St Petersburg in 1834 might be liable to think of them in Romantic, even gothic, terms, as symbols of the power of darkness and evil. Browning must have seen or heard wolves on his journey through the forests and would have reflected on Byron's *Mazeppa* where, in stanza XII, the hero, lashed to a horse, rushes madly through the woods pursued by the 'stealing, rustling step' and 'long gallop' of a troop of wolves. It was probably from a travel book that Tennyson learned the anecdote of the woman and the wolves, and wrung a friend's heart by the telling of it around 1839.[159] Unfortunately, our record of this incident is scant, and it would in any case be unwise to advance it as the earliest known version of the tale. However, Tennyson's story at that time apparently had both the woman and her husband in the sleigh, and thus diverged in at least one important respect from Browning's.

Let us look first at *Les Mystères de la Russie*. The publishing history of this work is somewhat obscure, but it seems to have been put together in 1844 from the manuscript notes of at least two witnesses, each referring back for a period of several years. Lacroix gives the following account, suggesting that it is true and not legendary. A woman is driving home from a neighbouring village with her three children in a one-horse sleigh. Wolves attack her, and she tries in vain to beat them off by driving faster and by screaming at them. You may expect her (intervenes Lacroix) to secure the children to the sleigh, whip the horse, and jump down among the wolves. But no: she throws each child in turn, and 'returns in triumph, safe and sound, beneath her conjugal roof.' 'That', concludes Lacroix, 'is what slavery does to a woman and a mother. Such facts are possible wherever a powerful cause of perversion is constantly at work upon the mind and morals of a people.'[160] This account clearly does have many things in common with Browning's; but it differs in several important respects. Browning's woman does not shout or urge on the horse; the poet, unlike Lacroix, makes no political judgment; in Browning, there is no talk of slavery; and, above all, in Lacroix there is no actual retaliation against the woman's behaviour. Were it for this last fact alone, Browning could hardly be said to have followed the version of *Les Mystères de la Russie*.

At about the same time as the Lacroix compilation there appeared the first edition of Charles Frederick Henningsen's anonymous *Revelations of Russia*[161] In it we find two variants on the wolf tale. The first is simply the essence of the thing: a woman gives her three children to the wolves. However, Henningsen adds two highly significant details here. One is that the event is said to have occurred a long time previously, in the reign of either Ivan the Terrible or Peter the Great; and the second that the Tsar 'was so indignant at the unnatural conduct of the heartless mother, that he ordered her to be cast to the wolves which he kept for his hunt'. The wolves strangled her, but left her body untouched. Henningsen obviously believed this to be a kind of myth, and suggested as its more likely factual origin his other account. Here, a colonel's wife was returning home with her two children and found herself beset by wolves. Hoping to save her weak younger son, and to prevent the beasts from killing her horses, she sacrificed the elder child. However, on reaching safety, she found the other one dead, frozen stiff in the spot where she had hidden him on the sleigh. Obviously, Browning cannot have been following either of the Henningsen accounts, since he has a carpenter, and not a tsar, as judge and his Loùscha is not a woman of rank. However, he does make his mother choose between the children, and save her favourite till last.

Our next record in historical progression must be Tennyson's again. As has earlier been described, in November 1849 he told the anecdote to friends and made it the basis of a philosophical discussion.[162] This account, noted at the time in the diary of one who participated in the ensuing debate, is strikingly different from Tennyson's own earlier version, and has two important new features: the woman has six, and not three children, and she is a lady in exile. This puts quite another complexion on the tale. However, we are told that Tennyson's account was 'borrowed from a Russian story', and it may well be that he invented the new details on the spot in an effort to divide opinion more equally. At all events, Browning clearly cannot have used this variant for his poem, even had he heard of it. Meanwhile, in 1854 a Boston magazine published yet another version of the story, in some travel notes by Professor D. Etienne de Lara.[163] Here it is related with some sympathy, as a 'painful circumstance' which actually took place 'some thirty miles from St Petersburg'. The woman is a peasant, returning to her village; she has four, and not three children; and her action in sacrificing each in turn to the wolves leaves her 'a maniac probably for life'. Although Browning evidently did not use this particular account, it is interesting because of its precise geographical location which corresponds closely to his own. Doubtless it, too, is a characteristically Petersburgian variant of the tale. The other interesting point is the sequel, which corresponds to a comment made half a century later by Edward Berdoe: 'we apprehend there is not a competent authority in brain troubles living who would not acquit

Loùscha on the ground of insanity'.[164] While this has no direct bearing on the Browning text, it shows that, long before *Ivàn Ivànovitch*, some commentators had what we might otherwise have conceitedly assumed to be modern scruples concerning the divine judgment on the woman.

We come now to the last known published account of the wolf story, by far the most detailed of all before Browning himself took it up. This is the 'dreadful anecdote of a peasant woman and her children' found in *The Englishwoman in Russia*, the report of a decade's residence in that country by an anonymous lady, perhaps Miss E. McCoy. Although the book appeared only in 1855, the account itself must relate to a period some years earlier. Again, it is given as if factually true. All the most familiar features are there: the mother was a peasant, travelling through the forest in winter in a one-horse sleigh; attacked by wolves, she sacrificed each of her three children in turn, and arrived 'almost insensible' at her destination. This much is presented in terms very similar to Browning's, including the significant detail that the 'affrighted steed' had become aware of the wolves before the mother or her children; compare the poet's

> Droug starts, stops, back go his ears, he snuffs,
> Snorts, — never such a snort! then plunges.... (ll. 119-20)

On the other hand, in common with one previous account, the Englishwoman makes the peasant whip her struggling horse — a detail foreign to Browning. It is also noticeable that, unlike Browning's Loukèria, this protagonist was travelling from her own hut to the neighbouring village. Nevertheless, the ending of the present text for the first time starts to resemble Browning's own. The woman was revived by a man who emerged from his hut. She told her gruesome story. '"And did you throw them *all* to the wolves, even the little baby you held in your arms?" exclaimed the horror-stricken peasant. "Yes, all!" was the reply. The words had scarcely escaped from the white lips of the miserable mother, when the man laid her dead at his feet with a single blow of the axe with which he was cleaving wood when she arrived.' Obviously, we here have Browning's tale in more than just the essence, even though the conclusion speaks not of a village trial but — as in another earlier version — the judgment of the Tsar. In this case, the Tsar pardoned the self-appointed executioner, 'wisely making allowance for his agitation and the sudden impulse with which horror and indignation at the unnatural act had inspired him'.

What, then, should we make of all this? Was DeVane right to think that Browning closely followed the Englishwoman's account, replacing only the Tsar of the 'original' by the village priest, and adding the character of the husband, Dmìtri?[165] Or should we rather imagine that the poet had access to yet another version of the tale, similar in some crucial details to the Englishwoman's, but related also to the Lara version in its geographical setting and to the Henningsen in its legendary context? Given that there is no sign whatever that Browning possessed or read any of the publications discussed, it seems wise to allow that the second alternative may be correct.[166] If so, he may have relied much more upon his own memory than is now commonly allowed.

Before attempting to demonstrate what one might call the poem's Russian authenticity, it is as well to consider for a moment how it was interpreted in English-speaking countries. Public comment on the piece was very mixed. A critic writing in the *Fortnightly Review* for July 1879 dismissed it as 'a piece of wild Russian folk-lore, wildly rendered in verse of quite appropriate rudeness'.[167] By contrast, Alexandra Orr published in the *Contemporary Review* for May 1879 a most sympathetic treatment of *Ivàn Ivànovitch*. (She did not, however, offer any explanation as to its origins.)[168] Private and sectional comment, though also mixed, was on the whole extravagant. In view of his importance as the chronicler of Tennyson's final judgment of the woman's actions in the story of the wolves, it is worth recording first some remarks by William Allingham pencilled into his personal copy of the *Dramatic Idyls. Ivàn Ivànovitch* in general, and the priest's verdict in particular, drew many exclamation marks from him together with notes like 'is this dramatic?', 'typically RB', and the final comment: 'wonderfully written wonderfully worthless'. To this Allingham added: 'Tennyson said to me, "I think the woman was right" — but that is not the question.'[169]

Most extraordinary was some early readers' reception of the dramatic contrast between Loùscha and Ivàn, which of course provokes an awkward moral dilemma. Amazing as it may seem to readers a century on, Christian propagandists of the period looked to the poem for guidance as educators. The Englishwoman Mrs Alexander Ireland seriously considered it in this light in one of her regular lecture topics on Browning, but was forced to conclude — without intended irony — that it was 'truly rather a *negative* study in parenthood'.[170] However, the American Charlotte M. Mason, again without a shred of irony, wrote a whole poem in praise of Browning's skill in distinguishing evil from good. Never since Shakespeare — nay, since Our Lord Himself — had the world seen such mastery as in this 'tale so horrible-piteous, show of human nature at worse'. As for the punishment which God called His chosen servant to mete out, was there any modern American woman who could truthfully say that she herself did not deserve it? Had she never left her children prey to wolves — the wolves, that is, of neglect? If the faults of a child were ignored, then the parent herself was guilty.[171] This thoroughly confused and rotten argument is adduced in order to underline the terrible dilemma that Browning's poem presents. It seems impossible to say that the woman was 'right', but as soon as you put 'rightness' on the carpenter's side, you risk falling into this Mason trap. And even if you stand back and say: the woman was 'wrong', but Ivàn was 'wrong' as well, you are still passing moral judgment, only of a more anarchical kind. It is tempting just to dismiss the poem, as posing a false alternative; but its dramatic and philosophical power is such that you are compelled to react. Most Browningites considered that they had no choice but to side with the judgment. Two other American women commentators agreed that 'Ivàn executed God's sentence on selfish motherhood.'[172] One bloodthirsty Briton spoke enthusiastically of 'the prompt axe of Ivàn, the terribly clear-sighted carpenter'.[173]

The problem is compounded for more sensible readers by the fact that Browning himself, who gave a dramatic reading of his 'idyl' before a distinguished audience on at least one occasion, was apparently quite pleased with it.[174] In attempting to understand why, a number of critics have emphasised the poet's search for that moment of truth which reveals latent character. In *Ivàn Ivànovitch* both the woman and the carpenter experience a crisis; the one (it is said) shows creature cowardice, the other divine valour.[175] Several authorities have pointed to the fact that Browning, in this poem as so often elsewhere, indulges his love of special pleading and paradox: he gives the woman the opportunity to present herself in the best light possible before having her head chopped off by God's judgment. One commentator has even called this method Homeric.[176] The poem has been described as typical of Browning's favourite thesis, in that he applauds 'the heart against the head, spontaneity against reflection, impulse against calculation'.[177] In more modern times, John Woolford has noted how Ivàn kills Loùscha precisely when she says that life must go on, and that she owes her life to him. 'The point is clearly that Loùscha's love of life has corroded into a hedonism that will protect life at all costs.'[178] From the point of view of the carpenter, this is clearly true: her final comment shocks him into action. But how did Browning intend it from the woman's point of view? What could she have meant? If all that the poet understood by it was that she had already got over the loss of her children, it may strike us as trivial and improbable. Could there even be an underlying sexual meaning to the story?

It is instructive to consider what the poet's closest friends and admirers thought of *Ivàn Ivànovitch*. The subject came up several times in the London Browning Society while the author was still alive (though not, alas, in his presence). In an immensely long paper read (or, as one hopes, summarised) before a meeting of the London

Browning Society on 27 April 1883, Miss E. Dickinson West considered what she called the poet's 'villains' and, towards the end, referred to the mother in *Ivàn Ivànovitch* as 'perhaps Browning's solitary *unredeemable* human being'. Loùscha's fault, she said, was 'merely the uncounteracted primary instinct of self-preservation', and as such was 'fitliest dealt with' by the hero's axe. 'We are satisfied to think', she observed, 'that the headless body and severed head are all that remain of 'Loùscha' when the strong-armed carpenter has dealt his righteous blow. And we feel that the dramatist is content thus to leave her.'[179] Perhaps because of the force of her judgment, but perhaps also because listeners at this point had woken up in the prospect of a speedy conclusion to her speech, *Ivàn Ivànovitch* was one of the chief points of contention during the discussion which followed. The Chairman himself, Rev. H.J. Bulkeley, M.A., allowed himself to remark that a lady friend of his, on hearing the subject for tonight, had exclaimed: 'I hope they'll mention that old villain who cut off the woman's head.' He wished to report this as an instance of opposing points of view in literary criticism. His own view was that Loùscha could have been redeemed, having done her best to save the children.[180] Frederick J. Furnivall retorted that he differed from Miss West on many points but agreed with her in this. 'Probably some of us would have acted as basely as Loùscha did', he admitted. 'In that case I trust another Ivàn would have cut our heads off too.'[181] In a subsequent letter the author herself reiterated the mother's guilt, adding: 'I suspect that Mr. Browning himself would hardly have scrupled to play the part of the carpenter if necessary!'[182]

And here, precisely, is the rub: would Browning have wielded the axe? A certain Mr J.J. Britton, himself a poet, was not satisfied with the West-Furnivall line and wrote a paper to protest. It was held for some time in reserve, but came up as a substitute for a quite different lecture due to have been given on 27 February 1885. The author being absent, it was read by a member of the Committee. Britton's line was really very daring. Having first picturesquely demonstrated Browning's narrative and dramatic skill, Britton threw down his challenge. Where was the *evidence* for Loùscha's guilt? Ivàn did not wait to hear it: he allowed her no trial, no cross-questioning. As there were no witnesses, everything would seem to have depended on her confession; yet this was not in fact so. Browning told us that she was *loved* in the village; how so, if she was of the kind to sacrifice her children? And what in fact had she done? She had tried her best to protect them, she had swooned away in terror when the last was gone, she had no time or inclination to concoct a lie and simply told what had happened. She had committed errors, it was true, but who in her situation could have remained without blame? The sensible Pomeshchik seemed to be on her side, and what would her husband Dmìtri have thought of the proud carpenter's action? 'On the whole', concluded Britton, 'I vote Loùscha guiltless — weak, but guiltless — and Ivàn Ivànovitch a most hot-headed and rash young man.' Perhaps what most irritated some listeners, however, was one final observation about the work itself, intended to be laudatory but actually double-edged: it was 'truly a notable poem of a great and eccentric master'.[183]

In the discussion which followed, several speakers adopted strongly differing positions. The Chairman, Augustine Birrell, claimed inside knowledge akin to Browning's own in that he 'had spent no less a period than one calendar month in Russia and made as many as two excursions into the interior'. In his view, the Browning Society should not play the Old Bailey. Life in a Russian village could not accommodate the freeing of the woman. Where would she have hidden? Who would ever have forgiven her? She would have become an old witch. Ivàn saw all this in prospect, and felled her. This fate, the Chairman piously opined, was in her better interest.[184] Dr Furnivall, not surprisingly, agreed, but at this point a surprising intervention was made by Dr Berdoe, future author of *The Browning Cyclopaedia*. He did not specially admire the poem. Its subject was terrifying, and it was impossible to believe that the woman could have acted rationally. The love of a mother for her children was so universal that no *man* could stand in judgment over her. Ivàn was a social purifier; and 'all the social purifiers he had met were pot-house humbugs, and were unfit to condemn erring women'. Surely those of Loùscha's own sex would only have pleaded for mercy.[185] After this, the level of debate declined into conventional generalities about the mother and Ivàn. But on the whole, Britton's own view prevailed and some excellent points were noted. What, for instance, would have been gained had Loùscha thrown herself to the wolves? How could divine law be reconciled with an impulse to murder? Why did Ivàn not wait for Dmìtri's return? And did he perhaps behead him also, for letting his wife and children drive without weapons?[186]

This same discussion was subsequently pursued in the Notes and Queries section of the Society's Papers. A member signing himself 'Job' took exception to Berdoe's refusal to condemn Loùscha on such muddled humanitarian grounds. She was obviously guilty, failing as she did to show herself a true mother. But, this writer added, 'Whether we should admire Ivàn is another question. I do not.'[187] To this Berdoe himself responded that he had of course meant that *men* should not judge the woman, for they are universally selfish and would certainly have behaved as badly as or worse than Loùscha under the same circumstances. No woman who was not insane could have acted as she did, and he was therefore 'inclined to attribute Loùscha's failing at the supreme moment of agony to an aberration of the intellect'.[188] Yet another contributor, however, asserted that Browning himself clearly showed the woman's guilt, through her own slips of tongue like: 'your mother flings.../Flings? I flung? Never.'[189] The debate continued — and continues a hundred years beyond the poet's death, confused still further by changed views on male and female morality.

But what, then, of the poem's 'Russianness'? Browning was never very widely read in Russia, though the great critic Mirskii hinted that he believed him to have had some influence on the course of modern Russian poetry: Maiakovskii's rhymes, he thought, resembled some of Browning's in their length and punning complexity, and Akhmatova could have written *Meeting at Night* and *Parting at Morning*.[190] As for the *Dramatic Idyls*, an anonymous reviewer in the *Ezhenedel'noe novoe vremia* (New Weekly Times) found the term 'idyl' inappropriate for Browning's subjects and their treatment, but only because their dramatic colouring and power so obviously transcended the expected confines of that genre. *Ivàn Ivànovitch* in particular had a timeless strength. 'One must turn to the history of the Greek gods in order to find an attitude of mind equal in moral simplicity to the childish and at the same time majestic view of the world in which the fatal blow is struck.' Similarly, the priest who justified that blow was not so much a Russian pope as an ancient seer of a primitive religion whose champion was the carpenter. Browning's purpose was not fact so much as hypothesis. His atmosphere was mournful and harsh, but his poetic manner was free. This ensured a happy fusion of the psychological material and its artistic expression.[191] By contrast, the influential *Vestnik Evropy* (Messenger of Europe) found the poem ignorant, long-drawn-out and stupid.[192] That this is scarcely so will be evident to most modern readers, save perhaps for the old priest's wordy tirade; but the Russians' failure to comment on the accuracy or otherwise of Browning's narrative may mean that the subject was already strange to them in 1879. It could thus have seemed unRussian and even rather shocking. There is some sign, however, that in its original form the tale as Browning knew it may have been still more bloodthirsty: in a letter which could have reference to *Ivàn Ivànovitch*, he declared, 'the story is true except in the infinitely less [*sic*, presumably for 'more'] revolting circumstances which I have softened away'.[193]

Perhaps, therefore, Browning did after all have access to a circumstantial report of the incidents described, or at least to an elaborate telling of the tale by whoever was his 'friend the Russ'. There are one or two curious indications that this might be so. Browning's poetic language is of course often odd, sometimes to the point of caprice; but there are places in *Ivàn Ivànovitch* where unusual English turns of phrase would seem natural if given literally in Russian. In line 84, for example, the expression 'deeper down' means 'further from St Petersburg'. In terms of an extent of forest, 'deep' is of course significant in English; but one feels that the Russian *glubokii* is much commoner in this sense. In line 99, it seems a little strange that the horse 'knows his way, by guess'; but the Russian word for 'guess', *dogadka,* can be expressive of perspicacity as well as of trial and error. The word 'border' in line 118 seems to mean less 'frontier' than 'territory'; in Russian, *krai* can have both senses. Although in using the endearment 'pigeons' of the mother's children (line 135) Browning may be striving consciously for local colour, the Russian *golubchiki* sounds more natural. Most intriguing, however, is Browning's use of a much-praised phrase at the very end of the poem. The carpenter is told he is pardoned, may go free. He is building his toy Kremlin and, as he looks up, has an acorn-cup in his mouth. 'How otherwise?' he asks. Now although this makes perfect sense, and is dramatically striking, it could not be thought of as very natural English. Besides, the phrase cannot easily be pronounced with anything between one's lips. By contrast, the exact equivalent in Russian, *kak inache,* is both a correct response and one which can be perfectly pronounced in the circumstance described.

All this is, of course, of relatively minor importance. In no single instance could it be categorically affirmed that Browning was dependent on a poorly translated Russian narrative. Nevertheless, these details could make more likely the existence of a 'friend the Russ'. More significant, perhaps, are certain features of Russian life which one imagines Browning could scarcely have recalled from over forty years before, even had he ever learnt them. There are a number of these; here are just a few. One wonders, first, how the poet knew the Russians' trick with wolves: to seize their tongues, to pull and not let go (ll. 215-17). Secondly, there is the matter of the saints' bones and other holy things kept in a bag around Terentiĭ's neck to ward off evil (ll. 179-82). Thirdly, the personification of the wolves as so many devils, and the supposed transformation of lame Màrpha into a she-wolf at night (ll. 188-94), would suppose a considerable knowledge on Browning's part of Slavonic werewolves and *volkodlaki.* Altogether, then, it seems likely that at least the narrative parts of the poem were thoroughly founded in a Russian source or sources, and perhaps only the more intellectual and vaguely western philosophical debate towards the end of the poem is truly Browning's own. That is not to say, of course, that he did not show great imagination and dramatic powers in versifying the whole.

There remains one crucial question: the judgment. How would this be seen from a Russian point of view? Why does the carpenter arrogate the right to execute the woman, and why does the priest believe this was, in effect, an act of God?

'It had to be:
I could no other: God it was bade "Act for me!"' (ll. 255-6)

'God bade me act for him: I dared not disobey!' (l. 289)

'...I proclaim
Ivàn Ivànovitch God's servant!' (ll. 381-2)

In one way, as has already been suggested, the triumph of this mad morality may seem purely characteristic of Browning. Were the question only philosophical, the judgment might be different; as it is, Ivàn feels instinctively that the woman is guilty, and kills her. In a totally different context, in *Mr. Sludge, 'The Medium'*, Browning appears to give a partial explanation of the need for varying reactions to the same phenomenon in varying circumstances. As Sludge tells his accuser, the possibility of turning clay to coin is not the same when affirmed by a poor boy as it is when viewed by scientists and thinkers (ll. 124-9):

Oh, with such philosophers
You're on your best behaviour! While the lad —
With him, in a trice, you settle likelihoods,
Nor doubt a moment how he got his prize:
In his case, you hear, judge and execute,
All in a breath: so would most men of sense.

However, in another way the final judgment in *Ivàn Ivànovitch* is very Russian. There was obviously no legal basis for condemning the woman, but rather a moral one. The question is therefore not so much: was the carpenter right in law to punish the woman? as: have we the moral right to punish him? This, in the last resort, is what sways the landowner and the people. In one sense, Ivàn and the priest have a horrible God (in Whom one suspects Browning of believing); but in another, the carpenter can be seen to have acted in a spirit of natural retaliation. He therefore must be morally pardoned, as a creature of instinct, just as the woman could be morally condemned. Now in Russian law — at least in its traditional basis — moral justice is seen as superior to legal justice. In a famous row with some French colleagues — Flaubert, Edmond de Goncourt and others, — Turgenev once argued that, whereas Western law was founded on rules and principles, Russian law was rooted in humanity.[194] By this he meant that human instincts, feelings and needs counted for more in the dispensation of justice than any predetermined legal code. As the village people sit round by the church and listen to their priest, they feel within them something of the anger, passion, and sense of betrayal which have led Ivàn Ivànovitch to raise his axe and slay the woman. If he has guilt, they share it; and they cannot punish an act in which they see themselves morally to have participated. They therefore acquiesce in his pardon, and the more Westernised lord is overruled and succumbs. Meanwhile, the carpenter's lack of any conscience in the matter, though horrible to any who abhor all killing, is merely the logical confirmation of this Russian point of view. Here, too, then, Browning has entered remarkably well into the Russian mind, even if his long apotheosis of the religious reaction to the woman's guilt may seem more Talmudic than Slav: letting 'life for life restore God's balance' (ll. 327-8) savours too much of 'an eye for an eye and a tooth for a tooth' to be typical of any Christian concept of justice, let alone a specifically Orthodox one. But Browning is a complex poet, and embraces in *Ivàn Ivànovitch* a many-sided and ambiguous picture of human behaviour and morality. He has not been afraid to graft foreign shoots upon the Russian tree in the interests of universality. Nor has he pruned untidy branches, such as the implication in ll. 61-74 and 242-8 that Loukèria and Ivàn have had something more than a neighbourly relationship. But to elaborate on that question would take us very far from the subject of Browning and Russia.

The rest is fairly brief. In his last ten years, Browning retained some interest in Russia, though he became increasingly preoccupied by things Semitic and Italian. He kept in touch with William Ralston, with whom he was by now on friendly terms: he read and enjoyed his publications, even without being sent them for possible comment, and it seems that he attended at least one function with a Russian flavour which Ralston organised in London in the May of 1879. In July that year Ralston gave Browning a recent Russian magazine, probably a copy of the *Vestnik Evropy* with its critique of *Ivàn Ivànovitch*.[195] Also in 1879, Browning was in Oxford for the Balliol May Ball at the same time as, or just before, Turgenev's reception of an honorary DCL. There is no record of their meeting.[196] A couple of years later, Ralston tried to secure Browning's presence, along with many other English writers, critics and journalists of distinction, at a dinner held at the Arts Club in honour of Turgenev, who was visiting the country at the time. Browning's physical movements made it impossible for him to attend, but he wrote from Venice after the event to say: 'How much I should have enjoyed an opportunity of again seeing Mr Tourgueneff — anybody who ever *did* see him will easily imagine: and I am grateful indeed for your invitation to share in the privilege, though prevented from profiting by it.'[197] At least Browning seems to have read Turgenev, late in life, as also some Tolstoi: his own or his sister's library contained French translations of *Zapiski okhotnika*, *Anna Karenina* and *Voina i mir* (War and Peace).[198] In this late period Browning also knew and had some correspondence with Mark André Rafalovich, a young Russo-French poet now residing in London. He praised the other's volumes of English poetry including *Tuberose and Meadow-Sweet* (1885) and *In Fancy Dress* (1886), declaring himself 'struck by much felicity in form and melodiousness in sound, to say nothing of not a few fine and delicate fancies'.[199] Another ongoing Russian connection was with Anton Rubinstein, whom Browning continued to admire and whose concerts he preferred to partying or socialising.[200] The feeling was mutual, besides: in 1884 Rubinstein wanted Browning to write some songs for him, though apparently without effect.[201] Finally, one may note that around 1883, while standing one day on the doorstep of his house in Warwick Crescent, talking to Edmund Gosse and contemplating the bitter east wind, Browning said that he felt really ill, more ill than he had ever felt since suffering a terrible headache in St Petersburg in 1834.[202]

All this, naturally, is superficial and anecdotal. More substantial, perhaps, was Browning's concern for Russian Jews: we are told that (unlike in 1846) he 'felt a warm interest' in their 'terrible crisis' during renewed persecution in the early 1880s.[203] Following in the wake of the assassination of Alexander II, massive anti-Jewish pogroms were reported in South Russia and the Ukraine throughout much of 1881. On Christmas Day that same year Polish Catholics sacked the Jewish ghetto in Warsaw, plundering shops and killing upwards of thirty persons.[204] News of such atrocities led the Anglo-Jewish Association to arrange a grand protest convention at the Mansion House in London on 1 February, 1882, in order to campaign, among other things, for official British intervention. The chief organiser of this was the Liberal M.P. John Simon, himself a Jew, but William Morris and Edward Burne-Jones were also active in enlisting the support of artists and intellectuals. Attracted perhaps by notices in the press, Browning attended the London rally, but meanwhile he had received a request from Oswald John Simon, the organiser's son and a Balliol man, to put his weighty name to a petition asking the Vice-Chancellor of Oxford University to call a public meeting on the Russian persecutions. (Matthew Arnold and Frederic Harrison were among those who had already signed.) And Browning magnanimously replied on 2 February: 'No words can sufficiently express my abomination of every species of religious intolerance, and execration of such an instance of it as the late outrages in Russia astonish us with. You are quite at liberty to add my name to the Oxford requisition.'[205] Browning certainly conveyed his anger over the fate of Russian Jews to the Jewish American poet and romancer Emma Lazarus, who visited him in London in the summer of the following year.[206] In return, she very probably spoke with him about Turgenev, whom she greatly admired and who had generously praised her own work in a famous letter of 1 August 1877 which she treasured ever afterwards. Perhaps she even showed this letter to Browning, since the envelope that had contained it was subsequently found in his papers.[207]

However, the main and last proof of any preoccupation with Russia in the final years before Browning's death in Venice in 1889 is his acquaintance with old Prince G.G. Gagarin. Grigorii Grigor'evich Gagarin had been educated in Italy and France and returned to reside in Venice after a long career as diplomat, soldier, and courtier. He had known Cavour and other Italian leaders whom the Brownings had admired; but a still more important bond of sympathy between the men was art: Gagarin's talents as a conservative painter and art historian had earned him for many years the influential position of Vice-President, under the Empress, of the Russian Academy of Arts. Browning had many conversations with Gagarin, whom he appreciated for his 'crusty-old-port flavour'.[208] A mutual acquaintance describes how[209]

On one never-to-be-forgotten evening the subject of music took the place of old-time politics. To the great surprise of the prince, the poet recalled to his memory, and sang in a low, sweet voice, a number of folk-songs and national airs he had caught by ear during his short stay in Russia, more than fifty years before. First one would sing and then the other; if one hesitated for a note or phrase, the other could generally supply the deficiency, and with great spirit and mutual delight they continued the curious tournament for quite an hour. It was evident that the old music took them back to the days of their youth. The Russian expressed himself amazed at the poet's musical memory. 'It is better than my own, on which I have hitherto piqued myself not a little', he said at the time, and he often referred to the experience of that evening as the most remarkable proof of memory he ever met with.

Browning's recollection of his Russian journey, reported over half a century after the event, is indeed strong testimony to the impact of that country on his life and thought, even if it never found so strong an echo in his other works as in the unique *Ivàn Ivànovitch*.

CHAPTER 4: Algernon Charles Swinburne (1837-1909)

Of a different generation from either Tennyson or Browning, Swinburne was early influenced by an intermediate stage in English culture: the Pre-Raphaelitism of Dante Gabriel and William Michael Rossetti. He first met Dante Gabriel in Oxford in 1857, when this Rossetti, Morris and Burne-Jones were painting frescoes in the Union Debating Chamber. They were immediately attracted to each other, although Rossetti, being significantly older than Swinburne, was naturally less demonstrative than he. Nor did Dante Gabriel (unlike William Michael) always share the younger man's professed republican zeal. As his niece Helen Rossetti Angeli would afterwards recall, 'He lived in a republic of his own, outside political ideals and creations. It was bread and wine to his brother William, who never forgot Swinburne's glorious republicanism, even when it lay damp and dank under the crushing dead-weight of Watts-Duntonry. Gabriel's rare incursions into political poesy consisted of sudden and violent outbursts of disgust, after which he relapsed into his own visions.'[1] 'Watts-Duntonry' may lie on the table for a time, but Swinburne's glorious (or inglorious) republicanism will be a leitmotif in our study of his Anglo-Russian attitudes. On the other hand it needs to be said immediately that his political views, like Dante Gabriel's, were never intended to form part of any movement. However passionately he felt, he could not join in with organised societies. Not for nothing has he been dubbed 'a rhetorical poet of republicanism'.[2] Yet he did always feel for things with passion, especially when he disapproved of them. As one who knew him explained, 'Swinburne never disliked anything — he always hated or loathed it'.[3]

At the outbreak of the Crimean War, the Eton-educated youth considered Russia his playing-field. According to his own subsequent, third-person account, 'After leaving Eton near the end of his seventeenth year he wanted to go into the army. Didn't he, poor chap! The Balaklava Charge eclipsed all other visions. To be prepared for such a chance as that, instead of being prepared for Oxford, was the one dream of his life. I am sure you won't deride it because he was but a little, slightly built chap.' His mother 'was not altogether against it', but asked for 'three days to think the matter over'. The outcome was refusal by the father; and not long afterwards the youth, determined to test his courage in a more immediate way than through dreams of desperate cavalry charges, climbed up Culver Cliff near Bonchurch and in the difficult ascent nearly succumbed (or so it would seem) to a desire for self-destruction. When everything was over, his mother remonstrated: 'Nobody ever thought you were a coward, my boy.'[4]

The closest that Swinburne ever got to the Crimea was in Germany, in fact. During a European tour with his military uncle Major-General the Hon. Thomas Ashburnham in the summer of 1855, he put up in Wiesbaden at the same house as a veteran of the Alma and Balaklava battles, Captain Hedworth Hylton Jolliffe (afterwards Baron Hylton). He believed his favourite sister Edith would be pleased to learn this fact — perhaps ironically since he went on to say that the captain, now far from the scene of war, nevertheless 'employs himself on a crusade against rabbits, and has a dog which kills them to admiration'.[5] Also while at Wiesbaden, Swinburne inspected the chapel built by the late Tsar Nicholas I for the burial of Elizaveta Mikhailovna, wife of the Duke of Bavaria. He was most impressed, particularly by her monument and the painted Orthodox rood-screen, and by the fact that one visited the place in woollen slippers (in true Russian style) so as not to scratch the marble floor.[6] The Anglo-Russian conflict of this period imprinted itself upon the young poet's imagination: there is a mention or two of the Crimean War in his unfinished novel conveniently known as *Lesbia Brandon*.[7] He did not, however, write about the conflict at the time, despite a popular myth: the poem 'Peace, Peace! How soon shall we forget', published in *Fraser's Magazine* for June 1856 (p. 659) under the initials A.C.S., was in fact by Major, afterwards Sir Anthony Cunningham Sterling.[8]

Although Swinburne's entry onto the field of international politics was not so precocious as this, his instinctively inimical attitude towards Russia during the Crimean War does seem to have led directly to the first mentions of that country in his writings. The earliest comes actually in a prose work, unpublished at the time but dating no doubt from the spring of 1865. This was the essay *Of Liberty and Loyalty*.[9] In it Swinburne attacked Thomas Carlyle and his 'disciple' John Ruskin (not here named specifically) for seeking to repudiate the principles of liberty, equality and fraternity. The sage of Chelsea was already a bête noire, though he admired the force and grandeur of his capricious ideas. The last two volumes of Carlyle's famous history of Frederick the Great came out in March this year. In a long passage of the penultimate volume, only marginally relevant to the Prussian monarch but typical of the line that Carlyle had been taking for many years already, he contrasted the character and destiny of the Russians and the Poles. Poles said ruefully, 'We are become latterly the peaceable stepping-stone of Russia into Europe, and out of it; — what may be called the door-mat of Russia, useful to her feet, when she is about paying visits or receiving them!' This, at least, is how Carlyle considered things should be expressed, and went on:[10]

The Poles put fine colours on all this; and are much contented with themselves. The Russians they regard as intrinsically an inferior barbarous people; and to this day you will hear indignant Polack Gentlemen bursting out in the same strain: 'Still barbarian, sir; no culture, no literature,' — inferior because they do not make verses equal to ours! How it may be with their verses, I will not decide: but the Russians are inconceivably superior in respect that they have, to a singular degree among Nations, the gift of obeying, of being commanded. Polack Chivalry sniffs at the mention of such a gift. Polack Chivalry got sore stripes for wanting this gift. And in the end, got striped to death, and flung out of the world, for continuing blind to the want of it, and never acquiring it. Beyond all the verses in Nature, it is essential to every Chivalry and Nation and Man.

Swinburne the republican refused to believe that the philosophy proposed by Carlyle and his followers could be anything other than bondage. They called it passive obedience or loyalty, but these two were not at all the same. Loyalty was the necessary counterbalance to any personal or public liberty, but it was not 'perfection of discipline and drill' or 'unreasoning submission'; it was itself a product of free will. In extolling the 'obedience' of the modern Russian army, Carlyle seemed to be praising not loyalty at all but the absence of anything 'that serves to distinguish man from beast or beast from machine'. The obedience in question had nothing to do with conscience, honour, love or faith; it was thoroughly inhuman and involuntary. For as long as the historian-philosopher had been talking of a Frederick or a Cromwell, the reader might suppose that he meant the loyalty of enthusiasm, heroism, devotion to a leader, but with his 'Russian gospel' there could no longer be any doubt: he meant 'the naked negative quality of non-resistance'. This, Swinburne added with deep irony, was 'the invaluable quality which has made Russia a nation, as the want of it has unmade Poland. This is what more than compensates for the want of culture, of art, of poetry; "they have not (forsooth) the gift of verses, but they have the gift of obedience".'[11] It is nevertheless clear throughout this essay that Swinburne felt a grudging respect for Carlyle, whose idiosyncratic and often capricious dogmas came with all the weight of his colossal personality. As yet our young republican did not actually despise the man whom, later, he would come to hate with all the force of his own considerable mind. Perhaps he was still reluctant, in his late twenties, to set himself up publicly as a political philosopher in opposition to Carlyle, let alone to the younger Ruskin with whom he had friendly personal relations. But, for the time being, he had at least enjoyed this opportunity to clarify his own thinking about Russia and its national attributes.

Not long afterwards, Swinburne brought Russia into his poem *The Litany of Nations*, first published in *Songs before Sunrise* (1871) but begun appreciably earlier. It has been argued that a significant antecedent for this was Leigh Hunt's *The Descent of Liberty: A Masque* (1815), in which divine freedom addresses the spirits of Europe's leading states and rewards Russia with a crown for defeating Bonaparte.[12] If that is so, Swinburne's poem comes to a completely different conclusion. A chorus of the nations of the earth invokes their mother Isis, asking that in all her majesty and beauty she remember still her poor afterbirth, the children of her grey-grown age: 'Thou that badest man be born, bid man be free.' There appear in turn Greece, Italy, Spain, France, Russia, Switzerland, Germany and England, before the chorus resumes the evils that beset humanity and beseeches Earth to hear and guide. Swinburne's characterisation of each country is predictable, though subtly announced — Greece good, Spain bad, France bloodily transformed, England free but destined to be freer still 'By the beacon-bright Republic far-off sighted'. The voice of Russia, however, is ambiguous, deliberately confusing the people's supposed slavery with their potential for universal dominion:[13]

RUSSIA

I am she whose hands are strong and her eyes blinded
    And lips athirst
Till upon the night of nations many-minded
    One bright day burst:
Till the myriad stars be molten into one light,
    And that light thine;
Till the soul of man be parcel of the sunlight,
    And thine of mine.
By the snows that blanch not him nor cleanse from slaughter
    Who slays his brother;
By the stains and by the chains on me thy daughter;
    (*Cho.*) Hear us, O mother.

A curious effect of this poem was that it contributed in one way or another to the unexpectedly favourable appreciation of *Songs before Sunrise* by I.S. Turgenev. In line perhaps with his quest to understand Dante Gabriel Rossetti, seen in conversation with Carlyle and William Allingham on 2 February 1871, Turgenev was able also to make the acquaintance of Swinburne.[14] It is not completely clear when this occurred, but it was apparently at a Pre-Raphaelite crush in Ford Madox Brown's studio one evening in June or July. As Edmund Gosse afterwards remembered it, Brown presented his guests in turn to Turgenev. 'Swinburne had prepared a compliment, but tripped over something on his way to the hearthrug, and in his vexation forgot what he meant to say.' Gosse assures us that Turgenev responded graciously, but the effect must have been comic in the extreme. By now Swinburne's legendary beauty had become somewhat faded, even a little ghastly and inhuman. His blue-green-grey eyes stared out of a pallid face, his shock of red hair was more like a balloon than a part of his own body. His handshake was podgy; and when he spoke, he stood erect, feet together, and started up a kind of delirium tremens in his arms and body. None of this could have impressed Brown's distinguished Russian guest. Swinburne was nevertheless more amiable than otherwise, and his eccentricities were quickly forgotten in the warmth and range of his talk.[15] Perhaps therefore he did say something, or at least reacted interestingly to Turgenev's own conversation. Certainly Turgenev — as will be seen — would later claim to have heard more than interesting phrases from Swinburne's lips, and it does not seem that they could have met again. It has been thought that they saw each other at Tummel Bridge near Pitlochry in August, but Swinburne probably arrived there only after Turgenev had gone.[16] This is, besides, a great pity, for the anti-royalist Turgenev missed thereby some other spicy comments by Swinburne with which he might have agreed. 'The Tummel is very pretty but much defiled by memories and memorials of the royal family,' he noted, drawing particular attention to the 'phallic emblem in stone' which Queen Victoria had ordered to be erected by the waterfalls, perhaps as a monument to the late Prince Albert's virility.[17]

Whatever effect Swinburne's person may have had upon Turgenev, the poetry excited him. In a letter of 28 August 1871, written not long after his return to Baden-Baden, he promised to acquaint his friend the poet Afanasii Fet with recent English verse. It was not exactly bewitching, he said, but it did have interest, and there was one 'very, very great lyrical talent — Swinburne'.[18] Writing a year later from Paris, on 29 October 1872, Turgenev told another Russian poet friend, Iakov Polonskii: 'The latest English poets — all those Rossettis, and so on, are terribly recherché. Only in Swinburne (Algernon) are there definite flashes of talent. He imitates Victor Hugo; but he has genuine passion and gusto, whereas in Hugo all this is often contrived. Get his "Songs before Sunrise"; there are occasional obscurities, but I daresay it will give you pleasure.'[19] In another letter to Fet of 1 August 1873, Turgenev repeated that Swinburne had definite strength, declaring him 'the most remarkable of contemporary English poets'.[20] And Guy de Maupassant, who related how Turgenev would call at Flaubert's during the 1870s armed with books of foreign poetry, translating them extempore for his French associates, cited three specific instances: Goethe, Pushkin — and Swinburne. Elsewhere he said: 'Turgenev often translated Swinburne poems for me, with a lively admiration. He criticised them, too. But every artist has faults. It is enough to be an artist.'[21] All these comments are the more remarkable for the fact that *Songs before Sunrise* contained, among many other most extraordinary things, *The Litany of Nations* with its none too complimentary treatment of Russia. One may surmise that, if Turgenev paid much attention to this particular piece, he was impressed by the very vagueness of Swinburne's presentation of Russia's decidedly uncertain future and, more especially, that he admired the overall pagan, anti-Christian spirit of the poem which (as in his own philosophy) portrays human beings as appendages of dubious significance upon the vast eternity of nature.

As far as can be told, the admiration was by no means mutual. The compliment which Gosse says became stuck on Swinburne's lips never disengaged itself — or at least not into print. To judge by the catalogue of a sale held in 1916, he possessed no works by Turgenev in his voluminous library (nor indeed any Russian books at all — unless of course the auctioneers did not think it worth while listing them).[22] Like most English writers of the period, his tastes in foreign literature were on the whole conventional, though he entertained a notorious adulation for Victor Hugo as Turgenev had realised. Through his interest in contemporary French literature he had at one point, curiously enough, come across a work by Gogol. This was the great comedy *Revizor* (The Inspector General), in an inept translation by Prosper Mérimée. Remembering the play many years afterwards, Swinburne would call it merely a 'slight social comedy or farce', but he admitted having found it at the time 'very witty, original, and amusing'.[23] However, that was perhaps the extent of his knowledge of Russian literature until very much later in life. Even in 1877, when recalling *Revizor*, he no longer knew its title or its author and needed to check these with a colleague. His idea then (which never came to fruition) was to collaborate with Edmund Gosse, William Michael Rossetti and others on a biographical dictionary of European dramatists. As well as English authors, there would be French, Italian, German, Scandinavian and Spanish sections, and 'if there are any Muscovites (dash and blank them), as I believe there are,' he said, 'we might apply to the Russophil Ralston.'[24] Similarly, in a long critique of John Nichol's *Tables of European Literature and History*, written about this same time, Swinburne failed to note that it included several Russians: Lomonosov, Derzhavin, Karamzin, Krylov, Pushkin, Lermontov, Herzen and (peculiarly) the traveller and diarist A.I. Turgenev whom Nichol may have confused with the novelist. Given that the spellings were often strange — like 'Kriroff' for Krylov and 'Pousckin' for Pushkin, — the Russian content of the *Tables* could scarcely be taken seriously, but the fact is that Swinburne chose to ignore its existence entirely.[25]

In the earlier years, things Russian were nevertheless kept in Swinburne's consciousness through friends. William Ralston he had known at least since 1862, and loved to listen to his public recitals of Russian stories. He attended one such occasion in the St George's Hall, surrounded in the front row by a bevy of half-admiring, half-taunting pre-Raphaelite ladies showing their enthusiasm. Among the tales they heard was 'one about a witch whose room was ornamented with the skulls of her victims'. The kinky poet was presumably delighted.[26] Swinburne could also have learnt of recent developments in Russia from an Oxford teacher whose friendship he greatly prized, the Italian patriot Aurelio Saffi. During his English exile Saffi had become a close associate of Alexander Herzen's, and himself wrote occasional pieces on Russia such as 'Le nazionalità slave e il panslavismo' (1859) and, much later, 'Per i profughi russi' (1884).[27] Swinburne would later dedicate two poems *In Memory of Aurelio Saffi*, written respectively in April 1890 and March 1896.[28]

Swinburne also of course received echoes of Russian critical attitudes to his poetry. Though not much noticed in Russia at the time, it started to impress some individual readers. In the autumn of 1872 he apparently received, through a third party, fulsome but intelligent praise from a certain Princess Orloff.[29] This was presumably the sensitive and cultured Ekaterina Nikolaevna Orlova, née Trubetskaya, wife of the Imperial Russian ambassador to France. Turgenev was perhaps a link here, since he had for long been friendly with the princess and her family. But other quite different rumours about Swinburne that would soon come to the poet's ear may also have originated with Turgenev. As the years went by, it became clear that the novelist's views of him were more complex than had at first appeared. Polonskii recalled a conversation in which he said of Swinburne 'He has power, but the power that irritates. He has fire, but lacks that artistic form, that measure, which is necessary to keep any lyricism, even the most fervent, in proper check. His appeal is that of a raving demagogue and revolutionary, but he isn't *popular*. There are those who run after him, but as they would run after scandal. He is read and liked by the young, by hotheads.' In a comparison with Maupassant, Turgenev further declared that if the Frenchman's depravity resembled that of Casanova, Swinburne's was more like that of the Marquis de Sade — both frenzied and insane. The rest of what he said was apparently censored.[30] Some may hesitate to accept this as an accurate report. Certainly Polonskii makes Turgenev state, for example, that he had never met the English poet, whereas we know that he had. Only recently, moreover, in a tantalisingly brief meeting with young George Moore at the Elysée Montmartre in Paris, Turgenev had reaffirmed his appreciation of Swinburne's genius despite (again) the imitation of Hugo.[31] The reference to de Sade in the Polonskii account is nevertheless convincing in relation to a host of other anecdotes.

The fact is that Swinburne was acquiring a quite scandalous reputation, both in England and abroad. How much of it was true is still a matter for debate. Dante Gabriel Rossetti is said to have described him as 'full of modern revolutionary fire and the courage of an ancient morality, whereof his personal conduct was as innocent as a child's'.[32] William Michael Rossetti was able to declare, 'As to indecency, Swinburne is not in his own conduct even up to the average of immorality', and according to another authority he was, 'from the sex point of view, as chaste as driven snow. All his "sins" were literary sins. His life was blameless.' It even seems that, in order to test this out, some of Swinburne's friends once put an actress in his bed, and all he did was talk to her of French literature.[33] Of similar inoffensiveness and fun was the plot, around 1859, to send him dressed as a *miss anglaise* to teach George Sand the degraded state of emancipated womanhood.[34] In a strong outburst of personal vanity Swinburne declared in a letter to Gosse of October 1879 how disgusted he was by the attempts of unnamed adversaries, once friends, to peddle him the reputation of a pederast and bestial with their 'obscene false anecdotes about my private eccentricities of indecent indulgence as exhibited in real or imaginary *lupanaria*'.[35]

On the other hand Gosse himself, who was criticised for not telling the truth about the Swinburne he had known, complained that one of the many constraints upon him had been a very heavy 'sexual embargo'.[36] He might have added: an embargo on drunkenness. Although undoubtedly exaggerated, reports of Swinburne's disorderly behaviour at the London Arts Club, jumping on committee members' hats and 'belching out blasphemy and bawdry', were too common to be untrue.[37] On the sexual plane, Swinburne certainly had unorthodox proclivities, in part but not exclusively intellectual. More seriously in the modern sense, no one who has read through his correspondence would have any doubt that he was fascinated by violence, and especially by corporal chastisement. He thought a few minutes' torment from the birch a preferable punishment for schoolboy misbehaviour to several hours' literary discomfort from impositions; and he also believed the absence of caning in continental teaching systems to be (as he put it) their 'fundamental' flaw.[38] In this respect at least he was certainly a sadist; and what is more, he delighted in de Sade. The promise of a loan of *Justine* from Richard Monckton Milnes had him 'in panting expectation', and in an extraordinary letter to the same correspondent, written in French in imitation of the Marquis, he expostulated: 'Voilà, je l'espère, une idée assez appétissante: manger tout vif un cul d'enfant cuit dans son propre sang, servi à l'huile, au lard, à la neige, et tout cela dans un même instant. Ah! monsieur, quel plaisir inexprimable que de réunir ainsi par un seul trait de génie Néron, Apicius, Orbilius, et Ivan-le-Terrible!'[39] It is true that the republican Swinburne tended to bring in the misdeeds of monarchs somewhat casually, after the fashion of Byron. He loved to make allusion to the Russian episodes in *Don Juan*, doubtless for their prurient information on the Great Catherine about whom he liked to joke.[40] It is also true that his self-parodic *Poeta loquitur*, written in 1880, suggests that one should not take everything he said too seriously:[41]

> In my poems, with ravishing rapture
>> Storm strikes me and strokes me and stings:
> But I'm scarcely the bird you might capture
>> Out of doors in the thick of such things.
>
> ....
>
> All the pale past's red record of history
>> Is dusty with damnable deeds;
>
> ....
>
> But my would-be maleficent verses
>> Are nothing but wind.

However, it is hard to take *this* too seriously, the more so as Swinburne never published the poem in his lifetime: who would ever have believed it?

It is against this background that one needs to read the story, supposedly told at a Goncourt dinner in Paris, of how Swinburne had served up to a homosexual friend his favourite but over-jealous monkey. Most of those present were shocked and sickened by this, but Turgenev, putting down his coffee, interrupted: 'I know Swinburne personally, and fairly well. It is definitely true that anything may be expected of him, as he is hardly a normal human being. I once asked him, in fun, which original and most improbable experience he would best enjoy, and he replied: "To take St Genevieve at the most passionate and ecstatic moment of her prayers, and to do so with her tacit approval."'[42] Wild as it may seem, the alleged remark about St Genevieve is consistent with similar and well-documented statements by the poet, with the probable proviso only that it would not have been he, but an imagined hero, who would take such pleasure in the saint. Swinburne had something of an obsession with saints and martyrs, from the time when he visited the grave of eleven thousand virgins in Cologne in 1855 to his comment in 1876 that St Theresa of Avila was 'the Christian Sappho'.[43] His preoccupation with disparate experiences conjointly undergone can be seen in many private letters. He loved to contrast supposedly natural functions with supposedly unnatural ones. In a characteristically pathetic letter to a friend on the pleasures of reciprocal swishing, he once made the interesting point that: 'The Russians with their daily use of it at meals and baths are more delicately civilised than we.'[44]

The context in which Turgenev made his reported remark about Swinburne and St Genevieve has nevertheless been garbled. It derives at second hand from the Russian artist A.A. Kharlamov, who in turn said that the monkey story was related by the playwright and librettist Ludovic Halévy, who had been told it by a friend, who had met Swinburne actually in the Isle of Wight. Kharlamov wished there could have been a stenographer present to record it in more exact detail, but in fact there was, in a sense — the diarist Edmond de Goncourt. It is clear that the conversation about Swinburne took place at Flaubert's apartment in the rue Murillo on Sunday 28 February 1875. Kharlamov was indeed in Paris at this time, occupied in painting his celebrated portrait of Turgenev. Turgenev does seem to have gone to Flaubert's on the evening in question, and it would have been quite natural for him to take Kharlamov along.[45] The painter would not, however, have been familiar with the other guests, nor accustomed to the sort of repartee that they indulged in. Goncourt tells us — and he is clearly right — that Maupassant, not Halévy, was the narrator of the shocking story about Swinburne. It even seems unlikely that Halévy ever mixed with Flaubert or the Goncourt circle during the period in question. Moreover, despite the very lurid notes in Goncourt's diary, the monkey is not said to have been offered as a dish — though some of the food that Maupassant ate at Swinburne's seemed of very dubious origin. Actually, the greater villain of the piece for Maupassant and company was the Welshman George Powell, Swinburne's host and friend.

The events reported by Maupassant occurred at Etretat in 1868, when the bard was holidaying in Powell's thatched flint cottage dubbed (sadically) 'Chaumière de Dolmancé'. Maupassant was also staying in the vicinity. While taking a swim in the morning of (as it seems) Friday 20 September, Swinburne was suddenly carried out to sea through a rocky archway by an undercurrent of the kind for which the local coast is renowned. Both Maupassant and Powell made independent efforts to save him, but he was meantime picked up over two miles from the shore by a fishing smack bound for neighbouring Yport. He afterwards described the incident as a 'lark', saying he had had no fear of octopuses, which do not attack, and had no religious thoughts on contemplating death.[46] This did not, however, stop him from writing a poem, *Ex-Voto*, which rehearsed his obviously frightening experience.[47] Powell invited Maupassant to dinner for his pains, and it was now that he saw old skeletons, the wizened hand of a parricide, obscene photographs and drawings — and the monkey, Nip. On another visit, he learnt that a servant had hanged this last so as not to have to keep cleaning up its mess.[48]

The monkey anecdote, with various accretions more or less sickening or obscene, continued to do the rounds of French literary society until at least as late as 1911. At that time Edmund Gosse resumed the story and, in correspondence with Henry James, discovered that in 1875-76 the American novelist had also heard tell of it at Flaubert's.[49] Somewhere along the line, Swinburne himself became aware of the much embroidered legend, as also perhaps of the fact that Maupassant was using various aspects of their encounter at Etretat for his stories *La Main de l'écorché* (1875) and *L'Anglais d'Etretat* (1882).[50] When the nasty rumours finally reached the French press and were echoed in England, Swinburne protested forcefully to the *World* of 6 December 1882 that practically everything was false from start to finish.[51]

We have come some way from the subject of Swinburne and Russia, but the sort of man that he was should by now be very evident. He was not afraid to stick his nose into anything that amused him, yet disliked to be reproached for doing so. In politics, as in other things, he was a curious mixture. By temperament not obviously political at all, he said more than once that he had no aspiration to be anything but a poet; but he expressed radical opinions on so many things that he early gained a reputation as a sort of Red and indeed in 1868 was invited to stand for Parliament on behalf of the Reform League. Mazzini, whom he revered above all others as a political reformer, advised him not to accept, but he continued to make potentially dangerous statements about revolutionary causes and was proud to be called a republican. He rejoiced, of course, in being unorthodox in politics as in every other experience. And yet he was in some ways closer to the Tories than to the Liberals, being himself of somewhat aristocratic tendencies. Indeed, he was further right than *The Times*, which he equated with the Irish *Skibbereen Eagle* for its royal 'We have our eye on Russia'. His own paper was the *Daily Telegraph*.[52] Not surprisingly, therefore, he was notoriously hostile to Gladstone whom he dubbed alternately as 'Gladsniff' and 'Mr Sadstone' and mocked in his poem 'All Is Gladness, All Is Joy'.[53] Indeed, it was not so much Liberalism as the actions of individual Liberals that so disgusted Swinburne. With regard to Anglo-Russian relations, at least, he asserted that 'the self-styled "Liberals" in this country have covered themselves with ...inexpressible ridicule and disgrace.'[54]

The reference here is to the Eastern Question of the mid-1870s. But the Eastern Question, for the British, started with the Bulgarian atrocities of 1876. This was a bad beginning for Swinburne, for the very word 'Bulgarian' amused him greatly, as a cognate of 'bugger'. As early as 1871 he said that leading organs of the press had 'proved their kinship to the most sanguinary tribe of Bulgarians' by ignoring his *Songs of the Sierras*. The phrase 'sanguinary Bulgarian' then became for him a standard term of abuse, a facetious euphemism for 'bloody bugger'.[55] It was perhaps not surprising that he should have difficulty in taking real Bulgarians seriously. His attention was first drawn to the Bulgarian issue, characteristically, by a circumstance that he found more derisory than otherwise. A man called (as the poet styled him) '*Sadick* Bey' was raping hundreds of girls — girls, note, and not boys; but in *Bulgarian* usage, no doubt (the poet imagined), 'girl' was a periphrasis for 'boy'.[56] This was at the beginning of 1876. Already by then, the Turks were putting down with what they asked the world to believe was a minimum of force a desperate Bulgarian insurrection. In June, news of pillage, burning, torture, rape, and the mutilation and murder of many thousands of children, women and old men began to shock Western readers as much as it had for long infuriated the Russian coreligionists of these Slavonic victims. The *Spectator*, the *Daily News* and then *The Times* carried ever more lurid reports.[57] Hard as it is to say, Swinburne showed not the slightest compassion for the suffering Bulgarians themselves; he used the current terminology — 'Bulgarian atrocity', and the like — only to characterise some literary misdeed or other of the *Contemporary Review*.[58]

What, if anything, can be said in Swinburne's defence? He was certainly not in general a heartless person: one has only to adduce his views on the Irish question, where his humanitarian sympathies extended *both* to the innocent victims of Republican extremists *and* to imprisoned Fenians themselves; indeed, his public and private views on Ireland were among the fairest and most progressive of his time. To compare his attitude to Russia and to Ireland is natural, besides, because the two were associated in his mind: on one occasion he referred to a Gaelic enemy as 'O'Brienoff'.[59] Perhaps, then, he was to some extent misinformed — or maybe blinded — as to the true nature of Turkish atrocities in Bulgaria? Certainly, he had come to be persuaded that Gladstonite liberals were committed to reverse the truth in everything: in their parlance, he asserted, truth became falsehood, and the Russian people were free. Later in life he would qualify a satirical attack on Gladstone's Irish policy with the words 'living as I do under a worse than Russian despotism'.[60] In other words, Swinburne found himself forced — or maybe forced himself — to believe that whoever was in favour of Russian rule deserved contempt and condemnation. Thus the Bulgarians, in appealing to the Tsar to save them, committed a greater crime in his eyes than any experienced by themselves. One needs to remember, finally, that Swinburne the atheist could not have any sympathy for Christians qua Christians, and particularly not for those in (for him) hypocritical Orthodox or Catholic rites. He once spoke of God's 'wallowing in human blood and revelling in human agony from Moscow to Valparaiso', and in calling his poem *Athens* an 'anti-Christian and anti-Russian ode' he said that if the Greeks themselves should laugh at it, this would prove only that 'modern Hellas is an annexe of the Kingdom of Bulgaria'.[61]

Swinburne's hostility to Russia was undoubtedly modelled upon, or at least to some extent influenced by, that of his old Oxford teacher Benjamin Jowett. He had immense admiration for Jowett — and also some fear of him — as a man, as a mind, and as a critic of his poetry.[62] Jowett had for long been deeply suspicious of Russia's international ambitions. Britain had never been sufficiently aware of them, right up to the outbreak of the Crimean War which, in his book, had been rendered necessary as much by the peace speeches of Cobden and Bright as by government policy. He believed that Russia was a 'semi-civilised intriguing power', which took advantage of every suitable occasion. During the Franco-Prussian War he saw it lurking in the wings, waiting for the slightest cue to come on stage. Long before the Bulgarian atrocities of 1876, he understood that England might easily be outwitted in the East by a Russia which would make a fuss over India in order to gain Constantinople.[63] His view of the atrocities themselves was very rational. On 17 October, 1876, he wrote a most remarkable letter to an unnamed friend who could well have been Swinburne. The English were 'spouting' about them, he said, as if they themselves had never committed similar crimes in India or Jamaica. They were lecturing the Turks without the least intention of doing anything about it. Meanwhile war came nearer day by day and Russia grew 'bolder and more openly treacherous'. Never was politician so deluded as Gladstone. Oh for a Palmerston again! Russia now might not seem so very strong, but in ten years' time it would rule, not just the Black Sea but the Mediterranean east of Italy. The eleventh hour had already struck; Russia must be stopped by force of arms. 'When the English people awake to the fact that for more than four months they and their government have been simply the dupes of Russia, their indignation will be great. But they will not know whom to blame — the opposition? the ministry? themselves?'[64]

None of this excuses Swinburne's own seemingly callous attitude, of course — although he was by no means alone in demonstrating it. A comment that he made to an American correspondent reveals a sensitive and conscious understanding of his own position. British feeling at large was against Russia as it had been against the North in the American Civil War — for reasons of self-interest and patriotism. In both instances, Swinburne found himself with some embarrassment to be on the same side as public opinion.[65]

Then, as now on the Eastern question, I found myself (an Englishman of the same class by birth and of the same opinions by instinct as Shelley and Landor and Byron) utterly opposed to the current of English radicalism — and yet, unable to deny, or disguise from myself, that the mass of Englishmen on my side had adopted the same view for reasons opposite to mine and on principles which I detested and despised. In such a case, it seems to me, the only thing for a loyal and honourable man to do is to hold fast to his own instincts and principles in spite of friend or foe, regardless of the reluctance and regret he must naturally feel to find himself arrayed (it may be) against men whom he respects, in the company of men whom he assuredly does not.

As this intriguing statement makes clear, Swinburne's views were based on what he took to be the instinct of his class. They were, essentially, loyal, in the sense that ancient British values should not be trampled over and destroyed, and had nothing to do with the dictatorship of the rabble. It is worth recalling that Queen Victoria herself, despite the recent marriage of her son the Duke of Edinburgh to the daughter of the Tsar, instinctively believed Russia's designs in the Balkans to be primarily imperial and exhorted Lord Beaconsfield to scotch them with force of arms; she said that, were she a man, she would enlist against the Russians, and at one point even threatened to abdicate if a British fleet was not sent to the Dardanelles.[66] Swinburne's own perspective was thus of the highest pedigree. It is, besides, a measure of the complexity of the Bulgarian debate that another leader in the anti-Russian camp was Karl Marx.[67]

As first-hand accounts of the atrocities came in, sixpenny and shilling pamphlets started to roll off the London and provincial presses in a frenzied war of words. Gladstone, boiling with zeal and rage, set the tone for the liberal and humanitarian side in his *Bulgarian Horrors, and the Question of the East*. Completed at Hawarden on 5 September 1876 and published soon afterwards by John Murray, this celebrated brochure (which, incidentally, was immediately translated into Russian and published in St Petersburg in many thousands of copies),[68] made a reasoned, double plea: for protest against the Turkish authorities, and for humanitarian relief in the Balkans. He followed it up with passionate speeches to gigantic meetings at Blackheath and elsewhere, and soon had the whole country astir. Admirers spoke of 'his magic voice and delivery', reducing knots of hecklers to rapt silence.[69] He said he was not so naive as to suppose that Russia had no selfish ambition, but the 'pulse of humanity' was at present throbbing through its people's veins.[70] He even went so far as to declare: 'The Emperor of Russia is a gentleman, and a great benefactor to his people, and I believe the people of Russia to be capable of as noble sentiments as any people in Europe.'[71] In this atmosphere, a Bulgarian

Relief Fund was set up of which Viscountess Strangford became prime mover, organising makeshift hospitals in Bulgaria itself under the most dangerous conditions.[72]

Gladstone was backed up by writers of varying emotional intensity. Some took the line: 'I told you so.' The historian Edward Freeman, who already in December 1875 had stated in the *Fortnightly Review* that he could never understand why the British should denounce the oppression of the Russian but 'uphold the far blacker oppression of the Turk', bounced back in October 1876 with talk of the 'bloody fields of Bulgaria' thanks to which the 'wicked power of the Turk' was now doomed: the great powers should simply come together to destroy him.[73] Other commentators, such as Humphry Sandwith, C.B., author of *Shall We Fight Russia? An Address to the Working Men of Great Britain*, were still more violently anti-Turk, though some pamphlets gave complex, even abstruse reasons why Britain should stand back and watch; such was *That Unconscionable Turk, and What to Do with Him*, by 'Veritatis Vindex'. Some good churchmen, including the Bishop of Lincoln (Christopher Wordsworth) jumped in with pamphlets like *The Mohammedan Woe and its Passing Away* in order to express the view that Biblical prophecy could be achieved by Russian successes in Turkey.[74] But the overall tone was changing. Impartial intellectuals started to bring out backgrounding brochures: in October and November there appeared, for instance, two separate editions of Henry Sutherland Edwards's *The Slavonian Provinces of Turkey: An Historical, Ethnological, and Political Guide to Questions at Issue in These Lands*, originally written for the *Pall Mall Gazette*. Some other moderate writers were appealing for calm. One of the most sensitive of these was H.A. Munro-Butler-Johnstone, who pleaded for 'friendly authoritative remonstrance, in order to bring about a new order of things in Turkey'. The Turks, after all, were human and could change. Britain should help them, he argued, not despise or destroy this great and noble people.[75]

The tide, then, was already turning and, as the year progressed, more and more writers joined a growing anti-Russian camp. The different stages of the public debate throughout this summer and autumn are vividly reflected in the pages of *Punch*. On 17 June it carried a cartoon called 'The Dogs of War' which shows a Russian holding back, but perhaps preparing to unleash, four Balkan hounds upon a re-treating Turk. An English bobby looks over the fence and says: 'Take care, my man! It might be awkward if you was to let 'em loose!' In a cartoon of 22 July the same dogs are seen leaping up at the Turk, while Europe's crowned heads and statesmen fold their arms and watch. In neither picture, interestingly enough, is there a specifically Bulgarian dog. On 5 August Turks are shown butchering Bulgarian women and children, and Britannia appeals to Disraeli to take action; but he will not do so as he cannot find any mention of atrocities in the official reports. The varying international perspectives on the crisis are neatly and satirically rendered in a piece on 12 August where Mr Punch considers 'The Eastern Question in the Future'. In the Russian view, by 1880 the Emperor will be crowned 'Czar of all the Russias, Greece, and both the Turkeys'. In the English view, the Balkan peoples will enjoy cheap omnibuses and penny ice-creams, and the Sultan will establish a Turkish House of Lords and a Constantinople underground railway. As for the Turks themselves, the future holds loans, loans, and more loans, to let them make war on everybody. However, by 4 November the public mood is vacillating again, as England's 'doubtful diplomacy' is seen to have driven all the oppressed peoples of the Turkish empire into the welcoming arms of the Bear, and on 2 December a cartoon 'Friends or Foes?' shows the Bear and the Lion face to face, wondering whether to fight, to go their different ways, or to proceed together down the road to the dismemberment of Turkey.[76]

Most pamphlets had by now become more or less openly hostile to the Tsar. *Holy Russia and Mr. Gladstone: A Protest*, by 'B.C.S.', claimed that half the British press must actually be owned by Russia, for people to have believed it for so long. Among the more remarkable authors who stood out against Russia and its schemes was Alfred Austin, publicist and poet (later to be laureate). He had for long been suspicious of the Tsar's international policies and had even sought out contact with dissidents like Bakunin.[77] He published two responses to Gladstone: *Tory Horrors; or, The Question of the Hour*, and *Russia before Europe*. His basic argument was cool and clever. Every English person, he averred, must be disgusted by Turkish misrule and wish it to be reformed. All Europe, indeed, was of this same opinion. The only difficulty was that Russia saw the liberation of the Balkans as its own special mission, and those who resisted Russian designs were thus inevitably considered Turkey-lovers and supporters of torture and infamy. The truth was the contrary, for the Bulgarian massacres lay ultimately 'at the door of Russian diplomacy and Russian ambition'.[78] Austin piled detail on historical detail to show that, if Russia did indeed free the Balkan peoples, then the Turks themselves would certainly be exterminated from the face of the earth. Nor should one believe, he said, that this was an anti-Moslem crusade. It was sheer aggrandisement: one had only to recall the fate of Christian Poland in order to predict the future. As he put it, 'a week of Bulgarian Horrors, even at their worst, is a small matter compared with a century of Russian Horrors and Polish Horrors'.[79] And let Gladstone beware: while he was idling away his time on pamphlets which should really be entitled 'Tory Horrors; or, The Question between Lord Beaconsfield and Myself', Britain could be heading for 'benevolent suicide'. While Gladstone was campaigning for humanity, English power and prestige might for ever disappear.[80]

Austin's pamphlets were enormously popular and influential. *Tory Horrors*, in particular, ran into many thousands of copies. The Queen herself spoke warmly of it to Lord Beaconsfield (formerly Disraeli) who, writing to inform Austin of this fact, declared: 'It is a spirited composition, and, what is rare in pamphlets in these days, it is true.' There is reason to believe that Swinburne, too, may have been impressed by Austin's arguments. He always took note of this colleague's judgments and had recently been most flattered by his favourable review of *Bothwell*.[81] The Eastern Question was certainly a point of clear agreement between them. As the initial pro-Russian stance had gathered impetus, Swinburne was increasingly alarmed by the current of Radical opinion in support of his bugbear. He could not countenance what he called 'this outbreak of English sympathy with suffering Bulgars', which extended even into quarters where he had previously been unable 'to find or awaken a spark on behalf of Italy, Hungary, or Poland'.[82]

Many, of course, have found such an attitude strange. Disregarding other people's hypocrisy, suffering Bulgarians would seem to fit very well with suffering Italians, suffering Hungarians and suffering Poles. As an ardent republican who always pretended to celebrate the fourteenth of July as the great feast-day of the year, and who not so long ago had composed an *Ode on the Proclamation of the French Republic, September 4th, 1870*,[83] Swinburne could presumably at least have wished a republic on the Bulgarians as he had wished one on other repressed peoples. His 'republicanism' seemed to have changed its definition during the last few years. Bernard Shaw would note, 'He was an odd phenomenon, this supporter of Dublin Castle who was a republican and regicide when Russia was in question', and William Michael Rossetti was one of many who would gladly have agreed with Cecil Lang's pithy formulation: 'The most cosmopolitan of English poets was transformed into the most parochial and chauvinistic of British jingoes.'[84] But Swinburne himself saw no contradiction, any more than the general British public did. In the French case, an Emperor had become extravagant and deserved to be removed; in the Russian, another Emperor was extending his sway and needed to be countered. It was a matter of practical politics, and the suffering of a people was not in itself a sufficient cause for action.

Friends who shared Swinburne's views on the Eastern Question but dared not openly proclaim them urged him to make a public declaration. For a long time he held off, but he was finally spurred into action by Carlyle's famous pro-Russian letter to a friend, published in *The Times* of 28 November, recommending 'that the unspeakable Turk should be immediately struck out of the question'. At first Swinburne considered sending a response to the press, but he had no influence with either *The Times* or the *Pall Mall Gazette* and feared that the only paper of which he thought much — the *Daily News* — would decline a letter of his own political persuasion. He therefore quickly saw that a pamphlet could be more appropriate and indeed the piece soon far outgrew the dimensions of a normal contribution to the press. As he wrote, he came under the influence of an article by Frederic Harrison called 'Cross and Crescent', published in the *Fortnightly Review* on 1 December.

Harrison began with a premise which, he said, was irrefutable: 'The existing rule of the Porte is scandalously evil, and its system abominably corrupt.' But he quickly pointed out that Turkey was not all bad, and still had intrinsic justification as well as practical usefulness for Europe. Where would things end if the powers were to annihilate whatever did not please them? It was not a question of dislodging the government of the Porte; it was potentially a new crusade, the extirpation of a race of millions of Mohammedans. No European nation had the right to undertake such a war, for 'The crimes in Bulgaria differ in degree, and not in kind, from the crimes of Christian nations.' With cool aplomb he asked: 'If the Turks are to be expelled from Europe, why are the Russians to be endured in Poland, or the Germans to be endured in Lorraine?' However, there was more. If the Turks were removed, who would take their place? The Russians, maybe? But 'the Russians are as capable of fanaticism for the Cross as Moslems of fanaticism for Islam.' In a marvellous concatenation of arguments, a tour de force of rationalism, Harrison went on to show that it could only be in the Russians' interest for Britain to raise a hypocritical Cross against the corrupt Crescent of Turkey.[85] Swinburne, of course, did not see things so peaceably, but he found the article by Harrison a breath of sanity in the face of liberal Russia-lovers. 'What a thoroughly and every way admirable paper on the Eastern business!' he expostulated to his friend Theodore Watts, who helped him place his own eventual brochure with the publishers Chatto and Windus.[86]

Note of an English Republican on the Muscovite Crusade was written in less than a week, beginning on 29 November, 1876. Its title was fixed from the start. Swinburne gladly put his own name to it, and sought to dedicate the work to his old friend Karl Blind, himself (as Swinburne believed) 'a Republican opponent of the Muscovite or Panslavonic Crusade at the repeated risk of his life even in London'. This did not, however, prove possible owing to scruples on the part of

Swinburne's publishers as well as to second thoughts of his own regarding a possible misinterpretation of his purpose by 'fellow' French republicans. He was in fact caused some embarrassment by a rumour of his original intention reaching the press, though this was luckily smoothed over by Blind's generosity.[87] Sending the finished manuscript to Watts on 5 December, Swinburne expressed a sense of urgency in wishing it to appear immediately and in no case later than Christmas. He even requested a specific colour for the cover, which must be either green or a sober red, and confessed he was 'as curious as a boy on his first rush into print' to see reviews of the pamphlet.[88] *Note of an English Republican on the Muscovite Crusade* was in fact published ten days earlier than Christmas, at the price of one shilling and (without explanation) with a pale blue cover like Gladstone's own — which had cost one and sixpence. Two thousand copies of it were printed in all. Although the meticulous Swinburne was displeased by textual blemishes introduced by the publisher or the printer and left uncorrected despite his insistent remonstrations, the visual effect of the *Note* is impressive.[89]

The tenor and substance of Swinburne's brochure should by now be obvious. The would-be modest author of the *Note* did seek to keep the play clean, as it were: he refrained from making a historical connection between the Bulgars and the 'universal European significance of their very name', and likewise forbore from any mention of Sadyk (alias Sadique) Pasha, the erstwhile Slavonic Turk whose cruel behaviour amply reflected the resemblance between his name and that of the Marquis himself.[90] This Polish-Ukrainian writer and adventurer turned Moslem, originally known as Michał Czajkowski, author of *The Moslem and the Christian; or, Adventures in the East* (1855), was of course the subject of Russian as well as of British taunts. Musorgskii could not not resist dubbing his fellow composer Tchaikovsky 'Sadyk Pasha'.[91] Currently Turkish ambassador to Paris, Sadyk Pasha was much in the news when Swinburne's *Note* appeared. He absolutely denied that any Bulgarians had been massacred. 'All that happened was in the most natural way,' he said, 'in regular fighting between disciplined troops and insurgents.'[92] Ignoring all this, Swinburne's pamphlet was a virulent yet reasoned attack upon the credibility of Russia, with the premise that one should 'have exactly as much reliance on the good intentions of a Czar as on the lachrymal gland of a crocodile' (p. 20). From Peter to Alexander, the Russian monarchs were a veritable 'House of Atreus' (p. 23). No more need be said about the anti-Russian side of the *Note*.

More interesting, perhaps, is its role as a refutation of Carlyle, the 'Ancient Enemy' and 'venerable Philobulgar', 'the filthy and virulent old Arch-Quack of Chelsea'.[93] He was too serious an opponent to be simply ignored. The public and private hostility between the two men was by now long-standing and bitter. Carlyle's view of Swinburne was reportedly that 'he sits in a cesspool and adds to it'. Swinburne responded that Carlyle was leader of a dirty, chattering bunch of apes; he was 'St Thomas Cloacinus' or 'T. Coprostom'.[94] Carlyle's complaint about Swinburne was the obvious and conventional one about his supposed immorality; Swinburne attacked Carlyle for his pretension and hypocrisy. The two men were complete opposites in what, for Swinburne, were the most important matters of all: poetry and republicanism.[95] But Swinburne still had some respect for Carlyle and hoped to achieve a deferential tone. He wanted his rejoinder to rest not on emotion, but on intellectual arguments based on political precedents.

One of these hinged upon atrocities perpetrated in 1865 by Edward John Eyre, Governor of Jamaica. Controversy over this had been raging among politicians and intellectuals for very many years. Already in December 1865 a reported clash between Gladstone and Tennyson exemplified the opposing points of view, the one attacking Eyre's unnecessary brutality, the other maintaining that savage people sometimes needed savage handling.[96] Nor was the parallel between Jamaica and Bulgaria, made by Swinburne in his pamphlet, a completely new one. As early as July 1876 W.T. Stead (whom Swinburne detested, incidentally, for his 'noisome adulation of Muscovite hypocrisy and tyranny') had angrily rejected the view that current Turkish atrocities could in any way be condoned by reference to the actions of Governor Eyre.[97] Swinburne himself felt personal animosity against Eyre, whose earlier exploits in Australia had made him a hero for British youth, and in 1872 he had applauded the forthright views of his mentor Benjamin Jowett on the British government's kid-glove treatment of Eyre: 'A generation ago', Jowett had expostulated angrily, 'we should have hanged him.'[98] Swinburne's publishers tried in vain to remove the references to Eyre, but did contrive to water them down a little. Such tampering with his text was doubly distressing as some friends of his, particularly Jowett, felt that he had already gone too far in deferring to Carlyle — given that gentleman's 'lust of tyranny' and 'letch for dirt' (phrases which Jowett either uttered or confirmed).[99] The link here with Carlyle is the abhorrent phrase 'beneficent whip' which Swinburne cites at the opening of his pamphlet (p. 4) and which derives obliquely from Carlyle's *Occasional Discourse on the Nigger Question*.[100] Purporting to be not actually by himself, and certainly not completely representative of his views, this extraordinary document was nevertheless launched upon a suspecting world with Carlyle's full authority in 1849. His voice comes through clearly in the proposition that black men — like whites, indeed, — must work if they are to eat, and that if they do not work they must be made to. This is why the whip could be beneficent, in the service of economic progress in the colonies.[101] It is interesting that the libertarian John Stuart Mill had immediately riposted with his own views on the 'Negro Question' in the same journal, *Fraser's Magazine*, which had first printed Carlyle's effusion. Later, Carlyle had been much angered by the prosecution of Eyre, and sought to help defend him, arguing that he was 'a just, humane, and valiant man'. The English had always loved order, and promptly suppressed sedition. What else had Eyre been guilty of?[102]

Although Swinburne used the Eyre issue as one important ground for attacking Carlyle and other 'Bulgarians', it should not be supposed that he himself felt as intensely about the West Indies as he did about Russia. In March 1881 he would be deeply gratified to learn that the great Herbert Spencer had read *The Muscovite Crusade* and considered it 'something to be preserved as an example of magnificent writing'; Carlyle's credo and 'absurd inconsistency' had been uncovered in it with 'extreme power and pungency'. But Swinburne was definitely not prepared to act on Spencer's suggestion that he turn his 'marvellous powers of expressing well-justified anger' in a public condemnation of Britain's own current behaviour in Afghanistan and southern Africa, making a 'scathing exposure of the contrast between our Christian creed and pagan doings, our professed philanthropy and our actual savagery'.[103] What Spencer had clearly failed to understand was that *The Muscovite Crusade* had been, primarily, a forceful attack on Russia and its English supporters, and only secondarily an attempt to show up British hypocrisy and colonial misrule.

The reviews of Swinburne's pamphlet, few in number, were unfavourable either by their overt hostility or by their condescension. On 23 December he read those in the 'weekly and weakly four' — the *Academy*, the *Athenaeum*, the *Examiner* and the *Spectator* — and approved of none. The first drew no specific response from him; the second he found merely 'civil'; the third was pretty-pretty, insincere; and the fourth, headed 'Swinburne versus Carlyle', he attacked for the 'imbecile insolence' and 'drivelling impertinence' with which it treated his views.[104] He must, however, have been pleased at least by the reaction of the *Gentleman's Magazine*, whose 'Sylvanus Urban', in his regular column of Table-Talk, was almost sycophantic in his praise for the pamphlet. It 'hits the nail on the head', we read, 'brings a breath of whirlwind to bear upon the controversy'. 'And it is interesting to watch the youngest and most fervent of our great poets casting his sword into the scale opposite to that which is weighted by Mr. Burne-Jones, Mr. Morris, Mr. Browning, Mr. Trollope, and Mr. Carlyle.'[105]

In a note (p. 13) added to his pamphlet not long before it was finished, Swinburne had associated Carlyle's 'crusade' with that of John Bright, the liberal politician and pacifist Quaker industrialist, who had once said that Savoy might perish but now argued that Bulgaria must live. This is perhaps the most obvious of several links between the *Note* and another work that Swinburne conceived while he was waiting for the pamphlet to be printed — *The Ballad of Bulgarie* — which is supposedly sung by a 'Perishing Savoyard'. Swinburne's good friend Edward Burne-Jones had had the temerity to send him a circular announcing the National Conference on the Eastern Question, the grand pro-Bulgarian rally held in the St James's Hall on 8 December. On reading about this gathering in the press, Swinburne was specially disappointed to find Dante Gabriel Rossetti's name listed among those present. He thought there must be a mistake, and indeed there was, but owing to this uncertainty he did not ask his publishers to send Dante Gabriel a copy of *Note of an English Republican on the Muscovite Crusade* (though he did have one sent to William Michael).[106] As for Swinburne's reactions to what really did happen at the meeting of 'philobulgars', he must have been angered to see that not only Gladstone but also Edward Freeman had been 'loudly cheered', but what most shocked the impressionable poet with a sense of tragic absurdity was the spectacle of Bright riding in to battle with the Russians against the Turks. As he told Theodore Watts,[107]

I would give anything ...for the hand of a great caricaturist at this moment, that I might draw that gallant crusader, the loyal Knight Sir John de Bright ...in the broad-brimmed basnet of his Plantagenet forefathers, laying his good lance in rest (with 'Ha! Beauséant. St. John for Birmingham and Our Blessed Lady of Cotton!') in defence of the Holy Sepulchre against miscreant worshippers of false Mahound.

Between 8 and 11 December, in fact, Swinburne composed and sent to the *Pall Mall Gazette* what he at that time was calling 'The Quest of Sir Bright de Brummagem'. Conceived as a sardonic 'ballad of Chivalry', the poem had little chance of success — as Swinburne knew full well — but Bright was again represented as fighting 'against the heathen dogs who worship Mahomet and Termagaunt, and pollute the Holy Sepulchre of his (Sir B.'s) Blessed Lord'. The fact that Swinburne used such whimsically irreligious phrases suggests that his own views at this time were as much emotional and anti-Liberal as intellectually pro-Turk.[108] He was nevertheless completely serious about his ballad. Not surprisingly, the *Pall Mall Gazette* ignored the poem entirely, although on 2 February it did review the *Note* (pp. 2-3), without particular enthusiasm. Perhaps it is just as well that it had not taken the *Ballad*: it could have mangled it. About this time the gazette reprinted as a pamphlet its own *Catechism on the Eastern Question* which, though in some ways useful, greatly misled its readers as to the nature of the interested parties. The Bulgarian, for instance, was described as 'a sort of Finn Slavonianized' (p. 11). When he realised that the *Pall Mall* (or the 'Dunghill') *Gazette* must be ignoring *The Ballad of Bulgarie*, Swinburne sent another copy of it to his literary adviser and associate Thomas Purnell, asking him to place it if he could in the *Globe* or in 'any other respectable anti-Russian paper of any note or standing'.[109]

This was on 27 December. Purnell drew a complete blank with the poem, and Swinburne's own approaches through friends came to nothing either. There was one moment of hope in late January when Sir Charles Dilke of the *Athenaeum*, the prominent Liberal parliamentarian, conveyed through Purnell a favourable personal reaction. He had been to Russia more than once, knew the way that country worked, and was deeply suspicious of the intentions of the Tsar. He had said as much in a speech to his Chelsea constituents on 9 January, conscious that he stood in this respect at some distance from Gladstone. But he was not sufficiently impressed by Swinburne's poem to consider it for publication in his magazine, and retained this copy of *The Ballad of Bulgarie* among his unactioned papers.[110] A disappointed Swinburne also considered printing the poem as a fly-sheet appendix to the *Muscovite Crusade*, perhaps 'with a comic head-and-tail piece'.[111] But nothing came of this idea either, and he was forced to shelve the thing. Obviously, it was quickly losing immediacy. In some respects, however, *The Ballad of Bulgarie* remained completely relevant during the Russo-Turkish War of 1877-78, and beyond into Anglo-Russian confrontation over Afghanistan in the 1880s. Swinburne's continuing cynicism about Tsarist motives and his perplexity at English Liberal views must have kept the poem's existence in his mind. Besides, the man whom he now called 'Billy the Bulgar' was always in the news.[112] Writing to Lord Houghton in December 1879, Swinburne chanced to mention Gladstone and then noted: 'That philobulgarious Christian's name reminds me of a ballad I wrote on Bright, himself, and Carlyle, at the time of the B--g-rian horrescent agitation.' He suggested that his correspondent might see it some day, contenting himself for now by quoting four lines — the invocation to Sts Penn and George — and giving the title which at that time stood as: 'The Quest of Sir Bright de Brummagem, Knight Templar: as it was recited on the Feast of Notre Dame des Bons Marchés, by a Perishing Savoyard: A Ballad of Bulgary.'[113]

The publishing history of *The Ballad of Bulgarie* is complicated, and can only be summarised here. In the commentary to his 1964 edition of the poem, Cecil Lang engagingly declared that it had never been published before — and then proceeded to list the various places in which it had already appeared in print.[114] In the age of desk-top publishing, it is doubtful if anyone will accept this ancient and once proper distinction between publication and private circulation in print. The fact is that *The Ballad of Bulgarie* was first privately printed by Edmund Gosse and Thomas J. Wise as early as 1893, during its author's lifetime, on the basis of a transcript made by Gosse in May 1877 from a copy of the poem lent to him by Swinburne.[115] Only twenty-five copies of this were made, and despite the participation of the honourable Gosse it is now considered as a Wise piracy.[116] Wise himself later allowed that Gosse had not wanted Swinburne to know of the poem's appearance, that it had certainly been printed without his technical consent, but that he had afterwards been informed of it to his 'considerable amusement and surprise'.[117] However, after Swinburne's death, Theodore Watts-Dunton hotly disputed the authenticity of the poem (among others printed by Wise), and threatened to denounce such 'damned ...forgeries and piracies' in the press. But he then recalled that Swinburne had sent just such a work to the *Pall Mall Gazette* in 1876, and reluctantly accepted Wise's suggestion that 'the P.M.G. people may have struck off a few copies before returning the MS. to S.' — an alarmingly different explanation from the one actually given in 1893.[118] Meanwhile, in 1896 an extract from the ballad had also appeared in the second volume of W. Robertson Nicoll and T.J. Wise's *Literary Anecdotes of the Nineteenth Century*, in Wise's chapter called 'A Contribution to the Bibliography of the Writings of Algernon Charles Swinburne'.[119] This was most definitely 'published', by Messrs Hodder and Stoughton; but the following year it was privately reprinted by Wise in a separate edition of his constituent essay, renamed *A Bibliographical List of the Scarcer Works and Uncollected Writings of Algernon Charles Swinburne*. Reference to the poem had also been made in R.J. Lister's *A Catalogue of a Portion of the Library of Edmund Gosse*, published in 1893. Quite a number of people must by now have known about *The Ballad of Bulgarie*, and it is as hard to believe that this never came to Swinburne's or Watts-Dunton's ears as it is to believe that they would have been amused by the piracy.

Two holograph manuscripts are known of *The Ballad of Bulgarie*, both at the British Library. Each has been deciphered and published in modern times, the one by Cecil Lang and the other by T.A.J. Burnett. The version taken by Lang is a fairly rough draft now in the Ashley Papers, which resurfaced in 1919 and which may or may not be the same as that from which Gosse transcribed the poem: there has been controversy on this.[120] The Burnett text is from the fair copy sent to Dilke, to which reference has already been made. Both printed texts are reasonably faithful to the originals, though Professor Lang had to supply punctuation and also rearranged the order of lines 69-80 in accordance with his interpretation of an authorial note 'penultimate' written between 'With offers to help in vain' and 'I don't mind writing — I do mind fighting'. The Dilke version lacks lines 69-74 of the Ashley holograph, but seems to show that Lang's order of lines 75-80 was not intended by Swinburne. My own text below is unashamedly bastard, being essentially the Dilke manuscript but with the original lines 69-74 reincorporated (in square brackets), with the division into stanzas removed, and with a few minor corrections based on the two manuscripts.[121] Little more need be said about the substance of the ballad. The reference to Fox is of course to George (1624-91), founder of the Society of Friends, and Penn is William (1644-1718), founder of Pennsylvania and another celebrated Quaker. With respect to the curious phrase in line 72, 'Like some in Denmark's ill', Professor Lang noted that, if he had correctly transcribed this, it might be 'a reference either to *Hamlet* or to Ruskin, whose home for many years had been (though it was no longer) at 163 Denmark Hill'.[122] Finally, Swinburne's own Latin ending, stating that the rest would not be very desirable, may imply that at one point he had written more; but there is no trace of any continuation in his manuscripts or letters. Here then is *The Ballad of Bulgarie*, with the title as it stood in the manuscript for Dilke:

> *The Quest of Sir Bright de Bromwicham,*
> *Knight Templar:*
> *A Ballad of Bulgaria.*
> *Sung on the Feast of Notre Dame de Bon-Marché,*
> *by a Perishing Savoyard*

The gentle Knight Sir John de Bright
    (Of Bromwicham was he),
Forth would he prance with lifted lance
    For love of Bulgarie.
No lance in hand for other land
    Sir Bright would ever take;
For wicked works, save those of Turks,
    No head of man would break;
But that Bulgarie should not be free,
    This made his high heart quake.   [10]
From spur to plume a star of doom
    (Few knights be like to him),
How shone from far that stormy star,
    His basnet broad of brim!
'Twas not for love of Cant above,
    Or Cotton's holy call;
But a lance would he break for Bulgary's sake,
    And Termagaunt should sprawl.
The mother-maid, Our Lady of Trade,

[20]

   His spurs on heel she bound;
She belted the brand for his knightly hand
   (Full wide the girth went round);
And the brand was bright as his name, to smite
   The spawn of false Mahound.
His basnet broad that all men awed
   No broader was to see,
From brim to brim that shadowed him
   As forth to fight rode he,
South-east by south, with his war-cry in mouth —

[30]

   'Saint John for Bulgarie!'
He had not ridden a mile but one
   When loud and loud cried he:
'Now who will stand at my right hand
   And beard the Turk for me?'
Up spake on this guise Sir William the Wise
   (The People's Knight was he):
'Oh, I will stand at thy stalwart hand
   And brave the Turk with thee.'
'Gramercy!' then quoth Sir Bright, 'by my troth!

[40]

   If better may not be,
Content I were (though I would not swear)
   To slang the Turk with thee;
But who will stand at my left hand
   And bang the Turk for me?'
Then out spake old Sir Thomas the bold
   (A Chelsea Knight was he;
On earth no knight was hardier wight,
   No man had seen him flee —
A stately sight of a grand old knight,

[50]

   As men of old might see):
'Lo, I will stand at thy quaking hand
   And smite the Turk for thee.'
And 'Marry, amen!' Sir Bright said then,
   'For better none might be;
But grieved I am, or God me — save,
   That I may not ride with thee
For the words thou hast said of fair Free Trade,
   My lady fair and free.'
Up then spake him True Thomas

[60]

   (And a scornful man was he):
'Wilt thou bide at the side of thy Bromwicham bride
   Or go to — Bulgarie?'
But up then spake him Wise William,
   Right softly then he spake:
'I deem it ill man's blood to spill,
   Though but for Bulgary's sake;
And meseems it were better ere weather wax wetter,
   Our homeward way to take;
[I don't mind writing — I do mind fighting.'

[70]

   (So spake the bold Sir Bill;
He don't mean outing — he does mean spouting,
   Like some in Denmark's ill.)
'We don't mean hitting — we don't mind spitting —
   For Turks have swords to kill,]

> For the Greek will not fight (which is far from right),
>   And the Russian has all to gain;
> Which I deeply regret should so happen — but yet
>   'Tis true, though it gives me pain;
> And methinks it were vulgar to cheat a poor Bulgar
>   With offers of help in vain.'   [80]
> 'Ha! Beauséant!' said Sir Bright, 'God's bread!
>   And by God's mother dear!
> By my halidom! nay, I will add, perfay!
>   What caitiff wights be here?
> Though Sir Thomas look black and Sir William hang back,
>   While tongue is mine to wag,
> By the help of Our Lady, though matters look shady,
>   It shall fight for the Red-Cross flag;
> Shout, gentlemen, for sweet Saint Penn!
>   Up, gallants, for Saint George!   [90]
> (His name in his day was Fox, by the way),
>   Till the Paynim fiend disgorge —
> Till he loosen his hold of the shrines of old
>   That yet his clutch is on,
> Of the Sepulchre Blest, by our arms repossessed
>   (As soon as his own shall be gone),
> And the Mount of might that's Olivet hight —
>   Strike, strike, for sweet Saint John!'
> *(Caetera non valde desiderantur.)*

Although Swinburne never managed to publish *The Ballad of Bulgarie*, he was glad at least to have brought out when he did his more prosaic *Note*. He hoped it would be listened to in high places, so much did he detest 'English Russophils and Muscovimaniacs'.[123] These kept popping up, like Carlyle with his new letter to *The Times* of 5 May 1877, in which he hoped that Turkey might be 'conquered by the Russians' and called the current British newspaper outcry against Russia 'no more respectable to me than the howling of Bedlam, proceeding, as it does, from the deepest ignorance, egoism, and paltry national jealousy'. The fact is that such outbursts still had influence. Even ruling Conservative opinion was divided, Lord Beaconsfield considering intervention but Lord Derby and most other Ministers urging neutrality. Encouraged in part by British inactivity, Russia had declared war on Turkey in the April of 1877 and rapidly advanced on Constantinople. With the open support of the Queen, Lord Beaconsfield made it known that England would not tolerate the complete destruction of Turkey. Early in 1878, at the height of British popular jingoism, he threatened to send ships through the Dardanelles in order to prove his intentions. Already it seemed too late: by the treaty of San Stefano, signed by Russia and Turkey on 3 March that year, Russian gains in the war zone were confirmed. However, Lord Beaconsfield stood firm among the European powers when, at the Congress of Berlin in June and July, he managed to protect British interests against Russian designs in his so-called 'peace with honour'. He also gained Cyprus for Britain. *Punch* again reflected nicely the national changes of mood. On 19 May 1877 it denied reports that the Earl of Beaconsfield was learning Russian and Mr Gladstone Turkish. Early in the following year it published a cartoon with the clever caption 'On the Dizzy Brink', showing Britannia being drawn by Lord Beaconsfield (that is, 'Dizzy' Disraeli) ever closer to the edge of a precipice, but refusing to tumble over into war; but on 13 April 1878 an enormous picture of a bear and a lion meeting on a precarious ledge spelled out the utmost gravity of England's national dilemma with the simple legend 'Which goes back?'[124]

Swinburne eagerly watched the progress of his pet aversion, Russia, during its war with Turkey and beyond. Late in 1877 there appeared in an English magazine a translation of what he later called 'some insolent lines addressed by "A Russian Poet to the Empress of India"'.[125] Although this has not yet been traced, it is almost certainly Turgenev's famous poem *Kroket v Vindzore* (Croquet at Windsor), which depicts the Queen at Windsor playing with Bulgarian heads instead of balls, and which was translated, among others, by Henry James for *The Nation* of 5 October 1876.[126] Swinburne was inflamed by this, and remained at fever pitch as infamy succeeded infamy. In the new year it was the turn of Edward Freeman. Freeman, who had caused some stir on Gladstone's side in the Bulgarian debate, reverted to his anti-Turkish stand in the *Gentleman's Magazine* for January 1878. Most Englishmen, he said, were quite incapable of understanding what was going on in Turkey. England must not become involved; Russia must certainly not be allowed to make advances in Europe; but we could let that country have, say, Armenia for its pains, and it would in any case, by its victory over 'the foul dominion of the Turk', gain 'the greatest moral position that any nation in Europe ever won'.[127] Swinburne, who had meanwhile written a series of sonnets on the Russo-Turkish War, was most annoyed that Andrew Chatto should refuse to publish them in the *Gentleman's Magazine*, and that this supposedly apolitical organ, once friendly to him, should be committed now to 'the Muscovite, Bulgarian, and Freedmaniac side of the question'.[128] In the end, the sonnets were published in the *Glasgow University Magazine* for February 1878 (p. 17), having been given to that organ through Professor John Nichol at a personal loss of £40![129] Not long afterwards they were reprinted, in a revised form, in the second series of *Poems and Ballads*. Swinburne was publicly 'preached at or verbally swished' for these poems in Glasgow by Rev. F.W. Farrar, leading him to exclaim to Lord Houghton: 'It is delightful to me just now to see the religious world openly avowing its Bulgarian proclivities.' Swift as he always was to disparage enemies in a string of colourful epithets, he rechristened this Farrar as 'the Rev. Flunkey Whoreson Fellator'.[130]

This group of sonnets consists of the two together called *The White Czar* ('Gehazi by the hue that sears thine hand', and 'Call for clear water, wash thine hands, be clean'), *Rizpah*, and *To Louis Kossuth 1877*. Swinburne has often been accused of jingoism in *The White Czar*,[131] but he again saw his reaction as purely patriotic. The first of these two sonnets was, he declared, a 'counterblast' to the 'insolent' Russian poem. In a somewhat contorted formula he argued that he, Swinburne, by no means royalist or imperialist, was well suited to respond, since 'an insult levelled by Muscovite lips at the ruler of England might perhaps be less unfitly than unofficially resented by an Englishman who was also a republican'.[132] The actual phrase 'the White Tsar' may seem strange today, but it was common enough in both Russia and England at the time and indeed was also used as the title of a poem by Longfellow — a playful yet serious piece about the ghost of Peter the Great, risen to free the Bosphorus and to liberate Slavonic Christians from the iron rule of the Sultan.[133] Gehazi, servant of Elisha, was stricken with a blanching skin disease known biblically as leprosy for having obtained money by false pretences. The reference to Pilate washing his hands of Jesus sounds very suspiciously like Turgenev's attack on Queen Victoria in *Kroket v Vindzore*.[134] Here then is Swinburne's *The White Czar*:[135]

THE WHITE CZAR

I

Gehazi by the hue that chills thy cheek
    And Pilate by the hue that sears thine hand
    Whence all earth's waters cannot wash the brand
That signs thy soul a manslayer's though thou speak
All Christ, with lips most murderous and most meek —
    Thou set thy foot where England's used to stand!
    Thou reach thy rod forth over Indian land!
Slave of the slaves that call thee lord, and weak
As their foul tongues who praise thee! son of them
Whose presence put the snows and stars to shame
    In centuries dead and damned that reek below
Curse-consecrated, crowned with crime and flame,
    To them that bare thee like them shalt thou go
    Forth of man's life — a leper white as snow.

II

Call for clear water, wash thine hands, be clean,
    Cry *What is truth?* O Pilate; thou shalt know
    Haply too soon, and gnash thy teeth for woe
Ere the outer darkness take thee round unseen

That hides the red ghosts of thy race obscene
    Bound nine times round with hell's most dolorous flow,
    And in its pools thy crownless head lie low
By his of Spain who dared an English queen
With half a world to hearten him for fight,
Till the wind gave his warriors and their might
    To shipwreck and the corpse-encumbered sea.
But thou, take heed, ere yet thy lips wax white,
    Lest as it was with Philip so it be,
    O white of name and red of hand, with thee.

The sonnet *Rizpah* is reasonably straightforward, being a generalised attack on Russia from the point of view of nations trodden down by it. Rizpah, whose sons were murdered by the Gibeonites with the complicity of King David, mourned for them and defended their bodies until David came and buried them. The reference to Rachel is of course to Herod's Massacre of the Innocents, claimed by the first Evangelist to be in fulfilment of Jeremiah's prophecy about Rachel weeping for her children.[136] Here is *Rizpah*:[137]

RIZPAH

How many sons, how many generations,
    For how long years hast thou bewept, and known
    Nor end of torment nor surcease of moan,
Rachel or Rizpah, wofullest of nations,
Crowned with the crowning sign of desolations,
    And couldst not even scare off with hand or groan
    Those carrion birds devouring bone by bone
The children of thy thousand tribulations?
Thou wast our warrior once; thy sons long dead
Against a foe less foul than this made head,
    Poland, in years that sound and shine afar;
Ere the east beheld in thy bright sword-blade's stead
    The rotten corpse-light of the Russian star
    That lights towards hell his bondslaves and their Czar.

The last sonnet in this sequence is *To Louis Kossuth 1877*. It was written after reading Kossuth's article in the *Contemporary Review* for December 1877 entitled 'Russian Aggression, as specially affecting Austro-Hungary and Turkey.'[138] The Hungarian patriot Lajos Kossuth was one of Swinburne's great heroes. After the Russian victory of August 1849 and the collapse of his revolutionary government, he had fled to Turkey. The authorities there refused to extradite him and he remained in exile in Turkey, England or Italy until his death in 1894. Swinburne the republican was grateful to Turkey for harbouring Kossuth, in 1876 was pleased to see him speaking out 'loud and clearly' in that country's favour over the Bulgarian question, and a year later rejoiced to read 'grand old Kossuth's glorious essay' in the *Contempo-*

rary Review. 'It supports me', he told a colleague, 'under the charge (from the lips of Radical friends) of having *ratted* to the Tory party and his lordship of Beaconsfield'.[139]

Walter Savage Landor, whose name is linked in this sonnet with Kossuth's, had published in the *Examiner* of 15 December 1849 a poem called 'Death in the battle is not death' which demonstrated his strong affection and reverence for him, as well as denouncing England for its failure to help the Hungarians. His later very moving piece on the same subject, 'There are some tears that only brave men shed', summarised the agony of a nation cheated of its hope of liberty.[140] Landor was, besides, an implacable enemy of Russia, over Turkey as well as over Hungary, and foresaw the need for the Crimean War some years before it occurred.[141] In his *Imaginary Conversation* between Nicholas I and Nesselrode, first published in 1851, he reverted to the theme of Russia as a bugbear, abandoned by him in this genre for many years.[142] There was also direct relevance to Nicholas I in his provocative poem *Tyrannicide* of December 1851, in which he recommended the assassination of despots, since 'Danger is not in action, but in sloth'.[143] In 1854 Landor brought out his satirical *Letters of an American, mainly on Russia and Revolution*, and in the *Examiner* for 10 March the following year he revelled in the opportune death of Nicholas I: 'He who trod upon the necks of millions is laid on his back and crept over by the earthworm. Rejoice, nations, rejoice!'[144] Swinburne must have taken all this to heart. He had visited Landor in Italy not long before his death in 1864, was profoundly influenced by him, and considered himself in some ways his successor.[145]

Here then is *To Kossuth, 1877*:[146]

TO LOUIS KOSSUTH
1877

Light of our fathers' eyes, and in our own
   Star of the unsetting sunset! for thy name,
   That on the front of noon was as a flame
In the great year nigh thirty years agone
When all the heavens of Europe shook and shone
   With stormy wind and lightning, keeps its fame
   And bears its witness all day through the same;
Not for past days and great deeds past alone,
Kossuth, we praise thee as our Landor praised,
But that now too we know thy voice upraised,
Thy voice, the trumpet of the truth of God,
   Thine hand, the thunder-bearer's, raised to smite
As with heaven's lightning for a sword and rod
   Men's heads abased before the Muscovite.

During all this time, Swinburne's health was breaking down from the effects of drink and whatever other dissolution may be properly imputed to him. Late in 1879 a nervously exhausted poet was taken in hand by his friend the critic Walter Theodore Watts (later Watts-Dunton), who was to look after him for the rest of his life. They settled together in comfortable and comforting suburban domesticity at The Pines, on Putney Hill, where, under Watts's care, Swinburne made a remarkable recovery. The common image offered of him at this period was of a prematurely aged man walking with staccato gait across the common in search of his daily pint of beer, oblivious to all passers-by except babies in perambulators, around whom he would march with adoring eyes.[147] George Bernard Shaw described him as a sort of 'pet animal' of Watts-Dunton, called upon to show his tricks. He was 'an old gentleman with the body of a boy, carrying a disproportionately large filbert shaped head. His eyes were like shirt buttons.'[148] However, Swinburne never ceased to be grateful to Watts, of whom William Michael Rossetti rightly said that he was 'a hero of friendship'.[149]

Swinburne also never really lost his sharpness, in a political sense. According to Mollie Panter-Downes, sparkling chronicler of his long habitation at The Pines, 'He was deeply interested in current affairs, but his impression of them came from the papers or was shaped in the ceaseless dialogue with Watts.' She is thus able to argue that: 'The poems Swinburne wrote on political topics during the eighties and the nineties were often as disconcerting to his admirers as they are mostly unreadable to us now.' However, even she, the irrepressible evocatrix of this last sad period in the poet's life, has to admit a certain continuity in one particular sphere of his wilder lucubrations. 'A solid rock in the tableau', she notes, 'was Swinburne's implacable hatred of the rulers of Russia.'[150] And so indeed it was. It would have been easy to suppose that Swinburne's anger against Russia had been quickened by his drink or whipped up by his *vice anglais*. But the nation that thought it ruled the waves detested Russia in sobriety, and Swinburne remained one with it. As for Watts-Dunton, he probably never recognised the depth of his friend's feeling against Russia. As late as 1896 he half-expected him to attack some recent Ottoman abominations and needed to be sharply reminded that Swinburne would never enter himself for 'the anti-Turkish cursing-and-swearing stakes'.[151]

So 'Watts-Duntonry' changed nothing in the poet's hatred for Russia. In the letter to Lord Houghton of December 1879 in which he had recalled the original purpose of *The Ballad of Bulgarie*, he reaffirmed his 'contemptuous abhorrence of the Anglo-Russolaters' and added: 'What a song will I not write when Alexander the Liberator descends from this world!'[152] Not long afterwards he cried to William Michael Rossetti: 'God send it soon to Alexander the Liberator and all his accursed race!'[153] The 'dawn of the Russian revolution' was, he hoped, now cracking.[154] The first post-Watts test for the poet's anti-Tsarist art came already in the summer of 1880, with the launch of Alexander's new yacht *Livadia*. This was an enormous ship built on commission at the yards of Elder and Co. in Fairfield, Glasgow, christened and launched on 6 July by the Duchess of Hamilton in the presence of Grand Duke Alexis. Flat-bottomed and of very shallow draught, the *Livadia* housed an Arabian Nights-style palace which infuriated Swinburne. The sequence of three sonnets that he devoted to it was completed on 30 September, a week before it was safely removed to anchorage. Here is *The Launch of the Livadia*, called by one critic 'the most powerful of all Swinburne's poems of hate, for the passion is held within bounds by a fine idea finely expressed'.[155]

THE LAUNCH OF THE LIVADIA

Mala soluta navis exit alite. — Hor.
Rigged with curses dark. — Milton.

I

Gold, and fair marbles, and again more gold,
　　And space of halls afloat that glance and gleam
　　Like the green heights of sunset heaven, or seem
The golden steeps of sunrise red and cold
On deserts where dark exile keeps the fold
　　Fast of the flocks of torment, where no beam
　　Falls of kind light or comfort save in dream,
These we far off behold not, who behold
The cordage woven of curses, and the decks
　　With mortal hate and mortal peril paven;
　　From stem to stern the lines of doom engraven
That mark for sure inevitable wrecks
Those sails predestinate, though no storm vex,
　　To miss on earth and find in hell their haven.

II

All curses be about her, and all ill
　　Go with her; heaven be dark above her way,
　　The gulf beneath her glad and sure of prey,
And, wheresoe'er her prow be pointed, still
The winds of heaven have all one evil will
　　Conspirant even as hearts of kings to slay
　　With mouths of kings to lie and smile and pray,
And chiefliest his whose wintrier breath makes chill
With more than winter's and more poisonous cold
　　The horror of his kingdom toward the north,
　　　The deserts of his kingdom toward the east.
And though death hide not in her direful hold
　　Be all stars adverse toward her that come forth
　　　Nightly, by day all hours till all have ceased:

III

Till all have ceased for ever, and the sum
   Be summed of all the sumless curses told
   Out on his head by all dark seasons rolled
Over its cursed and crowned existence, dumb
And blind and stark as though the snows made numb
   All sense within it, and all conscience cold,
   That hangs round hearts of less imperial mould
Like a snake feeding till their doomsday come.
O heart fast bound of frozen poison, be
All nature's as all true men's hearts to thee,
   A two-edged sword of judgment; hope be far
And fear at hand for pilot oversea
   With death for compass and despair for star,
   And the white foam a shroud for the White Czar.

September 30, 1880.

The Launch of the Livadia was first published in December 1880, in the collection *Studies in Song*. By that time, the ship itself had been holed on its maiden voyage in the Bay of Biscay, doubtless much to Swinburne's glee. But the poem did his book no good: critics in the *Academy*, the *Spectator* and elsewhere drew attention most to what he called these 'sonnets on that unhappy Muscovite wretch and his yacht'.[156] Not long afterwards, matters became still worse. As he told a sympathetic correspondent, 'The sonnets on the yacht of a certain unhappy wretch who since they were written has been sentenced and executed have, I am told, hopelessly ruined the chances of the book.'[157] In another sense, of course, the news that this remark half conceals was manna from heaven for Swinburne — the gruesome regicide of Alexander II in St Petersburg on 1/13 March 1881.

Already on 14 March, the day that England learnt of the event, our poet was composing his *Dysthanatos* on the assassinated Tsar. In letters to William Michael Rossetti of 14 and 17 March, dated also with the equivalents of these in the French Revolutionary calendar, he spoke of his 'Christian hilarity' and 'spiritual cordiality' over the death of a man justly 'condemned and executed'. He was even 'ready to make allowances for God.... If God will but persevere in this better path for some ten years or so, I feel as if Humanity, when impanelled as a jury to try the creator at the bar of his creation, might ultimately find him "Guilty — with extenuating circumstances".'[158] He denied that his attitude was one of inhuman exultation. To the mild objections of William Michael and others he retorted that the virtues of tyrannicide were not negated by Alexander's so-called 'reform of the condition of the serfs'. Only the most degraded serf would consider him a liberator. The 'jury of history' might find the emancipation an extenuating circumstance, but the Tsar 'deserved a hundred deaths' for the brutal repression of Poles, Circassians, and Turks by his 'hellish miscreant' M.N. Murav'ev.[159]

Such then were the fierce opinions that underlay the sonnet *Dysthanatos*. Named from a Greek word meaning either experiencing or causing a painful death, this was an 'expansion' of the lines by Juvenal on the fate of tyrants that Swinburne placed at its head. In view of the poor reception of his other recent sonnets, the poet was advised not to publish this new one. It did not in fact appear at the time, even though he felt it leant rather to mercy than otherwise. Indeed, he thought his plea that no free man should rejoice was the only irrational and objectionable aspect of the piece. 'I for one must confess that I was heartily glad', he told R.H. Horne some months later, for Alexander's 'non-judicial execution' rid the world of 'a hypocritical oppressor, worse than his father of infernal memory, insomuch as Nicholas at least was not inconsistent, and no hypocrite, but a steady straightforward servant of Hell all the days of his reign and life'.[160] Although Horne claimed to agree with Swinburne, and hoped that a chance to publish the sonnet might yet present itself, it was of course too late now to bring it out as an occasional piece: there could not be any other suitable opportunity, not even (as Swinburne put it) 'a fresh massacre of innocents' — among whom the poet hastened to add that he could never include 'any creature tainted by kinship with Czars or communion of any kind with the Russian government'.[161] He was clearly piqued not to have overridden the judgment of his advisers in March 1881, the more so as Dante Gabriel Rossetti's sonnet on the same subject — *Czar Alexander the Second (13th March 1881)* — seemed to him to show misplaced sympathy and, worse, a hankering after brutishness of the sort which (as Swinburne believed) marred much of his distinguished colleague's verse.[162] His own *Dysthanatos* was first published in *Tristram of Lyonesse and Other Poems* (1882), more than a year after the event that it celebrated. Here it is:[163]

DYSTHANATOS

Ad generem Cereris sine caede et vulnere pauci
Descendunt reges, aut sicca morte tyranni.

By no dry death another king goes down
    The way of kings. Yet may no free man's voice,
    For stern compassion and deep awe, rejoice
That one sign more is given against the crown,
That one more head those dark red waters drown
    Which rise round thrones whose trembling equipoise
    Is propped on sand and bloodshed and such toys
As human hearts that shrink at human frown.
The name writ red on Polish earth, the star

That was to outshine our England's in the far
   East heaven of empire — where is one that saith
Proud words now, prophesying of this White Czar?
    'In bloodless pangs few kings yield up their breath,
   Few tyrants perish by no violent death.'

March 14, 1881.

Almost a year after Alexander's demise, Swinburne found himself inspired to write an unexpected counterpart to *Dysthanatos*. On 2 March 1882 the latest of a surprising number of attempts on the life of Queen Victoria was made at Windsor station by one Roderick Maclean, a mentally disturbed grocer's assistant. The opportunity to compare two such different crowned heads was too good to be missed. Swinburne wrote his new sonnet on 8 March and gave it a Greek title to match that of the earlier one. *Euonymos*, which might imply 'of good or honoured name', here also has the sense 'well-named' since Victoria had emerged victorious over death. Taking this theme a step further, Swinburne prefaced his poem with a two-line epigraph in Greek, apparently not taken from any classical author and perhaps invented by himself, to the effect that strength and honour became this fearless heart whose very name derived from victory. Although the sonnet is as much about England as it is about Russia, it clearly shows the stark moral contrast with which Swinburne opposed these two countries. Here then is *Euonymos*, first printed immediately after *Dysthanatos* in *Tristram of Lyonesse, and Other Poems* (1882):[164]

EUONYMOS

A year ago red wrath and keen despair
   Spake, and the sole word from their darkness sent
   Laid low the lord not all omnipotent
Who stood most like a god of all that were
As gods for pride of power, till fire and air
   Made earth of all his godhead. Lightning rent
   The heart of empire's lurid firmament,
And laid the mortal core of manhood bare.
But when the calm crowned head that all revere
For valour higher than that which casts out fear,
   Since fear came near it never, comes near death,
Blind murder cowers before it, knowing that here
   No braver soul drew bright and queenly breath
   Since England wept upon Elizabeth.

March 8, 1882.

Just a few weeks earlier, on 23 January 1882, Swinburne had been provoked by recurring press reports into writing a sonnet *On the Russian Persecution of the Jews*. Ever since the accession of the new Tsar

Alexander III, outbreaks of violence against Jews had been occurring in the west and south of Russia with monotonous regularity. Various local authorities had refused to intervene, and the Emperor himself eventually took action which tended to worsen rather than alleviate the situation of the Jews. Russian correspondents to *The Times* had tended to blame the latter for bringing trouble on themselves, and on 23 January a quoted report from the *Journal de Saint-Pétersbourg* castigated the English newspapers for inflaming dissension, adding that: 'We can only suppose that the excellent relations created by the Gladstone Cabinet have lasted too long for some people.' Maybe it was this that so angered Swinburne. He did not perhaps yet know it at the time, but he was joining forces here with William Morris, who believed that his Eastern Question Association, so vociferous not long before in its support for Bulgaria, should be seen now to be impartial by accusing Russia of brutality. In view of what Morris had said so recently about his Queen and Britain's leading Semite ('the Jew wretch and that old Vic'), one wonders how he could properly have spoken either for his country or in favour of Russia's Jews, but together with Burne-Jones and other artistic crusaders he helped organise a grand meeting of protest at the Mansion House in London on 1 February this year.[165]

Swinburne was thus for once on the 'correct' intellectual side, but the overwhelming proof of anti-Semitism under Alexander III provided yet another opportunity to deride Russian barbarities. It should be said, however, that *On the Russian Persecution of the Jews* actually shows his own irreligion — or better, his humanity — as much as his hostility to Russia in particular. Here is the sonnet, which was published in the *Daily Telegraph* on 25 January, 1882, and reprinted that year in *Tristram of Lyonesse and Other Poems*.[166]

ON THE RUSSIAN PERSECUTION OF THE JEWS

O son of man, by lying tongues adored,
    By slaughterous hands of slaves with feet red-shod
    In carnage deep as ever Christian trod
Profaned with prayer and sacrifice abhorred
And incense from the trembling tyrant's horde,
    Brute worshippers or wielders of the rod,
    Most murderous even of all that call thee God,
Most treacherous even that ever called thee Lord;
Face loved of little children long ago,
    Head hated of the priests and rulers then,
        If thou see this, or hear these hounds of thine
        Run ravening as the Gadarean swine,
Say, was not this thy Passion, to foreknow
    In death's worst hour the works of Christian men?

January 23, 1882.

Whatever Watts's staying influence may have been upon his friend, it cannot be said that Swinburne's hatred for Russia ever abated much. Nor can it be said that he reacted any more from prejudice or ignorance. He read a great deal about Russia at this time. He was, for instance, disgusted by the authorities' treatment of Prince P.A. Kropotkin and his family, calling it 'enough to kindle a furnace-blast of pity and sympathetic rage in every human creature who has not a toadstool for a heart.'[167] On the other hand he did, perhaps, relax a little in his new environment of Victorian domesticity. In the cold winter of 1880-81 he called England 'Nova Zembla' and its climate 'Muscovite'. He described a snow-covered England as 'Siberia'. He jokingly referred to young Bertie Mason, subject of his innocently paedolatrous affection and the 'H.W.M.' of many poetic effusions, as 'H.M. the Czar of all the Pines'.[168] He could even joke about Bulgaria: in his extraordinary parodic *Last Words of a Seventh-Rate Poet*, written late in life, the narrator admits to having 'picked up' his poems 'on the banks of the Don, from the lips of a highly intelligent Bulgar'; one piece, rejected by his mistress, is actually entitled 'The Bride of Bulgaria'.[169] As Swinburne's poem seems in part a (light-hearted) satire on Browning, it may not be too far-fetched to suggest that the allusion here could be to that bard's early visit to Russia where he 'picked up' *Ivàn Ivànovitch*. As far as Bulgaria itself was concerned, a comment of Swinburne's to Edmund Gosse in 1893 is significant. Gosse had sent him his translation, just published, of the national poet and novelist Ivan Vazov's *Pod igoto* (Under the Yoke). Swinburne made haste to read it and replied: 'Many thanks for a very interesting and remarkable book. I am glad to know something more of the gallant Bulgarians than can be gathered from newspapers on the fresher and more trustworthy authority of fiction — almost always more really historic than history.'[170]

Swinburne also came to know some Russians in this period, who helped him see that not all was bleak and cruel in the empire of the Tsars — although, as émigrés, they must have reinforced his contempt for the autocracy. Frankly, they were also chiefly of professional use to him. He was, for instance, very glad to make the acquaintance of the Franco-Anglo-Russian poet and critic Mark André Rafalovich, who made a point of praising Pre-Raphaelites and their successors in the Russian press. Swinburne had occasion to write to Burne-Jones: 'Here is my young Rooshan raving about you again through a column of the Journal de St. Pétersbourg.'[171] One of what Swinburne called only two good notices of his *Mary Stuart* trilogy, 'the work of a Russian, written in French (in Russian it would not much have edified me)', was also probably by Rafalovich though it could just have been by his translator Tola Dorian.[172]

For a time, Swinburne was quite taken by this Mme Dorian. Formerly Princess Meshcherskaia, now married to a French deputy and banker, she resided in Paris with her husband, her ravishing small daughter and her extraordinary Slavonic steeds. She was also becoming an influential woman of letters. By her French translation of his ode *The Statue of Victor Hugo* she helped Swinburne to come closer to his beloved Master, and at dinner with the latter in Paris in November 1882 he was introduced to her personally. She then enabled him to keep in touch with the man he called 'mon maître' and 'mon père', and he asked her to bestow on the dying Hugo's great hand his own last kiss of love, devotion, and eternal thanks.[173] The depression that seized him when Hugo was finally no more is legendary. One may, however, add that his account of Hugo's genial reception of him in Tola Dorian's presence does not entirely tally with her own. Though keen enough on Swinburne's poetry, the old Frenchman was more frustrated by his visit than otherwise. After dinner Swinburne drank a toast to Hugo, throwing his empty glass over his shoulder. The master was perplexed, and for some time afterwards deplored the loss of one of his best wine-glasses.[174]

At all events, Swinburne was invited to Tola Dorian's house and made the acquaintance of her family and stud. He assured his friends that she was a 'Nihilist by creed and practice', which presumably excused her noble Russian origins. He really did have some sympathy with nihilism — or at least he was taken by the concept. In answer to an American enquiry in 1875 concerning his 'birth and career', he had emphasised among other things his 'quasi-Catholic' upbringing and his subsequent 'nihilism'. Although he was in fact a kind of humanist, he said, he did not object to being thought of as a 'clarified' (as opposed to a 'turbid') nihilist.[175] What exactly he meant by this is uncertain; perhaps he had in mind the 'pure' nihilism of a Bazarov (in Turgenev's novel *Ottsy i deti*), rather than any German-style complexity. Tola Dorian doubtless also informed Swinburne of the following that he had by now in Russia, as in France — which he supposed to be exclusively of the republican persuasion but which probably had nothing to do with politics. Swinburne corresponded with Mme Dorian on terms of admiration and friendship for a number of years, sent her his works and received copies of hers.[176] He was also very much impressed by her small daughter, Dora, photographs of whom he prized and showed off to friends. In the new year 1883 he described her as 'the daughter of a Russian princess by birth and nihilist by profession — as perhaps I need not have added, for I flatter myself that when I mention any Russian as a personal friend it can scarcely be requisite to specify which party in the empire has the honour of that Russian's adherence'.[177] Swinburne included a little poem called *To*

Dora Dorian in his *A Century of Roundels* (1883), celebrating in it this 'Child of two strong nations', symbol of hope that 'Men should yet be reconciled'.[178] As it turned out, France and Russia soon were; but Swinburne viewed that, of course, as treachery.

The new anti-British alliances of the later part of the nineteenth century greatly annoyed our poet. At first he was concerned about a possible pact between Russia and Bismarck's new Germany. At one point in his vigorous and bouncy ode *A Word for the Country*, written in the autumn of 1884, he again contrasted English freedom with Russian bondage and attacked the Tsar's international policies. He was proud of this piece, which he described as an adaptation of a medieval jingle from the North Country, and particularly wished his friends to like it.[179] The relevant stanza contains the climax of an argument by the poet's imaginary absolutist interlocutor, to which he then gives reply.[180]

> 'But we know, we believe it, we see it,
> Force only has power upon earth.'
> So be it! and ever so be it
> For souls that are bestial by birth!
> Let Prussian with Russian
> Exchange the kiss of slaves:
> But sea-folk are free folk
> By grace of winds and waves.

The theme of the sea and Britain's need to go on ruling it was developed further in Swinburne's *A Word for the Navy*. The history of the composition and publication of this ode is complicated and need only be summarised here. It has, besides, relatively little to do with Swinburne's hatred for Russia, but some aspects of it are of direct relevance. He wrote the poem originally in 1885, prepared it for publication in 1886, but apparently did not go through with it until early in 1887, when it came out as a special feature of Estelle Davenport Adams's collection *Sea Song and River Rhyme from Chaucer to Tennyson* (pp. vii-viii). He revived it in January 1896 as a popular penny pamphlet, with 'a few alterations rendered desirable by change of national circumstances', and brought it out in its definitive version only in 1904.[181] *A Word for the Navy* exhorted England to remember its maritime past and to strengthen its national resolve against enemies within and without. Among these, Russia, France and Prussia were the chief contestants. In Swinburne's own rough and fair manuscripts and in the proofs of the aborted edition of 1886, stanza iv of the poem reads:

> Smooth France, as a serpent for rancour,
> Strong Germany, girded with guile,

> Lay wait for thee riding at anchor
> On waters that whisper and smile.
> They deem thee or dream thee
> Less living now than dead,
> Deep sunken and drunken
> With sleep whence fear has fled.

There was thus no reference to Russia. However, in the published version of 1887 the first two lines of this were altered to read:

> Smooth France, as a serpent for rancour,
> Dark Muscovy, girded with guile.

In 1896 they were further revised to

> Smooth France, as a serpent for rancour,
> Strong Germany, girded with guile

and in 1904 they became definitively:[182]

> Dark Muscovy, reptile in rancour,
> Base Germany, blatant in guile.

In his discussion of these changes Thomas J. Wise found fit to comment: 'Had the poet survived to welcome the great Alliance of 1914 the words *Dark Muscovy* would doubtless have also been removed.'[183] That is as may be; but Muscovy for Swinburne was clearly as reptilious in 1904 as it had been in 1887. In the definitive text of the poem there is, besides, another reference to Russia, more than somewhat obscure, which seems to allude ironically to England's lack of response to the perpetual danger represented by its enemies:[184]

> Sleep thou: for thy past was so royal,
> Love hardly would bid thee take heed
> Were Russia not faithful and loyal
> Nor Germany guiltless of greed.
> No nation, in station
> Of story less than thou,
> Re-risen from prison,
> Can stand against thee now.

Back in the mid-1880s, meanwhile, Swinburne's anger at a nascent Franco-Russian entente was occasioned as much by the one partner as by the other. His republicanism and gallomania were deeply offended by the new régime in France, long since corrupt but now showing the ultimate in treachery by flirting with his arch-enemy. There follows a sequence of four previously unpublished or inadequately published pieces which, in their various ways, relate the poet's disgust for Russia and for France. They are extremely outspoken and vicious. According to one biographer, if they never appeared in print at the time it was that they 'were gingerly gathered up by Watts and dropped into a drawer out of sight before they could ignite anything or anybody'. After Swinburne's death, however (says the same authority), 'we note old Watts-Dunton digging out the manuscripts of the Russo-French poems and, perhaps reflecting that nothing could hurt Algernon now, selling them to the acquisitive and helpful Mr Thomas J. Wise.'[185] This is probably both unfair to Watts and not completely true of Swinburne. The poems were to some extent variants on each other and could not have all been published straight. The very fact that Swinburne kept using the same material shows that he himself was dissatisfied. Moreover, certain ideas and phrases included in them would be used in both *Russia: An Ode* (1890) and in later editions of *A Word for the Navy*, while others echoed his *Rondeaux parisiens*, dated August 1885 but first printed posthumously by Wise in 1917. These were in part an answer to French criticism of his morals, but constituted also a more general attack upon corruption and hypocrisy beyond the Channel; they contained the significant lines[186]

> Foul France must be whipped into silence, if ever again
> Fair France shall arise.

All four of the new pieces are published here, as accurately as possible, from Swinburne's own manuscripts at the British Library and the Humanities Research Center. The earliest in date is *The Russ and the Bulgar*, written or completed on 23 August 1886. The inspiration for this was actually not France so much as current events in Sofia. Following the terms of the Treaty of Berlin in 1878, Bulgaria had been granted an uneasy independence from Turkey, a constitution and a national assembly; in 1879 young Alexander of Battenberg was elected as its Prince. Much to the annoyance of Russia, Bulgaria had now tended to slip away from Slavonic control and into the camp of the Austrians. In this summer of 1886 Moscow, with the connivance of France, machinated to secure the abdication of the man whom Swinburne here designates 'the hero crowned'. Although this did not actually occur until September, its necessity had been assured by a military coup d'état in Sofia on 21 and 22 August. Here is the first of the sonnets:[187]

> The Russ and the Bulgar.
> August 23, 1886.

> Again the race for whom all wrong spells right,
>   The seed of servile treason, rears as red

> As ever yet it rose the serpent's head
> Whose hiss proclaims the present Muscovite.
> And that foul tribe, misborn of noisome night,
>   Whose worldwide shame is shameful to be said,
>   Whose name a nameless byword, seeks the bed
> Whose warmth still woos it toward the serpent's bite.
>
> But he, the hero crowned who bade the slaves
> Seek other than base ends & abject graves,
>   What part has he with knaves or slaves obscene?
> If there his part be played, & he cast forth
> By blasts of bitter treason from the north,
>   His place is higher, where hearts & names are clean.

Things here were somewhat obscure, and only three days later Swinburne made another attempt, omitting any reference to Bulgaria but spelling out quite clearly now the role of France in the new Russian assertiveness. He called it *The Russ and the Frenchman*. His holograph at the British Library is a fair copy, save that it was to have contained epigraphs, heavily scrawled out by himself, from Coleridge and Tennyson. The former seems indecipherable, but the Tennyson quotation is an apt line from *Maud*: 'Yet God's just wrath shall be wreaked on a giant liar.'[188]

> The Russ & the Frenchman.
>
> Again the race for whom all wrong spells right,
>   The seed of servile treason, rears as red
>   As ever yet it rose the serpent's head
> Whose hiss proclaims the present Muscovite.
> And France our friend, the friend of truth & right,
>   The friend of man, so late deject & dead
>   In shame, now full of insolence & bread,
> Roars rapture, yells derision, screams for spite.
>
> Imperial Caesar, bite but thou the heel
>   Of England, France, a fangless viper, licks
>   With tongue republican the foot that kicks
> At honour, shod with iron fraud & steel.
>   France, the whipped hound, yelps, cowering like a hare,
>   At Russia's heel — a bitch behind a bear.
>
> August 26, 1886

As a sort of variant on these two sonnets, Swinburne also wrote a third called *The Two Enemies*. Particularly dazzling in its imagery and vituperative power, this emphasised the dangers inherent in the possible entente between France and Russia and urged the English to restore themselves to strength, showering contempt on such hitherto improbable developments.[189]

The Two Enemies.
1886.

False France, yet writhing from the whip, aglow
   With poisonous hate & impotence of guile,
   Shoots froth at England, seeing her pass & smile
To hear the restless cock whose plumes lie low,
Who sees no dawn of Gallic sunrise, crow
   Forlorn defiance, vain & void & vile
   As even her plighted friendship, found erewhile
More perilous than her threatenings when a foe.
She crawls & spits & hisses, hearkening still:
If haply hate may have her ravenous will
   And Gaul win comfort of the Muscovite
Who slinks on southwards, lying & slaying: but we,
If aught of all that once was England be,
   May mock the bear's grip & the viper's bite.

Finally, in the spring of 1887 Swinburne took up again some of the material used in his three sonnets of the previous year and wrote a poem called *Russo-Gallia*. It is not clear if he both started and finished it on the stated date of 12 March. He apparently first conceived the thing as a sonnet, made a fair copy on a single side of paper, but was dissatisfied and later revised and extended it in rough copy on both sides of his paper so as to transform it into a double sonnet or, more accurately, an irregular poem of 28 lines. It is published here from what seems to have been intended as the final form of the manuscript, but one has to say that Swinburne must have still been unhappy with it and probably never copied it out again. Many earlier words and phrases are crossed through. For instance, France was first described as a 'strumpet & servant of a leprous lord', a slave 'by thieves & murderers whipped & whored'. The good 'lord' who remains in the poem is, of course, Victor Hugo, who had died on 22 May 1885. More interestingly, Swinburne abandoned the three vigorous lines with which his original sonnet was to end ('The tongue that licked Napoleon's footsole white/Beslavers now the ranker Muscovite/With love more loathsome than a leper's hide'), replacing them with lines that could develop the poem further. Likewise, he dropped a beautiful couplet in the new section ('A dream to laugh at when the shadows flee,/And orient sun transfigures earth & sea'), feeling perhaps that he was drifting too far from his political target. One may note, finally, that the ending of the piece caused him great difficulty and is not satisfactorily resolved. He tried, but was unable, to introduce the phrase 'unconquered England', and toyed with the concept of modern Britain being unknown to France, before leaving the poem with an ironic bathos that makes it more challenging but at the same time more mysterious and, frankly, less intelligible. Here then is the poem:[190]

Russo-Gallia.
March 12, 1887.

Falsehood, thy name is France! The land so late
   A hound at heel, with neck that loved the cord,
   A slave with stripes & kisses flushed and scored,
Now grunts & grovels at the Russian gate,
And spits at England all a harlot's hate.
   Quenched is the light that lit thee; dead the lord
   Whose lyre outsang the storm, outshone the sword.
At him too spit thy scorn: he too was great.

False prostitute, still flagrant from the whip
That Bismarck laid about thee, flank & hip,
   What see we now, who deemed thee purified?
The imperial foot of Russia lures thy lip;
   A lustier liar subdues thy servile pride;
   And shame bears witness how thy praisers lied.

Truth's very tongue must lie that praises thee;
   Love's very heart abjure the truthless trance
   Wherein thy sometime lovers held thee, France,
Less false than wind, less faithless than the sea.

Bulgaria treads down treason, & is free:
   Fine France & reptile Russia join the dance,
   The dance of death, whose masquers prowl & prance
And howl for hate of life that must not be.

Nay, what were freedom, what were man's first rights,
   If not by France conferred? The enfranchised slave
That snarls, but, snarling, hardly snaps or bites,
At England's heel, & licks the Muscovite's,
   Sees truth alone. From dreamland's darkling cave
   We stagger, blind with sunshine, toward the grave.

The imagery of this last poem in the set is peculiarly sadistic. It is the language of flogging. By coincidence or not, in the following year there appeared in London a curious book called *The Whippingham Papers*, stated to be 'chiefly by the Author of the 'Romance of Chastisement'. There is every reason to suppose that Swinburne wrote many of its contributions, both in verse and in prose.[191] Tucked away among prurient pieces on the doings of the Bumminghams and Birches is a pseudo-scientific section of 'Anecdotes, Extracts, and Original Contributions relating to Flagellation'. One of these concerns 'Whipping as a Punishment in Russia'. The source is at second or third hand, and the entry may of course not be by Swinburne at all, but he must have been cognisant of it. The style, besides, is reticent though realistic. A description of a knout is given — 'a bull's pizzle, to the end of which were fastened three thongs of an elk skin untanned', — followed by its bloody, mangling effect upon the backs of some poor unlicensed hawkers of tobacco and vodka. The author then notes that this is only a moderate punishment, for when the knout 'is ordered to be given with the utmost severity, the executioner striking the flank under the ribs, cuts the flesh to the very bowels'. To which he quite properly concludes: 'It is no wonder that many die of this cruel and inhuman punishment.'[192]

Out of all this, in a sense, came *Russia — An Ode*, with which in the July of 1890 Swinburne's hatred and contempt for that country rose to a frenzied peak. It is one of his most powerful and deeply-felt offerings. Nowhere had he been quite so savage and so brutally aggressive: the poem is an open call to sedition by the Russian anarchists, an extraordinarily violent 'interference in another country's affairs'. For most liberal English people, whatever their dislike of the Tsarist régime, whatever their disgust and distress at the persecution of young opponents of the Tsar, tyrannicide was no more excusable than, say, the murder of a harsh factory-owner or a pitiless judge; but Swinburne preached hatred, retaliation, even murder, so that Russia could be free. His poem is truly revolutionary. What caused him to be so extreme? *Russia: An Ode* was written, in fact, at the request of the Irish journalist, teacher and philologist E.J. Dillon who, under the pseudonym E.B. Lanin, had just published a devastating article on Russian prisons in the *Fortnightly Review*.[193] This was the latest instalment in a series that Dillon was contributing to the magazine; in another piece, on censorship, he described significantly how Russian officials spent their mornings blacking out pages of Swinburne, and in the afternoons tried their own feeble hand at lyric poetry.[194]

The subject of Russian law and order had been in the English air again for some time now and had been treated, for instance, by Robert Spence Watson in the influential new magazine *The Speaker*.[195] The special force of the Lanin study lies in the fact that, as opposed to most other contemporary accounts, its polyglot author drew almost exclusively on official Russian records and described the conditions of all kinds of prisoners, not just political ones. He built up a terrifying picture of floggings, filth and stench, overcrowding, starvation, nakedness in the freezing cold of winter. In particular, he dramatically evoked the plight of thousands who, completely innocent of any misdemeanour, found their unhappy way into this morass: soldiers detached from their units, peasants arbitrarily cast out from their commune, people who mislaid their passports, travelling pilgrims who got left behind by their friends. One young woman, studying medicine against her father's wishes in a distant town, was delivered back to him at his request — only dismembered and dead.[196] Worst of all, perhaps, was the destiny of those who were simply accompanying their convict relatives. Quoting again from an unimpeachable Russian source, Dillon related how 'The old men among them are beaten, the old women scoffed at and insulted, the girls and boys are violated and abused by convicts and guards.'[197] Swinburne would take careful note of this. Nor did Dillon spare the criminality of the prisoners themselves, spurred on by deprivation, drunkenness and (more often than one might expect) inactivity and boredom. 'Immorality', he noted, 'is practised on a scale unsuspected in the very worst of over-civilised European countries, and contemplated only in the penal code of the Old Testament.'[198] Again such remarks, not much elaborated in the text for reasons of Victorian sensibility, came over clearly enough to Swinburne.

The poet's response to Dillon's challenge was written in the fire of the moment. One who knew him well described his anger thus: 'There were times when he would work himself up into a passion of denunciation, when, trembling and quivering in every limb, he would in a fine frenzy of scorn annihilate those whom he conceived to be his enemies, and in scathing periods pour ridicule upon their works.'[199] Swinburne must have been in this kind of state when he penned *Russia: An Ode*. His first thought was to have the piece typeset as a brochure, but he had only proof copies made and gave it instead to the *Fortnightly Review* which gladly used it at the head of its August issue, preceding it with the author's note: '(Written after reading E.B. Lanin's account of "Russian Prisons.")'.[200] Appropriately enough, Swinburne's ode was incorporated in full the following year by Dillon's American publishers in a reprint of the *Fortnightly Review* series provocatively entitled *Russian Traits and Terrors*.[201] Here it is:

RUSSIA: AN ODE
1890

I

Out of hell a word comes hissing, dark as doom,
Fierce as fire, and foul as plague-polluted gloom;
Out of hell wherein the sinless damned endure
More than ever sin conceived of pains impure;
More than ever ground men's living souls to dust;
Worse than madness ever dreamed of murderous lust.
Since the world's wail first went up from lands and seas
Ears have heard not, tongues have told not things like these.
Dante, led by love's and hate's accordant spell
Down the deepest and the loathliest ways of hell,
Where beyond the brook of blood the rain was fire,
Where the scalps were masked with dung more deep than mire,
Saw not, where the filth was foulest, and the night
Darkest, depths whose fiends could match the Muscovite.
Set beside this truth, his deadliest vision seems
Pale and pure and painless as a virgin's dreams.

Maidens dead beneath the clasping lash, and wives
Rent with deadlier pangs than death — for shame survives,
Naked, mad, starved, scourged, spurned, frozen, fallen, deflowered,
Souls and bodies as by fangs of beasts devoured,
Sounds that hell would hear not, sights no thought could shape,
Limbs that feel as flame the ravenous grasp of rape,
Filth of raging crime and shame that crime enjoys,
Age made one with youth in torture, girls with boys,
These, and worse if aught be worse than these things are,
Prove thee regent, Russia — praise thy mercy, Czar.

II

Sons of man, men born of women, may we dare
Say they sin who dare be slain and dare not spare?
They who take their lives in hand and smile on death,
Holding life as less than sleep's most fitful breath,
So their life perchance or death may serve and speed
Faith and hope, that die if dream become not deed?
Nought is death and nought is life and nought is fate
Save for souls that love has clothed with fire of hate.
These behold them, weigh them, prove them, find them nought,
Save by light of hope and fire of burning thought.
What though sun be less than storm where these aspire,
Dawn than lightning, song than thunder, light than fire?
Help is none in heaven: hope sees no gentler star:
Earth is hell, and hell bows down before the Czar.
All its monstrous, murderous, lecherous births acclaim
Him whose empire lives to match its fiery fame.
Nay, perchance at sight or sense of deeds here done,
Here where men may lift up eyes to greet the sun,
Hell recoils heart-stricken: horror worse than hell
Darkens earth and sickens heaven; life knows the spell,
Shudders, quails, and sinks — or, filled with fierier breath,
Rises red in arms devised of darkling death.
Pity mad with passion, anguish mad with shame,
Call aloud on justice by her darker name;
Love grows hate for love's sake; life takes death for guide.
Night hath none but one red star — Tyrannicide.

III

'God or man, be swift; hope sickens with delay:
Smite, and send him howling down his father's way!
Fall, O fire of heaven, and smite as fire from hell
Halls wherein men's torturers, crowned and cowering, dwell!
These that crouch and shrink and shudder, girt with power —
These that reign, and dare not trust one trembling hour —
These omnipotent, whom terror curbs and drives —
These whose life reflects in fear their victims' lives —
These whose breath sheds poison worse than plague's thick breath —
These whose reign is ruin, these whose word is death,
These whose will turns heaven to hell, and day to night,
These, if God's hand smite not, how shall man's not smite?'
So from hearts by horror withered as by fire

Surge the strains of unappeasable desire;
Sounds that bid the darkness lighten, lit for death;
Bid the lips whose breath was doom yield up their breath;
Down the way of Czars, awhile in vain deferred,
Bid the Second Alexander light the Third.
How for shame shall men rebuke them? how may we
Blame, whose fathers died, and slew, to leave us free?
We, though all the world cry out upon them, know,
Were our strife as theirs, we could not strike but so;
Could not cower, and could not kiss the hands that smite;
Could not meet them armed in sunlit battle's light.
Dark as fear and red as hate though morning rise,
Life it is that conquers; death it is that dies.

The English press took a rather snooty view of the capricious bard's new poem. 'Mr. Swinburne's rage against Russia makes bad verses', opined the *Illustrated London News*, while the *Literary World* declared: 'We should hardly advise Mr. Swinburne to wander on to Russian territory for some little time to come. His "Russia: an Ode" ...is not calculated to awaken an enthusiasm for the author in the breast of Russian officials.'[202] On the other hand, a leading article in the *Speaker* simply noted that things in Russia were so bad now that 'even' (the word seems misplaced) 'Mr. Swinburne can chant the praises of the tyrannicide who makes a Czar his mark'.[203] The most interesting report of *Russia: An Ode* came in *Punch*, which on 16 August carried a cartoon by Harry Furniss showing Swinburne, as the poet told his sister Alice, 'tearing out my last few hairs in agony at finding that no member of the Tory Government had read or heard of my poem'. And he continued: 'I think it a capital caricature — and Walter and I have laughed over it all the more heartily for remembering how very imaginative an idea it is that I should have expected these worthy and useful and serviceable Tories to read or understand mine or any one's verses.'[204] The actual cartoon, a small but very vigorous one, is not quite as Swinburne describes it: his remaining hair is on end, and his arms are thrust outwards from a frail body in a dressing-gown, sprawled awkwardly in an armchair with a newspaper dropped to one side. The caption reads: 'Fancy Portrait of Algernon Charles Swinburne. On reading the Parliamentary report in Wednesday's *Times*. "*Mr. W.H. Smith*. I asked my colleagues near me whether they had seen or read the publication — (Mr. A.C. Swinburne's poem about Russia) and none of them had." "And this," exclaimed Algernon Charles Swinburne, the poet, "*this* is fame!"'

Though satirised and to some degree fictionalised, *Punch*'s ensuing report of the incident was founded on a genuine exchange that had taken place in Parliament during question time on Tuesday 5 August, with sequels the following week. The participants were Patrick

O'Brien, the Irish Home Rule Member for County Monaghan (North), also a Liverpool coal merchant; the Right Hon. William Henry Smith, First Lord of the Treasury and Leader of the House of Commons, also head of the not unheard-of booksellers W.H. Smith and Son; Sir Richard Everard Webster, barrister and QC, Attorney General and Conservative Member for Swinburne's own Isle of Wight; and Mr 'Order, order!', Speaker of the House. As Hansard relates it, O'Brien had given private notice to W.H. Smith a quarter of an hour before he put the question as to whether Russia had complained of Swinburne's poem, and whether Her Majesty's Government intended to prosecute either the author or his printer or publisher. He claimed that it contained 'a direct incitement to the assassination of the Czar' and misquoted a line: 'Night brings but one red star — tyrannicide!' The Speaker determined that 'This House has no control over a poet's opinions' (and allegedly also remarked that the matter in debate was 'only the fancy of a feather-brained poet'), but Smith responded none the less. In the few minutes at his disposal he had asked around his colleagues on the Government benches whether any 'had seen, or read, or heard of the publication', but none had. He further pointed out that the question should have been put down in writing. This O'Brien pledged to do, but when he revived it six days later the only answer that he received was the Speaker's 'Order, order!' On the following day he cleverly rephrased it so as to hear, first, if it was 'an indictable offence in England to encourage, persuade, or endeavour to persuade, any person or persons to murder a foreigner residing out of Her Majesty's dominions'. Learning from the Attorney General that it was, he then reverted to the Swinburne poem and asked again if anyone would be prosecuted for it. Unfortunately, the Speaker's 'Order, order!' was the only recorded reply.[205] But for those who heard or read these brief parliamentary exchanges the underlying intention of O'Brien's persistent questioning was all too embarrassingly clear: Irishmen might be imprisoned or even hanged if they proposed for Queen Victoria what Swinburne proposed for the Tsar.

As referring to *Russia: An Ode*, all this in one way diminishes the political force of the work. In another way, however, it heightens its value as a humanitarian and even quite daring appeal against despotism and tyranny. Although the Government seemed completely to ignore his poem at the time, there was one unfortunate consequence for Swinburne in the longer term. After Tennyson's death in 1892, he was for many the most obvious choice as Britain's poet laureate, but Gladstone, who had the matter in his charge, did not consider him suitable. Edmund Gosse supposed that this was because of Swinburne's professed animosity towards 'certain friendly foreign powers', which in turn has been interpreted as France and Russia. In particular, in 1892 the memory of *Russia: An Ode* was still very much alive.[206] It is therefore not surprising that this work should have had some influence upon sensitive young readers. The poet William Watson, for example, was deeply affected by it, calling it the final piece in which Swinburne 'sang with all his original fire.' As he wrote to Watts-Dunton after their colleague had died, 'No poem of my time thrilled me more, and it showed the man in his noblest light, as a great and fiery hater of oppression — the light in which I shall choose to think of him to the last'.[207] The sincerity of this statement is seen in Watson's own collection *The Year of Shame* (1897) in which, albeit less vehemently than Swinburne, he railed against the White Czar's treachery and condemned the Franco-Russian entente as an alliance between Venus and Mars.[208]

Despite being passed over for the laureateship, Swinburne was by now a grand old man of letters — at least for those who could not see his piteous frame. Many wrote to ask for his advice. Late in life, he was approached by Countess Benkendorf, the wife of the Russian ambassador to Great Britain, for an opinion on a projected four-act play by her young protégé Maurice Baring. At this time Baring, traveller, diplomat, poet, and future novelist, critic and authority on things Russian, was in his own words 'brimful of enthusiasm for Swinburne and Rossetti', simply 'intoxicated by Swinburne'.[209] However, as his biographer would later note, 'Once the first excess of youth has spent itself, a good deal of the work of writers like Swinburne ...leaves a once red-hot admirer as cold as a stone.'[210] Perhaps there was another reason, though, for Baring's loss of enthusiasm. Swinburne was clearly bored by the play, merely glanced at the Countess's letter (evidently reading 'Maurice' as 'Ma nièce'), and drafted a reply to the effect that he had no idea of its possible success, being cut off now from the world of letters. He did not, however, even get round to posting this response, which was found in his papers after his death together with Baring's manuscript.[211] It would doubtless be extravagant to suggest that Swinburne here was allowing his anti-Russian prejudice to condemn an innocent young Englishman's play, but it could have seemed that way to Countess Benkendorf. And what was Baring himself to make of it? Possibly even he retained a grudge, for in his celebrated *Outline of Russian Literature* he made the double-edged remark that, had Swinburne been a Russian, his 'politics alone would have been taken into consideration' by serious-minded critics like Belinskii.[212] In view of all this, it is most ironical to note that Coulson Kernahan dedicated to Baring his book *Swinburne as I Knew Him*, asserting of his subject: 'That he had read and admired work of yours, I have cause to know...'[213]

Baring's comment on Swinburne in relation to Russian literature is of interest because the bard was not, in fact, much appreciated in the land of the Tsars. A common Russian view of English poetry of the 1860s and later saw a clear divide between the so-called 'art-for-art's-sake' poetry of Tennyson and the 'Satanic school' said to have been founded by Swinburne. Proceeding in a direct line from Shelley, Swinburne seemed the 'passionate bard of pantheism and republicanism' and, in addition, of 'sensuality' (*chuvstvennost'*).[214] For this reason, for his anti-Russian politics, but more still for his complexity, Swinburne was never much translated into Russian. Konstantin Bal'mont, who extensively rendered works by foreign poets including many English ones, quoted lines from him — 'Miles and miles and miles of desolation,/Leagues on leagues on leagues without a change' — as a preface to his poem *Boloto* (The Marsh, 1903). But his attempts at actually translating Swinburne were not successful — at least in the opinion of the great Russian poet Pasternak. Pasternak himself became quite fascinated by Swinburne for a time, made a Russian version of the tragedy *Chastelard* and also began on *Mary Stuart*. His drafts of these have subsequently been lost, but his translation of the sonnet *John Ford* has been preserved in manuscript, along with his own comments and emendations. The concentration and intensity of Swinburne's high-flown style both attracted Pasternak and made his task in the end impracticable.[215]

It is hard to say what Swinburne himself knew or thought, if anything, of Russian literature in this later period. Needless to say, perhaps, a list of his 'Hundred Great Authors', supplied with some embarrassment in 1886 in response to a request from the *Pall Mall Gazette*, contained not a single Russian writer.[216] It does seem, however, that some of Tolstoi's works were familiar to him, though it could be rather that he was simply aware of them, given the great prominence of the man. On 29 June 1903 (old style) Sydney Carlyle Cockerell, formerly secretary to William Morris and the Kelmscott Press and afterwards Director of the Fitzwilliam Museum in Cambridge, visited Tolstoi at Iasnaia Poliana and was very kindly received. They spoke of Morris, Ruskin, Carlyle, Dickens, Shakespeare, science, religion and politics. The grand old Russian sage declared no sympathy for socialism, involving as it must do interference and coercion by government; his own views were more anarchical. He did, however, agree with the suggestion (originally Ruskin's) that to get rid of the problems of the East End one must first get rid of the West End.[217] Cockerell made extensive notes on all this at the time, which he afterwards sent to a number of acquaintances including Swinburne who was, of course, a lifelong devotee of Dickens. Heartily concurring with Tolstoi's view that Dickens's characters were like personal friends, Swinburne replied: 'The appreciation of so great a man as

Tolstoi — so glorious a genius and so glorious a personality — does what no other living man's could do: it adds a crowning ray of glory to the fame of Dickens.' Calling Tolstoi 'such a man of men', he concluded: 'genius will find out genius, and goodness will recognise goodness.'[218] It is a pity that Swinburne made no comment on Tolstoi's political and philosophical ideas, but it is obvious that he did not see him as a Russian at all, rather as an everyman. A love of Dickens was, for him, a touchstone of universality.

At all events, no isolated instance of Russian virtue could divert Swinburne from his path of acrimony. Most things Russian continued to antagonise him as the entente with France moved from promise into reality. In 1892, for instance, he even managed to complain that Gladstone was 'flirting' at Saint-Raphaël with the 'old' mother of the late Mariia Bashkirtseva, 'the Muscovite minx'.[219] On a more serious plane, when the newly-crowned Tsar Nicholas II paid a state visit to Paris in September 1896 Swinburne reviled 'the fawning, servile, prostitute hospitality of the strumpet Republic to "that excellent grand tyrant of the earth"' and, not content with quoting Shakespeare, went on to characterise France as the great whore of Ezekiel. He wished that the heavens would open up and destroy the Tsar and his friends.[220] Similarly, even though developments with respect to the Armenian question forced him at last to recognise 'Ottoman savageries', he believed that Russia, once again, was fundamentally to blame. There was room for a new ode. Nothing could be so 'horrible and infernal', he told Watts, 'as the Muscovite policy of hampering the intervention of Europe' to stop the criminal actions of the Turks which, when compared to the Russians, were 'as the brutality of a hunted beast to the devilry of an incarnate fiend'.[221]

Swinburne continued to observe Russia's fortunes as the years went by, gloating over its every setback and defeat and wishing it a cataclysmic rout. At the time of the Japanese War he wrote to William Michael Rossetti, citing Dickens: '"The still small voice is a-singing comic songs within me" every day that I read of a Russian reverse.' It was February 1904, a time when factions in St Petersburg already seemed set to topple the Tsar from within while Japan was crushing him from without. Swinburne foresaw a revolution which might even 'eclipse the French — in its beneficent and necessary result', and seemed to worry little that its terror, too, could be greater. Adding Russian endings to French names, he said for instance that he thought no latter-day vacillating Maratov could last as long as his celebrated ancestor.[222] Early in the following year he had cause to write a sonnet called *Czar Louis XVI. Adsit omen!* in which he railed against the cowardice of Nicholas II in the face of popular revolution. It was directly inspired by the Bloody Sunday massacre in St Petersburg on 22

January, 1905. The Tsar had deliberately remained at his country residence while his troops killed demonstrating workers in the capital. The people had thought him good, but now they were disabused. Swinburne read all this in the *Pall Mall Gazette* on 23 and 24 January, and shared the editor's horror. He wrote his poem in haste and gave it for publication in the paper as a centre feature on the very next day. This is how it read:[223]

CZAR LOUIS XVI
Adsit omen!

Peace on his lying lips, and on his hands
    Blood, smiled and cowered the tyrant, seeing afar
    His bondslaves perish and acclaim their Czar.
Now, sheltered scarce by Murder's loyal bands,
Clothed on with slaughters, naked else, he stands;
    He flies and stands not. Now the bloodred star
    That marks the face of midnight as a scar,
Tyranny, trembles on the brow it brands,
And shudders towards the pit where deathless death
    Leaves no life more for liars and slayers to live.
      Fly, coward, and cower, while time is thine to fly:
Cherish awhile thy terror-shortened breath.
    Not as thy grandsire died, if justice give
      Judgment, but slain by judgment thou shalt die.

January 24th, 1905.

Swinburne's sonnet appeared without comment on 25 January, but it is interesting that on the following day the *Pall Mall Gazette* carried a front-page editorial arguing that to compare Nicholas II to Louis XVI was to insult the Frenchman. Louis at least had died like a man; would the feeble Nicholas ever have the courage to do so? He had failed the Russian people, and fixed a great divide between themselves and him. Tsardom was now sick unto death — who knew how long it could last? While Swinburne had by no means invented the parallel with Louis XVI, this could have seemed a sort of snub to him. He had for long had an uneasy relationship with the paper, as has previously been seen. The sonnet, besides, was definitely not one of his best, what with its awkward opening enjambement and its exaggerated sense of drama in relation to the Tsar who was in fact, as the newspaper noted, a somewhat pathetic figure. Despite this, Swinburne was encouraged by the reactions of his neighbours on Putney Hill, 'simple and honest folk' who showed (he said) great sympathy with the sort of public attitudes that he was here expressing.[224] Moreover, the sonnet elicited a letter from his old associate in anti-Russian fervour, Karl Blind. 'I am rejoiced beyond expression', Swinburne replied, 'to find that you think my verdict on the equally contemptible and execrable Czar not only just but in some degree adequate to the occasion.'[225]

Nicholas II was the third Tsar in succession to be cursed by Swinburne. No one now in Britain sought to indict the poet for saying what everyone believed. Nor could the continuing cordial intercourse of European royalty do much to save the Emperor from the fate here willed upon him. England's throne had been allied to the Russian both in 1874, when Victoria's son Prince Alfred, Duke of Edinburgh, was married to Mariia Aleksandrovna, and twenty years later when her granddaughter Princess Alix of Hesse became the wife of the Tsarevich, soon to be Nicholas II. The Imperial couple's visit to Balmoral in September 1896 was used as an opportunity to gather together four generations of the British royal family. It is, however, cautionary to note that Queen Victoria was also grandmother to Kaiser Bill. But that is another story — as indeed is the cataclysm of 1917 which violently engulfed the last vestiges of Russian monarchy and introduced the world to Swinburne's own Vladimir Il'ich Maratov, not to speak of Iosif Vissarionovich Robesperskii. Our poet lived to see neither: it had been enough for him to damn the crimes of pre-Revolutionary Tsars.

NOTES

Very important: these Notes must be used in conjunction with the Bibliography, which is an essential key to understanding them; entries there are alphabetical, by author and title.

Notes to the Introduction

1. See Sewell, pp. 106-10, where this year is given; Moorman, *Later Years*, gives 1848. See also Morley, F.V., p. 166.

2. Hakluyt, vol. I, p. 54.

3. See Hakluyt, vol. I, p. 83.

4. See *Dictionary of National Biography*, vol. III, p. 912, vol. VI, p. 405, etc.; Alekseev, *Ln* 91, pp. 89-90; *Conversations on the History of Russia*, part (vol.) I, pp. 63-5.

5. *Canterbury Tales*, Prologue, l. 54. See Chaucer, p. 419, where 'reysed' is glossed as 'gone on a military expedition'.

6. *Canterbury Tales*, Squieres Tale, l. 10. See Chaucer, p. 628.

7. The story is recorded in Hakluyt, vol. I, pp. 254ff., 272ff., 307ff., 356ff. See also e.g. Cawley, *Voyagers*, p. 240; Alekseev, *Ln* 91, pp. 17-20.

8. Morgan and Coote, vol. II, p. 373; Hakluyt, vol. II, pp. 434-6; Putnam, p. 41, etc. Jenkinson's account of matrimonial manners in Russia was summarised, without comment, in Milton's *Moscovia* and adverted to, in somewhat garbled form, in Oliver Goldsmith's *Letters of a Citizen of the World*; see on this Brewster, *East-West*, pp. 19, 23.

9. Cawley, *Voyagers*, pp. 265-6; Alekseev, *Ln* 91, p. 20.

10. See Alekseev, *Ln* 91, pp. 36-8, 95-6; Brewster, *East-West*, p. 12.

11. See Brewster, *East-West*, pp. 15-16. Horsey's adventures in Russia were included in *Purchase his Pilgrimes* in 1625.

12. Burton, pp. 662 (3.2.2.1.), 827 (3.3.1.2.).

13. See Donne, pp. 175-6. 'E.G.' here is thought to be Edward Gilpin.

14. Drayton, vol. I, p. 14.

15. Innumerable references are given in Cawley, *Voyagers*, pp. 253-71.

16. Drayton, vol. III, p. 1033; note that the spelling *Poly-Olbion*, rather than *Poly-Albion*, is indeed used throughout this edition. See also Alekseev, *Ln* 91, p. 21.

17. Warner, 1602, pp. 282-3; see also ibid., p. 288 (ch. LXVIII); Morgan and Coote, vol. I, p. cxlix in pp. cxlix-clii; Alekseev, *Ln* 91, p. 21.

18. See Brody, pp. 141-216; Alekseev, *Ln* 91, pp. 35, 93-4; Cawley, *Voyagers*, pp. 253-4, 269.

19. See Hakluyt, vol. II, pp. 99-108; Major, vol. I, pp. cxlix-clvi; and cf. Morgan and Coote, vol. I, pp. 37-8, etc. Turbervile's *Certaine Letters in Verse*, first published in the author's own *Tragicall Tales* (1587), were reprinted in Hakluyt's *Voyages* in 1589.

20. James, R., pp. 243-4, 266-7. See also Unbegaun; Simmons and Unbegaun, pp. 123-5; Alekseev, *Ln* 91, pp. 29, 92. Larin includes (pp. 349-421) a facsimile of James's manuscript grammar and vocabulary.

21. James, R., p. xxv.

22. James, R., pp. 216-17.

23. James, R., pp. 222-3.

24. Shakespeare, *Measure for Measure*, II.i.144-5.

25. Shakespeare, *The Winter's Tale*, III.ii.120.

26. Shakespeare, *The Life of King Henry V*, III.vii.158-60.

27. Shakespeare, *Macbeth*, III.iv.100-6.

28. Shakespeare, *Love's Labour's Lost*, V.ii. See Alekseev, *Ln* 91, pp. 32, 93; Sorensen; Cawley, *Voyagers*, pp. 256, 263; Morgan and Coote, vol. I, p. xii, vol. II, p. 257.

29. Davenant, vol. I, p. 166; cf. Cawley, *Voyagers*, p. 256.

30. Heywood, vol. V, p. 16. Alekseev, *Ln* 91, p. 31, suggests that this may derive from a Russian proverb, but that seems intrinsically unlikely.

31. Heywood, vol. V, p. 65.

32. Sidney, pp. xliii-iv, xlix, 165-6, 458, 460. See also Cawley, *Voyagers*, p. 260; Alekseev, *Ln* 91, p. 22.

33. Nashe, folio E3, verso.

34. Nashe, folio G. The text has '*Ponuloi*', but I have taken this as a misprint for '*Pomiloi*'. In Russian, 'Lord, have mercy upon us' is '*Gospodi, pomilui nas*'.

35. *The Faerie Queene*, II.xi.26.6-8. See Spenser, vol. II, pp. 89-90.

36. *Tamburlaine the Great*, I.ii.299. See Marlowe, p. 16.

37. *The Jew of Malta*, IV.1581. See Marlowe, p. 283.

38. Belchier, D2, verso; see also on this Alekseev, *Ln* 91, p. 100, where the playwright's name has, however, been mangled as 'Dowbridge'.

39. *Temple of Fame*, ll. 53-4. See Pope, vol. I, p. 121.

40. *Tristram Shandy*, III.20. See Sterne, pp. 196-7.

41. Butler, pp. 36-7 (*Hudibras*, First Part, Canto II, ll. 249-98).

42. See Simmons, J., 'H.W. Ludolf'; Alekseev, *Ln* 91, pp. 45-6, 100-1.

43. Milton, *Paradise Lost*, XI.394-5.

44. Alekseev, *Ln* 91, 40-2, 98. See also Cawley, *Milton*, p. 43 and passim.

45. Milton, *Paradise Lost*, X.431-3.

46. Mottley, vol. I, p. 101.

47. Barrow, pp. 68-9. 86.

48. Evelyn, *Diary and Correspondence*, pp. 515-16; Evelyn, *Diary*, pp. 1022-5; *Conversations on the History of Russia*, part (vol.) II, p. 70; Putnam, p. 31; Barrow, pp. 80-1; Macaulay, vol. VI, pp. 358-66.

49. Barrow, p. 71.

50. See for instance Alekseev, *Ln* 91, pp. 67ff., 75, 104-5.

51. Richardson-Gardner, p. 53; Barrow, pp. 82-3; Alekseev, *Ln* 91, pp. 84-5 (illustration). The signboard of the Gravesend tavern later found its way to the Imperial Library in St Petersburg. There is, however, a slight problem here. The reverse of the board bears the legend 'HASTED'. As far as I can see, this cannot be a place-name, unless it is significantly misspelt.

52. Compare also Andrew Cherry's operatic drama *Peter the Great; or, The Wooden Walls* (1807) — though this is set in Russia — and the Anglo-Franco-Italian opera *Pietro il Grande*, produced at Covent Garden in 1852. See on this Cross, *Russian Theme*, pp. 13-14, 99; O'Driscoll, p. 121.

53. Congreve, p. 381.

54. Hill, A., vol. III, p. 184 in pp. 181-99.

55. Hill, A., vol. III, pp. 193-4.

56. Hill, A., vol. III, p. 185; this text differs considerably (but not substantially) from that of the first edition, ll. 85-90.

57. See Brewster, *Aaron Hill*, pp. 201-2, 205-6; Brewster, *East-West Passage*, pp. 24-5; Anderson, *Britain's Discovery*, p. 79; Alekseev, *Ln* 91, pp. 87-9, 109.

58. Hill, A., vol. III, pp. 39-40.

59. *The Seasons*, 'Winter', ll. 776-8. See Thomson, p. 156.

60. *The Seasons*, 'Winter', ll. 799-805. See Thomson, p. 157.

61. *The Seasons*, 'Winter', ll. 955-9. See Thomson, pp. 161-2. See also Longfellow, pp. 210-15.

62. Mottley, vol. I, p. 104.

63. See Bruce, p. 180, with reference to the year 1716.

64. I see that this point is also made in Crankshaw, p. 79.

65. Southey, *Complete Poetical Works*, p. 134; Longfellow, pp. 109-11.

66. Alekseev, *Ln* 91, 69, 76, 106-7.

67. Jonas Hanway, *An Historical Account of the British Trade over the Caspian Sea; with a Journal of Travels from London through Russia into Persia, and back again through Russia, Germany, and Holland...*, 4 vols, London, 1753; George Macartney, *An Account of an Embassy to Russia MDCCLXVII*, London, 1768; Sir Nathaniel William Wraxall, *Cursory Remarks Made in a Tour through some of the Northern Parts of Europe, particularly Copenhagen, Stockholm, and St. Petersburgh...*, London, 1775; William Richardson, *Anecdotes of the Russian Empire, in a Series of Letters written a few years ago from St. Petersburg*, London, 1784; Rev. William Coxe, *Travels into Poland, Russia, Sweden and Denmark, interspersed with Historical Relations and Political Enquiries...*, 3 vols, London, 1784-90; Andrew Swinton, *Travels into Norway, Denmark and Russia in the Years 1788, 1789, 1790, and 1791*, London, 1792; Sir John Carr, *A Northern Summer; or, Travels round the Baltic, through Denmark, Sweden, Russia, Prussia, and Part of Germany, in the Year 1804*, London (also Philadelphia), 1805; John Augustus Atkinson and James Walker, *A Picturesque Representation of the Manners, Customs, and Amusements of the Russians in One Hundred Coloured Plates; with an Accurate Explanation of Each Plate in English and French*, 3 vols, London, 1803-4, reprinted 1812; Edward Daniel Clarke, *Travels in Various Countries of Europe, Asia and Africa*, London, 1810.

68. Garrick, vol. III, p. 1229; cf. Alekseev, *Ln* 91, pp. 115, 171. No one yet appears to have identified the poet here referred to. On the general question of Russians in England in the eighteenth century, see the authoritative monograph by Cross, *'By the Banks of the Thames'*.

69. Cowper, p. 203 (book V, 'The Winter Morning Walk'); see also Longfellow, pp. 96-7. For a discussion of this poem, see Dawson.

70. Macartney, pp. 167-8; see on this Cross, 'Early English Specimens', p. 449.

71. Coxe, p. 203 in vol. II, pp. 196-209; see on this Cross, 'Early English Specimens', pp. 449-50.

72. See the title-pages of these two books, reproduced in Alekseev, *Ln* 91, p. 137.

73. Harris, James, *passim*.

74. See on this many works by Cross, e.g. 'Karamzin and England' and 'Early English Specimens'.

75. See Cross, *Russian Theme*, pp. 16-18, 98.

76. Coleridge, *Poetical Works*, pp. 39-40.

77. Campbell, T., *Poetical Works*, pp. 13-14; Longfellow, pp. 108-9.

78. See Cary, vol. I, pp. 93-5.

79. Hunt, *Poetical Works*, p. 176.

80. Hunt, *Table-Talk*, pp. 62, 106-7, 197-8.

81. Keats, p. 61.

82. Keats, p. 50. This prophetic poem was written in December 1816 and published in February 1817; Kościuszko died in October 1817.

83. See e.g. Ashton, vol. II, pp. 126-49; Vossler, passim.

84. See Ashton, vol. II, pp. 132, 147-9.

85. See on this Alekseev, *Ln* 91, pp. 160-4, 184-5; Cross, 'Early English Specimens', p. 453. The illustrator Hopwood may have been James the younger, or else William.

86. See on all this Alekseev, *Ln* 91, pp. 168, 186, 217, etc.; Cross, *Russian Theme*, pp. 18-23. Information on titles, dates and authors has been verified in Nicoll, A., and in other standard authorities.

87. For more details and examples than I give, see Alekseev, *Ln* 91, p. 372; Cross, *Russian Theme*, pp. 18-24, 101-4; Partridge, 'Slavonic Themes', pp. 428-9; Pasenko.

88. The full title of William Cowper's original, as readers of that time would have known, is *The Diverting History of John Gilpin, showing how he went farther than he intended, and came home safe again* (1782).

89. Alekseev, *Ln* 91, pp. 161, 372.

90. See on this Cross, *Russian Theme*, pp. 27-8, 108.

91. Harrison, R., p. 252.

92. Alekseev, *Ln* 91, pp. 250-2, 259; *Conversations on the History of Russia*, part (vol.) II, pp. 354-5.

93. See on this Partridge, 'Slavonic Themes', p. 429.

94. See Adams, W.H.D., p. 146; Waddington, *Turgenev and England*, pp. 104ff.

95. Badcock had earlier produced an English version of Karamzin's travels (1803).

96. See Hogg, p. 19.

97. *Punch; or, The London Charivari*, vol. XXVII, July 1854, p. 15. See on the possible effects of *Frankenstein* in Russia the intriguing article by Freeborn.

98. Shelley, *Hellas*, ll. 307-11. The other references are to *Alastor; or, The Spirit of Solitude*, ll. 352ff., etc.; *Prometheus Unbound*, III.i.63-7, ii.11-17; *Queen Mab*, IV. 33-89; and *Hellas*, ll. 264-77, 536-45, 948-9, 967-72. See Shelley, ed. Rogers, vol. I, pp. 90-1, 254-6, vol. II, p. 54; Shelley, ed. Hutchinson, pp. 244-5, 459-60, 465, 474-5, 774-5.

99. See Keats, p. 501. Only fragments of *The Castle-Builder* are known. The lines quoted were first published in 1912, the bulk of the poem in 1848.

100. Southey, *Common-Place Book*, series I, p. 435, series III, p. 251.

101. Southey, *Life and Correspondence*, vol. IV, p. 14.

102. Southey, *Selections*, vol. II, p. 314.

103. Southey, *Complete Poetical Works*, p. 202.

104. Southey, *Selections*, vol. II, pp. 302-3, and cf. p. 305.

105. Southey, *Selections*, vol. I, p. 90.

106. Southey, *Complete Poetical Works*, pp. 483-4; see also Longfellow, pp. 78-83.

107. Southey, *Complete Poetical Works*, pp. 206-7. Accompanying odes are dedicated to Frederick William IV of Prussia and the Prince Regent of England.

108. Southey, *Life and Correspondence*, vol. VI, pp. 150-1.

109. See Swinburne, *Letters*, ed. Lang, vol. III, p. 247.

110. Byron, p. 383 (*Don Juan*, IX, lxxii, lxxvii).

111. Byron, p. 382 (*Don Juan*, IX, lix).

112. Byron, p. 363 (*Don Juan*, VII, xv). See on this Alekseev, *Ln* 91, pp. 404-5, 454.

113. See Byron, pp. 234-40.

114. Campbell, T., *Life and Letters*, vol. II, pp. 7-11.

115. Campbell, T., *Poetical Works*, pp. 223-6.

116. Campbell, T., *Poetical Works*, pp. 218-22.

117. On this see e.g. Campbell, T., *Life and Letters*, vol. III, pp. 110ff., 444-5.

118. Robinson, *On Books*, ed. Morley, vol. I, p. 404. On Campbell's involvement with Poland see Partridge, 'Slavonic Themes', pp. 422-5.

119. See Campbell, T., *Life and Letters*, vol. III, p. 361.

120. Robinson, *On Books*, ed. Morley, vol. I, p. 230.

121. Moore, T., *Poetical Works*, vol. VII, pp. 238-9.

122. Moore, T., *Poetical Works*, vol. VII, pp. 215ff. For a discussion of this and other works by Moore, see Partridge, 'Slavonic Themes', pp. 429-32.

123. Moore, T., *Memoirs*, vol. III, p. 93.

124. Moore, T., *Memoirs*, vol. III, p. 262.

125. Struve, G., 'Russian Traveller', p. 342.

126. Moore, T., *Memoirs*, vol. VI, p. 5; Alekseev, *Ln* 91, pp. 738ff.

127. Moore, T., *Poetical Works*, vol. V, pp. 314-15.

128. Johnson, vol. I, pp. 394-5.

129. Johnson, vol. I, pp. 500-2; Lockhart, vol. III, pp. 21-2.

130. See Alekseev, *Ln* 91, pp. 266-7, 377; Partridge, 'Slavonic Themes', pp. 428-9.

131. Johnson, vol. II, pp. 981, 1003, 1006; Scott, Sir W., p. 11; Struve, G., 'Russian Friends', p. 309.

132. Scott, Sir W., pp. 11, 33, 47, 159, 166-8, 341, 337, 346, 380-1, 387, 397, 423, 447-8; Johnson, vol. II, pp. 1023, 1047, etc.; Rozov, pp. 300-2; Struve, G., 'Russian Friends', pp. 311, 316-17. There are letters of Walter Scott to Count Vl.P. Orlov-Davydov and D.V. Davydov for the years 1826-1828 in the department of manuscripts at the Russian State (Lenin) Library in Moscow (F479). Also there is a journal of young Orlov-Davydov, in English, in which he records meetings and conversations with Scott (F219, 90.43-6; 91.1-13).

133. Moore, T., *Memoirs*, vol. V, p. 5. Moore incorrectly refers to Davydov as 'Demidoff', doubtless because this name was better known to him.

134. Scott, Sir W., pp. 229-31, 233; Johnson, vol. II, pp. 1001-3; Partington, *Private Letter-Books*, p. 304; Struve, G., 'Russian Friends', p. 325; Struve, G., 'Scott Letters', pp. 479-82.

135. Scott, Sir W., pp. 537-8; Struve, G., 'Russian Friends', pp. 324-6.

136. Cited in Alekseev, *Ln* 91, p. 343.

137. See Johnson, vol. II, p. 1233.

138. See Bowring, L.B., pp. 117-25, 377.

139. See e.g. Cross, 'Early English Specimens', pp. 453-7.

140. Landor, *Imaginary Conversations*, vol. II, pp. 234-9, 316-23, 404-14; vol. V, pp. 74-8, 94-101, 219-37.

141. Bowring, J., 'Politics and Literature', pp. 80-1. Bowring was associated with the *Westminster Review* from its beginnings.

142. See General Register for 1827, pp. 160, 162-3, 167-8.

Notes to William Wordsworth

1. See e.g. Alekseev, *Ln* 91; Levin, *Ossian v russkoi literature*, 'Val'ter Skott v russkoi pechati'; Struve, G., 'Russian Friends', 'Scott Letters'; Struve, P., 'Walter Scott and Russia'; Simmons, E., *English Literature and Culture in Russia*.

2. See e.g. Gerbel', pp. xxviii, 195-7.

3. See Alekseev, *Ln* 91, p. 14.

4. See 'Sovremennaia angliiskaia literatura', *Literaturnaia gazeta*, 13 October 1830, p. 176 in pp. 175-80, 183-5; see also Alekseev, *Ln* 91, p. 815.

5. Belinskii, vol. IV, p. 432, vol. V, p. 13.

6. 'Pis'ma inogorodnogo podpishchika' (Letter XXIII of January 1851, and Letter XXVIII of February 1852), in Druzhinin, *Sobranie sochinenii*, vol. VI, pp. 481-2, 627; cf. vol. V, pp. 288, 292-3.

7. Druzhinin, *Sobranie sochinenii*, vol. IV, pp. 654-6.

8. Druzhinin, *Povesti. Dnevnik*, pp. 191, 216, 244, 245; *Sobranie sochinenii*, vol. IV, p. 656.

9. Dostoevskii, vol. XXIV, pp. 82, 411-12, 414. See Byron's *Don Juan*, 'Dedication', vi.6.

10. See Pushkin, vol. III, pp. 214, 803, 1205 (*Sonet*: 'Surovyi Dant ne preziral soneta'), vol. XI, pp. 73, 344, 538 ('V zreloi slovesnosti prikhodit vremia'), vol. XIV, p. 158; Simmons, E., 'La littérature', p. 105; Iakovlev, pp. 122-9, 132-7; Vatsuro, vol. II, pp. 51, 206.

11. Alekseev, *Ln* 91, p. 815; Iakovlev, pp. 124-5; Gerbel', pp. 197-8. Kozlov made many translations from English literature, especially from Moore and Byron.

12. Gerbel', p. 198.

13. Kropotkin, *Russian Literature*, p. 46. For a more objective comparison, see Partridge, 'Romanticism'.

14. Mirskii, p. 107. It is not completely clear if Mirskii had in mind the Kiukhel'beker poem of 1836 or that of 1837; see Kiukhel'beker, vol. I, pp. 291-2, 295-6.

15. See Kiukhel'beker, vol. I, pp. 214-15.

16. See Turgenev, I.S., *Sochineniia*, vol. I, pp. 102-27.

17. Wordsworth, *Letters*, 1967, p. 213.

18. Ellis, p. 254; Putnam, pp. 210, 251-2; see also Wordsworth, *Letters*, 1967, p. 213, etc.

19. Wordsworth, W., *Peter Bell*, p. ix; my quotations will be based on this edition, pp. 48-51, 483-7, 495, 613-15, and on Wordsworth, W., *Poetical Works*, ed. Selincourt and Darbishire, vol. II, revised ed., 1952, pp. 333-5, with notes pp. 527-9.

20. See Wordsworth, W., *Peter Bell*, pp. 3-17; Moorman, *Early Years*, pp. 392-4; *Later Years*, pp. 364-72.

21. On the history of the composition of this poem and the collection in which it appeared, see Wordsworth, W., *Poems, in Two Volumes*, pp. 3-5, 17, 75-7, 404, 437-8. See also *Poetical Works*, ed. Selincourt and Darbishire, vol. II, revised ed., 1952, pp. 149, 492, 539. No edition of the poem offers any explanation of the names supposedly associated with the redbreast in the countries in question. For the background to the poem and some commentaries on it, see Selincourt, *Dorothy Wordsworth*, p. 134; Siemens, p. 29; Magnus, p. 199; Pinion, p. 123; Lack, p. 131.

22. See Bewick, p. 207. Bewick was actually the engraver and editor, not the author of the text which was originally by Ralph Beilby. For other possible sources, see Bolton, J., 1794, plate 55 (and cf. Bolton, J., 1845, vol. II, p. 44); Montagu, p. 266; Lewin, vol. IV, p. 30. See also Shaver, p. 22.

23. The quotations here are adapted (by the removal of some unconvincing capital letters) from the Cornell Wordsworth 'reading text' of *The Fourteen-Book Prelude by William Wordsworth*, ed. W.J.B. Owen, Ithaca and London, 1985, pp. 138, 140, 143. The manuscript versions there transcribed (pp. 741, 749, 755, 757) show no significant variations from the text as quoted here, save that my reading of the facsimile of ll. 149-50 (p. 748) in conjunction with the editor's essay on dating (pp. 5-10) suggests to me that the term 'ant-hill' was introduced by Wordsworth only in the late 1830s. See also Wordsworth, W., *The Prelude*, ed. Selincourt.

24. Wordsworth, *Letters*, 1988, p. 43.

25. Cited here from Wordsworth, W., *Poetical Works*, ed. Selincourt and Darbishire, vol. IV, 1947, p. 123.

26. Cited from the text in Wordsworth, W., *Poetical Works*, ed. Selincourt and Darbishire, vol. V, revised ed., 1959, p. 256.

27. Cited from the text in Wordsworth, W., *Poetical Works*, ed. Selincourt and Darbishire, vol. V, revised ed., 1959, p. 203.

28. Wordsworth, *Letters*, 1969, pp. 475-6, 481, 484.

29. See Wordsworth, *Letters*, 1970, p. 142.

30. Significantly, Henry Wadsworth Longfellow would later anthologise it in his impressive book *Russia* (1878), a volume in the series *Poems of Places*; see Longfellow, pp. 8-9.

31. On the precise dating of these poems, see Wordsworth, W., *Shorter Poems*, ed. Ketcham, pp. 535-6.

32. See Wordsworth, *Letters*, 1978, pp. 178-9.

33. Wordsworth, *Letters*, 1979, p. 664. Southey's famous sonnet *Winter*, later much anthologised, opens: 'A wrinkled crabbèd man they picture thee,/Old Winter, with a ragged beard as grey/As the long moss upon the apple-tree;/Blue-lipt, an ice drop at thy sharp blue nose,/Close muffled up, and on thy dreary way/Plodding alone through sleet and drifting snows.' See Southey, *Complete Poetical Works*, p. 120.

34. See Wordsworth, W., *Shorter Poems*, ed. Ketcham, pp. 15, 177-80.

35. Quoted here from Wordsworth, W., *Shorter Poems*, ed. Ketcham, p. 185; cf. ibid., p. 197.

36. Wordsworth, W., *Shorter Poems*, ed. Ketcham, pp. 15-16, 187, 199.

37. Wordsworth, *Letters*, 1970, pp. 280-1.

38. Wordsworth, *Letters*, 1978, p. 178.

39. The titles and texts of the first two poems are as in Wordsworth, W., *Shorter Poems*, ed. Ketcham, pp. 206-8, except that I have preferred lower-case consistency with 'fathers ...sons' in l. 19 of 'Composed in Recollection...' These Cornell versions are, of course, bastard texts with no authorial justification; their great value is that they strip off previous editors' and publishers' errors and uncalled-for emendations, as well as Wordsworth's own later changes where these appear to detract from, rather than to enhance, the naturalness or freshness of his original inspiration. Sometimes, however, the new texts may seem controversial. An excellent example of this is seen in ll. 3-5 of 'Composed in Recollection...', which in definitive versions of the poem normally read:

> Hath painted Winter like a traveller old,
> Propped on a staff, and, through the sullen day,
> In hooded mantle, limping o'er the plain.

Which version is preferable here is chiefly a question of taste. Each has awkwardnesses. The standard text may lack some of the vigour of the original manuscript variants, but what the Cornell editor may not have noticed is that the alterations were dictated primarily by the need to remove the word 'shrunken', given that 'shrunk' is also used in l. 16. The text of the third poem in the sequence (*By Moscow self-devoted to a blaze*) is given here as in Wordsworth's *Poetical Works*, ed. Selincourt and Darbishire, vol. III, 1946, p. 142. It is interesting to note that Dorothy Wordsworth, in transcribing the piece for Henry Crabb Robinson soon after it was first composed, gave it in a very different form from the one with which her brother was finally satisfied. Here is the text as it stood on 21 December 1822:

> By self-devoted Moscow — by the blaze
> Of that dread sacrifice — by Russian blood
> Lavished in fight with desperate hardihood —
> The impassive elements no claim shall raise
> To rob our human nature of her praise.   5
> Enough was done and suffered to insure
> Final deliverance, absolute and pure;
> Enough for faith, tracking the beaten ways

> Of Providence. But now did the most High
> Exalt his still small voice, his wrath unshroud,   10
> And lay his justice bare to mortal eye;
> He who, of yore, by miracles spake aloud
> As openly that purpose here avow'd,
> Which only madness ventures to defy.

See Wordsworth, *Letters*, 1978, pp. 178-9. 'Aloud' in l. 12, instead of a scannable 'loud', was perhaps a slip in copying.

40. Wordsworth, Dorothy, *Journals*, vol. II, p. 33.

41. Wordsworth, Dorothy, *Journals*, vol. II, pp. 60, 93-4, etc., entries for July and August 1820.

42. Wordsworth, *Letters*, 1979, p. 187.

43. Moorman, *Later Years*, p. 79; Shaver, p. 208; cf. Wordsworth, *Letters*, 1967, p. 469. *Purchas his Pilgrimage* itself, which Wordsworth read in the third edition of 1617, does not, however, have a section on Russia and is devoted chiefly to religions; it should not be confused with *Purchase his Pilgrimes*, otherwise known as *Hakluytus Posthumus*.

44. Wordsworth, *Letters*, 1970, p. 152.

45. Wordsworth, *Letters*, 1978, p. 564.

46. Wordsworth, *Letters*, 1978, p. 669. Instead of 'feudal forms', the first — Selincourt — edition of Wordsworth's letters had 'feudal forces': see Wordsworth, *Letters*, ed. Selincourt, *The Later Years*, vol. I, p. 321. Alan G. Hill does not draw attention to the change.

47. See Shaver, p. 174.

48. Miege, p. 74.

49. See Wordsworth, *Letters*, 1979, p. 493.

50. See Lockhart, vol. IX, pp. 172-82; Johnson, vol. I, p. 681, II, pp. 1023, 1039, 1939, etc.; Scott, Sir W., p. 337.

51. Wordsworth, *Letters*, 1978, pp. 381-2.

52. Wordsworth, *Letters*, 1978, pp. 368-9, 627-8; cf. 1982, pp. 561-2.

53. Turgenev, A.I., *Arkhiv*, vol. I, p. 235; Alekseev, *Ln 91*, pp. 333-44, 817; Turgenev, A.I., *Pis'ma*, pp. 401, 414, etc.

54. Wordsworth, *Letters*, 1978, pp. 616, 623.

55. Hutchinson, pp. 366, 372, 376; Wordsworth, *Letters*, 1979, pp. 8, 155-6, 197, 254-5, 261, etc.

56. Wordsworth, *Letters*, 1978, p. 631; cf. ibid., pp. 651, 663, 688.

57. Wordsworth, *Letters*, 1978, p. 663; cf. ibid., pp. 664, 688-9, and Wordsworth, *Letters*, 1979, pp. 26, 56.

58. Wordsworth, *Letters*, 1979, p. 26. Wordsworth regularly used the word 'verse' for 'line', possibly owing to French influence. In the definitive text the poem has actually 376 lines.

59. Wordsworth, *Letters*, 1979, p. 56.

60. Wordsworth, *Letters*, 1978, pp. 650-3, 661-3, 687-90; see also *Letters*, 1979, pp. 35, 71, 145.

61. Wordsworth, *Letters*, 1979, pp. 6-8, 25-6, 32-3, 56-7, 59-60, 77, 84-6.

62. West, A., vol. I, p. 25.

63. There are references to a family of Gordons, possibly the one which interests us, in Turgenev, A.I., *Khronika*, p. 378, and in Turgenev, A.I., *Pis'ma*, p. 426.

64. See Turgenev, A.I., *Khronika*, p. 463; Turgenev, A.I., *Pis'ma*, pp. 390-1; Struve, G.,'Russian Traveller', p. 342; Partington, *Sir Walter's Post-Bag*, pp. 351, 355, 356, 363, 387.

65. Alekseev, *Ln 91*, pp. 355, 388; Struve, G.,'Russian Friends', pp. 343-4; Parker, p. 292.

66. Alekseev, *Ln 91*, p. 328.

67. See Alekseev, *Ln* 91, pp. 742, 815.

68. Wordsworth, *Letters*, 1979, p. 370.

69. Rydal Mount Visitors' Book, Dove Cottage; information kindly communicated by Dr Peter Laver in 1980.

70. See for instance Wordsworth, *Letters*, 1979, p. 387.

71. Wordsworth, *Letters*, 1988, p. 680.

72. See Moorman, *Later Years*, pp. 454-5.

73. Dove Cottage MSS Verse 78; see Siemens, p. 58.

74. Dove Cottage MSS Verse 81B; see Siemens, p. 64.

75. Dove Cottage MSS Verse 84; see Siemens, p. 68.

76. Dove Cottage MSS Verse 85; see Siemens, p. 71.

77. Dove Cottage MSS Verse 86; see Siemens, p. 77.

78. Wordsworth, *Letters*, 1978, p. 663.

79. This is given in the now standard form, found for instance in Wordsworth, W., *Poetical Works*, ed. Selincourt and Darbishire, vol. IV, 1947, pp. 183-94; this edition also has footnoted variants, and additional notes p. 441.

80. See Moorman, *Later Years*, p. 454.

81. See Coe, passim.

82. Wordsworth, C., vol. II, pp. 162-3.

83. See Putnam, p. xxii.

84. Alekseev, *Ln* 91, p. 174.

85. Robinson, *Diary*, vol. II, p. 632.

86. See Shaver, p. 37. The titles of the London and Dublin versions show trivial differences, but the text of each is identical. The story used by Wordsworth is in Book III, pp. 107-10. There is also a modern facsimile of the Dublin edition (London, 1970).

87. See Wordsworth, W., *Poetical Works*, ed. Selincourt and Darbishire, vol. IV, 1947, p. 441; Moorman, *Later Years*, p. 454.

88. Wordsworth, W., *Poetical Works*, ed. Selincourt and Darbishire, vol. IV, 1947, p. 441; see Bruce, pp. 86-9, 109-10.

89. See Bruce, pp. 107-10 (Book III).

90. Bruce, pp. 110-17.

91. Bruce, p. 161.

92. Bruce, p. 107.

93. See Vigor, pp. 13-16; see also Douhaire, passim.

94. Bruce, p. 106.

95. See for instance Andrew Simon Lamb, *Ina: A Lay of the Bruce's Heart*, Edinburgh, 1858; Charles Watts Whistler, *A Prince of Cornwall: A Story of Glastonbury and the West in the Days of Ina of Wessex*, London, 1904. Other publications with an Ina as heroine include Mrs Markham (pseud.), *Ina, and Other Fragments, in Verse*, Glasgow, 1834, which is set in Turkey and Arabia; Mira M. Radcliffe, *Ina, and Other Poems*, Liverpool, 1841; Mary Eliza Leslie, *Ina, and Other Poems*, Calcutta, 1856; R.F.H. (Rosa F. Hill), *The Lady Ina, and Other Poems*, London, 1865, whose title poem is set apparently in the Scottish border country; Katherine Valerio, *Ina: A Novel*, Boston (Mass.), 1871; Harriette E. Burch, *Ina and Kitty; or, The Little Flower Girl and her Friend*, London, 1892; Ila Floyd, *Ina: A Story*, Manchester and London, 1910.

96. See Dacre, vol. II, Preface.

97. See on this Cross, *The Tale*.

98. Wordsworth, *Letters*, 1979, p. 26.

99. Coe, p. 32.

100. Coe, p. 35.

101. See Wordsworth, W., *Poetical Works*, ed. Selincourt and Darbishire, vol. IV, 1947, pp. 188-9, 441.

102. Bruce, pp. 99-100.

103. Bruce, p. 100.

104. See Wordsworth, *Letters*, 1979, pp. 434-5; Moorman, *Later Years*, pp. 461-3; Wordsworth, W., *Poetical Works*, ed. Selincourt and Darbishire, vol. III, pp. 524-6; Struve, G., 'Russian Friends', pp. 344-5.

105. Wordsworth, W., *Poetical Works*, ed. Knight, vol. VII, p. 237; cf. also Coe, pp. 34-5.

106. Bruce, p. 98.

107. Bruce, pp. 120-1.

108. See e.g. Baring, *Russian People*, pp. 71-2.

109. Miege, pp. 70-2.

110. Batho, pp. 143-4.

111. See Shaver, p. 148.

112. Robinson, *Diary*, vol. II, p. 633.

113. Wordsworth, *Letters*, 1988, p. 479.

114. Wordsworth, *Letters*, 1988, pp. 384-5, 806.

115. Sewell, pp. 106-10; Wordsworth, *Letters*, 1988, p. 906.

116. Wordsworth, *Letters*, 1979, pp. 354, 651; Brookfield, p. 134; Tennyson, A., *Letters*, vol. I, p. 131; Tennyson, H., *Tennyson and Friends*, pp. 398-9, 402-3.

117. Tennyson, H., *Memoir*, vol. I, pp. 209-10; Abbott and Campbell, *Letters*, p. 172.

118. Tennyson, H., *Memoir*, vol. II, pp. 70-1, 288; Tennyson, A., *Letters*, vol. III, p. 415.

119. Tennyson, A., *Letters*, vol. I, pp. 238, 240.

120. Wordsworth, *Letters*, 1988, pp. 669, 687-8.

Notes to Alfred Tennyson

1. Allingham, p. 265 (entry for 30 March 1878).

2. Tennyson, C., 'Tennyson Papers', pp. 284-5.

3. See e.g. Hyde, pp. 32, 36. On the Emperor Paul's anglophobia, including threats about India, see e.g. Putnam, pp. 82, 300. For a contemporary English account of his assassination, see Carr, pp. 302-20.

4. Tennyson, C., and Dyson, p. 44: Campbell, N., vol. 1, items 223, 227, 279; Moore, G. (critic), pp. 3, 241.

5. Tennyson, C., and Dyson, pp. 37-8. The date of the Tsar's coronation was not brought forward, as is often stated in Tennyson literature.

6. McCabe, pp. 734-5.

7. McCabe, p. 735; Tennyson, H., *Memoir*, vol. II, pp. 147-8. See also Tennyson, C., *Alfred Tennyson,* pp. 8-9; Tennyson, A., *Letters*, vol. III, pp. 356-7. McCabe's original memorandum of his 1887 visit to Tennyson may be read in Gordon, vol. II, pp. 352-3. Although his account of the St Helens story is much briefer here than the one he published later, a close comparison of the two suggests that the expansion cannot have been his alone and must to some extent reflect what Tennyson actually said. One or two details in the earlier version even subsequently disappeared, notably that the English courier's name was Reynolds.

8. See e.g. Johnstone, vol. I, pp. 147-8, 155.

9. It is not possible to say if the anecdote was ever actually entered in the diary. It is not transcribed by Hallam in his own privately printed *Materials*, upon which the Memoir is for the most part based.

10. *Echoes of the 'Eighties*, p. 66.

11. Tennyson, C., and Dyson, pp. 37-8, 76-7; Martin, pp. 12-14, 114-15; Henderson, P.P., *Tennyson*, p. 3. Hoge, in Tennyson, E., *Journal*, p. 356, maintains (I think incorrectly) that the Bishop of Albany who came to Aldworth in 1873 was the Rt Rev. John J. Conroy.

12. On the recurrence at Somersby of the Napoleon and Wellington themes, see Tennyson, H., *Memoir*, vol. I, p. 5.

13. See Tennyson, A., *Poems*, ed. Ricks, vol. I, p. 164. Here and throughout, unless otherwise stated, I quote Tennyson's poetry in the texts now standardly received; by far the best recent edition is the splendid *Poems*, ed. Ricks, to which I refer readers for the sake of consistency.

14. See Tennyson, A., *Poems*, ed. Ricks, vol. I, p. 131.

15. See Tennyson, A., *Poems*, ed. Ricks, vol. I, p. 244, l. 15 and note, and p. 445, l. 126 and note (*The Palace of Art*; cf Tennyson, A., *Works*, pp. 898, 906.)

16. See Tennyson, A., *Poems*, ed. Ricks, vol. I, p. 25.

17. Tennyson, H., *Memoir,* vol. II, p. 164.

18. See Chancellor's Gold Medal, vol. I, prefatory note.

19. See the poem by Christopher Wordsworth in Chancellor's Gold Medal, pp. 145-53; it is anthologised (as *Moscow*) in Longfellow, pp. 87-8.

20. *Expedition*, p. 5. This brochure, from J.W. Clark's Cambridge Collection, carries no preface or hints of authorship and is identified as a Medal entry by the University Library catalogue alone; the attribution to Frere is from the American Union Catalog of Books. On the snow image, compare the anonymous and comic poem *Bonaparte's Journey to Moscow* (1813) discussed in the Introduction.

21. Some doubt is cast by Tennyson's assertion, late in life, that he tried for the competition in the year he won it (1829) only at his father's urging, considered as it was 'with the greatest contempt' (Tennyson, H., *Memoir*, vol. I, p. 46, vol. II, p. 355); if this is true, it may mean that he had not thought of entering for it in the previous year either. As Professor Ricks has sensibly suggested, however (*TLS*, 1969, p. 1002), the reluctance in 1829 may have been due precisely to the failed attempt in 1828. The poet's winning entry in 1829 was on the subject *Timbuctoo* (see Chancellor's Gold Medal, pp. 154-61).

22. *Times Literary Supplement,* 21 August 1969, p. 919, 28 August, p. 954, 11 September, p. 1002, 18 September, p. 1026.

23. Ibid. Professor Ricks's text, with which I for the most part concur, will now be found in Tennyson, A., *Poems*, ed. Ricks, vol. I, pp. 178-81.

24. See Tennyson, A., *Poems*, ed. Ricks, vol. I, pp. 169, III, p. 645.

25. Landor, *Poems*, vol. II, p. 185, where the writer and patriot's name is actually given in the mangled form 'Menincivicz'.

26. For a discussion of this, see Partridge. 'Slavonic Themes', p. 427.

27. See Tennyson, A., *Poems*, ed. Ricks, vol. I, pp. 497-8. Some critics, like J. Cuming Walters, believed that this sonnet was of equal value with the next one: see Walters, p. 309.

28. See Tennyson, A., *Poems*, ed. Ricks, vol. II, p. 249 (*The Princess: A Medley*, 1847, section IV, l. 552).

29. See Tennyson, A., *Poems*, ed. Ricks, vol. I, pp. 498-9.

30. Allingham, p. 303.

31. See Tennyson, A., *Poems*, ed. Ricks, vol. I, pp. 529-30.

32. See e.g. Carlyle, *Past and Present*, p. 136, and cf. Paul, pp. 15, 23-4.

33. Campbell, N., vol. I, item 3399; Tennyson, H., *Memoir*, vol. I, p. 123, vol. II, p. 346; Tennyson, A., *Letters*, vol. I, pp. 194-5, vol. II, p. 159, vol. III, p. 375; Tennyson, A., *Poems*, ed. Ricks, vol. II, p. 261 (ll. 367-8 of section V). Hallam Tennyson refers the reader to Hakluyt, meaning presumably the Anthony Jenkinson trip of 1557, of which there were several early nineteenth-century editions. See Hakluyt, vol. II, pp. 434-6, and cf. Major, vol. I, p. 94.

34. Venables, pp. 109-10.

35. Tennyson, C., *Alfred Tennyson*, p. 172.

36. Hill, F., p. 27; reprinted in Tennyson, A., *Letters*, vol. I, p. 312. 'Willie' is Colonel Cracroft's wife, and the Elmhirsts are the Rawnsleys' daughter and son-in-law.

37. Allingham, p. 314. Tennyson had Browning's *Dramatic Idyls* in his library.

38. See Tennyson, A., *Poems*, ed. Ricks, vol. II, p. 476, and p. 474 (*The Third of February, 1852*). The two poems were signed 'Merlin'. See also Tennyson, H., *Memoir,* vol. I, pp. 169, 343-6. On Tennyson's extreme patriotism, see e.g. Jenkinson, pp. 91-2; Minto, vol. I, p. 300; Gwynn, pp. 95-6. *Hands All Round* was later set to music by Emily Tennyson, and her version 'arranged' (that is, improved) by Charles Villiers Stanford, but it is noteworthy that the attacks upon specific foreign countries were smoothed out from the text of her song: see Tennyson, H., *Tennyson and Friends*, pp. 481-4.

39. Tennyson, E., *Letters*, p. 368; Stephen, vol. II, pp. 236-7.

40. See Tennyson, A., *Poems*, ed. Ricks, vol. II, pp. 499-500; cf. Tennyson, A., *Works*, p. 938.

41. Tennyson, H., *Memoir,* vol. I, p. 341; Tennyson, A., *Poems*, ed. Ricks, vol. II, p. 499.

42. Trinity Notebook 36, ff. 1-2 (Tennyson papers at Trinity College, Cambridge); this source also has a very different opening to the poem, and tails off at 'Sinope'.

43. Tennyson, H., *Memoir*, vol. I, p. 372; Tennyson, A., *Works,* p. 959; Tennyson, A., *Letters*, vol. II, p. 81; Tennyson, C., *Alfred Tennyson,* p. 280. For many interesting references to the war, see Tennyson, E., *Journal*, pp. 33-54.

44. Napier, p. 75.

45 Tennyson, A., *Letters*, vol. II, p. 87; Rader, p. 7; Browning, E.B., *Letters,* ed. Kenyon, vol. II, p. 171.

46. Tennyson, A., *Letters*, vol. II, pp. 83, 98.

47. On Bright's views on war and peace, and on England vs Russia in particular, see his relevant speeches in Bright, vol. I, pp. 441-535, vol. II, pp. 359-71.

48. 'International Law. Grotius *On War and Peace*', *Fraser's Magazine*, vol. XLIX, April 1854, pp. 479, 486-7.

49. Shee, pp. 212-13.

50. *Punch; or, The London Charivari*, vol. XXVI, p. 155; see also vol. XXVII, 4 November 1854, p. 217, vol. XXVIII, May 1855, p. 227.

51. See *Blackwood's Edinburgh Magazine*, vol. LXXVI, December 1854, p. 730; *Punch; or, The London Charivari*, vol. XXVII, 18 November 1854, p. 232; Swayne, 'Peace and Patriotism', p. 97.]

52. Marston, vol. II, p. 347.

53. See *Blackwood's Edinburgh Magazine*, vol. LXXVI, September 1854, pp. 302, 313-14. The Quaker group consisted of Joseph Sturge, Henry Pease and Robert Charleton. For more on this see e.g. Scott, R.C., pp. 107-11.

54. Swayne, 'Peace and War', pp. 597, 730 and passim; Swayne, 'Peace and Patriotism', pp. 103, 105, 107, 111. See also Collins; Schweik; Ricks, '"Peace and War"'. Ricks points out that Tennyson himself is cited in the dialogues, pp. 598, 714, and that he himself later used Irene/Irenaeus in the Epilogue to *The Charge of the Heavy Brigade*, added in 1885.

55. See Tennyson, A., *Poems*, ed. Ricks, vol. II, pp. 582-4; Tennyson, A., *Works,* p. 959; Tennyson, E., *Journal*, p. 33; Tennyson, H., *Memoir,* vol. I, pp. 372, 405.

56. See Tennyson, A., *Poems*, ed. Ricks, vol. II, pp. 528-9, 531-2 and note, 541, note; Trinity Notebook 36, ff. 3-52; Tennyson, *Works,* p. 958; Waller, pp. 194-7. For the line 'Now are they serf-like, horribly bland' we are entirely dependent upon the disreputable Thomas J. Wise, who published it in 1908 in his privately printed two-volume *Bibliography of Tennyson* (vol. I, p. 127.). Other sources do, however, confirm many other variants in the 'pre-natal' edition, no longer extant, but allegedly once owned by Coventry Patmore and described to Wise by Richard Herne Shepherd.

57. See Tennyson, A., *Tennyson Collection*, p. 23; Wise, *Bibliography of Tennyson*, pp. 126ff.

58. Tennyson, A., *Letters*, vol. II, p. 137. On the critical response to *Maud* in relation to the Crimean War, see also Colley, pp. 83-4. On the poem and its violent background, see the very different articles by M.C.C. Adams and J.R. Bennett, the one a sensitive treatment of what Tennyson understood as true heroism, the other a most informative attempt to extricate the poet from his own particular hero. See also the useful piece by O'Neill, who seeks to reconcile the whole.

59. Van Dyke, *Introduction*, p. 23.

60. Van Dyke, *Poetry*, pp. 124-8 (see also 2nd ed., p. 309); Van Dyke, *Introduction*, p. 23, and cf. pp. 25, 84.

61. See *Maud*, I, l. 370 in ll. 366-74 (Tennyson, A., *Poems*, ed. Ricks, vol. II, pp. 542-3); Knies, pp. 70, 77; Tennyson, H., *Memoir*, vol. I, pp. 403, 405, vol. II, p. 473.

62. Tennyson, E., *Letters,* pp. 70-1; Tennyson, E., *Journal*, pp. 40-1; Martin, p. 381; Tennyson, A., *Letters*, vol. II, p. 100; Rader, passim; Baum, pp. 134-43. The reference to a bird could be an imprecise quotation from a then unattributed poem by Tennyson himself: see Paden, p. 211.

63. Tennyson, H., *Memoir,* vol. I, p. 380; in the *Materials*, vol. II, pp. 105-6, the text is very slightly different. On Hood, see Tennyson, E., *Journal*, pp. 39-40, 266, 362; Colborne and Brine, 'Hood' (in alphabetical order).

64. See Tennyson, A., *Poems*, ed. Ricks, vol. III, p. 627; Tennyson, E., *Journal*, p. 38; Tennyson, H., *Memoir*, vol. I, p. 380. For the Tennysons' collaboration on songs, see Tennyson, E., *Letters*, p. 182.

65. Tennyson, E., *Journal*, p. 40; Tennyson, H., *Memoir,* vol. I, p. 380.

66. See *Blackwood's Edinburgh Magazine*, vol. LXXVI, December 1854, p. 696. *The Times* of 6 January slavishly repeated this (p. 8), long after the event!

67. Tennyson, H., *Memoir*, vol. I, p. 381; Tennyson, E., *Journal*, p. 40; Tennyson, E., *Letters,* p. 70. For good short accounts of the poem's composition and publication, see Sir Charles Tennyson's letter to the *Times Literary Supplement* of 15 July 1965, in reply to one from William Hardie of 3 June, and Wise, *Bibliography of Tennyson*, vol. I, pp. 143-8. A mass of material on *The Charge* is available on microfilm at the Tennyson Research Centre in Lincoln. The history of the different versions of the poem has been told at formidable length in the fine article by Shannon and Ricks. Tennyson's signed manuscript, claimed to be the 'earliest version' of *The Charge*, was offered for sale at auction in 1936: see *American Book-Prices Current*, 1936 (New York, 1937), p. 694.

68. See e.g. Lynn, pp. ix, 237. It must, however, be pointed out that one specialist who has carefully studied all the documents strongly argues that Nolan himself had misunderstood where the action was to take place: see Harris, John, pp. 202ff. A participant in the charge stated that Nolan had given the order twice, the first with verbal authority and the second with written, but nevertheless blamed him for believing in and conveying 'altogether the maddest and most extraordinary order ever given to cavalry': see Carew, pp. 43-4.

69. Carew, p. 43.

70. Russell, *Landing to Death*, p. 231.

71. Adye, p. 107; cf. Swayne, 'Peace and Patriotism', p. 110. Tennyson had wanted to write a poem about the troopship *Birkenhead*, but was forestalled by Francis Doyle's *The Loss of the 'Birkenhead'*: see Tennyson, A., *Letters*, vol. III, p. 389; cf. also M.C. Tyndall's *The Loss of the 'Birkenhead', off the Coast of Africa* and Frances Anne Kemble's *The Wreck of the Birkenhead, a British Transport Vessel Lost on the Coast of Africa: A Ballad*. Mark Twain was no doubt thinking actually of this disaster when he sardonically wished that Tennyson had devoted his talent to a description of the wreck of the *Berkeley Castle*, a troopship which (as Twain believed) sank in a storm off the Crimea: see Howe, p. 254.

72. For an exhaustive description and discussion of the charge of the Light Brigade and its aftermath, see Kinglake, vol. IV, pp. 206-396. See also the *Times* reports of the engagement, 13 and 14 November 1854; Russell, *Landing to Death*, pp. 225-7, 230-2, etc.; Farquharson, pp. 43-4, 47; Dodd, pp. 256-60; Lynn, pp. 233-52. I am particularly indebted to Cecil Woodham-Smith's *The Reason Why*, one of the most remarkable popular history-books ever written. As an example of the difficulties involved in establishing how many troops took part in the charge, one may cite the fact that Dodd's *Pictorial History* records on one page 'barely 670 horsemen' and on the next 'somewhat under 700' (pp. 257-8).

73. *Punch; or, The London Charivari*, vol. XXVII, 25 November 1854, p. 213.

74. 'The Battle of Balaklava', *Punch; or, The London Charivari*, vol. XXVII, 25 November 1854, p. 219.

75. Compare Tennyson, H., *Memoir*, vol. I, p. 381. See on this also McGann, pp. 221, 252. McGann argues that the Light Brigade charge was a class matter, arising out of Public School values, but this is not completely sustained by the facts.

76. See Tennyson, A., *Poems*, ed. Ricks, vol. II, p. 489, and cf. p. 490.

77. See e.g. Gowing, p. 39.

78. See Tennyson, A., *Poems*, ed. Ricks, vol. II, p. 511; Rawnsley, p. 139. Tennyson always repudiated the concept of his having borrowed things, preferring the word 'parallelism'. An identical experience could occur to different people at different places and times, he said. Natural speech had certain rhythms, just as it had certain phrases: a scholar had once told him he had found two lines of Tennyson, practically word for word, in an unknown Chinese poem never before translated. (See Tennyson, A., *Letters*, vol. III, pp. 238-40).

79. Tennyson, E., *Letters*, p. 70; Tennyson, A., *Letters*, vol. II, pp. 100-2; see also McGann, pp. 221, 252.

80. *Examiner*, 9 December 1854, p. 780 (the poem is signed 'A.T.'); Tennyson, A., *Letters*, vol. II, pp. 100-2. See also Wise, *Bibliography of Tennyson*, vol. I, pp. 125, 143-4; Tennyson, H., *Memoir*, vol. I, p. 381. In the *Maud; and Other Poems* text a transitional phase was seen in the line: '"Charge," was the captain's cry'. With respect to the number of men at first thought to have taken part in the charge, there is actually a slight discrepancy in the different sources due, perhaps, to a misreading: sometimes the figure 605 is given, sometimes 607. On the whole complex issue of the various manuscripts and alterations, see Shannon and Ricks, especially pp. 2-5.

81. Tennyson, H., *Memoir*, vol. I, pp. 386-7; Tennyson, H., *Materials*, vol. IV, p. 504c (the *Memoir*, vol. I, pp. 409-10, omits reference to 'blundered'); Tennyson, A., *Letters*, vol. II, pp. 108, 114, 117; Tennyson, E., *Letters*, p. 79, note; Golden, pp. 18-20, corrected from the original correspondence at Harvard. When at Farringford, Tuckerman had criticised the 'hundred'/'blundered' rhyme on the basis of a newspaper comment, not realising that the poem was by Tennyson! Perhaps as a peace-offering, he gave the Englishman a fine edition of Webster's dictionary, bound in Russia leather which made his smoking-attic fragrant. He seemingly also offered him asylum in America, should the Russians overrun the whole of Europe. See Tennyson. A., *Letters*, vol. II, pp. 105, 113.

82. See e.g. Tennyson, H., *Memoir*, vol. I, pp. 385-8; Tennyson, A., *Tennyson Collection*, p. 23. Information on Rev. C.E. Hadow, and a copy of his letter, have been kindly provided by Mrs Clare Brown, Archivist at Rhodes House Library. He afterwards thanked Tennyson for the copies, and was glad to be sent more: see Tennyson, H., *Materials*, vol. II, pp. 111-13; Tennyson, E., *Journal*, p. 54. There is conflicting information as to how many copies were sent, how many arrived, and what the soldiers did with them. Thomas J. Wise informs us (*Bibliography of Tennyson*, vol. I, pp. 125, 143) that only one thousand copies of the quarto were

made in all, but J. Cuming Walters says (pp. 81-2) that the author sent one thousand to the men at Sebastopol and two hundred others to the chaplain who had first inspired this production, only these were lost at sea. For a more recent attempt to resolves the matter, see Shannon and Ricks, pp. 7-10.

83. Tennyson, A., *Letters*, vol. II, pp. 117-21, 132-3; Tennyson, H., *Memoir*, vol. I, pp. 385-7, 411; Tennyson, E., *Journal*, pp. 49, 54; Tennyson, E., *Letters*, pp. 79, 86; Walters, p. 82. Tennyson elsewhere said that his motive for distributing copies of *The Charge* in the Crimea and at Scutari was a request from Lady Franklin (see Tennyson, A., *Works*, p. 937).

84. See Tennyson, A., *Poems*, ed. Ricks, vol. II, pp. 511-13. I have changed Ricks's reading 'Their's' to the more natural 'Theirs', which is found, for example, in the Trinity College manuscript and in that used for the poem's original publication in the *Examiner* (Tennyson Research Centre, Lincoln, P61 (b)). In 1856 the practically definitive text was incorporated in a book entitled *In honorem. Songs of the Brave: Poems and Odes by Campbell, Wolfe, Collins, Byron, Tennyson, [Burns], and Mackay* (at pp. 31-5; see also Wise, *Tennyson*, vol. I, p. 147). This finely produced anthology had illustrations by A. Huttula and George Thomas depicting the preparations for battle, the charge itself, and the tragic, disordered return. *The Charge of the Light Brigade* was naturally also anthologised in Henry Wadsworth Longfellow's comprehensive volume *Russia* (1878), from his series *Poems of Places*: see Longfellow, pp. 38-40.

85. Tennyson, A., *Letters*, vol. II, pp. 104, 114; Tennyson, H., *Memoir*, vol. I, pp. 409-10; Tennyson, C., *Alfred Tennyson*, p. 288; Tyree, p. 75; Dobell, *Life and Letters*, vol. I, p. 401.

86. *Punch; or, The London Charivari*, vol. XXVIII, 17 February 1855, p. 67. The poem is by Tom Taylor.

87. Tennyson, E., *Letters*, p. 72; Tennyson, A., *Letters*, vol. II, p. 107.

88. As well as a few anonymous poets, these included W.C. Bennett, Alexander Smith and Sydney Dobell, Lord Ellesmere, Richard Chenevix-Trench, Walter Whitmore-Jones, Edmund Peel, John Sumner Gibson, John Dryden Pigott, Alfred Knott, John Duff Schomberg, Helen MacGregor, Caroline Hayward, and John Westland Marston. The poems devoted to the charge of the Light Brigade will form the subject of a later study.

89. It is, however, interesting to note that Tennyson's *The Charge of the Light Brigade* was not collected in the *Illustrated Crimean War Song Book of the Allies*, published later in 1855 together with *A Brief Account of the War to the Fall of Sebastopol*. This interesting miscellany of popular pieces, some old, some new, some anonymous and some by named authors like George Linley, C.W. Glover, J.E. Carpenter and the book's publisher, Alexander Kirkaldy, did have songs about the battle of the Alma, Inkerman, even the Baltic campaign, but failed to celebrate Balaklava. Not everyone in Britain transformed the Light Brigade's débâcle into a myth of victory.

90. See Tennyson, A., *Letters*, vol. II, pp. 134, 152.

91. Among the earliest engravings of the engagement were those in the *Illustrated London News* (18 November 1854, p. 501, and 23 December 1854, supplement, pp. 676-7).

92. Reid, vol. I, p. 512.

93. Tennyson, A., *Letters*, vol. II, pp. 119-20; Tennyson, H., *Memoir*, vol. I, p. 400; Tennyson, C., *Alfred Tennyson*, pp. 287-9.

94. Tennyson, A., *Letters*, vol. II, pp. 107-8.

95. See Churton, *Anti-Maud*; see also e.g. *Punch*, 18 August 1855, p. 69. *The Charge* itself was said by Hallam Tennyson to have been reprinted in *Punch*, but I can find no trace of it; see Tennyson, H., *Materials*, vol. II, p. 115. There may have been confusion with the fact that *Punch* quite often took the poem off in later years. The attribution of *Anti-Maud* to William Cox Bennett, made by T.J. Wise

and others (see e.g. Wise, *Bibliography of Tennyson*, vol. I, p. 142) may have arisen from a misunderstanding. Bennett did write at least one poem *about* Tennyson's *Maud*, but in the most generous and laudatory terms, speaking for instance of the laureate's 'sweet sway' (see his 'Written in Tennyson's "Maud"', *Illustrated London Magazine*, vol. V, October 1855, p. 194; Tennyson, A., *Letters*, vol. II, pp. 120, 129). He also composed, for the first anniversary of the charge, a poem which has echoes of Tennyson and takes exactly the same line as he (W.C. Bennett, 'Balaclava. — October 25th. 1854', *Illustrated London Magazine*, vol. V, November 1855, p. 238). It is possible that the author of *Anti-Maud* was its original printer, Edward Churton of 26 Holles Street, Cavendish Square, who self-published books on travel, the nobility, and bibliophily, and eventually emigrated to New Zealand. (He should not be confused with the divine of this same name.) Among better-known literary personalities, William Edmonstoune Aytoun may be a contender. More research is called for on this fascinating subject.

96. Tennyson, A., *Letters*, vol. II, p. 116.

97. Tennyson, A., *Letters*, vol. II, p. 112.

98. *Jackson's Oxford Journal*, 23 June 1855, p. 5; Oxford University *Calendar*, 1856, p. 275; Tennyson, H., *Memoir*, vol. I, p. 384; Tennyson, E., *Journal*, p. 46; Tennyson, A., *Letters*, p. 114.

99. *Examiner*, 23 June 1855, pp. 390-1; Young, J.C., p. 413. Cf. the once popular setting by Mrs Robert Arkwright of 'If you're waking, call me early', from Tennyson's *The May Queen*.

100. Knies, pp. 46, 48.

101. Tennyson, H., *Materials*, vol. II, pp. 111-14, *Memoir*, vol. II, p. 298, *Tennyson and Friends*, p. 269.

102. Ricks, *Tennyson*, p. 244.

103. Tennyson, H., *Memoir*, vol. I, p. 389; Tennyson, A., *Poems*, ed. Ricks, vol. III, p. 647, where there is comment on a proposal by Professor W.D. Paden, never followed up. The two poems, signed 'T.', are entitled *On Hearing that the News of the Czar's Death was Applauded in a Theatre* and *On Hearing the Czar's Death called 'A Judgment from God'*. They seem very un-Tennysonian both in manner and in mood.

104. Tennyson, E., *Letters*, pp. 96-8.

105. See Tennyson, A., *Poems*, ed. Ricks, vol. II, p. 605.

106. Tennyson, E., *Letters*, pp. 225; Tennyson, E., *Journal*, p. 282.

107. See Tennyson, E., *Journal*, pp. 266, 362; Tennyson, A., *Letters*, vol. III, p. 326.

108. Tennyson, A., *Letters*, pp. 170, 250-1; Tennyson, H., *Memoir*, vol. I, p. 490.

109. Tennyson, E., *Letters*, p. 264; Tennyson, E., *Journal*, pp. 313-14; Tennyson, H., *Memoir*, vol. II, p. 101.

110. Dobell, *Poetical Works*, vol. II, p. 381 in pp. 379-88.

111. See on all this Waddington, *Turgenev and England*, pp. 164, 198-9, 201.

112. See Tennyson, A., *Letters*, vol. II, p. 523; Alekseev, 'Angliiskii iazyk', p. 132. W.R.S. Ralston's book *Krilof and his Fables* was published in 1869.

113. Kropotkin, *Russian Literature*, p. 205.

114. Druzhinin, *Povesti. Dnevnik*, pp. 205, 353, *Sobranie sochinenii*, vol. VI, p. 556. Mikhailov translated e.g. *Godiva* (*Sovremennik*, September 1859, section I, pp. 5-8), and Pleshcheev *The May Queen* and *Dora* (*Otechestvennye zapiski*, February 1871, section I, pp. 369-74, January 1873, section I, pp. 33-9).

115. Tennyson, E., *Journal*, pp. 313-14.

116. For the Tennysons' reports of and reactions to Turgenev's visit in 1871, see Tennyson, H., *Memoir*, vol. II, pp. 106-7, and Tennyson, E., *Journal*, pp. 324-5. Further discussion of Turgenev's side of things will be found in Waddington, *Turgenev and England*, pp. 198-205.

117. See Petrov and Fridliand, vol. I, pp. 413-14, where the story involves Nicholas I rather than Alexander II.

118. Baring, *Outline*, pp. 165-7.

119. Tennyson, H., *Memoir,* vol. II p. 106, where Turgenev's novel is referred to as *Lisa* since Ralston's translation gave it the heroine's name.

120. See Tennyson, A., *Poems*, ed. Ricks, vol. II, p. 528. Note, however, that while this quotation is particularly apposite to Blackgang, Tennyson's son Hallam actually associated it with their own Freshwater: see Tennyson, H., *Memoir*, vol. II, p. 370. On the Tennysons' consciousness of Blackgang, see Tennyson, E., *Journal*, pp. 50, 68.

121. Reminiscence of Arthur Coleridge, in his manuscript notes on Tennyson at the Lincoln Research Centre; Tennyson, H., *Memoir,* vol. II, pp. 414-15.

122. Tennyson, H., *Memoir,* vol. II, pp. 106, 109, 147-8; Campbell, N., vol. I, entries 1851, 3368; Tennyson, C., and Dyson, p. 201; Tennyson, E., *Journal*, pp. 330-1. On Tennyson and novels, see e.g. Tennyson, A., *Letters*, vol. III, pp. 175, 316, 324, 326, 332, 341-2, 381, 400; Tennyson, E., *Journal*, p. 106; Tennyson, E., *Letters*, pp. 223, 260; Tennyson, H., *Memoir,* vol. I, p. 488. See also Boyesen, p. 615.

123. Knies, pp. 128, 130.

124. See Irving, *Annals 1871-1887*, p. 1152.

125. Tennyson, E., *Journal*, p. 369.

126. Dyson and Tennyson, pp. 92-4. According to Thomas J. Wise, forty copies of the *Welcome* were printed separately for private distribution, and when they were exhausted a few more were made: see Wise, *Bibliography of Tennyson*, vol. I, pp. 225-6. Others believe these to have been fictitious, having been published more probably by Wise himself around 1895: see Partington, *Thomas J. Wise*, p. 342. In one way Tennyson had been spurred into writing his poem by some doggerel addressed to him on 24 January by *Punch*, accompanied by a not entirely respectful cartoon on the marriage entitled 'The Latest in "Russia Bonds".'

127. Irving, *Annals 1871-1887*, p. 1147.

128. Gladstone, M., pp. 89-90; Tennyson, A., *Letters*, vol. III, p. 74; Tennyson, E., *Letters*, pp. 305-6; Tennyson, E., *Journal*, p. 369; Tennyson, H., *Memoir,* vol. II, pp. 155-6; Dyson and Tennyson, pp. 92-4 (which includes the Windsor holograph of the poem whose more logical punctuation I have followed at one or two points; otherwise the text here concords with that in Tennyson, A., *Poems*, ed. Ricks, vol. III, pp. 5-7). The poem originally had 'plains' instead of 'palms' in the fourth line of the second stanza: see Tennyson, A., *Tennyson Collection*, p. 35. According to Wise (*Bibliography of Tennyson*, vol. I, p. 225), Tennyson himself wanted 'palms', but one wonders if this was not a misreading which for some reason has stuck, since 'sultry palms' is faintly absurd when speaking of India.

129. Tennyson, E., *Letters*, p. 306; Tennyson, H., *Memoir*, vol. II, p. 156. Tennyson almost certainly took the reference to Gytha from Freeman, *History*, vol. IV (1871), pp. 159-60: he used this work not long afterwards for his verse drama *Harold* (see *Works,* p. 652). Unfortunately, he failed to read the appendix note to the story of Gytha's marriage to 'Valdimar King of Holmgard', which enumerates the problems involved in giving credit to the legend (Freeman, *History*, vol. IV, pp. 754-5). Interestingly, the subject of Harold (or rather of Harolds), Gytha, and their possible intermarriage with Kievan rulers had been treated only recently by the Russian poet and anglophile Count A.K. Tolstoi, in his ballads *Pesnia o Garal'de i Iaroslavne* (The Song of Harold and Iaroslavna, 1869) and *Tri poboishcha* (Three Slaughters, 1869) and in Act II of his verse tragedy *Tsar' Boris* (1870): see Tolstoi, A.K., vol. I, pp. 263-77, 754-5, vol. II, pp. 442, 688.

130. See Austin, *Lyrical Poems*, pp. 64-7.

131. Tennyson, A., *Letters*, vol. III, pp. 104, 113-15, 118.

132. Gladstone, M., pp. 111-12; Tennyson, A., *Letters*, vol. III, pp. 135-6, 138.

133. *Punch; or, The London Charivari*, vol. LXXI, 4 November 1876, p. 198. This is a little puzzling: the lines quoted, in parody of Tennyson's *In Memoriam A.H.H.*, xxvii, had already been coined much earlier by A.H. Clough.

134. Gladstone, M., pp. 135-6; Tennyson, A., *Letters*, vol. III, pp. 155-6.

135. Tennyson, A., *Letters*, vol. III, pp. 306, 333, 358, and cf. p. 446.

136. Allingham, p. 265; Tennyson, A., *Poems*, ed. Ricks, vol. III, p. 25; cf. Tennyson, C., *Alfred Tennyson*, p. 442.

137. Novikova, *Is Russia Wrong?*, pp. 70, 82-3.

138. See Thackeray, vol. IX, pp. 186-7 (*The Book of Snobs*, 1848, ch. XXXVIII).

139. Thornbury, vol. II, pp. 317-21; see also Longfellow, pp. 156-61, etc.

140. *Nineteenth Century*, vol. I, no. 3, May 1877, where Tennyson's 'Montenegro', p. 359, is followed by W.E. Gladstone, 'Montenegro: A Sketch', pp. 360-79. See Tennyson, H., *Memoir*, vol. II, p. 217; Stillman, vol. II, p. 162; Shannon, R.T., p. 218.

141. See Tennyson, A., *Poems*, ed. Ricks, vol. III, pp. 23-4, *Works,* p. 533; Tennyson, A., *Letters*, vol. III, p. 146. *Montenegro* proved very popular with readers. In 1881 it was anthologised, as the sole chosen sonnet by Tennyson, in Samuel Waddington's *English Sonnets by Living Writers* (2nd ed., p. 7). In the following year Hall Caine reprinted it in his *Sonnets of Three Centuries* (Caine, *Sonnets*, p. 128), and in 1887 William Sharp included it as one of only two by Tennyson in his *Sonnets of This Century*, the other being, significantly enough, that written *On Hearing of the Outbreak of the Polish Insurrection* (Sharp, *Sonnets*, pp. 222-3).

142. Gladstone, M., pp. 158, 160; Tennyson, A., *Letters*, vol. III, pp. 171, 175-6.

143. See on this Turgenev, I.S., *Pis'ma*, vol. XII (2), pp. 261, 557; Letkova, p. 461; Waddington, *Turgenev and England*, p. 279.

144. See Tennyson, A., *Poems*, ed. Ricks, vol. II, p. 475, III, p. 98.

145. Allingham, p. 297.

146. Waddington, *Turgenev and England*, pp. 285-8.

147. 'The Charge of the Heavy Brigade at Balaclava. October 25th, 1854', *Macmillan's Magazine*, vol. XLV, March 1882, pp. 337-9. The poem heads the issue and has notes, p. 339, on the 'three hundred' and the 'three'. *The Heavy Brigade* caused Tennyson some slight embarrassment with his publishers, the *Nineteenth Century* claiming that he should have offered it to them, he claiming that he had, but that they had refused: see Tennyson, A., *Letters*, vol. III, pp. 220-1.

148. Tennyson, H., *Materials*, vol. IV, pp. 503-4; Tennyson, A., *Works,* pp. 569, 993-4; Kinglake, vol. IV, pp. 149-50. Scarlett's heroic mettle was seen also during the Light Brigade's engagement, when he was all for charging down the valley of death with the Heavies; he actually set off at a gallop, but turned back on hearing that Lucan had told his men not to follow him (*Dictionary of National Biography*).

149. See Kinglake, vol. IV, pp. 128-206, especially pp. 134, 140-4, 148-50, and cf. Lynn, pp. 224-32. In his published account of the battle, Kinglake cautiously estimated that there were at least 2000 Russians (vol. IV, pp. 140-1).

150. Tennyson, H., *Memoir,* vol. I, p. 380.

151. Tennyson, H., *Memoir*, vol. II, p. 297. Hamley would later briefly mention Tennyson in his book *The War in the Crimea* (pp. 122-3), though more in connection with the Light Brigade than with the Heavy.

152. See *The Times* for 13 and 14 November 1854; Russell, *Landing to Death*, pp. 227-9; see also Hamley, pp. 112-14.

153. See the note in Tennyson, A., *Poems*, ed. Ricks, vol. III, p. 93.

154. Tennyson, A., *Works,* p. 937; Tennyson, C., and Dyson, p. 201; Swayne, 'Peace and Patriotism', p. 107; Carew, p. 43; Adye, pp. 102-3.
155. See Tennyson, A., *Poems*, ed. Ricks, vol. III, pp. 93-5.
156. Van Dyke, *Introduction*, p. 68.
157. See Tennyson, A., *Poems*, ed. Ricks, vol. III, pp. 95-7; Tennyson, H., *Memoir*, vol. II, pp. 319-20, 400.
158. Tennyson, H., *Memoir,* vol. II, p. 298.
159. Tennyson, H., *Memoir*, pp. 40-1. Tennyson, A., *Works*, p. 993.
160. Tennyson, H., *Memoir,* vol. II, pp. 296, 303.
161. Tennyson, H., *Memoir*, pp. 282-4; Tennyson, C., *Alfred Tennyson,* p. 470; Tennyson, A., *Letters*, vol. III, pp. 259-60; West, A., vol. II, pp. 171-3; Gladstone, M., pp. 294-5; Morley, J., *Gladstone*, vol. III, pp. 116-17; McCabe, p. 736; reminiscence of Arthur Coleridge, in his manuscript notes on Tennyson at the Lincoln Research Centre; Domett, p. 270; Grant Duff, vol. II, p. 246; *Graphic,* 29 September 1883, p. 22.
162. Tennyson, H., *Memoir,* vol. I, p. 487, *Echoes of the 'Eighties*, pp. 65-6.
163. Tennyson, H., *Tennyson and Friends*, p. 256; O'Connor, p. 256; Tennyson, A., *Letters*, vol. III, p. 267. There are two pictures of 'Karenina' in Wheatcroft, pp. 128, 148.
164. Tennyson, A., *Letters*, vol. III, p. 379; Tennyson, H., *Memoir*, vol. II, p. 348. For a discussion of Arnold's article, see Mainwaring.
165. Arnold, pp. 783, 785, 790-1.
166. See Stead, pp. 430-1.
167. Copy at the Tennyson Research Centre. On Tennyson's new interest in novels, see Tennyson, H., *Memoir,* vol. II, p. 372.
168. Tennyson, H., *Memoir,* vol. II, p. 349; Tennyson, A., *Letters*, vol. III, pp. 175, 316, 381, etc.
169. Gordon, vol. II, p. 350; Tennyson, A., *Letters*, vol. III, p. 300.
170. See Burnaby, pp. 168-9, 288. Burnaby attached many appendices showing the Russian troop advances into Afghan territory and, eventually, towards India. His subsequent book *On Horseback through Asia* was more anti-Russian still.
171. *British Annual Register*, 1885, pp. 21, 83.
172. See Broemel, passim.
173. See Tennyson, A., *Poems*, ed. Ricks, vol. III, pp. 131-3; Tennyson, A., *Letters*, vol. III, pp. 311-12, 316. The titles were, respectively, 'The Fleet (On Its Reported Insufficiency' and '"The Truth about the Navy." A Warning by Lord Tennyson.'
174. Tennyson, A., *Letters*, vol. III, pp. 299-300.
175. See Tennyson, A., *Poems*, ed. Ricks, vol. III, p. 153 (ll. 115-16).
176. Tennyson, A., *Letters*, vol. III, pp. 324, 351.
177. Tennyson, A., *Letters*, vol. III, p. 380.
178 Tennyson, H., *Memoir*, vol. II, p. 349.
179. See also Morris, *Letters*, ed. Henderson, p. 158.
180. Dillon, 'Jews in Russia', p. 509; on the persecution of Jews in Russia in 1890, see also Frye, pp. 135, 153.
181. See the unsigned anti-Russian article 'The Jews in Russia', *The Speaker*, 13 December 1890, p. 647.
182. See 'The Tsar and the Jews', *Contemporary Review*, vol. LIX, March 1891, pp. 309-26.
183. Tennyson, A., *Letters*, vol. III, p. 430; Tennyson, H., *Memoir,* vol. II, p. 391. There is a variant draft of this letter at the Research Centre in Lincoln.
184. See Tennyson, A., *Poems*, ed. Ricks, vol. III, p. 97; Tennyson, H., *Memoir,* vol. II, pp. 314, 325-6, 378.
185. Tennyson, H., *Memoir,* vol. II, p. 355, *Tennyson and Friends,* pp. 268-9; Walters, p. 82.

186. Tennyson, H., *Memoir,* vol. II, pp. 297-8.

187. Tennyson, A., *Letters,* vol. III, pp. 110-11; Tennyson, H., *Memoir,* vol. I, p. 388; *Illustrated London News,* 30 October 1875, p. 442.

188. See on the constitution of the Society Lummis and Wynn, pp. 311-12.

189. *Punch; or, The London Charivari,* 26 April 1890, p. 196. See also 'Allowed to Starve, ibid., 10 May 1890, p. 221, with the cartoon 'One of the Six Hundred'.

190. See Maxwell, pp. 153, 156; *St James's Gazette,* 8 May 1890, p. 9, 9 May, p. 5, 12 May, p. 3.

191. See Chapman-Huston, p. 81; Orel, *Kipling,* vol. I, p. 120.

192. *St James's Gazette,* 28 April 1890, p. 3. Reprinted in *Week's News* for 24 May 1890, in *Werner's Readings and Recitations,* New York, no. 2, 1890, pp. 189-90, in *Home News* for 2 May 1892, and in an obscure Manchester volume of 1908, this poem was for some reason never collected properly until 1919 — in Rudyard Kipling, *Verse: Inclusive Edition 1885-1918.* See Martindell, pp. 115, 160; Livingston, *Bibliography of Kipling,* pp. 73, 393; Stewart, pp. 257-8. By mistake but puzzlingly, the poem is customarily given the date 1891: see the text in Kipling, vol. XXXV, pp. 187-9, or in *Rudyard Kipling's Verse: Definitive Edition,* London, 1940, pp. 200-2. See also Maxwell, pp. 156-7.

193. See on this Weygandt, pp. 113-15.

194. This penultimate stanza, found in the *St James's Gazette* and other early texts, was removed by the author for his collected edition of 1919. Kipling's signed manuscript contains the full text and is prefaced by an eight-line prose note summarising the Balaclava Committee's announcement of 8 April 1890. See *American Book-Prices Current,* New York, 1921, p. 973; Martindell, pp. 115, 160; Chandler, p. 147.

195. Carrington, p. 179; Kipling, *Letters,* vol. II, pp. 17, 19-20, 34.

196. Kipling, *Letters,* vol. II, p. 33; Tennyson, H., *Memoir,* vol. II, p. 392 (where the text is paraphrased); this exchange is not included in Tennyson's collected letters. Kipling's *The Flag of England* was first published in the *National Observer* on 4 April 1891 and reprinted in the *St James's Gazette* six days later. See Livingston, *Bibliography of Kipling,* pp. 115, 124; Chandler, p. 73.

197. Tennyson, E., *Letters,* pp. 277, 349 (where the visitor's name is incorrectly given as Stiegler); Tennyson, H., *Tennyson and Friends,* p. 211; Ricks, *Tennyson,* p. 244; Jennings, p. 155; Maxwell, pp. 150-2, 157. See also Tennyson, C., *Stars and Markets,* p. 169. In some sources Gouraud's name is found as Gourand; I have not been able to ascertain his exact identity, although he was the author of at least one learned article on the phonograph (*Journal of the Society of Arts,* vol. XXXVII, 1889, pp. 23ff.) Some said that Tennyson recited his own verse jarringly, unnaturally, even without proper attention to the punctuation of his lines, but others found his manner fresh, melodious and winning: see Tennyson, A., *Letters,* vol. III, pp. 436-7, 445; Richards and Elliott, p. 347.

198. Maxwell, pp. 153-6; *St James's Gazette,* 20 May 1890, p. 8.

199. Maxwell, p. 154. Gouraud publicised his work with a *Lecture on the Phonograph and its Practical Applications to Military and Other Purposes* (Aldershot, 1890). There has been considerable discussion as to who, if anyone, actually sounded the charge of the Light Brigade: see Lynn, pp. 239-40; Maxwell, p. 154; *Pall Mall Gazette,* 4 August 1890, p. 4. There is much confusion over Landfrey's name: Lummis and Wynn, pp. 258-9, call him Martin Leonard Lanfried.

200. Maxwell, p. 154.

201. See Tennyson, H., *Memoir,* vol. II, p. 378. The 'story' that Hallam read seems likely to have been 'Reminiscences of a Balaclava Hero', which was collected in the annual handwritten 'Odds and Ends' of the St Paul's Literary and Educational Society at Easter 1890 (vol. XXXVI, ff. 503-11) and doubtless then

reported in the *Manchester City News* and elsewhere. I am indebted for this information to Jean M. Ayton, Archivist in the Department of Libraries and Theatres of Manchester City Council.

202. Dyson and Tennyson, p. 143.

203. Tennyson, H., *Memoir*, pp. 429-30; Tennyson, A., *Letters*, vol. III, p. 449; Tennyson, A., *Works,* p. XXXVI.

Notes to Robert Browning

1. Morley, J., *Recollections*, vol. I, p. 312.

2. See Berdoe, pp. 327-31; DeVane, *Browning Handbook*, pp. 39ff.

3. See e.g. Porter and Clarke, p. 531.

4. Pearsall, p. 24.

5. Sarianna Browning's copy of this book is at the Armstrong Browning Library, Waco, Texas; see Kelley and Coley, p. 50.

6. See Maynard, pp. 89-90; *Baylor Browning Interests*, no. 27, 1981, p. 42 (item 426); Wanley, p. 54. Browning's copy of Wanley is at the Armstrong Browning Library.

7. Browning, V., pp. 40-9; *The Last Ride Together* (ll. 47-8, 108). The edition of Browning used mainly for this chapter is *Poems*, ed. Pettigrew. Also consulted have been three ambitious projects not yet completed: the editions by Woolford and Karlin (*The Poems of Browning*), Ian Jack et al. (*The Poetical Works of Robert Browning*), and Roma A. King et al. (*The Complete Works of Robert Browning*).

8. *Paracelsus*, I, ll. 813-14; Browning, V., pp. 46-9; Maynard, pp. 164, 365, 459.

9. Maynard, pp. 120-1, 128, 420; Orr, *Life and Letters*, pp. 64-5.

10. Orr, *Life and Letters*, p. 60. Known in England as Benckhausen or Benkhausen, the consul's name will as from now be given in a correct transliteration from the Russian: Benkgauzen.

11. Commonly known in the West as Lieven; again given here in a more correct form from the Russian. Although not of literary interest, the many publications of letters from and to Princess Liven are a precious source of knowledge on Anglo-Russian relations in the first half of the nineteenth century; see Zamoyska.

12. On Benkgauzen, see Maynard, pp. 127, 419-20; *British Imperial Calendar*, 1833, 1834, 1835; Griffin, p. 61; Alekseev, 'British Manuscripts', p. 456; Lieven, pp. 178, 370-1, 375; Viazemskii, pp. 247, 255.

13. Browning, V., p. 15; Bolton, F., p. 3.

14. Maynard, p. 127.

15. Rothschild, pp. 18-19; Morton, F,, pp. 52ff; Reeves, pp. 75, 178. Some sources give the figure £6,629,166, but this was probably the amount actually due in 1834.

16. British Library MSS Add. 41271, ff. 240-1, and 48485, f. 73; Public Record Office FO 182/5, ff. 33-5 (cf. also FO 65/213), copies of a despatch to Lord Palmerston from the British Ambassador in St Petersburg; Rothschild Archives (London) 109/31-7, private letters, January-March 1834, letters of 14 January, 3 March, etc., and 89/0, letters to Rothschilds from the Russian Minister of Finance; Maynard, pp. 419-20; *British Annual Register*, 1834, p. 462.

17. Reeves, p. 194.

18. Reeves, p. 195.

19. Lieven, pp. 370-1; British Library MSS Add. 41271, f. 240.

20. Allingham, p. 179; Browning, E.B., *Elizabeth Barrett to Miss Mitford*, p. 250. Vivienne Browning (p. 46) asserts that the poet's letters to Sarianna were destroyed owing to their compromising references to Jemima. For whatever reason,

their loss is a minor tragedy for students of Russian history and customs. The expression '*Wanderjahr*' is Edmund Gosse's (see his *Robert Browning*, p. 33).

21. Maynard, p. 122. In Griffin (p. 61) and in Browning, R. and E.B., *Brownings' Correspondence*, ed. Kelley et al., vol. III, p. xiii, the date is given as 1 March, but this was probably the day the men set sail for the continent. The best general account of Browning's Russian trip, superseded in only a few particulars, will be found in Bolton, F., pp. 1-14.

22. See Irvine and Honan, pp. 5, 64. Maynard (pp. 45ff.) does his best to set Browning's relations with his mother in their nineteenth-century context. The Bible is pictured in Maynard, p. 122; see also his pp. 127, 420. Browning's Russian exit passport at the Armstrong Browning Library (see also Maynard, pp. 7, 392) describes his height as 'medium', notes no special marks, and makes no comment in the space for a description of his nose.

23. *Wege-Karte durch den grösten und wichtigsten Theil Europa's, von London bis Moscau, und von Stockholm bis Neapel* (Berlin, 1830); see *Baylor Browning Interests*, no. 27 (1981), p. 27 (item 251). The copy of the map at the Armstrong Browning Library is inscribed 'Robert Browning. London. 1834.'

24. See e.g. Griffin, pp. 61-2; Maynard, p. 420. The references are to *How They Brought the Good News from Ghent to Aix*, to *Sordello*, V, ll. 134-9, and to *Colombe's Birthday*, Act I. The editors of the Brownings' complete correspondence confidently assert that the men travelled 'via Ostend, Rotterdam, Castle Ravestein, Cleves, Aix-la-Chapelle' (Browning, R. and E.B., *Brownings' Correspondence*, vol. III, p. xiii). They may of course be right, but I believe they are not. There has been much confusion in Browning research concerning Aachen, otherwise known as Aix-la-Chapelle or just Aix. According to one young commentator, Browning and Benkgauzen made a detour to Aix-*en-Provence*! (See the third-year student research essays, Armstrong Browning Library.)

25. Allingham, p. 179; passport at the Armstrong Browning Library.

26. Reeves, p. 95.

27. Orr, *Life and Letters*, p. 60; for a similar description of the roads in Russia, see Venables, p. 20.

28. Browning, R. and E.B., *Brownings' Correspondence*, vol. IV, p. 67; Browning, R., *Letters Collected by Wise*, ed. Hood, p. 1.

29. Griffin, p. 62.

30. Cf. e.g. Venables, pp. 3-5; Oliphant, pp. 1-2.

31. Opening lines of *A Forest Thought*, written in 1837 but not published until after Browning's death. See Orr, *Life and Letters*, pp. 60-1, footnote; McCoy, p. 20. See also Browning, R., *Poems*, ed. Woolford and Karlin, vol. I, p. 342, where it is suggested not quite convincingly that Browning was influenced by similar descriptions of parent trees and saplings in Mary Wollstonecraft's *A Short Residence in Sweden, Norway, and Denmark* (1796).

32. The two quotations which follow are from *Ivàn Ivànovitch* (ll. 19-26, 113-16), in e.g. Browning, R., *Works*, introd. Kenyon, vol. IX, pp. 234-55; see Appendix Two. On the Russian verst-poles, generally wooden but made of marble in the environs of St Petersburg, see Morton, E., p. 114, and Paul, p. 91.

33. British Library MSS Add. 41271, f. 240 (Bligh to Palmerston), tells us that Benkgauzen reached St Petersburg 'about a fortnight' before 16/28 March, that is, around 2/14 March. (In the nineteenth century the Russian calendar was twelve days behind the Western.) This despatch of 16/28 March, which must have gone post-haste, was received in London in the afternoon of 14 April, a period of 17 days.

34. Orr, *Life and Letters*, p. 61; Vengerova, 'Robert Brouning', p. 112; Lieven, p. 375.

35. Allingham, p. 179.

36. Maynard, p. 420.

37. Exit passport at the Armstrong Browning Library, Russian and Prussian stamps on the reverse.

38. Gosse, *Robert Browning*, p. 78.

39. See the article by Kelly, p. 41 and passim; Venables, pp. 189-90; Kohl, vol. II, pp. 125ff.; Gilbert, pp. 78-82. An identical fair (though not on the ice) took place in the week after Easter, but Browning had already left Russia by that period.

40. Browning, R. and E.B., *Letters*, ed. Kintner, vol. I, pp. 149-50; Orr, *Life and Letters*, p. 61, note. The drama is usually placed around 1843. Whether or not with inside knowledge, a contemporary Russian critic who had lived and worked in England spoke of it as having been written specifically in 1840 and as being simply unpublished, not lost: see Vengerova, 'Robert Brouning', pp. 112-13.

41. Rothschild Archives (London) 109, where various files have letters of 1833-4 expressing the fears of English merchants at St Petersburg. See also Kohl, vol. I, pp. 77, 208-9, vol. II, p. 360.

42. Kohl, vol. I, p. 363.

43. British Library MSS Add. 41271, f. 241 verso.

44. Kohl, vol. I, pp. 208-10, vol. II, pp. 15-16; Paul, pp. 26-7; Gilbert, p. 54; Venables, p. 8.

45. Jenkins, pp. 108ff.; see also Brewster, *East-West*, pp. 37-40. Borrow's versions of these poems were included in his *Targum...*

46. Jenkins, p. 114.

47. Browning, R. and E.B., *Letters*, ed. Kintner, vol. I, p. 148. On Wylie, see e.g.the *Dictionary of National Biography* and Putnam, p. 388.

48. *Alumni cantabrigienses* gives such a John Waring as having been admitted pensioner in 1812 and matriculated in 1813; these would be the right dates for the Foreign Office Waring, who was born in 1795 or late 1794. See *Foreign Office List*, January 1866, p. 178, also the lists for 1856, 1865, 1869. The authority for Browning's acquaintance with a real-life Waring, not substantiated by any primary material, is Griffin, p. 63; see also DeVane, *Browning Handbook*, pp. 118-19. On Domett see Maynard, p. 412; Domett, pp. 63-4; and the *Dictionary of National Biography*.

49. The phrase is Maynard's: see his p. 100.

50. Baring, *Russian People*, p. 17. The reference is to *Michel Strogoff* (1876), Verne's far-fetched but most exciting novel about Russia and Siberia.

51. Browning, R. and E.B., *Letters*, ed. Kintner, vol. I, p. 428.

52. *Encyclopaedia Britannica*, 9th ed., vol. VII, 1877, p. 166; Henningsen, vol. II, p. 37.

53. Kohl, vol. I, pp. 382-3; Henningsen, vol. II, p. 37.

54. Venables, p. 19; Henningsen, vol. II, p. 6. As an example of the ignorance and carelessness of early Browning critics, one may cite the belief of Charlotte Porter and Helen A. Clarke that the highway from St Petersburg to Moscow mentioned in *Ivàn Ivànovitch* was the modern Nevskii Prospect which linked these two cities at a distance of four versts! (See Browning, R., *Agamemnon*, pp. 304-5.)

55. See e.g. Bolton, F., p. 9.

56. Alekseev, *Ln* 91, pp. 524-8, 565-6.

57. Griffin, pp. 63, 266; *The Ring and the Book*, 'Guido' (ll. 270-5). 1 have not been able to verify whether one of the two paintings is indeed a copy of the other. Both are listed without comment, as originals, in the museum catalogues.

58. *The Dial*, 16 August 1917, p. 120. Extensive correspondence with dealers and leading galleries has failed to trace these works.

59. See Browning, R., *Poems*, ed. Pettigrew, vol. I, pp. 1084-5; *Poems*, ed. Woolford and Karlin, vol. I, p. 3; *Poetical Works*, ed. Jack, vol. III, pp. 244-5; Griffin, p. 73; Ritchie, p. 221.

60. Griffin, p. 63; Venables, p. 192; Kohl, vol. II, pp. 37-8, 40, 56-7.

61. Reeves, p. 208.

62. Lieven, p. 375.

63. Reeves, pp. 202, 208-11; Rothschild Archives 109/36, private letters, Lionel to his parents, Paris, 24 May 1834.

64. Vengerova, 'Robert Brauning i ego poeziia', p. 157 (p. 111 in the later edition).

65. Browning, R. and E.B., *Brownings' Correspondence*, vol. I, p. 9. As the editors point out, the specific context of this letter is somewhat problematical, but the meaning is obvious enough.

66. Browning, E.B., *Barretts at Hope End:*, pp. 115, 176-7; Browning, E.B., *Letters*, ed. Kenyon, vol. I, p. 189. Others have speculated that coal was involved.

67. Browning, R. and E.B., *Brownings' Correspondence*, vol. III, pp. 65, 69.

68. Browning, E.B., *Letters*, ed. Kenyon, vol. I, p. 244.

69. Browning, R. and E.B., *Brownings' Correspondence*, vol. IX, pp. 128-9.

70. Browning, R. and E.B., *Brownings' Correspondence*, vol. IX, p. 230; Browning, E.B., *Letters*, ed. Kenyon, vol. I, pp. 216, 463, vol. II, p. 27.

71. Browning, R. and E.B., *Brownings' Correspondence*, vol. V, p. 117, vol. IX, p. 88; Browning, E.B., *Letters*, ed. Kenyon, vol. I, p. 88. For the first of these allusions Kelley and Hudson refer in a note (*Brownings' Correspondence*, vol. V, p. 118) to Catherine *I* of Russia, but I think that would have needed to be specified. For most people, 'the Empress Catherine' would mean Catherine the Great.

72. Browning, R. and E.B., *Brownings' Correspondence*, vol. VII, p. 53; Browning, E.B., *Invisible Friends*, p. 72. On Elizabeth's knowledge of Alexander I, see also *Brownings' Correspondence*, vol. IX, p. 304.]

73. Browning, R. and E.B., *Brownings' Correspondence*, vol. VII, pp. 49, 51; Browning, E.B., *Invisible Friends*, p. 62.

74. Browning, R. and E.B., *Brownings' Correspondence*, vol. IX, pp. 151-2.

75. See the article by Lee, who later in 1854 published a fuller account of his experiences in his book *The Last Days of Alexander, and the First Days of Nicholas (Emperors of Russia)*.

76. Wolf, *Montefiore*, pp. 128ff.

77. Browning, R. and E.B., *Letters*, ed. Kintner, vol. I, pp. 473, 490, 506-7.

78. The references and quotations are from I, ll. 707ff., II, ll. 399ff., 416-17, 640-6.

79. Browning, E.B., *Letters*, ed. Kenyon, vol. I, p. 391.

80. Browning, E.B., *Letters*, ed. Kenyon, vol. I, pp. 360, 378, 452, vol. II, p. 41; Browning, E.B., *Letters to her Sister*, pp. 105-6, 151; Hewlett, p. 260.

81. Browning, E.B., *Letters*, ed. Kenyon, vol. II, p. 61; Hewlett, p. 288.

82. Browning, E.B., *Letters to her Sister*, pp. 149-50. See also Browning, E.B., *Letters*, ed. Kenyon, vol. II, pp. 47-8, 51-2.

83. Browning, E.B., *Letters*, ed. Kenyon, vol. II, pp. 128, 130.

84. Browning, E.B., *Letters*, ed. Kenyon, vol. II, p. 133.

85. McAleer, p. 597; cf. p. 600.

86. Browning, R. and E.B., *Letters to George Barrett*, p. 203.

87. Browning, E.B., *Letters*, ed. Kenyon, vol. II, pp. 186, 203; Browning, E.B., *Letters to her Sister*, p. 213; cf. Kelley and Hudson, p. 442.

88. Browning, E.B., *Letters to her Sister*, p. 208; Taplin, p. 287.

89. Browning, E.B., *Letters*, ed. Kenyon, vol. II, p. 124.

90. Browning, E.B., *Letters to her Sister*, pp. 205, 207; Browning, E.B., *Letters*, ed. Kenyon, vol. II, pp. 181, 183, 186, 193, 202-4; Hewlett, pp. 305-7; Taplin, pp. 287-8; Browning, E.B., *Letters to Ogilvy*, pp. 116, 123.

91. Hewlett, p. 305.

92. Browning, E.B., *Letters*, ed. Kenyon, vol. II, p. 183.

93. Browning, E.B., *Letters*, ed. Kenyon, vol. II, p. 171.

94. Browning, E.B., *Letters to Ogilvy*, pp. 133-4.

95. Browning, E.B., *Letters to Ogilvy*, p. 133.

96. Letter to Mrs Sunderland, Armstrong Browning Library. A synopsis of and brief extract from this letter, printed originally in a Christies sale catalogue of 23 June 1976 (lot 159), will be found in Kelley and Hudson, pp. 80, 442; the whole is as yet unpublished.

97. Browning, E.B., *Letters*, ed. Kenyon, vol. II, p. 185.

98. Hudson, R., p. 155.

99. Browning, E.B., *Letters*, ed. Kenyon, vol. II, pp. 188-9.

100. Browning, E.B., *Letters*, ed. Kenyon, vol. II, p. 203; Irvine and Honan, pp. 325-6.

101. *The Browning Society's Papers*, Part VII, Monthly Abstract of Proceedings, Fourth Session, 1884-85, p. 41, no. 57. The member, signing himself G.H.R., must have been G.H. Rendall, Principal of University College, Liverpool.

102. Browning, E.B., *Letters*, ed. Kenyon, vol. II, p. 226.

103. Browning, E.B., *Letters to her Sister*, pp. 270, 287; Hewlett, pp. 333, 338.

104. Browning, E.B., *Letters to her Sister*, pp. 293, 312; Irvine and Honan, pp. 331-4, 356. See also Knies, p. 91.

105. British Library MSS Ashley 5718.

106. Hewlett, p. 367.

107. Browning, E.B., *Letters*, ed. Kenyon, vol. II, pp. 410-12, 440; Browning, E.B., *Letters to Ogilvy*, pp. 168-9.

108. Letter of Browning to Ralston, 23 November 1865. The Browning-Ralston correspondence is listed in Kelley and Hudson, pp. 417-18; several of the items are at the Armstrong Browning Library.

109. See Browning's letter to Ralston of April 1874, Armstrong Browning Library, and also Kelley and Hudson, pp. 417-18.

110. Browning, R., *Dearest Isa*, pp. 274, 298, 333.

111. Haweis, p. 33.

112. Kelley and Hudson, p. 238; Browning, R., *Letters Collected by Wise*, ed. Hood, pp. 116-17, 125, 136; Browning, R., *Dearest Isa:*, pp. 274, 298.

113. Conway, vol. II, pp. 163ff.

114. The details may be read in Waddington, *Turgenev and England*, chapters 9-12; on Turgenev and Browning, see pp. 177-8, 217-18. It should be noted that the title of Philip Stafford Moxom's book *Two Masters: Browning and Turgenief* (Boston, 1912) is purely fortuitous, there being no parallels drawn between the writers.

115. Browning, E.B., *Letters*, ed. Kenyon, vol. I, p. 233, vol. II, pp. 75-6, 228-30; Browning, E.B., *Letters to her Sister*, p. 244; Browning, E.B., *Letters to Ogilvy*, pp. 78-9; Kelley and Hudson, p. 250.

116. Waddington, 'Two Unpublished Letters of Browning', pp. 35-6; Library of Congress, MSS Acc. 3786, Robert Browning Papers, vol. 2, p. 89, letter of Pauline Viardot to Robert Browning, 1 February [1871].

117. Hallé, pp. 126-7.

118. Carlyle, *New Letters*, vol. II, p. 272, letter of Carlyle to his brother John, 26 November 1870.

119. Browning, R., *Dearest Isa*, p. 360.

120. Turgenev, I.S., *Lettres inédites*, pp. 178-81. I have not been able to discover a reliable source for the frequently repeated statement that Turgenev was impressed by Browning's handshake: see e.g. Henderson, P.P., *Swinburne*, pp. 148-9, according to whom Turgenev in some as yet unidentified letter 'mentions meeting Browning and describes him as a vigorous white-bearded man with a handshake like an electric shock'.

121. Sewell, p. 183. Some details of Browning's poem *Donald*, written in 1882, may have been inspired by Pen's ability to massacre grouse during this visit

to Pitlochry: see Browning, R., *Poems*, ed. Pettigrew, vol. II, pp. 661-2, 1085. *Donald*, incidentally, is an excellent example of a poem which, like *Ivàn Ivànovitch*, matured in the poet's mind only half a century after the events that it describes, resurrecting observations made many decades before.

122. See Dowson, p. 146, a letter to Arthur Moore of about 31 March 1890. Dowson thought that the same held true for the works of Henry James and Emile Bourget.

123. Wilson, D.A., and MacArthur, pp. 232-4; National Library of Scotland (Edinburgh), MSS Carlyle Papers, 1770, ff. 41-2, letter to Carlyle concerning Turgenev and William Ralston; Tennyson, H., *Memoir*, vol. II, pp. 106-7, 109.

124. Shannon, R.T., pp. 204, 218. See also Davis, p. 37; Thompson, p. 245.

125. See on this e.g. Morris, *Collected Letters*, vol. I, p. 338.

126. It was reported in *The Times* of 9 December 1876, p. 7, that Dante Gabriel Rossetti was on the platform at the Conference, but this proved to be pure invention.

127. See on this *The Times*, 8 December 1876, p. 9.

128. Kelley and Hudson, p. 157.

129. Armstrong, pp. 72-3.

130. Armstrong, pp. 71-2. It has been thought that this letter, which has no year, belongs to 1877, but 1878 seems more likely. It is, however, possible that a letter of Browning to an unnamed correspondent, dated 7 April 1877 and 'sending money for a subscription and best wishes for a new campaign' is a reply to this: see Kelley and Hudson, p. 158.

131. See Browning, R., *Poems*, ed. Pettigrew, vol. II, p. 966.

132. Gladstone, M., p. 135; Tennyson, A., *Letters*, vol. III, p. 74. See also Browning, R., *Poems*, ed. Pettigrew, vol. II, p. 958 and notes p. 1145, where it is urged that the anti-Semitism is uncharacteristic of the poet. The reference is to 4 April 1878.

133. Morris, *Collected Letters*, vol. I, pp. 386, 421.

134. See Browning, R., *Poems*, ed. Pettigrew, vol. II, p. 1145.

135. See, for instance, Burnaby, pp. 47, 69.

136. See *Punch; or, The London Charivari*, vol. LXXII, 2 and 9 June 1877, pp. 249-50, 263. The series began on 21 April, pp. 177-8, and continued either weekly or fortnightly until 14 July (vol. LXXIII, pp. 11-12). The author is identified by *Punch*'s office ledger for April 1877-January 1884.

137. Bolton, F., p. 2; Orr, *Life and Letters*, pp. 307-8; Irvine and Honan, pp. 494-5; Browning, R., *Letters Collected by Wise*, ed. Hood, p. 209; Browning, R., *New Letters*, pp. 248-9. The full text of *Ivàn Ivànovitch* will be found in Appendix Two; it is given in the now standard form, found for instance in Browning, R., *Works*, introd. Kenyon, vol. IX, pp. 234-55.

138. See e.g. Bolton, F., p. 2; DeVane, *Browning Handbook*, pp. 437-8.

139. *Baylor Bulletin*, vol. XXX, no. 4, December 1927, p. 33. There was never any response to this query.

140. Orr, *Life and Letters*, p. 312; Bolton, F., pp. 2-3; Irvine and Honan, p. 496.

141. Vengerova, 'Robert Brauning i ego poeziia', pp. 181-2 (pp. 144-5) in the later edition); cf. Symons, pp. 186-7.

142. Orr, *Life and Letters*, p. 312. On all linguistic aspects of the poem one may usefully consult the thesis by Wolfe.

143. Sala, vol. I, p. 363; Barry, passim; Wallace, ch. XV, pp. 23ff. (in the edition of 1905 ch. XXI, vol. I, pp. 401ff.); cf. Alekseev, 'Die Quellen', p. 418.

144. See Turgenev, I.S., *Sochineniia*, vol. IV, p. 476.

145. See Viardot, *Les Jésuites*. In the States around 1940 the name Ivàn Ivànovitch was used by the Schering Corporation to advertise its laxative, Saraka, — or rather, to advertise the only sort of person who could be regular without it!

146. See Browning, R., *Agamemnon*, p. 305.

147. *Les Reliques vivantes*, originally published in *Le Temps* in 1874, gave its title to a collection of pieces by Turgenev published in Paris by Hetzel in 1876.

148. See Alekseev, 'Die Quellen', also his 'Zur Entstehungsgeschichte'.

149. See e.g. *Ezhenedel'noe novoe vremia*, vol. II, 10 May 1879, col. 109; Vengerova, 'Robert Brauning i ego poeziia', p. 181 (p. 145 in the later edition).

150. Alekseev, 'Die Quellen', pp. 425-6, 'Zur Entstehungsgeschichte', pp. 60-1.

151. DeVane, *Browning Handbook*, pp. 438-9.

152. Allingham, p. 314. I have carefully checked the annual indexes of *The Mirror* from its origins to the date of Tennyson's first telling of the story and beyond, and cannot substantiate Allingham's statement that he had seen it there.

153. Griffin, p. 64; Berdoe, p. 228. It is possible that the remark in Berdoe's *Browning Cyclopaedia* has less to do with the story as the poet tells it than with variations of the kind noted in the Goncourt diary for 2 January 1869, namely that the French government was throwing its ministers to be eaten by the opposition just as a Russian, in his sledge, would stave off wolves by sacrificing first his food, then his blankets, then his boots; see Goncourt, vol. II, p. 479. Contemporary cartoons treated a similar theme, and one should note that in more recent times the expression 'to throw the baby out of the sleigh' has been used for example to describe Rommel's behaviour to the Italians. See, however, Sim, p. 192, where it is stated that *Ivàn Ivànovitch* relates 'one of the wolf stories Browning brought back from his Russian trip in 1833 [sic], recalled out of the capacious storehouse of his brain forty years later'. Perhaps, too, one should mention at this point a red herring fished up by the eccentric Franklin H. Head in 'Some Methods of Browning, as Illustrated by the Poem of Ivàn Ivànovitch'. This claims that Browning took his subject from Holinshed and adduces a long narrative to prove it (pp. 67-72). The wife of Llewellyn Griffiths sacrifices her four children to marauding wolves near Cardigan and is killed by Owen ApJones; good King Rufus pardons ApJones and makes him captain of a hundred men. I confess to having searched for this in various editions of Holinshed, just in case, but assure readers there was no point in doing so; the hoax is made obvious enough by the tongue-in-cheek way that Head prefaces it: he says, for instance (p. 67), that the surname Jones is an unusual one in Wales, making it probable that Holinshed's ApJones was an ancestor of Rev. Jenkin Lloyd Jones, then president of the Chicago Browning Club.

154. Orr, *Handbook*, p. 311; Ireland, p. 46; cf. Porter and Clarke, p. 532.

155. Browning, R., *Agamemnon*, p. 304.

156. See Bolton, F., pp. 15-16. The story is not found mentioned in Andreev's index to the subjects of fairy tales, based on the Aarne system. I have tried unsuccessfully to obtain a book called *Wolf Stories*, published in London in 1866, the only noted copy of which would appear to have been destroyed by bombing at the British Museum during World War II. Nor does there seem to be a source for the tale in antiquity; there is no reference to it in Eckels.

157. See e.g. *Notes and Queries,* 11th series vol. II, July-December 1910, pp. 28, 318, vol. CLXXIV, January-June 1938, pp. 216, 245, 316, and cf. Knox, pp. 383-4. A. Joseph Armstrong, founder of the Armstrong Browning Library, had some interesting correspondence with Armand Hammer concerning statements in his book *The Quest of the Romanoff Treasure* (New York, 1936, pp. 149-52). On the one hand, Hammer recounted a version of the wolf tale which he claimed to have first met in a primer read as a schoolboy in Connecticut, but on the other he said he was informed that wolves do not attack human beings unless they are wounded or dying. Armstrong collected a considerable file on this subject, to which are appended relevant essays written by third-year Baylor University students in 1964 and later; see this file at the Armstrong Browning Library, and in particular Hammer's letter to Armstrong of 2 July 1936.

158. Kohl, vol. II, p. 250.

159. Tennyson, C., *Alfred Tennyson*, p. 172.

160. Lacroix, pp. 323-4.

161. Henningsen's book first appeared in 1844 and was published in a revised form in 1846. The 1846 preface (vol. I, pp. vi-vii) suggests that Lacroix may have copied things from Henningsen; but this is obviously not the case with the wolf story. The two Henningsen accounts cited here are taken from the 3rd revised edition, vol. II, pp. 73-4.

162. Hill, F., p. 27.

163. Lara, p. 238.

164. Berdoe, pp. 228-9.

165. DeVane, *Browning Handbook*, pp. 438-9. Frances Bolton, in a well-researched thesis of 1934, cogently argued the similarities between *Ivàn Ivànovitch* and the account by the Englishwoman in Russia, while accepting that there were a few significant differences such as the circumstances of a pardon for the carpenter: see Bolton, F., pp. 18-21.

166. The Kelley and Coley reconstruction of Browning's library shows no trace of these travel accounts. One should be cautious of accepting the frequently held view that Browning took his names from *The Englishwoman in Russia* or used this for his information on the German and French influence in that country; he would have found out all this for himself during his stay in St Petersburg.

167. Cited in Litzinger and Smalley, p. 459, where the reviewer is tentatively identified as Grant Allen.

168. See Orr, 'Dramatic Idyls', pp. 293-7. For other contemporary criticism in Britain, see Bolton, F., pp. 31-2; *Athenaeum*, 10 May 1879, pp. 593-5; Symons, pp. 186-7. For a useful general discussion of *Ivàn Ivànovitch* as a poem, see Bolton, F., pp. 24-31. Among more recent articles in English one may note those by Slinn and Drew, which look in quite different ways at the philosophical and moral problems posed by *Ivàn Ivànovitch*.

169. See Allingham's copy of the book at the Armstrong Browning Library, M 116, and cf. his own *Diary*, p. 314.

170. Ireland, pp. 46-7.

171. See the Mason poem.

172. Browning, R., *Agamemnon*, p. 304.

173. Ireland, p. 46.

174. Gladstone, M., p. 204.

175. Smith, G.C.M., p. 292.

176. Cummings, p. 409; see also e.g. DeVane, *Browning's Parleyings*, p. 10.

177. Chadwick, p. 261.

178. Woolford, 'Dramatic Idyls', p. 22.

179. West, Miss E.D., p. 431.

180. *The Browning Society's Papers*, 1881-4, Monthly Abstract of Proceedings, p. 69.

181. *The Browning Society's Papers*, 1881-4, Monthly Abstract of Proceedings, p. 71.

182. *The Browning Society's Papers*, 1881-4, Monthly Abstract of Proceedings, p. 73.

183. *The Browning Society's Papers*, Part VII, Monthly Abstract of Proceedings, Fourth Session, 27 February 1885, pp. 29-31.

184. *The Browning Society's Papers*, Part VII, Monthly Abstract of Proceedings, Fourth Session, 27 February 1885, p. 31.

185. *The Browning Society's Papers*, Part VII, Monthly Abstract of Proceedings, Fourth Session, 27 February 1885, pp. 31-2.

186. *The Browning Society's Papers*, Part VII, Monthly Abstract of Proceedings, Fourth Session, 27 February 1885, pp. 32-3.

187. *The Browning Society's Papers*, Part VII, Monthly Abstract of Proceedings, Fourth Session, 1884-85, p. 65, no. 65.

188. *The Browning Society's Papers*, Part VII, Monthly Abstract of Proceedings, Fourth Session, 1884-85, p. 87, no. 90.

189. *The Browning Society's Papers*, Part VII, Monthly Abstract of Proceedings, Fourth Session, 1884-85, pp. 65-6, no. 67. The reference is to ll. 168-9 of *Ivàn Ivànovitch*.

190. Mirskii, pp. 488, 499. On the reception of Robert Browning's poetry in Russia, see especially the articles by Vengerova and the book by Klimenko. Some Russian translations from his poetry appear in *Antologiia novoi angliiskoi poezii*, ed. M. Gutner, Leningrad, 1937, pp. 27-63.

191. 'Dramaticheskaia idilliia Roberta Brouninga iz russkoi zhizni', *Ezhenedel'noe novoe vremia*, vol. II, 10 May 1879, cols 108-15. This also included the first Russian translations from Browning's poem.

192. Regnard, pp. 350-2. Regnard was admittedly a Frenchman, corresponding from London!

193. Kelley and Hudson, p. 238, fragment of a lost letter whose date and recipient are unknown.

194. Goncourt, vol. II, pp. 1124-5; see also Waddington, 'Turgenev and George Eliot', pp. 756-7.

195. Letters of Browning to Ralston, 8 April 1874, 5 May and 30 July 1879; Kelley and Hudson, p. 418. Several, but not all, of the Browning-Ralston items are at the Armstrong Browning Library.

196. Forbes, E.M., pp. 861-2, 869; Griffin, p. 279. Browning's name is not given in the guest-lists of any function that Turgenev attended, and he probably in fact left Oxford and Balliol just before the novelist arrived there; he himself was due to receive an Hon. LL.D. about that time, but from the University of Cambridge. See also A. H. Sayce to Browning, Queen's College, 9 June 1879, in Young, R.A., p. 292. On Turgenev's own stay in Oxford, see Waddington, *Turgenev and England*, ch. 14.

197. Letter of Browning to Ralston of 24 October 1881, Armstrong Browning Library; cf. Kelley and Hudson, p. 418. The spelling of Turgenev's name in Browning's letter is not clear: it could read 'Tourquereff'.

198. *The Browning Collections*, Sotheby's sale of 1913, lots 1163-5, p. 136; Woolford, *Sale Catalogues*, p. 165. The Armstrong Browning Library has Turgenev's *Mémoires d'un seigneur russe*, trans. Charrière, 2 vols. (Paris, 1885) — a late edition of the first French version of *Zapiski okhotnika*, originally published in one volume in 1854, — and also a copy of *Katia* (1887), a translation of Tolstoi's *Semeinoe schast'e* (Family Happiness).

199. Letter of 2 March 1887. Browning's known letters to Rafalovich are listed in Kelley and Hudson, p. 417; several are at the Armstrong Browning Library. See also Armstrong, p. 128.

200. See undated letter of Robert Browning to Mrs Charles Skirrow (Sunday, spring 1881?), Armstrong Browning Library. Here as elsewhere, he spells the pianist's name 'Rubenstein'.

201. Browning, R., *Browning's Trumpeter*, p. 94.

202. Gosse, *Robert Browning*, p. 78.

203. Armstrong, pp. 91-2.

204. Irving, *Annals 1871-1887*, p. 1366.

205. *Poet Lore*, vol. II, no. 2, 1890, p. 103, following an article by Oswald John Simon in the London *Jewish Chronicle*; Armstrong, pp. 91-2. See also *The Critic: A Weekly Review of Literature and the Arts*, New York, n.s. vol. XIII, 11 January 1890, p. 22; Jacob, p. 166; Morris, *Letters*, ed. Henderson, p. 158; Morris, *Collected Letters*, vol. II, pp. 95-6; *The Times*, 2 and 3 February 1882.

206. Jacob, pp. 165-72; Kelley and Hudson, pp. 184, 355.

207. It is at the Library of Congress, Washington, MSS Acc. 3786. On Emma Lazarus and Turgenev, see e.g. Jacob, pp. 57-60.

208. Bronson, p. 578; letters of Browning to Mrs and Miss Bronson, 4 January and 7 February 1889, Armstrong Browning Library. Browning twice refers to Gagarin (as 'Gargarin') in his letters to Bronson, the editors of which say that the Gagarin in question was 'Prince Léon'; but Grigory Grigor'evich (1810-93) must certainly be meant. See Browning, R., *More than Friend*, pp. 88-90, 156; this book reprints the Bronson article.

209. Bronson, pp. 578-9.

Notes to Algernon Charles Swinburne

1. Angeli, p. 97.

2. Thompson, p. 339, and cf. ibid., pp. 311-12, 374.

3. Watts-Dunton, C., *Home Life*, p. 91.

4. Leith, pp. 13-17; Swinburne, *Letters*, ed. Lang, vol. III, p. 13, VI, pp. 37, 251-3. See also Lafourcade, *La Jeunesse*, vol. I, pp. 103-4, 109.

5. Swinburne, *Letters*, ed. Lang, vol. I, p. 5.

6. Swinburne, *Letters*, ed. Lang, vol. I, p. 5.

7. See Swinburne, *Lesbia Brandon*, p. 46, and cf. pp. 182, 521, 578-9.

8. See Wise, *Bibliography of Swinburne*, vol. II, pp. 370-1. The mistake was made by Wise, owing largely to whose ignorance (or more often whose machinations) various poems at various times have been wrongly attributed to Swinburne.

9. In his preface to the first (posthumous) edition of *Liberty and Loyalty* in 1909, Sir Edmund Gosse argued cogently that it belonged to the summer of 1866 (see Wise, *Bibliography of Swinburne*, vol. II, pp. 43-4), but the connection with Carlyle makes March or April 1865 much more probable. It is also relevant to note that in a letter of March 1865 Swinburne mentioned together, though in a different context, a number of past and present public figures referred to in the essay: see Swinburne, *Letters*, ed. Lang, vol. I, pp. 114-17.

10. Carlyle, *History of Friedrich II.*, vol. IX, pp. 296-7 (book XXI, ch. III).

11. Swinburne, *Complete Works* (Bonchurch), vol. XVI, pp. 44-6.

12. Partridge, 'Slavonic Themes', p. 438.

13. See Swinburne, *Complete Works* (Bonchurch), vol. II, p. 133 in pp. 130-6. *The Litany of Nations* is at pp. 73-81 in *Songs before Sunrise*.

14. Wilson and Macarthur, p. 233. What follows is from Gosse, 'A Memory of Tourgenieff'. On the party at Brown's, see Waddington, *Turgenev and England*, pp. 187-91. There I guess (p. 188) that it took place on 8 June, but Swinburne may well have been at Henley then; a more likely date may be between 3 July, when he probably returned to London, and 29 July, when Turgenev left. See Swinburne, *Letters*, ed. Lang, vol. II, pp. 152-4; Turgenev, I.S., *Pis'ma*, vol. IX, p. 114.

15. Gosse, *Life of Swinburne*, pp. 200-2, 296.

16. See Waddington, *Turgenev and England*, p. 218.

17. Swinburne, *Letters*, ed. Lang, vol. II, pp. 156-8.

18. Turgenev, I.S., *Pis'ma*, vol. IX, p. 125.

19. Turgenev, I.S., *Pis'ma*, vol. X, p. 8.

20. Turgenev, I.S., *Pis'ma*, vol. X, p. 128.

21. Maupassant, 'Gustave Flaubert', p. 120; 'Notes sur Swinburne', p. x.

22. See Swinburne, *Catalogue*.

23. Swinburne, *Letters*, ed. Lang, vol. IV, pp. 23-4. *L'Inspecteur général* was included in Mérimée's volume *Les Deux héritages* (Paris, 1853).

24. Swinburne, *Letters*, ed. Lang, vol. IV, pp. 23-4.

25. Swinburne, *Letters*, ed. Lang, vol. III, pp. 163ff., 175-6; Nichol, *Tables*, VI, VII and VIII.

26. Friswell, L.H., pp. 79-82; see also e.g. Hudson, D., *Munby*, pp. 127-8.

27. *Pensiero e Azione*, 16 April 1859, reprinted in Saffi, vol. V, pp. 139-41, and *Il Dovere*, 21 December 1884, reprinted in Saffi, vol. XI, pp. 416-17. See also Lafourcade, *La Jeunesse*, vol. I, pp. 117-18; Panter-Downes, p. 121.

28. See Swinburne, *Complete Works* (Bonchurch), vol. VI, pp. 171-4, 289; cf. *Poems*, 1904, vol. VI, pp. 238-41, 382.

29. Swinburne, *Letters*, ed. Lang, vol. II, p. 198.

30. Polonskii, p. 572; the passage was first published in the journal *Niva* in 1884. See also Rossetti, W.M., *Diary*, pp. 71-2, where Turgenev is said to have made a comment about Swinburne's lips which 'startled' the company after dinner at Dante Gabriel Rossetti's on 23 June 1871.

31. Moore, G., 'Turgueneff', p. 237.

32. Caine, *Recollections*, pp. 173-4.

33. Rossetti, W.M., *Selected Letters*, pp. 150-1; Compton-Rickett, pp. 150-1.

34. Swinburne, *Letters*, ed. Lang, vol. I, pp. 76-7. The Trevelyan Papers should still have a pictorial record of this.

35. Swinburne, *Letters*, ed. Lang, vol. IV, p. 107.

36. Charteris, p. 411.

37. See Rossetti, W.M., *Diary,* pp. 5-6, 16-17; Hudson, D., *Munby*, pp. 233-4, 270, 289; Kernahan, pp. 40-3; Hardman, pp. 78-80; Swinburne, *Letters*, ed. Lang, vol. II, pp. 20-1, and VI, p. 242 (Gosse's account); Henderson, P.P., *Swinburne*, pp. 115, 152, 161-2; Lafourcade, *La Jeunesse*, vol. I, pp. 237-8.

38. Swinburne, *Letters*, ed. Lang, vol. I, pp. 291, 293-4.

39. Swinburne, *Letters*, ed. Lang, vol. I, p. 82; see also Rossetti, D.G., *Letters*, ed. Doughty and Wahl, vol. II, p. 510.

40. See Swinburne, *Letters*, ed. Lang, vol. III, pp. 247, 284.

41. See Swinburne, *Complete Works* (Bonchurch), vol. V, pp. 296-7.

42. Usov, pp. 1051-2.

43. Swinburne, *Letters*, ed. Lang, vol. I, p. 3, vol. III, p. 117.

44. Swinburne, *Letters*, ed. Lang, vol. I, p. 260; see also e.g. ibid., p. 291.

45. See Turgenev, I.S., *Pis'ma*, vol. XI, pp. 23, 25, 28, etc.

46. Swinburne, *Letters*, ed. Lang, vol. I, pp. 308-10; Rossetti, W.M., *Rossetti Papers 1862 to 1870*, p. 335.

47. First published in the *Athenaeum* of 2 June 1877, p. 703, and reprinted in the second series of *Poems and Ballads*; 1878, pp. 116-22, it will be found in Swinburne, *Complete Works* (Bonchurch), vol. III, pp. 74-7.

48. Maupassant, 'Notes sur Swinburne', pp. vii-x; Goncourt, vol. II, pp. 1044-7, and cf. vol. III, p. 251.

49. See Gosse, 'Swinburne at Étretat', pp. 462-4; Charteris, pp. 329, 342-3; James, H., *Letters*, vol. IV, pp. 630-4, 640; James, H., *Letters to Gosse*, pp. 279-83.

50. See also Maupassant, 'Notes sur Swinburne', pp. viii-ix, and Steegmuller, pp. 35-7, 67-8, 351-4. Steegmuller suggests (p. 70) that the figure of a monkey in Maupassant's *Le Docteur Héraclius Gloss* must also have derived from the association with Powell and Swinburne.

51. See the *World*, 6 December 1882, p. 18 (also the report on 29 November); Swinburne, *Letters*, ed. Lang, vol. IV, pp. 318-19. Among the innumerable other references to the Etretat affair, see e.g. Swinburne, *Letters*, ed. Lang, vol. I, pp. 308-10, vol. VI, pp. 253-4; Lafourcade, *La Jeunesse*, vol. I, p. 234; Leith, pp. 238-9.

52. Watts-Dunton, C., *Home Life*, p. 110.

53. See Swinburne, *Letters*, ed. Lang, vol. I, pp. 306-7, vol. III, pp. 13, 82, vol. IV, pp. 32, 40, etc.; Swinburne, *Ballade of Truthful Charles*, p. 8; Wise, *A Swinburne Library*, p. 133. See also British Library, Ashley MS 5077.

54. Swinburne, *Letters*, ed. Lang, vol. IV, p. 65.

55. Swinburne, *Letters*, ed. Lang, vol. II, pp. 150, 274, vol. III, pp. 223, 236, 245, 246.

56. Swinburne, *Letters*, ed. Lang, vol. III, p. 122.

57. The *Daily News* took credit for announcing the full extent of the troubles in its famous piece 'The Assassinations at Constantinople — Moslem Atrocities in Bulgaria', published on 23 June, but the *Spectator*, annoyed that its own relevant article of 3 June should have been overlooked, reprinted it as a pamphlet called *'The First Alarm' respecting the Bulgarian Outrages.*

58. Swinburne, *Letters*, ed. Lang, vol. III, pp. 204-5, 209-10, 216, 219.

59. Swinburne, *Letters*, ed. Lang, vol. VI, p. 71; see also e.g. vol. V, pp. 8-10, 14-15, 188-91, and Swinburne, *Complete Works* (Bonchurch), vol. XX, pp. 81-4.

60. Swinburne, *Letters*, ed. Lang, vol. V, p. 229, VI, p. 292.

61. Swinburne, *Letters*, ed. Lang, vol. IV, p. 211, VI, p. 200.

62. Swinburne, *Letters*, ed. Hake and Compton-Rickett, pp. 48ff.

63. Abbott and Campbell, *Letters*, pp. 64, 69-70, 91, 95.

64. Abbott and Campbell, *Letters*, pp. 79-80; and cf. pp. 81-3.

65. Swinburne, *Letters*, ed. Lang, vol. III, p. 304.

66. See e.g. Thompson, pp. 254-5; Gernsheim, p. 155.

67. For a discussion of this, see e.g. Thompson, p. 262.

68. See Sumner, p. 187.

69. West, A., vol. II, pp. 75-6.

70. Gladstone, W.E., *Speech at Blackheath*, pp. 25-6; see also Gladstone, M., p. 109.

71. Cited in Sinclair, p. 1.

72. She was later their chronicler, publishing in September 1877 a *Report on the Bulgarian Relief Fund, with a Statement of Distribution and Expenditure.*

73. Freeman, 'True Eastern Question', p. 747, and 'Present Aspects', pp. 409, 411.

74. See on this and many other aspects of the Bulgarian debate the most excellent book by R.T. Shannon; see also his bibliography there, pp. 282-96.

75. Munro, *Eastern Question*, p. 50, *The Turks*, p. 48.

76. See *Punch; or, The London Charivari*, vol. LXX, pp. 247, vol. LXXI, pp. 29, 51, 68, 193, 241, and cf. p. 277.

77. See Austin, *Autobiography*, vol. I, pp. 163-4, vol. II, pp. 54-5, 66-8.

78. Austin, *Tory Horrors*, p. 28.

79. Austin, *Russia before Europe*, p. 64.

80. Austin, *Tory Horrors*, p. 32.

81. Austin, *Autobiography*, vol. II, pp. 2-4, 110; Swinburne, *Letters*, ed. Lang, vol. II, pp. 38, 46, 304-5, vol. III, p. 58, vol. V, pp. 17-18, vol. VI, p. 180.

82. Swinburne, *Letters*, ed. Lang, vol. III, p. 228; see also p. 304.

83. See Swinburne, *Complete Works* (Bonchurch), vol. II, pp. 333-43, IV, p. 313; Swinburne, *Letters*, ed. Lang, vol. II, pp. 125, 186, VI, pp. 254-5.

84. *Bookman*, vol. XXXVI, June 1909, pp. 127, 129; Swinburne, *Letters*, ed. Lang, vol. I, p. xxviii.

85. Harrison, F., pp. 709, 719-20.

86. Swinburne, *Letters*, ed. Lang, vol. III, pp. 221-5, 233. On the Christian/Moslem difficulty, see also Abbott and Campbell, *Letters*, p. 101.

87. Swinburne, *Letters*, ed. Lang, vol. III, pp. 224, 226-7, 232, 237-8.

88. Swinburne, *Letters*, ed. Lang, vol. III, p. 237.

89. See Algernon Charles Swinburne, *Note of an English Republican on the Muscovite Crusade*, London: Chatto and Windus, 1876, reprinted in Swinburne, *Complete Works* (Bonchurch), vol. XV, pp. 411-29.; Swinburne, *Letters*, ed. Lang, vol. III, pp. 234-5, 237. See also Wise, *Bibliography of Swinburne*, vol. I, pp. 264, 267; Swinburne, *Complete Works* (Bonchurch), vol. XX, pp. 142-3.

90. Swinburne, *Letters*, ed. Lang, vol. III, p. 225, IV, pp. 203-4.

91. Musorgskii, pp. 110-11, 259; Brown, vol. I, p. 282.
92. 'An Ottoman Statesman', *The Times*, 9 January 1877, p. 5, col. e.
93. Swinburne, *Letters*, ed. Lang, vol. III, pp. 225, 239, 252, V, p. 21.
94. Wilson and MacArthur, pp. 137-8; Swinburne, *Letters*, ed. Lang, vol. II, pp. 274-8, vol. III, pp. 252, etc., vol. V, p. 69.
95. Swinburne, *Letters*, ed. Lang, vol. IV, p. 208. See also Wise, *A Swinburne Library*, pp. 107-8.
96. Symonds, pp. 1-2. Tennyson vigorously supported Eyre's actions, both at the time and afterwards: see Tennyson, E., *Letters*, pp. 197-8; Tennyson, A., *Letters*, vol. II, pp. 415-16, 421-2, 428-9.
97. *Northern Echo*, Darlington, 13 July 1876, pp. 2-3, cited in Shannon, R.T., p. 206; Swinburne, *Letters*, ed. Lang, vol. V, p. 205.
98. Abbott and Campbell, *Life and Letters*, vol. II, p. 34; Swinburne, *Letters*, ed. Lang, vol. III, pp. 239-40.
99. Swinburne, *Letters*, ed. Lang, vol. III, p. 232-4, and cf. p. 250.
100. See here also Swinburne, *Letters*, ed. Lang, vol. V, p. 206.
101. See Carlyle, *Occasional Discourse*, passim.
102. See Irving, *Annals 1837-1871*, p. 751.
103. Duncan, p. 220.
104. Swinburne, *Letters*, ed. Lang, vol. III, pp. 242-3, 246, 250. See *Spectator*, 23 December 1876, pp. 1606-7; the unsigned author of this review was Meredith Townsend.
105. *Gentleman's Magazine*, vol. CCXL, January 1877, p. 124.
106. Swinburne, *Letters*, ed. Lang, vol. III, pp. 232, 234, 237, 249-50; Rossetti, D.G., *Family-Letters*, vol. II, p. 339; Rossetti, D.G., *Letters*, ed. Doughty and Wahl, vol. III, p. 1466. See also *The Times*, 9 December 1876, p. 7.
107. Swinburne, *Letters*, ed. Lang, vol. III, p. 228.
108. See Swinburne, *Letters*, ed. Lang, vol. III, pp. 229-30.
109. Swinburne, *Letters*, ed. Lang, vol. III, p. 245; vol. V, pp. 153, etc.
110. British Library MSS Add. 43949, ff. 37-41. See Burnett, pp. 276-7; Waddington, *Turgenev and England*, pp. 153-4.
111. Swinburne, *Letters*, ed. Lang, vol. III, pp. 276, 282.
112. Swinburne, *Letters*, ed. Lang, vol. IV, p. 34.
113. Swinburne, *Letters*, ed. Lang, vol. IV, pp. 118-19. The only important difference from the text that I print later was the reading 'Strike, gentlemen' instead of 'Shout, gentlemen' in line 89.
114. See Swinburne, *New Writings*, pp. 188-9.
115. See Swinburne, *Letters*, ed. Gosse and Wise, vol. I, pp. 286-7, and *Complete Works* (Bonchurch), vol. XX, pp. 254-7; Wise, *A Swinburne Library*, pp. 154-5. Edmund Gosse's transcript of *The Ballad of Bulgarie* is at the Brotherton Library of Leeds University.
116 Wise Exhibition, p. 6. The cover of the catalogue of this April Fools Day celebration of the work of T.J. Wise, held at the Humanities Research Center of the University of Texas in 1959, tells all in the Latin tag: 'Nihil tetigit quod non ornavit.'
117. Wise, *Bibliography of Swinburne*, vol. I, p. 450; Swinburne, *Complete Works* (Bonchurch), vol. XX, p. 257; Carter and Pollard, 2nd ed., p. 290.
118. See Partington, *Thomas J. Wise*, pp. 171, 175.
119. Nicoll and Wise, vol. II, pp. 346-8.
120. See Swinburne, *New Writings*, p. 189; Burnett, pp. 276-9; Wise, *Bibliography of Swinburne*, vol. II, p. 399. This draft at the British Library is Ashley A1930.
121. For comparison, see Swinburne, *New Writings*, pp. 17-19, and Burnett, pp. 279-82.
122. Swinburne, *New Writings*, p. 190. 'Like some in Denmark's ill' does ap-

pear to be a correct reading in the British Library draft, where it replaces something crossed out which makes even less sense. (See Ashley A1930, f. 138 verso).

123. Swinburne, *Letters*, ed. Lang, vol. III, p. 331.

124. *Punch; or, The London Charivari*, vol. LXXII, 19 May 1877, p. 227; vol. LXXIV, 19 January 1878, p. 19, 13 April 1878, pp. 162-3. An excellent discussion of the history of the Eastern Question will be found in Thompson, pp. 230-1, 244-63.

125. See Swinburne, *Poems and Ballads*, 2nd series, 1878, p. 189; cf. Swinburne, *Poems*, 1904, vol. III, p. 129, and *Complete Works* (Bonchurch), vol. III, p. 121.

126. See on this the article by Žekulin. Despite a long and careful search, I have not been able to find the translation referred to by Swinburne. It is not in the *Gentleman's Magazine*, as he could appear to be hinting, nor yet in any journal covered by the Wellesley Index or Poole. Although Swinburne speaks merely of 1877, the date of his comments suggests that the poem came out near the end of that year, and indeed on 29 December *Punch* published a cartoon by Sambourne called 'Planting the Hughenden Tree' which contains a possible echo of Turgenev's *Kroket v Vindzore*: the Queen is planting trees for Lord Beaconsfield, oblivious of the war that rages over Bulgaria. See *Punch; or, The London Charivari*, vol. LXXIII, 29 December 1877, p. 290. Turgenev's poem was first suggested as the origin of Swinburne's remarks by a Russian critic called N. Vasil'ev; M.P. Alekseev, the great Soviet polymath, argued that this was unlikely and proposed instead Apollon Maikov's *The Empress of India*, published in the *Russkii vestnik* in 1877. However, there is no sign that this poem was ever translated into English at the time. See Alekseev, 'Sibirskaia ssylka', p. 190; the Vasil'ev references that Alekseev gives are *Sbornik 'Tvorchestvo'*, Kazan, 1909, p. 135, and *Vestnik Evropy*, 1909, no. 8, p. 520.

127. Freeman, 'Terms of Peace', p. 93.

128. Swinburne, *Letters*. ed. Lang, vol. IV, pp. 36, 41. It is clear that 'Freedmaniac' does refer to Freeman.

129. Swinburne, *Letters*, ed. Lang, vol. IV, p. 41.

130. Swinburne, *Letters*, ed. Lang, vol. IV, pp. 45-6.

131. See e.g. Chew, p. 152.

132. Swinburne, *Poems and Ballads*, 2nd series, 1878, p. 189; cf. Swinburne, *Poems*, 1904, vol. III, p. 129, and *Complete Works* (Bonchurch), vol. III, p. 121.

133. H.W. Longfellow, 'The White Czar', *Atlantic Monthly*, vol. XLI, March 1878, pp. 365-6; reprinted in Longfellow, pp. 218-20.

134. For the biblical references, see 2 Kings 5.20-7 and Matthew 27.24-5.

135. The text is taken from the definitive Swinburne, *Complete Works* (Bonchurch), vol. III, pp. 121-2; cf. Swinburne, *Poems and Ballads*, 2nd series, 1878, pp. 189-91, and *Poems*, 1904, vol. III, pp. 129-30.

136. For these biblical references, see 2 Samuel 21.8-14; Matthew 2.16-18; Jeremiah 31.15. Tennyson, after Swinburne, wrote a poem called *Rizpah*, which Swinburne in fact much admired, but there is no connection between the two pieces other than the name and mother's love of Rizpah. See Swinburne, *Letters*, ed. Lang, vol. IV, pp. 177, 192.

137. The text is taken from Swinburne, *Complete Works* (Bonchurch), vol. III, p. 123; cf. Swinburne, *Poems and Ballads*, 2nd series, 1878, p. 192, and *Poems*, 1904, vol. III, p. 131.

138. For details, see Bibliography.

139. Swinburne, *Letters*, ed. Lang, vol. IV, p. 32; see also ibid., pp. 203-4, 237, 259-61, and vol. III, p. 240. In February 1878 Kossuth published another article in the *Contemporary Review*, 'What is in Store for Europe, and especially for Austria-Hungary'; for details, see Bibliography.

140. Landor, *Poems*, vol. II, p. 229.

141. Super, pp. 349-50, 380, 392, 416-17.
142. See Landor, *Imaginary Conversations*, vol. VI, pp. 397-411.
143. Landor, *Poems*, vol. II, pp. 248-9; Elwin, p. 401.
144. Super, pp. 421, 423, 596.
145. See Elwin, p. 383; Super, pp. 430, 508-9, 597.
146. The text is taken from Swinburne, *Complete Works* (Bonchurch), vol. III, p. 124; cf. Swinburne, *Poems and Ballads*, 2nd series, 1878, p. 193, and *Poems*, 1904, vol. III, p. 132.
147. Compton-Rickett, pp. 143-4.
148. Cited in Partington, *Thomas J. Wise*, p. 318.
149. Hake and Compton-Rickett, *Watts-Dunton*, vol. II, pp. 101-3, 182-3, 217.
150. Panter-Downes, pp. 123-4, 132.
151. Swinburne, *Letters*, ed. Lang, vol. VI, p. 114.
152. Swinburne, *Letters*, ed. Lang, vol. IV, p. 119.
153. Swinburne, *Letters*, ed. Lang, vol. IV, p. 128.
154. Swinburne, *Letters*, ed. Lang, vol. IV, pp. 130-1, 262.
155. Chew, p. 158. The text is taken from the definitive Swinburne, *Complete Works* (Bonchurch), vol. IV, pp. 314-15; cf. Swinburne, *Poems*, 1904, vol. V, pp. 74-6.
156. Swinburne, *Letters*, ed. Lang, vol. IV, pp. 185-7, 231.
157. Swinburne, *Letters*, ed. Lang, vol. IV, p. 205.
158. Swinburne, *Letters*, ed. Lang, vol. IV, pp. 202-3.
159. Swinburne, *Letters*, ed. Lang, vol. IV, pp. 203-4, 237, 259-61; Rossetti, W.M., *Selected Letters*, pp. 393, 395.
160. Swinburne, *Letters*, ed. Lang, vol. IV, pp. 259-60.
161. Swinburne, *Letters*, ed. Lang, vol. IV, p. 261.
162. Swinburne, *Letters*, ed. Lang, vol. IV, p. 237. Dante Gabriel Rossetti's sonnet (see Rossetti, D.G., *Collected Works*, ed. W.M. Rossetti, 1886, vol. I, p. 342; *Works*, ed. W.M. Rossetti, 1911, p. 233) goes like this:

From him did forty million serfs, endow'd
Each with six feet of death-due soil, receive
Rich freeborn lifelong land, whereon to sheave
Their country's harvest. These to-day aloud
Demand of Heaven a Father's blood, — sore bow'd
With tears and thrilled with wrath; who, while they grieve,
On every guilty head would fain achieve
All torment by his edicts disallow'd.
He stayed the knout's red-ravening fangs; and first
Of Russian traitors, his own murderers go
White to the tomb. While he, — laid foully low
With limbs red-rent, with festering brain which erst
Willed kingly freedom, — 'gainst the deed accurst
To God bears witness of his people's woe.

163. The text is taken from the definitive Swinburne, *Complete Works* (Bonchurch), vol. V, p. 118; cf. Swinburne, *Poems*, 1904, vol. V, p. 243. In Swinburne's *Letters*, ed. Lang, vol. IV, p. 259 (13 February 1882) the poem is given with the emendation 'darkling' for 'dark red'.
164. The two sonnets are at pp. 222-3. The text of *Euonymos* used here is taken from Swinburne, *Complete Works* (Bonchurch), vol. V, p. 119; cf. Swinburne, *Poems*, 1904, vol. V, p. 244.
165. See Morris, *Collected Letters*, vol. I, p. 421, vol. II, pp. 95-6.
166. At p. 224. The text here is taken from Swinburne, *Complete Works* (Bonchurch), vol. V, p. 120; cf. Swinburne, *Poems*, 1904, vol. V, p. 245. The manuscript, written on Swinburne's habitual blue foolscap paper, is at the Harry

Ransom Humanities Research Center, The University of Texas at Austin. *On the Russian Persecution of the Jews* was selected by William Sharp in 1887 as one of only five pieces by Swinburne for his anthology *Sonnets of this Century*: see Sharp, *Sonnets*, p. 214.

167. Swinburne, *Letters*, ed. Lang, vol. IV, p. 262.

168. Swinburne, *Letters*, ed. Lang, vol. IV, pp. 189, 192, 309, V, pp. 130-1; cf. vol. I, p. 232.

169. See Swinburne, *Complete Works* (Bonchurch), vol. V, p. 285 in pp. 278-91; cf. *Poems*, 1904, vol. V, pp. 407, 413.

170. Swinburne, *Letters*, ed. Lang, vol. VI, pp. 62-3.

171. Swinburne, *Letters*, ed. Lang, vol. IV, p. 287.

172. Swinburne, *Letters*, ed. Lang, vol. IV, p. 265.

173. Swinburne, *Letters*, ed. Lang, vol. V, p. 107.

174. Watts-Dunton, C., 'My Recollections', pp. 222-3, and *Home Life*, pp. 224-6.

175. Swinburne, *Letters*, ed. Lang, vol. III, pp. 13-14.

176. Swinburne, *Letters*, ed. Lang, vol. IV, pp. 217, 236, 275, 315-18, 323, V, pp. 51, 78-9, 104-5, 126-7.

177. Swinburne, *Letters*, ed. Lang, vol. V, p. 1.

178. See Swinburne, *Complete Works* (Bonchurch), vol. V, p. 45; cf. *Poems*, 1904, vol. V, p. 160.

179. Swinburne, *Letters*, ed. Lang, vol. V, p. 90.

180. *A Word for the Country* was first published in *A Midsummer Holiday and Other Poems*, 1884; the quotation here is from Swinburne, *Complete Works* (Bonchurch), vol. VI, p. 47 in pp. 44-9.

181. See Swinburne, *Letters*, ed. Lang, vol. V, pp. 128, 148, 199, 203, 205, 207, vol. VI, p. 95; *A Channel Passage and Other Poems*, 1904, pp. 95-101; *Poems*, 1904, vol. VI, pp. 342-5; Wise, *Bibliography of Swinburne*, vol. II, pp. 267, 397. Although the aborted 1886 text seems authentic, a second so-called 1887 edition was a Wise forgery produced perhaps in 1890: see Wise Exhibition, p. 10; Partington, *Thomas J. Wise*, p. 345. Swinburne's own fair copy of the poem, clearly dated 1885 (and not 1886, as is commonly stated) is at the Harry Ransom Humanities Research Center, The University of Texas at Austin.

182. See Swinburne, *Complete Works* (Bonchurch), vol. VI, p. 253 in pp. 252-5; cf. *Works*, 1904, vol. VI, p. 343. On the variants, see also Livingston, *Swinburne's Proof Sheets*, pp. 25-9.

183. See Wise, *Bibliography of Swinburne*, vol. I, pp. 365-86 (the quotation is from p. 382), vol. II, p. 267; Swinburne, *Poems*, 1904, vol. VI, p. 343; Nicoll and Wise, vol. II, pp. 338-9; Swinburne, *Complete Works* (Bonchurch), vol. XX, pp. 217-29.

184. Swinburne, *Poems*, 1904, vol. VI, p. 344; *Complete Works* (Bonchurch), vol. VI, p. 254 in pp. 252-5.

185. Panter-Downes, p. 135. See also Lafourcade, *Swinburne*, p. 280; Hare, p. 198.

186. Swinburne, *New Writings*, p. 25; cf. Swinburne, *Complete Works* (Bonchurch), vol. XX, pp. 397-401.

187. 'The Russ and the Bulgar', British Library, Ashley MS 4390. See also Wise, *Swinburne Library*, p. 125, and *Ashley Library*, vol. VI, p. 159.

188. 'The Russ and the Frenchman', British Library, Ashley MS A1956. See also *Ashley Library*, vol. VII, p. 7; Wise, *A Swinburne Library*, p. 190.

189. Harry Ransom Humanities Research Center, The University of Texas at Austin: Swinburne, Works, 'The Two Enemies. 1886.' This is a fair copy, written by Swinburne on a single sheet of blue foolscap paper, but not signed or more specifically dated. It is published here by kind permission of the Center.

190. 'Russo-Gallia', British Library, Ashley MS A1958, recto and verso. See

also *Ashley Library*, vol. VII, p. 9; Wise, *A Swinburne Library*, p. 192. The reading 'fine France' in the fourth stanza is doubtful; but note that Wise's 'fair France', though possible in sense, is impossible to read from the manuscript.

191. See Wise, *Bibliography of Swinburne*, vol. II, p. 271.

192. See Swinburne, *Whippingham Papers*, pp. 10-11 in the separately paginated section of 'Anecdotes'.

193. See Dillon, *Eclipse*, p. 46. There was some mystery, or perhaps mystification, at the time concerning the identity of 'E.B. Lanin'. While there is now every reason to believe that it was Dillon's pseudonym alone, his book *Russian Traits and Terrors* carried on its title-page the confident assertion: 'by E.B. Lanin, the Collective Signature of Several Writers in the *Fortnightly Review*.'

194. See Dillon, *Russian Traits*, p. 279.

195. 'Russian Prison Atrocities', *The Speaker*, 29 March 1890, p. 33.

196. Dillon, 'Russian Prisons', p. 41.

197. Dillon, 'Russian Prisons', p. 43.

198. Dillon, 'Russian Prisons', p. 26. It is, perhaps, important to note that Dillon's piece on Russian prisons was thoroughly corroborated in the November issue of the *Fortnightly Review* by the personal experiences of the revolutionary Feliks Volkhovskii ('My life in Russian prisons', pp. 782-94).

199. Watts-Dunton, W.T., p. 15.

200. See *Fortnightly Review*, new series vol. XLIX (old series vol. LV), August 1890, pp. 165-7; Wise, *A Swinburne Library*, p. 144; Livingston, *Swinburne's Proof Sheets*, p. 20.

201. Dillon, *Russian Traits*, pp. 137-40, appendix to ch. V. The poem was also included in part in the subsequent British edition of this work, renamed *Russian Characteristics* (London, 1892). It was later reprinted in Swinburne's *A Channel Passage and Other Poems*, 1904 (pp. 130-5), and in his six-volume *Poems* of that same year (vol. VI, pp. 366-9). See Wise, *Bibliography of Swinburne*, vol. I, pp. 428-32, vol. II, p. 289. The connection between the Lanin article and Swinburne's poem, as well as the general background to both, is discussed in Alekseev, 'Sibirskaia ssylka', where much of Swinburne's piece is also translated into Russian. According to Wise, the manuscript of *Russia: An Ode* differed from the published text in many instances: see Wise, *Bibliography of Swinburne*, vol. I, p. 432; see also Swinburne, *Complete Works* (Bonchurch), vol. XX, pp. 248-9. By contrast, the published text itself remained remarkably consistent, indeed practically identical, with the *Fortnightly* text. The text used here is that of Swinburne, *Complete Works* (Bonchurch), vol. VI, pp. 274-7.

202. *Illustrated London News*, 9 August 1890, p. 178; *Literary World*, 8 August 1890, p. 111.

203. *Speaker*, 2 August 1890, p. 119.

204. Swinburne, *Letters*, ed. Lang, vol. V, pp. 286-7. See *Punch; or The London Charivari*, 16 August 1890, pp. 83-4. The accompanying article, by Lucy, is called 'Essence of Parliament'.

205. See *Hansard's Parliamentary Debates*, third series, vol. CCCXLVII, 17 July-5 August 1890, col. 1921, vol. CCCXLVIII, 6-18 August 1890, cols 525, 720-1; *Pall Mall Gazette*, 7 August 1890, p. 4 (and cf. 6 August, p. 2). For a discussion of *Russia: An Ode* and its reception in *Punch*, the House of Commons, and elsewhere, see also Hyder, p. 216.

206. See Gosse, *Life of Swinburne*, pp. 276-7; Kernahan, pp. 55-6; Hyder, p. 222.

207. Hake and Compton-Rickett, *Watts-Dunton*, vol. II, p. 147; Panter-Downes, p. 133.

208. See Watson, pp. 49-50 ('To Russia'), 63-4 ('On a Certain European Alliance'), 65-6 ('To Our Sovereign Lady').

209. Baring, *Puppet Show*, pp. 126, 139.

210. Smyth, p. 228.

211. Swinburne, *Letters*, ed. Lang, vol. VI, p. 258. Without giving any reason, Clara Watts-Dunton states that this affair must belong to the period 1897 to 1903 (see her *Home Life*, pp. 234-5); it cannot in fact date from earlier than 1902, when Count Aleksandr Konstantinovich Benkendorf took up his appointment as ambassador in London.

212. See Baring, *Outline*, p. 147.

213. Kernahan, p. v.

214. Gerbel', p. xxx.

215. See the article by Rashkovskaia and Rashkovskii.

216. See Swinburne's letters to the *Pall Mall Gazette* of 26 and 27 January 1886; Swinburne, *Letters*, ed. Lang, vol. V, pp. 131-6; Wise, *Bibliography of Swinburne*, vol. II, p. 263.

217. See Meynell, pp. 78-86; Tolstoi, L.N., vol. LXXXVIII, p. 300.

218. Swinburne, *Letters*, ed. Lang, vol. VI, p. 171; cf. Meynell, pp. 87-8.

219. Swinburne, *Letters*, ed. Lang, vol. VI, p. 26. Gladstone had a very high regard for the posthumously published *Journal* of the tragic young artist Mariia Konstantinovna Baskirtseva (1860-84); he had been in correspondence with the mother since 1889, when he reviewed the *Journal*, and met her at Valescure, Saint-Raphael, on 9 February 1892. (I am indebted for this information to the kindness of Professor Colin Matthew.)

220. Swinburne, *Letters*, ed. Lang, vol. VI, pp. 114-15.

221. Swinburne, *Letters*, ed. Lang, vol. VI, p. 114.

222. Swinburne, *Letters*, ed. Lang, vol. VI, p. 179.

223. *Pall Mall Gazette*, 25 January 1905, p. 7; see also ibid., 23 January, p. 1, 24 January, p. 1. 'Czar Louis XVI. *Adsit omen!*' was reprinted in the *Living Age* on 11 February 1905, and in 1910 was posthumously incorporated by T.J. Wise, with one trivial punctuation mistake, in *The Ballade of Truthful Charles, and Other Poems*, p. 14. The sonnet was for some reason not included in the Bonchurch edition of Swinburne's complete works. See also Wise, *Bibliography of Swinburne*, vol. II, p. 317, and Swinburne, *Letters*, ed. Lang, vol. VI, p. 190, where there is the misprint 'absit'.

224. Swinburne, *Letters*, ed. Lang, vol. VI, p. 190.

225. Swinburne, *Letters*, ed. Lang, vol. VI, p. 190.

BIBLIOGRAPHY

Very important: this Bibliography is an essential companion to the Notes, comprising as it does an alphabetical list of books, articles and theses therein cited. A few other works of general interest have been included, although most items consulted but not actually referred to have had to be omitted. Also excluded are standard works of reference such as dictionaries, encyclopaedias, official publications, dictionaries of biography, and editions of certain great authors like Shakespeare and Milton.

ABBOTT, Evelyn, and Lewis CAMPBELL. *The Life and Letters of Benjamin Jowett, M.A., Master of Balliol College, Oxford.* 2 vols, London, 1897.

ABBOTT, Evelyn, and Lewis CAMPBELL (eds). *Letters of Benjamin Jowett, M.A., Master of Balliol College, Oxford.* London, 1899.

ABEL, George. *Gordon, and Other Poems.* Published privately, London, no date.

ADAMS, Michael C.C. 'Tennyson's Crimean War Poetry: A Cross-Cultural Approach.' *Journal of the History of Ideas*, vol. XL, no. 3, July-September 1979, pp. 405-22.

ADAMS, W.H. Davenport. *The Isle of Wight: Its History, Topography, and Antiquities...* New, revised ed., London, 1884.

ADKINS, Nelson F. 'Tennyson's "Charge of the Heavy Brigade": A Bibliographical Note.' *Notes and Queries*, vol. CLXVII, 15 September 1934, pp. 189-90, and reply by 'Olybrius', ibid., 13 October 1934, p. 266.

ADYE, Lieut-Col. (later Sir) John Miller. *A Review of the Crimean War, to the Winter of 1854-5.* London, 1860 (reprint 1973).

ALEKSEEV, Mikhail Pavlovich. 'Sibirskaia ssylka i angliiskii poet' [Siberian Exile and an English Poet]. *Sibirskie ogni: literaturno-khudozhestvennyi i nauchno-obshchestvennyi zhurnal*, vol. VII, no. 4, July-August 1928, pp. 182-93.

ALEKSEEV, Mikhail Pavlovich. 'Die Quellen zum Idyll "Ivan Ivanovitsch" von Rob. Browning.' *Juhrbucher für Kultur und Geschichte der Slaven*, n.s. vol. V, 1930, pp. 417-27.

ALEKSEEV, Mikhail Pavlovich. 'Zur Entstehungsgeschichte der *Dramatic Idyls* von Robert Browning.' *Englische Studien*, vol. LXVI, no. 1, 1931, pp. 54-64.

ALEKSEEV, Mikhail Pavlovich. 'Angliiskii iazyk v Rossii i russkii iazyk v Anglii' [English in Russia and Russian in England]. *Uchenye zapiski Leningradskogo gosudarstvennogo universiteta*, no. 72 (Seriia filologicheskikh nauk, no. 9), 1944, pp. 77-137.

ALEKSEEV, Mikhail Pavlovich. 'British Manuscripts in Russia.' *Times Literary Supplement*, 21 September 1946, p. 456.

ALEKSEEV, Mikhail Pavlovich. *Literaturnoe nasledstvo*, tom 91: *Russko-angliiskie literaturnye svyazi (XVIII vek-pervaia polovina XIX veka)* [Russo-English Literary Connections in the 18th Century and First Half of the 19th Century], ed. V.R. Shcherbina, I.S. Zil'bershtein et al. from research by M.P. Alekseev. Moscow, 1982.

ALLINGHAM, William. *A Diary*, ed. Helen Allingham and D. Radford. London. 1907.

ANDERSON, Matthew Smith. *Britain's Discovery of Russia, 1553-1815.* London, 1958.

ANDREEV, Nikolay Petrovich. *Ukazatel' skazochnykh siuzhetov po sisteme Aarne* [Index to the Subjects of Fairy-Tales, on the Aarne System]. Leningrad, 1929.

ANGELI, Helen Rossetti. *Dante Gabriel Rossetti: His Friends and Enemies.* London, 1949.

ARMSTRONG, A. Joseph. 'Intimate Glimpses from Browning's Letter File.' *Baylor Bulletin*, vol. XXXVII, nos 3-4, September 1934.

ARNOLD, Matthew. 'Count Leo Tolstoi.' *Fortnightly Review*, n.s. vol. XLII (o.s. vol. XLVIII), December 1887, pp. 783-99.

ASHTON, John. *English Caricature and Satire on Napoleon I.* 2 vols, London, 1884.

AUSTIN, Alfred. *Tory Horrors; or, The Question of the Hour: A Letter to the Right Hon. W.E. Gladstone, M.P.* London, 1876.

AUSTIN, Alfred. *Russia Before Europe.* London, 1876.

AUSTIN, Alfred. *Lyrical Poems.* London, 1891.

AUSTIN, Alfred. *The Autobiography of Alfred Austin, Poet Laureate, 1835-1910.* 2 vols, London, 1911.

BARING, Maurice. *The Russian People.* London, 1911.

BARING, Maurice. *An Outline of Russian Literature.* London, 1914.

BARING, Maurice. *The Puppet Show of Memory.* London, 1922.

BARON, Samuel H. 'A Guide to Published and Unpublished Documents on Anglo-Russian Relations in the Sixteenth Century in British Archives.' *Canadian-American Slavic Studies*, vol. XI, no. 3, Fall 1977, pp. 354-87.

BARON, Samuel H. 'Osip Nepea and the Opening of Anglo-Russian Commercial Relations.' *Oxford Slavonic Papers*, n.s. vol. XI, 1978, pp. 42-63.

BARRATT, Glynn R.V. *Russophobia in New Zealand 1838-1908.* Palmerston North, 1981.

BARROW, Sir John [unsigned]. *A Memoir of the Life of Peter the Great.* London, 1832.

BARRY, Herbert. *Ivan at Home; or, Pictures of Russian Life.* London, 1872.

BATHO, Edith C. *The Later Wordsworth.* Cambridge, 1933.

BAUM, Paull Franklin. *Tennyson Sixty Years After.* Hamden and London, 1963.

BELCHIER, Dabridgcourt. *Hans Beer-Pot his invisible Comedie, of See me, and See me not; acted in the Low Countries, by an honest Company of Health-Drinkers.* London, 1618.

BELINSKII, Vissarion Grigor'evich. *Polnoe sobranie sochinenii* [Complete Works]. 13 vols, Moscow, 1953-59.

BENNETT, James R. 'The Historical Abuse of Literature: Tennyson's *Maud: A Monodrama* and the Crimean War.' *English Studies*, vol. LXII, no. 1, January 1981, pp. 34-45.

BENNETT, William Cox. *War Songs.* London, 1855.

BERDOE, Edward. *The Browning Cyclopaedia.* London, 1906.

BEWICK, Thomas. *History of British Birds; the Figures engraved on wood by T. Bewick. Volume I, containing the History and Description of Land Birds.* Newcastle, 1797.

BEZOBRAZOVA, E. D. (signing T.S.; the attribution is from the *Wellesley Index*). 'Contemporary Life and Thought in Russia.' *Contemporary Review*, vol. XXXII, June 1878, pp. 599-624.

BLIND, Karl. 'Young Turkey.' *Fortnightly Review*, n.s. vol. LX (o.s. vol. LXVI), December 1896, pp. 830-43.

BOLTON, Frances. 'Robert Browning's *Dramatic Idyls*.' Unpublished PhD thesis, Yale University, 1934.

BOLTON, James. *Harmonia Ruralis; or, An Essay towards a Natural History of British Song Birds*. Vol. I, privately printed, Stannary, near Halifax, 1794. Also new, revised ed., 2 vols, London, 1845.

BORROW, George Henry. *Targum; or, Metrical Translations from Thirty Languages and Dialects; and The Talisman, from the Russian of Alexander Pushkin, with other Pieces*. London, [1892]. (Originally in two separate volumes, St Petersburg, 1835, and published first together that same year in London.)

BOWRING, John. *Rossiiskaia antologiia* [Russian Anthology]: *Specimens of the Russian Poets, with Preliminary Remarks and Biographical Notices*. Privately printed, London, 1821. *Rossiiskaia antologiia: Specimens of the Russian Poets, with Introductory Remarks; Part the Second*. Privately printed, London, 1823.

BOWRING, John [unsigned, but attributed with considerable probability]. ['Politics and Literature of Russia.' (Title in table of contents only.)] *Westminster Review*, vol. I, January 1824, pp. 80-101.

BOWRING, Lewin B. (ed.) *Autobiographical Recollections of Sir John Bowring, with a Brief Memoir*. London, 1877.

BOYESEN, Hjalmar Hjorth. 'Reminiscences of Tourgueneff.' *Harper's Weekly*, 29 September 1883, p. 615.

BREWSTER, Dorothy. *Aaron Hill: Poet, Dramatist, Projector*. New York, 1913.

BREWSTER, Dorothy. *East-West Passage: A Study in Literary Relationships*. London, 1954.

BRIGHT, John. *Speeches on Questions of Public Policy by John Bright, M.P.*, ed. James E. Thorold Rogers. 2 vols, London, 1868.

BRODY, Ervin C. *The Demetrius Legend and its Literary Treatment in the Age of the Baroque*. Rutherford, Madison and Teaneck, 1972.

BROEMEL, F. and P. *The Break-up of Nihilism in Russia. Female Nihilists*. London, 1885.

BRONSON, Katharine de Kay. 'Browning in Venice.' *The Century: A Popular Quarterly*, New York, vol. LXIII, February 1902, pp. 572-84.

BROOKFIELD, Frances Mary. *The Cambridge 'Apostles'*. London and New York, 1906.

BROWN, David. *Tchaikovsky: A Biographical and Critical Study*. 4 vols, London, 1978-91. Vol. I: *The Early Years (1840-1874)*, 1978; vol. II: *The Crisis Years (1874-1878)*, 1982.

BROWNING, Elizabeth Barrett. *The Letters of Elizabeth Barrett Browning*, ed. with Biographical Additions by Frederic G. Kenyon. 2nd ed., 2 vols, London, 1897.

BROWNING, Elizabeth Barrett. *Elizabeth Barrett Browning: Letters to her Sister, 1846-1859*, ed. Leonard Huxley. London, 1929.

BROWNING, Elizabeth Barrett. *Invisible Friends: The Correspondence of Elizabeth Barrett Barrett and Benjamin Robert Haydon, 1842-1845*, ed. Willard Bissell Pope. Cambridge (Mass.), 1972.

BROWNING, Elizabeth Barrett. *Elizabeth Barrett Browning's Letters to Mrs. David Ogilvy, 1849-1861, with Recollections by Mrs. Ogilvy*, ed. Peter N. Heydon and Philip Kelley. New York, 1973.

BROWNING, Elizabeth Barrett. *Elizabeth Barrett to Miss Mitford: The Unpublished Letters of Elizabeth Barrett Barrett to Mary Russell Mitford*, ed. and introd. Betty Miller. London, 1954.

BROWNING, Elizabeth Barrett. *The Barretts at Hope End: The Early Diary of Elizabeth Barrett Browning*, ed. and introd. Elizabeth Berridge. London, 1974.

BROWNING, Robert. *The Agamemnon of Aeschylus — La Saisiaz — Dramatic Idyls — Jocoseria*, ed. Charlotte Porter and Helen A. Clarke. New York, 1898. (Also another edition, 1910.)

BROWNING, Robert. *The Works of Robert Browning*, introd. Frederic G. Kenyon. 10 vols, London, 1912.

BROWNING, Robert. *The Poems*, ed. John Pettigrew. 2 vols, London and New Haven (Conn.), 1981.

BROWNING, Robert. *The Complete Works of Robert Browning, with Variant Readings and Annotations*, ed. Roma A. King, Jr, et al. Athens (Ohio) and Waco (Texas), 1969 and ongoing. (14 vols planned.)

BROWNING, Robert. *The Poems of Browning*, ed. John Woolford and Daniel Karlin. London and New York, 1991 and ongoing. (An unspecified number of volumes planned.)

BROWNING, Robert. *The Poetical Works of Robert Browning*, ed. Ian Jack, Rowena Fowler and Margaret Smith. Oxford, 1983 and ongoing. (An unspecified number of volumes planned.)

BROWNING, Robert. *Letters of Robert Browning Collected by Thomas J. Wise*, ed. and introd. Thurman L. Hood, New Haven (Conn.) and London, 1933; new ed., New York, 1973.

BROWNING, Robert. *Dearest Isa: Robert Browning's Letters to Isabella Blagden*, ed. Edward C. McAleer. Austin (Texas) and Edinburgh, 1951.

BROWNING, Robert. *New Letters of Robert Browning*, ed. William Clyde DeVane and Kenneth Leslie Knickerbocker. London, 1951.

BROWNING, Robert. *Browning's Trumpeter: The Correspondence of Robert Browning and Frederick J. Furnivall, 1872-1889*, ed. William S. Peterson. Washington, 1979.

BROWNING, Robert. *More than Friend: The Letters of Robert Browning to Katharine de Kay Bronson*, ed. Michael Meredith with Rita S. Humphrey. Waco (Texas) and Winfield (Kansas), 1985.

BROWNING, Robert and Elizabeth Barrett. *The Brownings' Correspondence*, ed. Philip Kelley, Ronald Hudson and Scott Lewis. Winfield (Kansas), 1984 and ongoing. [14 complete printed volumes are planned, after which an electronic format will be used in combination with further volumes of selected letters; note that this edition contains letters to the Brownings as well as from them.]

BROWNING, Robert and Elizabeth Barrett. *The Letters of Robert Browning and Elizabeth Barrett Barrett, 1845-1846*. 2 vols, ed. Elvan Kintner, Cambridge (Mass.), 1969.

BROWNING, Robert and Elizabeth Barrett. *Letters of the Brownings to George Barrett*, ed. Paul Landis with Ronald E. Freeman. Urbana (Illinois), 1958.

BROWNING, Vivienne. *My Browning Family Album*. London, 1979.

BRUCE, Peter Henry. *Memoirs of Peter Henry Bruce, Esq., a Military Officer, in the Services of Prussia, Russia, and Great Britain; Containing an Account of his Travels in Germany, Russia, Tartary, Turkey, the West Indies, &c., as also, Several very Interesting Private Anecdotes of the Czar, Peter I. of Russia*. London, 1782; reprinted Dublin, 1783. [The titles of the London and Dublin versions show trivial differences, but the text of each is identical. There is also a German translation, Leipzig, 1784, and a modern facsimile of the Dublin reprint (London, 1970).]

BURNABY, Frederic Gustavus. *A Ride to Khiva: Travels and Adventures in Central Asia*, by Fred Burnaby, Captain, Royal Horse Guards. London, 1876.

BURNETT, T.A.J. 'Swinburne's "The Ballad of Bulgarie".' *Modern Language Review*, vol. LXIV, no. 2, April 1969, pp. 276-82.

BURTON, Robert. *The Anatomy of Melancholy, now for the first time with the Latin completely given in Translation and embodied in an All-English Text*, ed. Floyd Dell and Paul Jordan-Smith. New York, 1948.

BUTLER, Samuel. *Hudibras*, ed. John Wilders. Oxford, 1967.

BYRON, George Gordon, Lord. *The Poetical Works of Lord Byron*. New revised ed., Edinburgh, [1869].

CAINE, Sir Thomas Henry Hall (ed.) *Sonnets of Three Centuries: A Selection including many Examples hitherto Unpublished*. London, 1882.

CAINE, Sir Thomas Henry Hall. *Recollections of Rossetti*. Definitive ed., London, 1928.

CAMPBELL, Nancie (comp.) *Tennyson in Lincoln: A Catalogue of the Collections in the Research Centre*. 2 vols, Lincoln, 1971-73.

CAMPBELL, Thomas. *The Complete Poetical Works of Thomas Campbell*, ed. J. Logie Robertson. London, New York and Toronto, 1907.

CAMPBELL, Thomas. *Life and Letters of Thomas Campbell*, ed. William Beattie. 3 vols, London, 1849.

CAREW, Peter. 'One of "The Six Hundred".' *Blackwood's Magazine*, vol. CCLIX, January 1946, pp. 40-50.

CARLYLE, Thomas. *Occasional Discourse on the Nigger Question, communicated by T. Carlyle*. London, 1853. (Originally published in *Fraser's Magazine*, vol. XL, December 1849, pp. 670-9, but with 'Negro' in the title.)

CARLYLE, Thomas. *History of Friedrich II. of Prussia, called Frederick the Great*. 10 vols, London, [1888]. (Originally 6 vols, 1858-65.)

CARLYLE, Thomas. *Past and Present*. London, 1888.

CARLYLE, Thomas. *New Letters of Thomas Carlyle*, ed. Alexander Carlyle. 2 vols, London and New York, 1904.

CARR, John. *A Northern Summer; or, Travels round the Baltic, through Denmark, Sweden, Russia, Prussia, and Part of Germany, in the Year 1804*. London, 1805.

CARRINGTON, Charles E. *Rudyard Kipling: His Life and Work*. Revised ed., London, 1978 (originally 1955).

CARTER, John Waynflete, and Graham POLLARD. *An Enquiry into the Nature of Certain Nineteenth Century Pamphlets*. London and New York, 1934; 2nd ed., London and Berkeley, 1983.

CARY, Rev. Henry (ed.) *Memoir of the Rev. Henry Francis Cary, M.A., Translator of Dante, with his Literary Journal and Letters*. 2 vols, London, 1847.

CAWLEY, Robert Ralston. *The Voyagers and Elizabethan Drama*. Boston (Mass.) and London, 1938.

CAWLEY, Robert Ralston. *Milton and the Literature of Travel*. Princeton, 1951.

CHADWICK, John White. 'Luria.' Paper read before the Boston Browning Society on 23 January 1894, pp. 249-63 in *The Boston Browning Society Papers, Selected to Represent the Work of the Society*, New York and London, 1900.

Chancellor's Gold Medal. *A Complete Collection of the English Poems Which Have Obtained the Chancellor's Gold Medal in the University of Cambridge*. New and enlarged ed., vol. I, Cambridge, 1859; vol. II: *1859-1893*, London, 1894.

CHANDLER, Lloyd H. (comp.) *A Summary of the Work of Rudyard Kipling, Including Items Ascribed to Him*. New York, 1930.

CHAPMAN-HUSTON, Wellesley William Desmond Mountjoy. *The Lost Historian: A Memoir of Sir Sidney Low*. London, 1936.

CHARTERIS, Evan. *The Life and Letters of Sir Edmund Gosse*. London, 1931.

CHAUCER, Geoffrey. *The Complete Works of Geoffrey Chaucer, Edited from Numerous Manuscripts* by the Rev. Walter W. Skeat. Oxford, [1894].

CHEW, Samuel Claggett. *Swinburne*. London, 1931.

CHURTON. Edward (certainly the publisher, perhaps the author). *Anti-Maud, by a Poet of the People*. London, 1855.

COBDEN, Richard. *Russia*. London, [1835].

COBDEN, Richard. *What Next and Next?* London, 1856.

COE, Charles Norton. 'Wordsworth's "The Russian Fugitive".' *Modern Language Notes*, vol. LXIV, January 1949, pp. 31-6.

COLBORNE, J., and F. BRINE, Captains the Hon. *Graves and Epitaphs of our Fallen Heroes in the Crimea and Scutari.* London, [1864].

COLERIDGE, Samuel Taylor. *The Poetical Works of Samuel Taylor Coleridge*, ed. James Dyke Campbell. London, 1914.

COLLEY, Ann C. *Tennyson and Madness.* Athens (Georgia), 1983.

COLLINS, Winston. '"Maud": Tennyson's Point of War.' *Tennyson Research Bulletin*, vol. II, no. 3, November 1974, pp. 126-8.

COMPTON-RICKETT, Arthur. *I Look Back: Memories of Fifty Years.* London, 1933.

CONGREVE, William. *The Works of Congreve: Comedies; Incognita; Poems*, ed. F.W. Bateson. London, 1930.

Conversations on the History of Russia. 2 parts (vols), London, [1855].

CONWAY, Moncure Daniel. *Autobiography: Memories and Experiences.* 2 vols, London, 1904.

COWPER, William. *The Poetical Works of William Cowper*, ed. H.S. Milford, 4th ed., London, 1934.

COX, Edward Godfrey. *A Reference Guide to the Literature of Travel, including Voyages, Geographical Descriptions, Adventures, Shipwrecks and Expeditions.* Vol. I: *The Old World*, Seattle, 1935. (University of Washington Publications in Language and Literature, vol. IX, November 1935.)

COXE, Rev. William. *Travels into Poland, Russia, Sweden, and Denmark, interspersed with Historical Relations and Political Enquiries...* 3 vols, London, 1784-90.

CRANKSHAW, Edward. *Russia and Britain.* London, [1943].

CRIMEA. *The Illustrated Crimean War Song Book of the Allies, with a Brief Account of the War to the Fall of Sebastopol. (Dedicated to the Gallant Heroes of the East.)* London, [1855].

CROSS, Anthony G. 'Karamzin and England.' *Slavonic and East European Review*, vol. XLIII, 1965, pp. 91-115.

CROSS, Anthony G. (ed.) *Russia under Western Eyes, 1517-1825.* London, 1971.

CROSS, Anthony G. 'Early English Specimens of the Russian Poets.' *Canadian-American Slavic Studies*, vol. IX, no. 4, winter 1975, pp. 449-62.

CROSS, Anthony G. 'British Knowledge of Russian Culture (1698-1801).' *Canadian-American Slavic Studies*, vol. XIII, no. 4, winter 1979, pp. 412-35.

CROSS, Anthony G. *'By the Banks of the Thames': Russians in Eighteenth-Century Britain.* Newtonville (Mass.), 1980.

CROSS, Anthony G. '"O thou, great monarch of a pow'rful reign!": English Bards and Russian Tsars.' *Oxford Slavonic Papers*, n.s. vol. XV, 1982, pp. 80-94.

CROSS, Anthony G. *The Tale of the Russian Daughter and her Suffocated Lover.* University of Birmingham Slavonic Monographs, no. 13, Birmingham, 1982.

CROSS, Anthony G. *The Russian Theme in English Literature from the Sixteenth Century to 1980: An Introductory Survey and a Bibliography.* Oxford, 1985.

CUMMINGS, Prentiss. 'Homer and Browning.' *Boston Browning Society Papers*, 1896, pp. 388-410.

DACRE, Barbarina, Lady (née Wilmot, afterwards Ogle Brand). *Dramas, Translations and Occasional Poems.* 2 vols, privately printed, London, 1821.

DAVENANT, William. *The Dramatic Works of Sir William Davenant, with Prefatory Memoir and Notes.* 5 vols, Edinburgh and London, 1872-74.

DAVIS, Arthur Kyle, Jr. 'William Morris and the Eastern Question. With a

Fugitive Political Poem by Morris.' In *Humanistic Studies in Honor of John Calvin Metcalf* (University of Virginia Studies, vol. I), Charlottesville, 1941, pp. 28-47.

DAWSON, P.M.S. 'Cowper and the Russian Ice-Palace.' *Review of English Studies*, vol. XXXI, 1980, pp. 440-3.

DeVANE, William Clyde. *A Browning Handbook*. 2nd ed., New York, 1955 (originally 1935).

DeVANE, William Clyde. *Browning's Parleyings: The Autobiography of a Mind*. New York, 1964.

DILLON, Emile Joseph (writing as E.B. Lanin). 'Russian Prisons: The Simple Truth.' *Fortnightly Review*, n.s. vol. XLVIII (o.s. vol. LIV), July 1890, pp. 20-43.

DILLON, Emile Joseph (writing as E.B. Lanin). 'The Jews in Russia.' *Fortnightly Review*, n.s. vol. XLVIII (o.s. vol. LIV), October 1890, pp. 480-509.

DILLON, Emile Joseph (writing as E.B. Lanin). *Russian Traits and Terrors: A Faithful Picture of the Russia of To-day, by E.B. Lanin, the Collective Signature of Several Writers in the 'Fortnightly Review', with an Ode by Algernon Charles Swinburne*. Boston (Mass.), 1891.

DILLON, Emile Joseph. *The Eclipse of Russia*. London and Toronto, 1918.

DOBELL, Sydney Thompson. *England in Time of War*. London, 1856.

DOBELL, Sydney Thompson. *The Poetical Works of Sydney Dobell, with Introductory Notice and Memoir*, ed. John Nichol. 2 vols, London, 1875.

DOBELL, Sydney Thompson. *The Life and Letters of Sydney Dobell*, edited by E.J. [Emily Jolly]. 2 vols, London, 1878.

DODD, George [unsigned]. *Pictorial History of the Russian War, 1854-5-6, with Maps, Plans, and Wood Engravings*. Edinburgh and London, 1856.

DOMETT, Alfred. *The Diary of Alfred Domett, 1872-1885*, ed. E.A. Horsman. London, 1953.

DONNE, John, Dean of St Paul's. *Complete Poetry and Selected Prose*, ed. John Hayward. London, 1929.

DOSTOEVSKII, Fiodor Mikhaylovich. *Polnoe sobranie sochinenii v tridtsati tomakh* [Complete Works in Thirty Volumes]. Leningrad, 1972-90.

DOUHAIRE, Pierre-Paul. *Les de Lacroix. Histoire du temps de Pierre le Grand et d'Elisabeth Pétrowna*. Paris, 1861.

DOWSON, Ernest. *The Letters of Ernest Dowson*, ed. Desmond Flower and Henry Maas. London, 1967.

DRAYTON, Michael. *The Works of Michael Drayton, Esq; a celebrated Poet in the Reigns of Queen Elizabeth, King James I. and Charles I*. 4 vols, London, 1753.

DREW, Philip. '"The Raw Material of Moral Sentiment": Another View of "Ivàn Ivànovitch".' *Browning Society Notes*, vol. V, no. 2, July 1975, pp. 3-6.

DRUZHININ, A.V. *Sobranie sochinenii* [Collected Works], ed. N.V. Gerbel'. 6 vols, St Petersburg, 1865-67.

DRUZHININ, A.V. *Povesti. Dnevnik*, ed. B.F. Egorov and V.A. Zhdanov. Moscow, 1986.

DUNCAN, David. *The Life and Letters of Herbert Spencer*. London, 1908.

DYSON, Hope, and Charles TENNYSON (eds). *Dear and Honoured Lady: The Correspondence between Queen Victoria and Alfred Tennyson*. London, 1969.

Echoes of the 'Eighties: Leaves from the Diary of a Victorian Lady, introd. Wilfred Partington. London, [1921].

ECKELS, Richard Preston. 'Greek Wolf-Lore.' Unpublished PhD thesis, University of Pennsylvania, 1937.

ELLIS, Amanda M. *Rebels and Conservatives: Dorothy and William Wordsworth and their Circle*. Bloomington (Indiana) and London, 1968.

ELWIN, Malcolm. *Landor: A Replevin*. London, 1958.

EVANS, Sir George De Lacy. *On the Designs of Russia*. London, 1828.

EVELYN, John. *Diary and Correspondence of John Evelyn, F.R.S., to which is Subjoined the Private Correspondence between King Charles I and Sir Edward Nicholas and between Sir Edward Hyde, afterwards Earl of Clarendon, and Sir Richard Browne*, ed. William Bray. London, [1906].

EVELYN, John. *The Diary of John Evelyn*, ed. E.S. de Beer. London, 1959.

The Expedition of Napoleon Buonaparte into Russia. 'Secundus, sed linus secundior.' Cambridge, 1828.

FARQUHARSON, Robert Stuart [unsigned]. *Crimean Campaigning and Russian Imprisonment*, by one of the 'Six Hundred'. Dundee, 1889.

FORBES, Archibald. 'The Battle of Balaclava.' *Contemporary Review*, vol. LIX, March 1891, pp. 428-40.

FORBES, Eveline M. (née Farwell). 'A Visit to Balliol, 1879.' *Nineteenth Century and After*, vol. XC, November 1921, pp. 861-70.

FORSTETTER, Michel (ed.) *Voyageurs en Russie. Textes choisis du Xe au XXe siècle*. Vevey, 1947.

FREEBORN, Richard. 'Frankenstein's Last Journey.' *Oxford Slavonic Papers*, n.s. vol. XVIII, 1985, pp. 102-19.

FREEMAN, Edward Augustus. *The History of the Norman Conquest of England, its Causes and its Results*. 5 vols, Oxford, 1867-76.

FREEMAN, Edward Augustus. 'The True Eastern Question.' *Fortnightly Review*, n.s. vol. XVIII (o.s. vol. XXIV), December 1875, pp. 747-69.

FREEMAN, Edward Augustus. 'Present Aspects of the Eastern Question.' *Fortnightly Review*, n.s. vol. XX (o.s. vol. XXVI), October 1876, pp. 409-23.

FREEMAN, Edward Augustus. 'Terms of Peace.' *Gentleman's Magazine*, vol. CCXLII, January 1878, pp. 78-93.

FRISWELL, James Hain (ed.) *Songs of the War, by the Best Writers*. London, 1855.

FRISWELL, Laura Hain. *In the Sixties and Seventies: Impressions of Literary People and Others*. Boston (Mass.), 1906.

FRYE, H. Hamilton. *The Annals of our Time: A Diurnal of Events Social and Political, Home and Foreign*. Vol. III, part I: *From the Date of the Fiftieth Anniversary of the Accession of Queen Victoria to the End of the Year 1890*. London and New York, 1891. [See also under IRVING.]

GARRICK, David. *The Letters of David Garrick*, ed. David M. Little and George M. Kahrl. 3 vols, London, 1963.

General Register for 1827. Anon. 'Europe in 1827. IV. Russia.' *Constable's Miscellany of Original and Selected Publications in the Various Departments of Literature, Science, and the Arts*, vol. XXII: The General Register for 1827, Edinburgh and London, 1828, pp. 160-8.

GERBEL', Nikolay Vasil'evich (ed.) *Angliiskie poety v biografiiakh i obraztsakh* [English Poets in Biographies and Examples]. St Petersburg, 1875.

GERNSHEIM, Helmut and Alison. *Queen Victoria: A Biography in Word and Picture*. London, 1959.

GIBBS, Peter. *Crimean Blunder: The Story of War with Russia a Hundred Years ago*. London, 1960.

GILBERT, Linney. *Russia Illustrated*. London, [1844].

GLADSTONE, Mary (later Mrs Harry Drew). *Mary Gladstone (Mrs. Drew): Her Diaries and Letters*, ed. Lucy Masterman. London, 1930.

GLADSTONE, William Ewart. *Bulgarian Horrors and the Question of the East*. London, 1876.

GLADSTONE, William Ewart. *A Speech Delivered at Blackheath, on Saturday, September 9th, 1876; together with Letters on the Question of the East*. London, 1876.

GLADSTONE, William Ewart. 'Montenegro: A Sketch.' *Nineteenth Century*, vol. I, no. 3, May 1877, pp. 360-79.

GLEASON, John Howes. *The Genesis of Russophobia in Great Britain: A Study of the Interaction of Policy and Opinion*. Harvard Historical Studies, vol. LVII, Cambridge (Mass.), 1950; new ed., New York: Octagon Books, 1972.

GOLDEN, Samuel A. *Frederick Goddard Tuckerman: An American Sonneteer*. University of Maine Bulletin, April 1952.

GONCOURT, Edmond and Jules de. *Journal. Mémoires de la vie littéraire*, ed. Robert Ricatte. 4 vols, Paris, 1956.

GORDON, Armistead Churchill (ed.) *Memories and Memorials of William Gordon McCabe*. 2 vols, Richmond (Virginia), 1925.

GOSSE, Sir Edmund William. *Robert Browning: Personalia*. London, 1890. (Made up largely of articles previously published in the *Century Magazine*, December 1881, and the *New Review*, January 1890.)

GOSSE, Sir Edmund William. 'Swinburne at Étretat.' *Cornhill Magazine*, n.s. vol. XXXIII, October 1912, pp. 457-68.

GOSSE, Sir Edmund William. *The Life of Algernon Charles Swinburne*. London, 1917. (Also published as vol. XIX of the Bonchurch edition of Swinburne's works.)

GOSSE, Sir Edmund William. 'A Memory of Tourgenieff.' *London Mercury*, vol. XVII, February 1928, p. 403.

GOVE, A. *Sir Charles Napier in the Mediterranean and the Baltic, and Elsewhere, Being a Warning to Sailors and Soldiers, and an Appeal to the Legislature*. No. 1 (no more published), London, 1856.

GOWING, J. [unsigned]. *A Soldier's Experience: Things not Generally Known, Showing the Price of War in Blood and Treasure...*, by one of the Royal Fusiliers. Privately printed, Colchester, [1883].

GRANT DUFF, Rt. Hon. Sir Mountstuart E. *Notes from a Diary, 1892-1895*. 2 vols, London, 1904.

GRIFFIN, William Hall. *The Life of Robert Browning, with Notices of his Writings, his Family, and his Friends*, completed and edited by Harry Christopher Minchin. 3rd ed., revised and enlarged, London, [1938].

GWYNN, Stephen. *Tennyson: A Critical Study*. London, Glasgow and Dublin, 1899.

HAKE, Thomas Gordon, and Arthur COMPTON-RICKETT. *The Life and Letters of Theodore Watts-Dunton, including Some Personal Reminiscences by Clara Watts-Dunton*. 2 vols, London and New York, 1916.

HAKLUYT, Richard. *The Principal Navigations, Voyages, Traffiques and Discoveries of the English Nation, made by Sea or overland to the Remote and farthest distant Quarters of the Earth at any Time within the Compass of these 1600 Years*. Slightly modernised text, 8 vols, London, Toronto and New York, 1927.

HALLÉ, C.E. and M. (eds). *Life and Letters of Sir Charles Hallé*. London, 1896.

HAMLEY, General Edward. *The War in the Crimea*. London, 1891.

HARDMAN, Sir William. *A Mid-Victorian Pepys: the Letters and Memoirs of Sir William Hardman, M.A., F.R.G.S.*, ed. S.M. Ellis. London, 1923.

HARE, Humphrey. *Swinburne: A Biographical Approach*. London, 1949.

HARRIS, James. 'Some Account of Literature in Russia, and of its Progress towards being Civilized.' Appendix, Part the Fourth, pp. 560-71 in vol. II of this author's *Philological Inquiries in Three Parts*, 2 vols, London, 1781.

HARRIS, John. *The Gallant Six Hundred: A Tragedy of Obsessions*. London, 1973.

HARRISON, Frederic. 'Cross and Crescent.' *Fortnightly Review*, n.s. vol. XX (o.s. vol. XXVI), December 1876, pp. 709-30.

HARRISON, Robert. *Notes of a Nine Years' Residence in Russia, from 1844 to 1853; with notices of the Tzars Nicholas I and Alexander II*. London, 1855.

HAWEIS, H.R. 'Rubinstein.' *Fortnightly Review*, n.s. vol. LVII (o.s. vol. LXIII), January 1895, pp. 27-36.

HEAD, Franklin H. 'Some Methods of Browning, as Illustrated by the Poem of Ivan Ivanovitch.' In Head's *Studies in Medieval and Modern History*, pp. 57-74. Chicago, [1899].

HENDERSON, Philip Prichard. *Swinburne: The Portrait of a Poet*. London, 1974.

HENDERSON, Philip Prichard. *Tennyson: Poet and Prophet*. London, 1978.

HENDERSON, W. Brooks Drayton. *Swinburne and Landor: A Study of their Spiritual Relationship and its Effect on Swinburne's Moral and Poetic Development*. London, 1918.

HENNINGSEN, Charles Frederick [unsigned]. *Revelations of Russia; or, The Emperor Nicholas and his Empire, in 1844*. By one who has seen and describes. 2 vols, London, 1844. [This later became *Revelations of Russia in 1846*, by an English Resident. 3rd revised ed., 2 vols, London, 1846.]

HEWLETT, Dorothy. *Elizabeth Barrett Browning: A Life*. New York, 1952.

HEYWOOD, Thomas. *The Dramatic Works of Thomas Heywood, now first Collected, with Illustrative Notes and with a Memoir of the Author*. 6 vols, London, 1874.

HILL, Aaron. *The Works of the Late Aaron Hill, Esq; in four Volumes, consisting of Letters on Various Subjects, and of Original Poems, Moral and Facetious; with an Essay on the Art of Acting*. 4 vols, London, 1753.

HILL, Sir Francis. 'The Cracroft Diary.' *Tennyson Research Bulletin*, vol. III, no. 1, November 1977, pp. 26-9.

HOGE, James O. 'Emily Tennyson's Narrative for her Sons.' *Texas Studies in Literature and Language*, vol. XIV, no. 1, spring 1972, pp. 93-106.

HOGG, Thomas Jefferson. *Memoirs of Prince Alexy Haimatoff*, ed. Sidney Scott. London, 1952.

HOWE, Mark Antony De Wolfe. *Memories of a Hostess: A Chronicle of Eminent Friendships drawn chiefly from the Diaries of Mrs. James T. Fields*. London, 1923 (originally Boston, Mass., 1922).

HUDSON, Derek. *Munby, Man of Two Worlds: The Life and Diaries of Arthur J. Munby, 1828-1910*. London, 1972.

HUDSON, Ronald. 'Elizabeth Barrett Browning and her Brother Alfred: Some Unpublished Letters.' *Browning Institute Studies*, no. 2, 1974, pp. 135-60.

HUNT, James Henry Leigh. *The Poetical Works of Leigh Hunt, containing many Pieces now first Collected*. London, 1844.

HUNT, James Henry Leigh. *Table-Talk, to which are added Imaginary Conversations of Pope and Swift*. London, 1851.

HUTCHINSON, Sara. *The Letters of Sara Hutchinson from 1800 to 1835*, ed. Kathleen Coburn. London, 1954.

HYDE, H. Montgomery. *Princess Lieven*. London, 1938.

HYDER, Clyde Kenneth. *Swinburne's Literary Career and Fame*. Durham (North Carolina), 1933.

IAKOVLEV, N.V. 'Iz razyskanii o literaturnykh istochnikakh v tvorchestve Pushkina [Gleanings on Pushkin's Literary Sources]. I. Sonety Pushkina v sravnitel'no-istoricheskom osveshchenii [Pushkin's Sonnets in a Comparative-Historical Light]. II. Perevod Pushkina iz poemy Vordsvorta "Ekskursiia" [Pushkin's Translation from Wordsworth's Poem *The Excursion*.].' In *Pushkin v mirovoi literature. Sbornik statei*, Leningrad, 1926, pp. 113-37.]

IRELAND, Mrs Alexander. 'Some Remarks on Browning's Treatment of Parenthood.' *Papers of the London Browning Society*, part XII (vol. III, part I), no. LIX, 28 March 1890, pp. 46-52.

IRVINE, William, and Park HONAN. *The Book, the Ring, and the Poet*. New York and London, 1974.

IRVING, Joseph. *The Annals of our Time: A Diurnal of Events, Social and Political, Home and Foreign, from the Accession of Queen Victoria, June 20, 1837, to the Peace of Versailles, February 28, 1871*. New, revised ed., London, 1880. [See also below, and under FRYE.]

IRVING, Joseph. *The Annals of our Time: A Diurnal of Events Social and Political, Home and Foreign, from February 24, 1871, to the Jubilee, June 20, 1887*. London and New York, 1889. [See also above, and under FRYE.]

JACOB, H.E. *The World of Emma Lazarus*. New York, 1949.

JAMES, Henry. *Letters*, ed. Leon Edel. 4 vols, Cambridge (Mass.) and London, 1974-84.

JAMES, Henry. *Selected Letters of Henry James to Edmund Gosse, 1882-1915: A Literary Friendship*, ed. Rayburn S. Moore. Baton Rouge and London, 1988.

JAMES, Richard. *The Poems, etc., of Richard James, B.D. (1592-1638), now for the first time Collected and Edited, with Introduction, Notes and Illustrations and an Etching*, by the Rev. Alexander B. Grosart.... Privately printed, London, 1880.

JENKINS, Herbert. *Life of George Borrow*. London, 1912.

JENKINSON, Arthur. *Alfred, Lord Tennyson, Poet Laureate: A Brief Study of his Life and Poetry*. London, 1892.

JENNINGS, Henry J. *Lord Tennyson: A Biographical Sketch*. London, 1884.

JOHNSON, Edgar. *Sir Walter Scott: The Great Unknown*. 2 vols (vol. I: *1771-1821*; vol. II: *1821-1832*), London, 1970.

JOHNSTONE, Catherine Laura [Signed C. Joyneville.] *The Life and Times of Alexander I, Emperor of All the Russias*. 3 vols, London, 1875.

JORDAN, John E. *De Quincey to Wordsworth: A Biography of a Relationship; with the Letters of Thomas De Quincey to the Wordsworth Family*. Berkeley and Los Angeles, 1962.

KEATS, John. *The Poetical Works of John Keats*, ed. H.W. Garrod. 2nd ed., Oxford, 1958.

KELLEY, Philip, and Betty A. COLEY (comps). *The Browning Collections: A Reconstruction, with Other Memorabilia*. Waco (Texas), Winfield (Kansas) and London, 1984.

KELLEY, Philip, and Ronald HUDSON (comps). *The Brownings' Correspondence: A Checklist*. New York, 1978.

KELLY, Catriona. 'From Pulcinella to Petrushka: The History of the Russian Glove Puppet Theatre.' *Oxford Slavonic Papers*, n.s. vol. XXI, 1988, pp. 41-63.

KERNAHAN, John Coulson. *Swinburne as I Knew Him, with Some Unpublished Letters from the Poet to his Cousin the Hon. Lady Henniker Heaton*. London, 1919.

KINGLAKE, Alexander William. *The Invasion of the Crimea: Its Origin, and an Account of its Progress down to the Death of Lord Raglan*. 8 vols, Edinburgh and London, 1863-87.

KIPLING, Rudyard. *Complete Works in Prose and Verse*. 35 vols, London, 1937-39. (Sussex Edition.)

KIPLING, Rudyard. *Rudyard Kipling's Verse: Definitive Edition*. London, 1940.

KIPLING, Rudyard. *The Letters of Rudyard Kipling*, ed. Thomas Pinney. 4 vols, Basingstoke and London, 1990 proceeding.

KLIMENKO, Ekaterina Innokent'evna. *Tvorchestvo Roberta Brauninga*. Leningrad, 1967.

KNIES, Earl A. (ed.) *Tennyson at Aldworth: The Diary of James Henry Mangles*. Athens (Ohio) and London, 1984.

KNIGHT, William. *The Life of William Wordsworth*. 3 vols, Edinburgh, 1889 (vols IX-XI of *The Poetical Works of William Wordsworth*, edited by Knight).

KNOX, Thomas W. *The Boy Travellers in the Russian Empire*. New York, 1887.

KOHL, J.G. *Russia and the Russians in 1842*. 2 vols, London, 1842.

KOSSUTH, Louis. 'Russian Aggression, as Specially Affecting Austro-Hungary and Turkey.' *Contemporary Review*, vol. XXXI, December 1877, pp. 1-24.

KOSSUTH, Louis. 'What is in Store for Europe, and Especially for Austria-Hungary.' *Contemporary Review*, vol. XXXI, February 1878, pp. 555-64.

KRASIŃSKI, Count Walerjan Skorobohaty. *Russia, Poland, and Europe; or, The Inevitable Consequence of the Present War. A Sequel to the Pamphlet Entitled 'Russia and Europe'*. London, 1854.

KROPOTKIN, Prince Piotr Alekseevich. 'The Russian Revolutionary Party.' *Fortnightly Review*, n.s. vol. XXXI (o.s. vol. XXXVII), May 1882, pp. 654-71.

KROPOTKIN, Prince Piotr Alekseevich. *Russian Literature: Ideals and Realities*. London, 1916 (originally 1905).

KIUKHEL'BEKER, Vil'gel'm Karlovich. *Izbrannye proizvedeniia v dvukh tomakh* [Selected Works in 2 Vols]. Moscow and Leningrad, 1967.

LACK, David Lambert. *The Life of the Robin*. 4th ed., London, 1965.

LACROIX, Frédéric (ed.) *Les Mystères de la Russie, tableau politique et moral de l'empire russe...; ouvrage rédigé d'après les manuscrits d'un diplomate et d'un voyageur par M. Frédéric Lacroix*. Paris, 1845.

LAFOURCADE, Georges. *La Jeunesse de Swinburne (1837-1867)*. 2 vols (vol. I: *La Vie*; vol. II: *L'Œuvre*), Paris and Oxford, 1928.

LAFOURCADE, Georges. *Swinburne: A Literary Biography*. London, 1932.

LAMBERT, Andrew D. *The Crimean War: British Grand Strategy, 1853-56*. Manchester and New York, 1990.

LANDOR, Walter Savage. *Imaginary Conversations by Walter Savage Landor*, with Bibliographical and Explanatory Notes by Charles G. Crump. 6 vols, London, 1891-1901.

LANDOR, Walter Savage. *Poems, Dialogues in Verse, and Epigrams by Walter Savage Landor*, ed. Charles G. Crump. 2 vols, London, 1903.

LANIN, E.B.: see DILLON.

LARA, D. Etienne de. 'Russia and the Russians.' *Gleason's Pictorial Drawing-Room Companion*, Boston (Mass.), vol. VI, 15 April 1854, section I, p. 238.

LARIN, B.A. *Russko-angliiskii slovar'-dnevnik Richarda Dzhemsa (1618-1619gg.)* [Richard James's Russian-English Dictionary-Diary, 1518-19.] Leningrad, 1959.

LEE, Robert. 'The Last Days of the Emperor Alexander.' *Athenaeum*, 2 and 9 August 1845, pp. 766-8, 792-5.

LEITH, Mary Charlotte Julia, Mrs Disney. *The Boyhood of Algernon Charles Swinburne: Personal Recollections by his Cousin, Mrs. Disney Leith, with Extracts from Some of his Private Letters*. London, 1917.

LETKOVA, E.P. 'Ob I.S. Turgeneve. (Iz vospominanii kursistki.)' [On Turgenev (from the Recollections of a Female Student)], in *Sbornik "K svetu". Nauchno-literaturnyi sbornik*, St Petersburg, 1904, pp. 449-65.

LEVIN, Iurii Davydovich. 'Val'ter Skott v russkoi pechati. 1811-1833. Materialy dlia bibliografii' [Walter Scott in the Russian Press, 1811-33: Materials for a Bibliography]. In *Epokha romantizma. Iz istorii mezhdunarodnykh sviazei russkoi literatury* [The Romantic Period; from the History of Russian Literature and its International Connections], Leningrad, 1975, pp. 29-67.

LEVIN, Iurii Davydovich. *Ossian v russkoi literature. Konets XVIII — pervaia tret' XIX veka* [Ossian in Russian Literature from the Late 18th Century to the 1830s], Leningrad, 1980.

LEWIN, W. *The Birds of Great Britain, systematically arranged, accurately engraved, and painted from Nature; with Descriptions, including the Natural History of each Bird.* 8 vols, London, 1800-01.

LIEVEN, Princess Daria (Doroteya) Khristoforovna. *Letters of Dorothea, Princess Lieven, during her Residence in London, 1812-1834*, ed. Lionel G. Robinson. London, 1902.

LITZINGER, Boyd, and Donald SMALLEY (eds). *Browning: The Critical Heritage*. London, 1970.

LIVINGSTON, Flora Virginia Milner. *Swinburne's Proof Sheets and American First Editions: Bibliographical Data Relating to a Few of the Publications of Algernon Charles Swinburne, with Notes on the Priority of Certain Claimants to the Distinction of 'Editio Princeps'.* Privately printed, Cambridge (Mass.), 1920.

LIVINGSTON, Flora Virginia Milner. *Bibliography of the Works of Rudyard Kipling*. New York, 1927.

LOCKHART, John Gibson. *The Life of Sir Walter Scott.* 10 vols, Edinburgh, 1902-03.

LONGFELLOW, Henry Wadsworth (ed.) *Poems of Places: Russia.* Boston (Mass.), 1878.

LUMMIS, Canon William Murrell, and Kenneth G. WYNN. *Honour the Light Brigade: A Record of the Services of Officers, Non-Commissioned Officers and Men of the five Light Cavalry Regiments, which Made up the Light Brigade at Balaclava on October 25th 1854 and Saw Service in the Crimea from September 1854 to the End of the War.* London, 1973.

LUSHINGTON, Franklin. *Points of War. I. II. III. IV.* Cambridge, 1854.

LUSHINGTON, Henry and Franklin. *La Nation Boutiquière and Other Poems, Chiefly Political,* by Henry Lushington, with a Preface; *Points of War,* by Franklin Lushington. Cambridge, 1855.

LUSHINGTON, Vernon. *How Shall the Strong Man Use his Strength? or, The Right and Duty of War, with Application to the Present Crisis.* London, 1855.

LYNN, Escott. *Blair of Balaclava: A Hero of the Light Brigade.* London, 1911.

MACARTNEY, George, Lord [unsigned]. *An Account of an Embassy to Russia MDCCLXVII.* Privately printed, London, 1768.

MACAULAY, Thomas Babington, Lord. *The Works of Lord Macaulay.* 12 vols, London, 1898.

MAGNUS, Laurie. *A Primer of Wordsworth, with a Critical Essay.* London, 1897.

MAINWARING, Marion. 'Arnold and Tolstoi.' *Nineteenth-Century Fiction,* vol. VI, no. 4, March 1952, pp. 269-74.

MAJOR, R.H. (trans. and ed.) *Notes upon Russia; being a Translation of the Earliest Account of that Country, entitled Rerum Moscoviticarum Commentarii, by the Baron Sigismund von Herberstein, Ambassador from the Court of Germany to the Grand Prince Vasiley Ivanovich, in the years 1517 and 1526.* 2 vols, London, 1851-52. (Hakluyt Society.)

MARLOWE, Christopher. *The Works of Christopher Marlowe,* ed. C.F. Tucker Brooke. Oxford, 1910.

MARRIOTT, Sir J.A.R. *Anglo-Russian Relations, 1689-1943.* London, 1944.

MARSTON, John Westland. *The Dramatic and Poetical Works of Westland Marston.* 2 vols, London, 1876.

MARTIN, Robert Bernard. *Tennyson: The Unquiet Heart.* Oxford, 1980.

MARTINDELL, E.W. *A Bibliography of the Works of Rudyard Kipling (1881-1923).* New ed., much enlarged, London, 1923.

MASEFIELD, John. *Natalie Maisie and Pavilastukay: Two Tales in Verse.* London and Toronto, 1942.

MASON, Charlotte M. 'Browning's "Ivàn Ivànovitch",' by the Editor. *Parents' Review,* vol. XX, no. 8, August 1909, pp. 577-8.

MAUPASSANT, Guy de. 'Gustave Flaubert. (Suite et fin.)' *La Revue politique et littéraire*, 26 January 1884, p. 120.

MAUPASSANT, Guy de. 'Notes sur Algernon Charles Swinburne.' Preface, pp. v-xxvi, to *Poèmes et Ballades de A.C. Swinburne*, trans. Gabriel Mourey. Paris, 1891.

MAXWELL, Bennett. 'The Steytler Recordings of Alfred, Lord Tennyson: A History.' *Tennyson Research Bulletin*, vol. III, no. 4, November 1980, pp. 150-7.

MAYNARD, John. *Browning's Youth*. Cambridge (Mass.), 1977.

McALEER, Edward C. 'New Letters from Mrs. Browning to Isa Blagden.' *Publications of the Modern Language Association*, vol. LXVI, 1951.

McCABE, William Gordon. 'Personal Recollections of Alfred, Lord Tennyson.' *Century Illustrated Monthly Magazine*, vol. LXIII (n.s. vol. XLI), March 1902, pp. 722-37.

McCOY, Miss E. [?] *The Englishwoman in Russia: Impressions of the Society and Manners of the Russians at Home*. By a Lady, ten years resident in that country. London, 1855.

McGANN, Jerome J. 'Tennyson and the Histories of Criticism.' *Review* (Charlottesville, Virginia), vol. IV, 1982, pp. 219-53.

MERRY, Robert. *Paulina; or, The Russian Daughter. A Poem in Two Books*, by Robert Merry, Esq., Member of the Royal Academy of Florence, late La Crusca. London, 1787.

MEYNELL, Viola (ed.) *Friends of a Lifetime: Letters to Sydney Carlyle Cockerell*. London, 1940.

MIDDLETON, Kenneth William Bruce. *Britain and Russia: An Historical Essay*. London, [1947].

MIEGE, Guy [unsigned]. *A Relation of the Embassies from his Sacred Majestie Charles II to the Great Duke of Muscovie, the King of Sweden, and the King of Denmark, performed by the Right Hoble the Earle of Carlisle in the Years 1663 and 1664; written by an Attendant on the Embassies...* London, 1669.

MILL, John Stuart [signed 'D.'] 'The Negro Question.' *Fraser's Magazine*, vol. XLI, January 1850, pp. 25-31.

MILLMAN, Richard. *Britain and the Eastern Question, 1875-1878*. Oxford, 1979.

MINTO, W. (ed.) *Autobiographical Notes of the Life of William Bell Scott, H.R.S.A., LL.D., and Notices of his Artistic and Poetic Circle of Friends, 1830 to 1882*. 2 vols, London, 1892.

MIRSKII, D.S. *A History of Russian Literature*, ed. Francis J. Whitfield. London, 1949.

MONTAGU, George. *A Dictionary of British Birds; being a Reprint of Montagu's Ornithological Dictionary, etc.*, ed. Edward Newman. London, [1881; originally 1802].

MOORE, George (Augustus) [the Anglo-Irish author]. 'Turgueneff.' *Fortnightly Review*, n.s. vol. XLIII, 1 February 1888, pp. 237-51. (Reprinted in Moore's *Impressions and Opinions*, London, 1913, pp. 44-65.)

MOORE, George [critic]. 'A Critical and Bibliographical Study of the Somersby Library of Doctor George Clayton Tennyson.' Unpublished MA thesis, University of Nottingham, October 1966.

MOORE, Thomas [unsigned]. *Tom Crib's Memorial to the Congress, with a Preface, Notes, and Appendix*. By One of the Fancy. London, 1819.

MOORE, Thomas. *The Poetical Works of Thomas Moore, Collected by himself*. 10 vols, London, 1840-41.

MOORE, Thomas. *Memoirs, Journal, and Correspondence of Thomas Moore*, ed. Rt. Hon. Lord John Russell. 8 vols, London, 1853-56.

MOORMAN, Mary. *William Wordsworth: A Biography. The Early Years, 1770-1803*. Oxford, 1957.

The Later Years, 1803-1850. Oxford, 1965; corrected reprint 1966.

MORGAN, Edward Delmar, and Charles Henry COOTE (eds). *Early Voyages and Travels to Russia and Persia by Anthony Jenkinson and Other Englishmen, with Some Account of the First Intercourse of the English with Russia and Central Asia by Way of the Caspian Sea*. 2 vols, London, 1886. (Hakluyt Society publications, nos 72-73.)

MORLEY, F.V. *Dora Wordsworth: Her Book*. London, 1924.

MORLEY, John, Viscount. *The Life of William Ewart Gladstone*. 3 vols, London, 1903.

MORLEY, John, Viscount. *Recollections*. 2 vols, London, 1917.

MORRIS, William. *The Letters of William Morris to his Family and Friends*, ed. Philip Henderson. London, 1978 (originally 1950).

MORRIS, William. *The Collected Letters of William Morris*, ed. Norman Kelvin. Princeton (New Jersey) and Guildford (Surrey), 1984 and ongoing.

MORTON, Edward. *Travels in Russia and a Residence at St. Petersburgh and Odessa*. London, 1830.

MORTON, Frederic. *The Rothschilds: A Family Portrait*. London, 1962.

MOTTLEY, John. *The History of the Life of Peter I., Emperor of Russia*. 3 vols, London, 1739.

MOXOM, Philip Stafford. *Two Masters: Browning and Turgenief*. Boston (Mass.), 1912.

MUNRO-BUTLER-JOHNSTONE, H.A. *The Eastern Question*. London, 1875.

MUNRO-BUTLER-JOHNSTONE, H.A. *The Turks: Their Character, Manners, and Institutions, as Bearing on the Eastern Question*. Oxford and London, 1876.

MUSORGSKII, Modest Petrovich. *Pis'ma*. Moscow, 1981.

NAPIER, George G. *The Homes and Haunts of Alfred Lord Tennyson, Poet Laureate*. Glasgow, 1892.

NASHE [here actually NASH], Thomas. *Have with You to Saffron Walden, 1596*. Menston (Yorkshire), 1971. (Being a facsimile of the London, 1596, edition of Nashe's *Haue with you to Saffron-walden; or, Gabriell Harueys Hunt is vp; containing a full Answere to the eldest Sonne of the Halter-maker; or, Nashe his Confutation of the sinfull Doctor.*)

NERHOOD, Harry W. *To Russia and Return: An Annotated Bibliography of Travelers' English-Language Accounts from the Ninth Century to the Present*. Columbus, 1968.

NICHOL, John. *Tables of European Literature and History, A.D. 200-1876*. Glasgow, 1877. (Also *Tables of European History, Literature, Science, and Art, from A.D. 200 to 1909; and of American History, Literature, and Art*, revised and updated by William R. Jack. 5th ed., Glasgow, 1909.)

NICHOL, John. *Thomas Carlyle*. 2nd ed., London, 1901.

NICOLL, Allardyce. *A History of English Drama, 1660-1900*. Vol. IV: *Early Nineteenth Century Drama, 1800-1850*. Cambridge, 1955.

NICOLL, W. Robertson, and WISE, Thomas J. (eds). *Literary Anecdotes of the Nineteenth Century: Contributions towards a Literary History of the Period*. 2 vols, London, 1895-96.

NOVIKOVA, Ol'ga Alekseevna [née Kireeva; pseud. 'O.K.'] *Is Russia Wrong? A Series of Letters*. By a Russian Lady, with a Preface by J.A. Froude, M.A. 2nd ed., London, 1878.

NOVIKOVA, Ol'ga Alekseevna [née Kireeva; pseud. 'O.K.'] *Friends or Foes? A Sequel to 'Is Russia Wrong?'* By a Russian Lady. London, 1878.

O'CONNOR, V.C. Scott. 'Tennyson and his Friends at Freshwater.' *Century Illustrated Monthly Magazine*, vol. LV (n.s. vol. XXXIII), December 1897, pp. 240-68.

O'DRISCOLL, W. Justin. *A Memoir of Daniel Maclise, R.A.* London, 1871.

OLIPHANT, Laurence. *The Russian Shores of the Black Sea in the Autumn of 1852.* 4th ed., Edinburgh and London, 1854.

O'NEILL, James Norman. 'Anthem for a Doomed Youth: An Interdisciplinary Study of Tennyson's *Maud* and the Crimean War.' *Tennyson Research Bulletin*, vol. V, no. 4, November 1990, pp. 166-81.

OREL, Harold. 'The Russian Novel in Victorian England: 1831-1917.' Unpublished PhD thesis, University of Michigan, 1952.

OREL, Harold. 'The Forgotten Ambassadors: Russian Fiction in Victorian England.' *American Slavic and East European Review*, vol. XII, 1953, pp. 371-7.

OREL, Harold. 'Victorians and the Russian Novel: A Bibliography.' *Bulletin of Bibliography and Magazine Notes*, vol. XXI, no. 3, January-April 1954, pp. 61-3, no. 4, May-August 1954, pp. 78-81.

OREL, Harold. 'English Critics and the Russian Novel, 1850-1917.' *Slavonic and East European Review*, vol. XXXIII, 1955, pp. 457-69.

OREL, Harold (ed.) *Kipling: Interviews and Recollections.* 2 vols, London, 1983.

ORLOV-DAVYDOV, Count V. [unsigned]. *An Appeal on the Eastern Question to the Senatus Academicus of the Royal College of Edinburgh*, by a Russian, quondam civis Bibliothecae Edinensis. Edinburgh, 1854.

ORR, Alexandra, Mrs Sutherland. 'Mr Browning's Dramatic Idyls.' *Contemporary Review*, vol. XXXV, May 1879, pp. 289-302.

ORR, Alexandra, Mrs Sutherland. *A Handbook to the Works of Robert Browning.* 6th, revised ed., London, 1892.

ORR, Alexandra, Mrs Sutherland. *Life and Letters of Robert Browning.* New ed., revised and in part rewritten by Frederic G. Kenyon. London, 1908.

PADEN, W.D. 'Twenty New Poems Attributed to Tennyson, Praed and Landor. Part One.' *Victorian Studies*, vol. IV, March 1961, pp. 195-218.

PANTER-DOWNES, Mollie. *At The Pines: Swinburne and Watts-Dunton in Putney.* London, 1971.

PARKER, W.M. 'Burns, Scott, and Turgenev: A Remarkable Linkage.' *Notes and Queries*, vol. CLXXVI, 29 April 1939, pp. 291-2.

PARTINGTON, Wilfred (ed.) *The Private Letter-Books of Sir Walter Scott: Selections from the Abbotsford Manuscripts; with a Letter to the Reader from Hugh Walpole.* London, 1930.

PARTINGTON, Wilfred (ed.). *Sir Walter's Post-Bag: More Stories and Sidelights from his Unpublished Letter-Books.* London, 1932.

PARTINGTON, Wilfred. *Thomas J. Wise in the Original Cloth: The Life and Record of the Forger of the Nineteenth-Century Pamphlets.* London, 1946. (In large part a revised and updated edition of the same author's *Forging Ahead: The True Story of the Upward Progress of Thomas James Wise, Prince of Book Collectors, Bibliographer Extraordinary and Otherwise*, New York, 1939.)

PARTRIDGE, Monica. 'Slavonic Themes in English Poetry of the 19th century.' *Slavonic and East European Review*, vol. XLI, June 1963, pp. 420-41.

PARTRIDGE, Monica. 'Romanticism and the Concept of Communication in a Slavonic and a Non-Slavonic Literature.' *Renaissance and Modern Studies*, vol. XVII, 1973, pp. 62-82.

PASENKO, V.A. 'Otechestvennaia voina v literature na inostrannykh iazykakh (1812-1813g.). Materialy dlia bibliograficheskogo ukazatelia' [The Patriotic War in Literature in Foreign Languages, 1812-13: Materials for a Bibliographical Checklist]. *Bibliograficheskie izvestiia*, 1913, no. 1, pp. 71-8, no. 2, pp. 148-59, no. 3, pp. 240-51.

PAUL, Rev. Robert Bateman. *Journal of a Tour to Moscow in the Summer of 1836.* London, 1836.

PEARSALL, Robert Brainard. *Robert Browning.* New York, 1974.

PENNINGTON, W.H. *Sea, Camp, and Stage: Incidents in the Life of a Survivor of the Balaclava Light Brigade*. Bristol, 1906.

PETROV, S.M., and V.G. FRIDLIAND. *I.S. Turgenev v vospominaniiakh sovremennikov* [Turgenev in the Reminiscences of his Contemporaries]. 2 vols, Moscow, 1983.

PHELPS, Gilbert. *The Russian Novel in English Fiction*. London, 1956.

PHELPS, Gilbert. 'The Early Phases of British Interest in Russian Literature.' *Slavonic and East European Review*, vol. XXXVI, June 1958, pp. 418-33.

PINION, F.B. *A Wordsworth Companion: Survey and Assessment*. London, 1984.

POLONSKII, Iakov Petrovich. *Na vysotakh spiritizma* [On the Heights of Spiritualism]. St Petersburg, 1889.

POPE, Alexander. *The Poetical Works of Alexander Pope*, ed. Charles Cowden Clarke. 2 vols, Edinburgh, 1863.

PORTER, Charlotte, and CLARKE, Helen A. *Browning Study Programmes*. Vol. II, second series, New York, 1900.

PURCHAS, Samuel. *Hakluytus Posthumus; or, Purchase his Pilgrimes, contayning a History of the World in Sea Voyages and Land Travells by Englishmen and Others*. 20 vols, Glasgow, 1905-07. (A reprint of the 4-volume edition of 1625.)

PUSHKIN, Aleksandr Sergeevich. *Polnoe sobranie sochinenii* [Complete Works], ed. V.D. Bonch-Bruevich et al. 16 vols, Leningrad, 1937-49. (Jubilee Edition.)

PUTNAM, Peter (ed.) *Seven Britons in Imperial Russia, 1698-1812*. Princeton, 1952.

RADER, Ralph Wilson. *Tennyson's* Maud: *The Biographical Genesis*. Berkeley and Los Angeles, 1963.

RALSTON, William Ralston Shedden-. 'Russian Idylls.' *Contemporary Review*, vol. XXIII, April 1874, pp. 734-45.

RASHKOVSKAIA, M.A., and E.B. RASHKOVSKII. 'Sonet Suinberna v perevode Borisa Pasternaka' [A Swinburne Sonnet in Boris Pasternak's Translation]. *Izvestiia AN SSSR*, Seriia literatury i iazyka, vol. XLIII, no. 6, 1984, pp. 544-50.

RAWNSLEY, Rev. H.D. *Memories of the Tennysons*. Glasgow, 1900.

REEVES, John. *The Rothschilds: The Financial Rulers of Nations*. London, 1887.

REGNARD, Albert-Adrien. Review of Robert Browning's *Dramatic Idyls* in 'Nauka i literatura v sovremennoi Anglii' [Science and Literature in Contemporary England]. *Vestnik Evropy*, no. 7, July 1879, pp. 346-52.

REID, Sir Thomas Wemyss. *The Life, Letters, and Friendships of Richard Monckton Milnes, First Lord Houghton*. 2nd ed., 2 vols, London, 1890.

RICHARDS, Laura E., and ELLIOTT, Maud Howe. *Julia Ward Howe, 1819-1910*. Boston and New York, 1925.

RICHARDSON-GARDNER, Robert. *A Trip to St. Petersburg*. London, 1872.

RICKS, Christopher. '"Peace and War" and "Maud".' *Notes and Queries*, vol. CCVII (n.s. vol. IX), no. 6, June 1962, p. 230.

RICKS, Christopher. 'The Tennyson Manuscripts.' *Times Literary Supplement*, 21 August 1969, pp. 918-22 (and cf. 28 August, p. 954, 11 September, p. 1002, and 18 September, p. 1026).

RICKS, Christopher. *Tennyson*. London and New York, 1972.

RITCHIE, Anne Isabella Thackeray, Lady. *Records of Tennyson, Ruskin and Browning*. 2nd ed., London, 1893.

ROBINSON, Henry Crabb. *Diary, Reminiscences, and Correspondence of Henry Crabb Robinson, Barrister-at-Law, F.S.A.*, ed. Thomas Sadler. 3 vols, London, 1869.

ROBINSON, Henry Crabb. *Henry Crabb Robinson on Books and their Writers*, ed. Edith J. Morley. 3 vols, London, 1938.

ROSSETTI, Dante Gabriel. *The Collected Works of Dante Gabriel Rossetti*, ed. William Michael Rossetti. 2 vols, London, 1886.

ROSSETTI, Dante Gabriel. *The Works of Dante Gabriel Rossetti*, ed. William M. Rossetti. Revised and enlarged ed., London, 1911.

ROSSETTI, Dante Gabriel. *Dante Gabriel Rossetti: His Family-Letters, with a Memoir by William Michael Rossetti.* 2 vols, London, 1895.

ROSSETTI, Dante Gabriel. *Letters of Dante Gabriel Rossetti*, ed. Oswald Doughty and John Robert Wahl. 4 vols, London, 1965-67.

ROSSETTI, William Michael (comp.) *Rossetti Papers 1862 to 1870.* London, 1903.

ROSSETTI, William Michael. *The Diary of W.M. Rossetti, 1870-1873*, ed. Odette Bornand. Oxford, 1977.

ROSSETTI, William Michael. *Selected Letters of William Michael Rossetti*, edited by Roger W. Peattie. University Park (Pennsylvania) and London, 1990.

ROTHSCHILD. *A Century of Finance, 1804 to 1904: The London House of Rothschild.* London, 1905.

ROZOV, Zoja. 'Denis Davydov and Walter Scott.' *Slavonic Year-Book* (vol. XIX of *Slavonic and East European Review*), 1939-1940, pp. 300-2.

RUSSELL, Sir William Howard. *The War: From the Landing at Gallipoli to the Death of Lord Raglan*; by W.H. Russell, correspondent of 'The Times.' London, 1855. [See also below.]

RUSSELL, Sir William Howard. *The War: From the Death of Lord Raglan to the Evacuation of the Crimea; with Additions and Corrections.* London, 1856. (These two volumes jointly became *The British Expedition to the Crimea*, revised ed., 1858, 1877.)

SAFFI, Aurelio. *Ricordi e scritti.* 14 vols, Forlì, 1898-1914.

SALA, George Augustus. *The Life and Adventures of George Augustus Sala, Written by Himself.* 2 vols, London, 1895.

SCHWEIK, Robert C. 'The "Peace or War" Passages in Tennyson's "Maud".' *Notes and Queries*, vol. CCV (n.s. vol. VII), no. 12, December 1960, pp. 457-8.

SCOTT, Richenda C. *Quakers in Russia.* London, 1964.

SCOTT, Sir Walter. *The Journal of Sir Walter Scott*, ed. William Eric Kinloch Anderson. Oxford, 1972.

SELBY, John Millin. *The Thin Red Line of Balaclava.* London, 1970. (Published in New York as *Balaclava: Gentlemen's Battle.*)

SELINCOURT, Ernest de. *Dorothy Wordsworth: A Biography.* Oxford, 1933.

SEWELL, Elizabeth Missing. *The Autobiography of Elizabeth M. Sewell, edited by her niece*, Eleanor L. Sewell. London, New York, etc., 1907.

SHANNON, Edgar F., Jr, and Christopher RICKS. '"The Charge of the Light Brigade": The Creation of a Poem.' In *Studies in Bibliography*, ed. Fredson Bowers, vol. XXXVIII, Charlottesville, 1985, pp. 1-44.

SHANNON, Richard T. *Gladstone and the Bulgarian Agitation, 1876.* 2nd ed., Hassocks (Sussex). 1975.

SHARP, William (ed.) *Sonnets of This Century, Edited and Arranged, with a Critical Introduction on the Sonnet, by William Sharp.* London, 1887.

SHAVER, Chester Linn and Alice C. *Wordsworth's Library: A Catalogue, including a List of Books Housed by Wordsworth for Coleridge from c. 1810 to c. 1830.* New York and London, 1979.

SHAW, Thomas Budge. 'Púshkin, the Russian Poet.' *Blackwood's Edinburgh Magazine*, June-August 1845, vol. LVII, pp. 657-78, vol. LVIII, pp. 28-43, 140-56.

SHEE, William Archer. *My Contemporaries, 1830-1870.* London, 1893.

SHELLEY, Percy Bysshe. *The Complete Poetical Works of Percy Bysshe*

Shelley, ed. Thomas Hutchinson. London, New York and Toronto, 1956 (originally 1905).

SHELLEY, Percy Bysshe. *The Complete Poetical Works of Percy Bysshe Shelley*, ed. Neville Rogers. Vols I-II, London, 1972-75.

SIDNEY, Sir Philip. *The Poems of Sir Philip Sidney*, ed. William A. Ringler, Jr. Oxford, 1962.

SIEMENS, Reynold. *The Wordsworth Collection: A Catalogue; Dove Cottage Papers Facsimiles of the University of Alberta*. Edmonton (Alberta), 1971.

SIM, Frances M. *Robert Browning: Poet and Philosopher 1850-1889*. London, 1923.

SIMMONS, Ernest Joseph. *English Literature and Culture in Russia (1553-1840)*. Harvard Studies in Comparative Literature, vol. XII. Cambridge (Mass.), 1935; reprint 1964.

SIMMONS, Ernest Joseph. 'La Littérature anglaise et Pouchkine.' *Revue de littérature comparée*, 1937, pp. 79-107.

SIMMONS, John S.G. 'H.W. Ludolf and the Printing of his *Grammatica Russica* at Oxford in 1696.' *Oxford Slavonic Papers*, vol. I, 1950, pp. 104-29.

SIMMONS, John S.G., and B.O. UNBEGAUN. 'Slavonic Manuscript Vocabularies in the Bodleian Library.' *Oxford Slavonic Papers*, vol. II, 1951, pp. 119-27.

SINCLAIR, Sir Tollemache. *Audi alteram partem. — Strike, but hear. A Defence of Russia and the Christians of Turkey; including a Sketch of the Eastern Question, from 1686 to September, 1877, with its Best Solution, 'The Reconstruction of the Greek Empire,' and Strictures on their Opponents; with an Original Cartoon of the Turkish Atrocities, a Map of Turkey, and several Caricatures*. Also a separately paginated *Appendix* to the same. London, [1877].

SLINN, E. Warwick. 'The Judgement of Instinct in "Ivàn Ivànovitch".' *Browning Society Notes*, vol. IV, no. 1, March 1974, pp. 3-9.

SMITH, Alexander, and Sydney Thompson DOBELL (called here 'the author of *Balder* and *The Roman*'). *Sonnets on the War*. London, 1855.

SMITH, G.C. Moore. 'Browning. "Ivàn Ivànovitch."' *National Home-Reading Union Magazine*, vol. XVI, no. 9, 7 June 1905, pp. 292-4.

SMITH, Sir Thomas (not actually the author). *Sir Thomas Smithes Voiage and Entertainment in Rushia; with the Tragicall Ends of two Emperors, and one Empresse, within one Moneth during his being there, and the Miraculous Preservation of the now Raigning Emperor, esteemed dead for 18 Yeares...* London, 1605.

SMYTH, Ethel. *Maurice Baring*. London, 1938.

SORENSEN, Fred. '"The Masque of the Muscovites" in *Love's Labour's Lost'.' *Modern Language Notes*, vol. L, December 1935, pp. 499-501.

SOUTHEY, Robert. *The Life and Correspondence of Robert Southey*, edited by his Son, Rev. Charles Cuthbert. 6 vols, London, 1849-50.

SOUTHEY, Robert. *The Complete Poetical Works of Robert Southey, LL.D. (late Poet Laureate), collected by himself*. New ed., New York, 1860. (Based chiefly on the 10-vol. London edition of 1837-38.)

SOUTHEY, Robert. *Southey's Common-Place Book*, edited by his Son-in-Law, John Wood Warter, B.D.. Four series, London, 1849-51.

SOUTHEY, Robert. *Selections from the Letters of Robert Southey, &c., &c., &c.*, edited by his Son-in-Law, John Wood Warter, B.D. 4 vols, London, 1856.

SPENSER, Edmund. *The Poetical Works of Edmund Spenser*, ed. Charles Cowden Clarke. 5 vols, Edinburgh, 1862-65.

STANMORE, Lord. *Sidney Herbert, Lord Herbert of Lea: A Memoir*. 2 vols, London, 1906.

STEAD, William Thomas. *Truth about Russia*. London, 1888.

STEEGMULLER, Francis. *Maupassant*. London, 1950.

STEPHEN, Sir Leslie. *Studies of a Biographer*. 4 vols, London, 1898.

STERNE, Laurence. *The Life and Opinions of Tristram Shandy*, ed. James Aiken Work. Indianapolis, 1940 (reprinted 1979).

STEWART, James McG. *Rudyard Kipling: A Bibliographical Catalogue*. Toronto, 1959.

STILLMAN, William James. *The Autobiography of a Journalist*. 2 vols, London, 1901.

STRUVE, Gleb. 'A Russian Traveller in Scotland in 1828: Alexander Turgenev.' *Blackwood's Magazine*, vol. CCLVIII, November 1945, pp. 342-9.

STRUVE, Gleb. 'Russian Friends and Correspondents of Sir Walter Scott.' *Comparative Literature*, vol. II, 1950, pp. 307-26.

STRUVE, Gleb. 'Scott Letters Discovered in Russia.' *Bulletin of the John Rylands Library, Manchester*, vol. XXVIII, no. 2, December 1944, pp. 477-84.

STRUVE, Peter. 'Walter Scott and Russia.' *Slavonic (and East European) Review*, vol. XI, January 1933, pp. 397-410.

SUMNER, Benedict Humphrey. *Russia and the Balkans, 1870-1880*. Hamden and London, 1962 (originally Oxford, 1937).

SUPER, R.H. *Walter Savage Landor: A Biography*. London, 1957.

SWAYNE, George Carless [unsigned]. 'Peace and War: A Dialogue', *Blackwood's Edinburgh Magazine*, vol. LXXVI, November 1854, pp. 589-98; 'Peace and War: Dialogue the Second', ibid., December 1854, pp. 714-30. See also Tlepolemus (i.e. G.C. Swayne), 'Peace and Patriotism: A Letter to Irenaeus', ibid., vol. LXXVII, January 1855, pp. 97-111.

SWINBURNE, Algernon Charles. *Note of an English Republican on the Muscovite Crusade*. London, 1876.

SWINBURNE, Algernon Charles. *Poems and Ballads*. Second series, London, 1878.

SWINBURNE, Algernon Charles [presumed author of a considerable part]. *The Whippingham Papers: A Collection of Contributions in Prose and Verse.*, chiefly by the Author of the 'Romance of Chastisement.' London, 1888.

SWINBURNE, Algernon Charles. 'Recollections of Professor Jowett.' *Nineteenth Century*, vol. XXXIV, December 1893, pp. 912-21.

SWINBURNE, Algernon Charles. *The Ballad of Bulgarie*. London, 1893. [Pirated by Thomas J. Wise with the naive connivance of Edmund Gosse.]

SWINBURNE, Algernon Charles. *A Channel Passage and Other Poems*. London, 1904,

SWINBURNE, Algernon Charles. *The Poems of Algernon Charles Swinburne*, 6 vols, London, 1904.

SWINBURNE, Algernon Charles. *Of Liberty and Loyalty*. Privately printed for T.J. Wise, London, 1909.

SWINBURNE, Algernon Charles. *The Ballade of Truthful Charles, and Other Poems*. Privately printed [for Thomas James Wise], London, 1910.

SWINBURNE, Algernon Charles. *Catalogue of the Library of Algernon Charles Swinburne, Esq. Deceased*. Sotheby, Wilkinson and Hodge, London, 19 June 1916.

SWINBURNE, Algernon Charles. *The Complete Works of Algernon Charles Swinburne*, ed. Sir Edmund Gosse and Thomas James Wise. (Bonchurch edition.) 20 vols, London and New York, 1925-27. [Vol. XVIII is actually *Letters* (1927), vol. XIX Gosse's *Life* of Swinburne (1927), and vol. XX Wise's *Bibliography* (1927).]

SWINBURNE, Algernon Charles. *Lesbia Brandon [with] An Historical and Critical Commentary, being largely a Study (and Elevation) of Swinburne as a Novelist*, ed. Randolph Hughes. London, 1952.

SWINBURNE, Algernon Charles. *New Writings by Swinburne, or Miscellanea nova et curiosa; being a Medley of Poems, Critical Essays, Hoaxes and Burlesques*, ed. Cecil Y. Lang. Syracuse (N.Y.), 1964.

SWINBURNE, Algernon Charles. *The Letters of Algernon Charles Swinburne,* ed. Edmund Gosse and Thomas James Wise. 2 vols, London, 1918.

SWINBURNE, Algernon Charles. *The Letters of Algernon Charles Swinburne, with Some Personal Recollections,* ed. Thomas Hake and Arthur Compton-Rickett. London, 1918.

SWINBURNE, Algernon Charles. *The Swinburne Letters,* ed. Cecil Y. Lang. 6 vols, New Haven (Conn.) and London, 1959-62.

SYMONDS, John Addington. *Letters and Papers of John Addington Symonds,* coll. and ed. Horatio F. Brown. London, 1923.

SYMONS, Arthur. *An Introduction to the Study of Browning.* London, 1886.

T. 'Two Sonnets.' [*On Hearing that the News of the Czar's Death was Applauded in a Theatre* and *On Hearing the Czar's Death called 'A Judgment from God'.*] *Examiner,* 17 March 1855, p. 165.

TAPLIN, Gardner Blake. *The Life of Elizabeth Barrett Browning.* New Haven (Conn.) and London, 1957.

TENNYSON, Alfred, Lord. *The Works of Tennyson, with Notes by the Author,* ed. with Memoir by Hallam, Lord Tennyson. London, 1913.

TENNYSON, Alfred, Lord. *The Poems of Tennyson in Three Volumes; Second Edition Incorporating the Trinity College Manuscripts,* ed. Christopher Ricks. 3 vols, London, 1987. (This clumsily titled but marvellously authoritative work replaces Ricks's earlier convenient one-volume edition of *The Poems of Tennyson,* London, 1969.)

TENNYSON, Alfred, Lord. *The Tennyson Collection, Presented to the University of Virginia in Honor of Edgar Finley Shannon, Jr.* Charlottesville, 1961.

TENNYSON, Alfred, Lord. *The Letters of Alfred Lord Tennyson,* ed. Cecil Y. Lang and Edgar F. Shannon, Jr. 3 vols, Oxford, 1982-90.

TENNYSON, Sir Charles. 'Tennyson Papers. I. Alfred's Father.' *Cornhill Magazine,* vol. CLIII, March 1936, pp. 283-305.

TENNYSON, Sir Charles. *Alfred Tennyson, by his Grandson.* London and New York, 1949.

TENNYSON, Sir Charles. *Stars and Markets.* London, 1957.

TENNYSON, Sir Charles. Letter to the *Times Literary Supplement,* 15 July 1965.

TENNYSON, Sir Charles, and Hope DYSON. *The Tennysons: Background to Genius.* London, 1974.

TENNYSON, Emily, Lady. *The Letters of Emily Lady Tennyson,* ed. and introd. James O. Hoge. University Park (Penn.) and London, 1974.

TENNYSON, Emily, Lady. *Lady Tennyson's Journal,* ed. James O. Hoge. Charlottesville, 1981.

TENNYSON, Hallam, Lord. *Materials for a Life of A.T., Collected for my Children.* 4 vols, privately printed, [1895].

TENNYSON, Hallam, Lord. *Alfred Lord Tennyson: A Memoir, by his Son.* 2 vols, London, 1897. (Used here in preference to the single vol. ed., London, 1899.)

TENNYSON, Hallam, Lord (ed.) *Tennyson and his Friends.* London, 1911.

THACKERAY, William Makepeace. *The Works of William Makepeace Thackeray, with Biographical Introductions by his Daughter Lady Ritchie.* 26 vols, London, 1911.

THOMPSON, E.P. *William Morris: Romantic to Revolutionary.* London, 1955.

THOMSON, James (18th century). *The Poetical Works of James Thomson,* ed. Charles Cowden Clarke. Edinburgh, 1863.

THORNBURY, Walter. *Criss-Cross Journeys.* 2 vols, 1873.

TOLSTOI, Aleksey Konstantinovich. *Sobranie sochinenii v chetyrekh tomakh* [Collected Works]. 4 vols, Moscow, 1963-64.

TOLSTOI, Lev Nikolaevich. *Polnoe sobranie sochinenii* [Complete Works]. 90 vols, Moscow and Leningrad, 1928-58.

TUPPER, Martin Farquhar. *A Batch of War Ballads*. London, 1854.

TUPPER, Martin Farquhar. *Lyrics of the Heart and Mind*. London, 1855.

TURGENEV, Aleksandr Ivanovich. *Pis'ma Aleksandra Ivanovicha Turgeneva k Nikolaiu Ivanovichu Turgenevu. Lettres d'Alexandre Tourgueneff à son frère Nicolas*. Leipzig, 1872.

TURGENEV, Aleksandr Ivanovich. *Arkhiv brat'ev Turgenevykh* [Archives of the Turgenev Brothers], 6th series. *Perepiska Aleksandra Ivanovicha Turgeneva s kn. Petrom Andreevichem Viazemskim* [Correspondence of A.I. Turgenev with Prince P.A. Viazemskii], vol. I: *1814-1833 gody* [1814-33], ed. N.K. Kul'man. Petrograd, 1921.

TURGENEV, Aleksandr Ivanovich. *Khronika russkogo. Dnevniki (1825-1826gg.)* [Chronicle of a Russian; Diaries 1825-26], ed. M.I. Gillel'son. Moscow and Leningrad, 1964.

TURGENEV, Ivan Sergeevich. *Polnoe sobranie sochinenii i pisem* [Complete Works and Letters]. 28 vols, Moscow and Leningrad, 1960-68; *Sochineniia* [Works], 15 vols, *Pis'ma* [Letters], 13 vols. (A second, revised edition is in progress; it is occasionally referred to in this book.)

TURGENEV, Ivan Sergeevich. Ivan Tourguénev. *Nouvelle correspondance inédite*, ed. Alexandre Zviguilsky. 2 vols, Paris, 1971-72.

TURGENEV, Ivan Sergeevich. *Lettres inédites de Tourguénev à Pauline Viardot et à sa famille*, ed. Henri Granjard and Alexandre Zviguilsky. Lausanne, 1972.

TYREE, Donald W. 'A Bibliographical Item on "The Charge of the Light Brigade".' *Tennyson Research Bulletin*, vol. II, no. 2, November 1973, p. 75.

UNBEGAUN, B.O. 'The Language of Muscovite Russia in Oxford Vocabularies.' *Oxford Slavonic Papers*, vol. X, 1962, pp. 46-59.

URQUHART, David. *The War of Ignorance: A Prognostication*. London, 1854.

USOV, Sergei Alekseevich [signed S.U.] 'Mozaika. (Iz starykh zapisnykh knizhek)' [A Mosaic from Old Notebooks]. *Istoricheskii vestnik*, vol. CXXX, December 1912, pp. 1051-2.

VAN DYKE, Henry. *The Poetry of Tennyson*. London, 1890; also 2nd ed., 1892.

VAN DYKE, Henry. *An Introduction to the Poems of Tennyson*. Boston (Mass.) and London, 1903.

VATSURO, V.E., et al. (eds). *A.S. Pushkin v vospominaniiakh sovremennikov*. 2 vols, Moscow, 1985.

VENABLES, Rev. Richard Lister. *Domestic Scenes in Russia: in a Series of Letters Describing a Year's Residence in that Country, Chiefly in the Interior*. 2nd, revised ed., London, 1856 (originally 1839).

VENGEROVA, Zinaida A. 'Robert Brauning i ego poeziia' [Robert Browning and his Poetry (a review of *The Poetical Works*, 16 vols, London, 1888)]. *Vestnik Evropy*, 1893, no. 9, September, pp. 150-87; reprinted in Vengerova's *Literaturnye kharakteristiki*, St Petersburg, 1897, pp. 102-52.

VENGEROVA, Zinaida A. 'Robert Brouning.' In the same author's *Sobranie sochinenii*, vol. I, *Angliiskie pisateli XIX veka* [Nineteenth-Century English Writers, vol. I of Collected Works], St Petersburg, 1913, pp. 103-47. (This article is different from the above.)

VIARDOT, Louis. *Les Jésuites jugés par les rois, les évêques et le Pape; nouvelle histoire de l'ordre, écrite sur les documents originaux. Histoire de Dmitri, étude sur la situation des serfs en Russie*. Paris, 1857.

VIGOR, Jane (formerly Lady Rondeau, formerly Ward, née Goodwin; here unsigned). *Letters from a Lady, who Resided some Years in Russia, to her Friend in England; with Historical Notes* (originally 1775). 2nd ed., London, 1777, which contains also: *Eleven Additional Letters from Russia in the Reign of Peter II, by the late Mrs. Vigor, never before published, with a Preface and Notes.*

VOSSLER, H.A. *With Napoleon in Russia, 1812: The Diary of Lt H.A. Vossler, a Soldier of the Grand Army, 1812-13*, trans. Walter Wallich. London, 1969.

VIAZEMSKII, P.A. *Zapisnye knizhki (1813-1848)* [Notebooks, 1813-48], ed. V.S. Nechaeva. Moscow, 1963.

WADDINGTON, Patrick. 'Turgenev and George Eliot: A Literary Friendship.' *Modern Language Review*, vol. LXVI, no. 4, October 1971, pp. 751-9.

WADDINGTON, Patrick. 'Two Unpublished Letters of Robert Browning to Pauline Viardot-Garcia.' *English Language Notes*, vol. XIII, no. 1, September 1975, pp. 35-7.

WADDINGTON, Patrick. *Turgenev and England*. London and New York, 1980.

WADDINGTON, Patrick. 'Browning and Russia.' *Baylor Browning Interests*, no. 28, Waco, October 1985.

WADDINGTON, Patrick. *Tennyson and Russia*. Lincoln, 1987. (Tennyson Society Monographs, no. 11.)

WADDINGTON, Samuel (ed.) *English Sonnets by Living Writers, Selected and Arranged, with a Note on the History of the 'Sonnet' by Samuel Waddington.* London, 1881; 2nd enlarged ed., 1884.

WALLACE, Sir Donald Mackenzie. *Russia*. London, [1877]. (Also new and enlarged ed., 2 vols, London, 1905.)

WALLER, John O. *A Circle of Friends: The Tennysons and the Lushingtons of Park House*. Columbus, Ohio, 1986.

WALTERS, John Cuming. *Tennyson: Poet, Philosopher, Idealist; Studies of the Life, Work, and Teaching of the Poet Laureate*. London, 1893.

WANLEY, Nathaniel. *The Wonders of the Little World; or, A General and Complete History of Man*. London, 1677.

WARNER, William. *Albions England: A Continued Historie of the same Kingdome, from the Originals of the first Inhabitants thereof...* London, 1602. (Also consulted: *Albions England; the third time corrected and augmented; continuing an History of the same Countrey and Kingdome, from the Originals of the first Inhabitants of the same...* London, 1592.]

WATSON, William. *The Year of Shame*, with an Introduction by the Bishop of Hereford. London and New York, 1897.

WATTS-DUNTON, Clara. 'My Recollections of Swinburne.' *Nineteenth Century and After*, vol. XC, July-December 1921, pp. 219-29 (first part).

WATTS-DUNTON, Clara. *The Home Life of Swinburne*. London, 1922.

WATTS-DUNTON, Walter Theodore. *Old Familiar Faces*. London, 1916.

WEST, Sir Algernon. *Recollections, 1832 to 1886*. 2 vols, London, 1899.

WEST, Miss E. Dickinson. 'One Aspect of Browning's Villains.' *The Browning Society's Papers*, 1881-4, part IV, no. XXI, 27 April 1883, pp. 411-34; see also Monthly Abstract of Proceedings, 15th Meeting, 27 April 1883, pp. 69-73.

WEYGANDT, Ann Matlack. *Kipling's Reading and its Influence on his Poetry*. Philadelphia, 1939.

WHEATCROFT, Andrew. *The Tennyson Album: A Biography in Original Photographs*. London, Boston (Mass.) and Henley, 1980.

WILSON, David Alec. *Carlyle to Threescore-and-Ten (1853-1865)*. London, 1929.

WILSON, David Alec, and David Wilson MacARTHUR. *Carlyle in Old Age (1865-1881)*. London, 1934.

WILSON, Francesca Mary. *Muscovy: Russia through Foreign Eyes, 1553-1900*. London, 1970.

WINTON, James [unsigned, but attributed in British Library copy]. *Bonaparte's Journey to Moscow. (In the Manner of John Gilpin.)* London, [1813].

Wise Exhibition. *Various Extraordinary Books Procured by Thomas J. Wise, and now Displayed on All Fools Day in Observance of the Centenary of his Birth.* (Catalogue of the Exhibition.) Harry Ransom Humanities Research Center, The University of Texas at Austin, 1 April 1959.

WISE, Thomas James. *A Bibliographical List of the Scarcer Works and Uncollected Writings of A.C. Swinburne.* Privately printed, London, 1897. (Earlier published as an appendix to vol. II of W. Robertson Nicoll and T.J. Wise's *Literary Anecdotes of the Nineteenth Century: Contributions towards a Literary History of the Period,* 2 vols, London, 1895-96.)

WISE, Thomas James [unsigned]. *A Bibliography of the Writings of Alfred, Lord Tennyson.* 2 vols, privately printed, London, 1908.

WISE, Thomas James. *A Bibliography of the Writings in Prose and Verse of Algernon Charles Swinburne.* 2 vols, privately printed, London, 1919-20; reprinted 1966. (Also published as vol. XX of the Bonchurch edition of Swinburne's works.)

WISE, Thomas James. *A Swinburne Library: A Catalogue of Printed Books, Manuscripts and Autograph Letters by Algernon Charles Swinburne.* Privately printed, London, 1925. (See also vol. XX of the Bonchurch edition of Swinburne.)

WISE, Thomas James. *The Ashley Library: A Catalogue of Printed Books, Manuscripts and Autograph Letters Collected by Thomas James Wise.* 11 vols, privately printed, London, 1922-36.

WOLF, Lucien. *Sir Moses Montefiore: A Centennial Biography.* London, 1884.

WOLFE, Edward Lester. 'Browning's "Dramatic Idyls, First and Second Series": A Critical Text with Annotations and Introduction.' Unpublished PhD thesis, University of Pennsylvania, 1968.

WOODHAM-SMITH, Cecil Blanche. *The Reason Why.* London, 1953.

WOOLFORD, John (ed.) *Sale Catalogues of the Libraries of Eminent Persons.* Vol. VI, London, 1972.

WOOLFORD, John. 'Dramatic Idyls: The Case-Law of Extremity.' *Browning Society Notes,* vol. VI, no. 2, July 1976, pp. 18-28.

WORDSWORTH, Christopher. *Memoirs of William Wordsworth, Poet-Laureate, D.C.L.* 2 vols, London, 1851.

WORDSWORTH, Dorothy. *Journals of Dorothy Wordsworth,* ed. Ernest de Selincourt. 2 vols, London, 1941.

WORDSWORTH, William. *The Poetical Works of William Wordsworth,* ed. William Knight. 11 vols (Works, vols I-VIII; Life, vols IX-XI), Edinburgh, 1882-89.

WORDSWORTH, William. *The Poetical Works of William Wordsworth,* ed. Ernest de Selincourt and Helen Darbishire. 5 vols, Oxford, 1940-49; revised ed., Oxford, 1952-59.

WORDSWORTH, William. *The Prelude; or, Growth of a Poet's Mind,* ed. Ernest de Selincourt. Oxford, 1926.

WORDSWORTH, William. Poems, in Two Volumes, *and Other Poems, 1800-1807, by William Wordsworth,* ed. Jared Curtis. Ithaca, 1983. (A volume in the series The Cornell Wordsworth.)

WORDSWORTH, William. Peter Bell *by William Wordsworth,* ed. John E. Jordan. Ithaca and London, 1985. (A volume in the series The Cornell Wordsworth.)

WORDSWORTH, William. *The Fourteen-Book* Prelude *by William Wordsworth,* ed. W.J.B. Owen. Ithaca and London, 1985. (A volume in the series The Cornell Wordsworth.)

WORDSWORTH, William. *Shorter Poems, 1807-1820, by William Words-*

worth, ed. Carl H. Ketcham. Ithaca and London, 1989. (A volume in the series The Cornell Wordsworth.)

WORDSWORTH, William. *The Prose Works of William Wordsworth, for the first time collected, with Additions from Unpublished Manuscripts*, ed. Rev. Alexander B. Grosart. 3 vols, London, 1876.

WORDSWORTH, William. *The Prose Works of William Wordsworth*, ed. W.J.B. Owen and Jane Worthington Smyser. 3 vols, Oxford, 1974.

WORDSWORTH, William and Dorothy. *The Letters of William and Dorothy Wordsworth*, ed. Ernest de Selincourt:

> *The Early Letters of William and Dorothy Wordsworth, 1787-1805*. Oxford, 1935.
>
> *The Letters of William and Dorothy Wordsworth: The Middle Years, 1806-1820*. 2 vols (1806-1811; 1811-1820), Oxford, 1937.
>
> *The Letters of William and Dorothy Wordsworth: The Later Years, 1821-1850*. 3 vols (1821-30; 1831-40; 1841-50), Oxford, 1939.

WORDSWORTH, William and Dorothy. *The Letters of William and Dorothy Wordsworth*, arranged and edited by the late Ernest de Selincourt. 2nd ed., revised and in some cases enlarged by various editors. The titles of the volumes in this series are so confusing that they are referred to in my notes by their year of publication, as follows:

> Wordsworth, *Letters*, 1967=vol. I: *The Early Years 1787-1805*, ed. Chester L. Shaver. Oxford, 1967;
>
> Wordsworth, *Letters*, 1969=vol. II: *The Middle Years*; part I: *1806-1811*, ed. Mary Moorman. Oxford, 1969;
>
> Wordsworth, *Letters*, 1970=vol. III: *The Middle Years*, part II: *1812-1820*, ed. Mary Moorman and Alan G. Hill. Oxford, 1970;
>
> Wordsworth, *Letters*, 1978=vol. IV: *The Later Years*, part I: *1821-1828*, ed. Alan G. Hill. Oxford, 1978 [N.B. this volume was incorrectly numbered III];
>
> Wordsworth, *Letters*, 1979=vol. V: *The Later Years*, part II: *1829-1834*, ed. Alan G. Hill. Oxford, 1979;
>
> Wordsworth, *Letters*, 1982=vol. VI: *The Later Years*, part III: *1835-1839*, ed. Alan G. Hill. Oxford, 1982;
>
> Wordsworth, *Letters*, 1988=vol. VII: *The Later Years*, part IV: *1840-1853*, ed. Alan G. Hill. Oxford, 1988.

YOUNG, Julian Charles. *A Memoir of Charles Mayne Young, Tragedian, with Extracts from his Son's Journal*. London and New York, 1871.

YOUNG, Roland A. 'Miscellaneous Letters of Robert Browning.' Unpublished MA thesis, Baylor University, Waco, Texas, 1933.

ZAMOYSKA, Priscilla, Countess. *Arch Intriguer: A Biography of Dorothea de Lieven*. London, 1957.

ŽEKULIN, Nicholas G. 'Turgenev's *Króket v Vindzore* ('Croquet at Windsor').' *New Zealand Slavonic Journal*, 1983, pp. 85-103.

APPENDIX ONE

William Wordsworth, *The Russian Fugitive*

<u>PART I</u>

ENOUGH of rose-bud lips, and eyes
   Like harebells bathed in dew,
Of cheek that with carnation vies,
   And veins of violet hue;
Earth wants not beauty that may scorn   5
   A likening to frail flowers;
Yea, to the stars, if they were born
   For seasons and for hours.

Through Moscow's gates, with gold unbarred,
   Stepped One at dead of night,   10
Whom such high beauty could not guard
   From meditated blight;
By stealth she passed, and fled as fast
   As doth the hunted fawn,
Nor stopped, till in the dappling east   15
   Appeared unwelcome dawn.

Seven days she lurked in brake and field,
   Seven nights her course renewed,
Sustained by what her scrip might yield,
   Or berries of the wood;   20
At length, in darkness travelling on,
   When lowly doors were shut,
The haven of her hope she won,
   Her Foster-mother's hut.

'To put your love to dangerous proof   25
   I come,' said she, 'from far;
For I have left my Father's roof,
   In terror of the Czar.'
No answer did the Matron give,
   No second look she cast,   30
But hung upon the Fugitive,
   Embracing and embraced.

She led the Lady to a seat
   Beside the glimmering fire,
Bathed duteously her wayworn feet,   35
   Prevented each desire:—
The cricket chirped, the house-dog dozed,
   And on that simple bed,
Where she in childhood had reposed,
   Now rests her weary head.   40

When she, whose couch had been the sod,
   Whose curtain pine or thorn,
Had breathed a sigh of thanks to God,
   Who comforts the forlorn;
While over her the Matron bent   45
   Sleep.sealed her eyes, and stole
Feeling from limbs with travel spent,
   And trouble from the soul.

Refreshed, the Wanderer rose at morn,
   And soon again was dight   50
In those unworthy vestments worn
   Through long and perilous flight;
And 'O beloved Nurse,' she said,
   'My thanks with silent tears
Have unto Heaven and You been paid: 55
   Now listen to my fears!

'Have you forgot' — and here she smiled —
   'The babbling flatteries
You lavished on me when a child
   Disporting round your knees?   60
I was your lambkin, and your bird,
   Your star, your gem, your flower;
Light words, that were more lightly heard
   In many a cloudless hour!

'The blossom you so fondly praised   65
   Is come to bitter fruit;
A mighty One upon me gazed;
   I spurned his lawless suit,
And must be hidden from his wrath:
   You, Foster-father dear,   70
Will guide me in my forward path;
   I may not tarry here!

'I cannot bring to utter woe
   Your proved fidelity.' —
'Dear child, sweet Mistress, say not so!   75
   For you we both would die.'
'Nay, nay, I come with semblance feigned
   And cheek embrowned by art;
Yet, being inwardly unstained,
   With courage will depart.'   80

'But whither would you, could you, flee?
  A poor Man's counsel take;
The Holy Virgin gives to me
  A thought for your dear sake;
Rest, shielded by our Lady's grace,   85
  And soon shall you be led
Forth to a safe abiding-place,
  Where never foot doth tread.'

PART II

THE dwelling of this faithful pair
  In a straggling village stood,   90
For One who breathed unquiet air
  A dangerous neighbourhood;
But wide around lay forest ground
  With thickets rough and blind;
And pine-trees made a heavy shade   95
  Impervious to the wind.

And there, sequestered from the sight,
  Was spread a treacherous swamp,
On which the noonday sun shed light
  As from a lonely lamp;   100
And midway in the unsafe morass,
  A single Island rose
Of firm dry ground, with healthful grass
  Adorned, and shady boughs.

The Woodman knew, for such the craft   105
  This Russian vassal plied,
That never fowler's gun, nor shaft
  Of archer, there was tried;
A sanctuary seemed the spot
  From an intrusion free;   110
And there he planned an artful Cot
  For perfect secrecy.

With earnest pains unchecked by dread
  Of Power's far-stretching hand,
The bold good Man his labour sped   115
  At Nature's pure command;
Heart-soothed, and busy as a wren,
  While, in a hollow nook,
She moulds her sight-eluding den
  Above a murmuring brook.   120

His task accomplished to his mind,
  The twain ere break of day
Creep forth, and through the forest wind
  Their solitary way;
Few words they speak, nor dare to slack   125
  Their pace from mile to mile,
Till they have crossed the quaking marsh,
  And reached the lonely Isle.

The sun above the pine-trees showed
   A bright and cheerful face;   130
And Ina looked for her abode,
   The promised hiding-place;
She sought in vain, the Woodman smiled;
   No threshold could be seen,
Nor roof, nor window; — all seemed wild   135
   As it had ever been.

Advancing, you might guess an hour,
   The front with such nice care
Is masked, 'if house it be or bower,'
   But in they entered are;   140
As shaggy as were wall and roof
   With branches intertwined,
So smooth was all within, air-proof,
   And delicately lined:

And hearth was there, and maple dish,   145
   And cups in seemly rows,
And couch — all ready to a wish
   For nurture or repose;
And Heaven doth to her virtue grant
   That there she may abide   150
In solitude, with every want
   By cautious love supplied.

No queen before a shouting crowd
   Led on in bridal state,
E'er struggled with a heart so proud,   155
   Entering her palace gate;
Rejoiced to bid the world farewell,
   No saintly anchoress
E'er took possession of her cell
   With deeper thankfulness.   160

'Father of all, upon thy care
   And mercy am I thrown;
Be thou my safeguard!' — such her prayer
   When she was left alone,
Kneeling amid the wilderness   165
   When joy had passed away,
And smiles, fond efforts of distress
   To hide what they betray!

The prayer is heard, the Saints have seen,
   Diffused through form and face,   170
Resolves devotedly serene;
   That monumental grace
Of Faith, which doth all passions tame
   That Reason *should* control;
And shows in the untrembling frame   175
   A statue of the soul.

<u>*PART III*</u>

'Tis sung in ancient minstrelsy
   That Phœbus wont to wear
The leaves of any pleasant tree
   Around his golden hair;   180
Till Daphne, desperate with pursuit
   Of his imperious love,
At her own prayer transformed, took root,
   A laurel in the grove.

Then did the Penitent adorn   185
   His brow with laurel green;
And 'mid his bright locks never shorn
   No meaner leaf was seen;
And poets sage, through every age,
   About their temples wound   190
The bay; and conquerors thanked the Gods,
   With laurel chaplets crowned.

Into the mists of fabling Time
   So far runs back the praise
Of Beauty, that disdains to climb   195
   Along forbidden ways;
That scorns temptation; power defies
   Where mutual love is not;
And to the tomb for rescue flies
   When life would be a blot.   200

To this fair Votaress a fate
   More mild doth Heaven ordain
Upon her Island desolate;
   And words, not breathed in vain,
Might tell what intercourse she found,   205
   Her silence to endear;
What birds she tamed, what flowers the ground
   Sent forth her peace to cheer.

To one mute Presence, above all,
   Her soothed affections clung,   210
A picture on the cabin wall
   By Russian usage hung —
The Mother-maid, whose countenance bright
   With love abridged the day;
And, communed with by taper light,   215
   Chased spectral fears away.

And oft, as either Guardian came,
   The joy in that retreat
Might any common friendship shame,
   So high their hearts would beat;   220
And to the lone Recluse, whate'er
   They brought, each visiting
Was like the crowding of the year
   With a new burst of spring.

But, when she of her Parents thought,   225
 The pang was hard to bear;
And, if with all things not enwrought,
 That trouble still is near.
Before her flight she had not dared
 Their constancy to prove,   230
Too much the heroic Daughter feared
 The weakness of their love.

Dark is the past to them, and dark
 The future still must be,
Till pitying Saints conduct her bark   235
 Into a safer sea —
Or gentle Nature close her eyes,
 And set her Spirit free
From the altar of this sacrifice,
 In vestal purity.   240

Yet, when above the forest-glooms
 The white swans southward passed,
High as the pitch of their swift plumes
 Her fancy rode the blast;
And bore her toward the fields of France, 245
 Her Father's native land,
To mingle in the rustic dance,
 The happiest of the band!

Of those belovèd fields she oft
 Had heard her Father tell   250
In phrase that now with echoes soft
 Haunted her lonely cell;
She saw the hereditary bowers,
 She heard the ancestral stream;
The Kremlin and its haughty towers   255
 Forgotten like a dream!

PART IV

THE ever-changing Moon had traced
 Twelve times her monthly round,
When through the unfrequented Waste
 Was heard a startling sound;   260
A shout thrice sent from one who chased
 At speed a wounded deer,
Bounding through branches interlaced,
 And where the wood was clear.

The fainting creature took the marsh,   265
 And toward the Island fled,
While plovers screamed with tumult harsh
 Above his antlered head;
This, Ina saw; and, pale with fear,
 Shrunk to her citadel;   270
The desperate deer rushed on, and near
 The tangled covert fell.

Across the marsh, the game in view,
   The Hunter followed fast,
Nor paused, till o'er the stag he blew   275
   A death-proclaiming blast;
Then, resting on her upright mind,
   Came forth the Maid — 'In me
Behold,' she said, 'a stricken Hind
   Pursued by destiny!   280

'From your deportment, Sir! I deem
   That you have worn a sword,
And will not hold in light esteem
   A suffering woman's word;
There is my covert, there perchance   285
   I might have lain concealed,
My fortunes hid, my countenance
   Not even to you revealed.

'Tears might be shed, and I might pray,
   Crouching and terrified,   290
That what has been unveiled to-day,
   You would in mystery hide;
But I will not defile with dust
   The knee that bends to adore
The God in heaven; — attend, be just;   295
   This ask I, and no more!

'I speak not of the winter's cold
   For summer's heat exchanged,
While I have lodged in this rough hold,
   From social life estranged;   300
Nor yet of trouble and alarms:
   High Heaven is my defence;
And every season has soft arms
   For injured Innocence.

'From Moscow to the Wilderness   305
   It was my choice to come,
Lest virtue should be harbourless,
   And honour want a home;
And happy were I, if the Czar
   Retain his lawless will,   310
To end life here like this poor deer,
   Or a lamb on a green hill.'

'Are you the Maid,' the Stranger cried,
   'From Gallic parents sprung,
Whose vanishing was rumoured wide,   315
   Sad theme for every tongue;
Who foiled an Emperor's eager quest?
   You, Lady, forced to wear
These rude habiliments, and rest
   Your head in this dark lair!'   320

But wonder, pity, soon were quelled;
   And in her face and mien
The soul's pure brightness he beheld
   Without a veil between:
He loved, he hoped, — a holy flame   325
   Kindled 'mid rapturous tears;
The passion of a moment came
   As on the wings of years.

'Such bounty is no gift of chance,'
   Exclaimed he: 'righteous Heaven,   330
Preparing your deliverance,
   To me the charge hath given.
The Czar full oft in words and deeds
   Is stormy and self-willed;
But, when the Lady Catherine pleads,   335
   His violence is stilled.

'Leave open to my wish the course,
   And I to her will go;
From that humane and heavenly source
   Good, only good, can flow.'   340
Faint sanction given, the Cavalier
   Was eager to depart,
Though question followed question, dear
   To the Maiden's filial heart.

Light was his step, — his hopes, more light, 345
   Kept pace with his desires;
And the fifth morning gave him sight
   Of Moscow's glittering spires.
He sued:— heart-smitten by the wrong,
   To the lorn Fugitive   350
The Emperor sent a pledge as strong
   As sovereign power could give.

0 more than mighty change! If e'er
   Amazement rose to pain,
And joy's excess produced a fear   355
   Of something void and vain;
'Twas when the Parents, who had mourned
   So long the lost as dead,
Beheld their only Child returned
   The household floor to tread.   360

Soon gratitude gave way to love
   Within the Maiden's breast;
Delivered and Deliverer move
   In bridal garments drest;
Meek Catherine had her own reward;   365
   The Czar bestowed a dower;
And universal Moscow shared
   The triumph of that hour.

Flowers strewed the ground; the nuptial feast
   Was held with costly state; 370
And there, 'mid many a noble guest,
   The Foster-parents sate;
Encouraged by the imperial eye,
   They shrank not into shade;
Great was their bliss, the honour high 375
   To them and nature paid!

APPENDIX TWO

Robert Browning, *Ivàn Ivànovitch*

'THEY tell me, your carpenters,' quoth I to my friend the Russ,
'Make a simple hatchet serve as a tool-box serves with us.
Arm but each man with his axe, 'tis a hammer and saw and plane
And chisel, and — what know I else? We should imitate in vain
The mastery wherewithal, by a flourish of just the adze,   5
He cleaves, clamps, dovetails in, — no need of our nails and brads, —
The manageable pine: 'tis said he could shave himself
With the axe, — so all adroit, now a giant and now an elf,
Does he work and play at once!'
                        Quoth my friend the Russ to me,
'Ay, that and more beside on occasion! It scarce may be   10
You never heard tell a tale told children, time out of mind,
By father and mother and nurse, for a moral that's behind,
Which children quickly seize. If the incident happened at all,
We place it in Peter's time when hearts were great not small,
Germanised, Frenchified. I wager 'tis old to you   15
As the story of Adam and Eve, and possibly quite as true.'

In the deep of our land, 'tis said, a village from out the woods
Emerged on the great main-road 'twixt two great solitudes.
Through forestry right and left, black verst and verst of pine,
From village to village runs the road's long wide bare line.   20
Clearance and clearance break the else-unconquered growth
Of pine and all that breeds and broods there, leaving loth
Man's inch of masterdom, — spot of life, spirt of fire, —
To star the dark and dread, lest light and rule expire
Throughout the monstrous wild, a-hungered to resume   25
Its ancient sway, suck back the world into its womb:
Defrauded by man's craft which clove from North to South
This highway broad and straight e'en from the Neva's mouth
To Moscow's gates of gold. So, spot of life and spirt
Of fire aforesaid, burn, each village death-begirt   30
By wall and wall of pine — unprobed undreamed abyss.

Early one winter morn, in such a village as this,
Snow-whitened everywhere except the middle road
Ice-roughed by track of sledge, there worked by his abode
Ivàn Ivànovitch, the carpenter, employed   35

On a huge shipmast trunk; his axe now trimmed and toyed
With branch and twig, and now some chop athwart the bole
Changed bole to billets, bared at once the sap and soul.
About him, watched the work his neighbours sheepskin-clad;
Each bearded mouth puffed steam, each grey eye twinkled glad   40
To see the sturdy arm which, never stopping play,
Proved strong man's blood still boils, freeze winter as he may.
Sudden, a burst of bells. Out of the road, on edge
Of the hamlet — horse's hoofs galloping. 'How, a sledge?
What's here?' cried all as — in, up to the open space,   45
Workyard and market-ground, folk's common meeting-place, —
Stumbled on, till he fell, in one last bound for life,
A horse: and, at his heels, a sledge held — 'Dmìtri's wife!
Back without Dmìtri too! and children — where are they?
Only a frozen corpse!'
                They drew it forth : then — 'Nay,   50
Not dead, though like to die! Gone hence a month ago:
Home again, this rough jaunt — alone through night and snow —
What can the cause be? Hark — Droug, old horse, how he groans:
His day's done! Chafe away, keep chafing, for she moans:
She's coming to! Give here: see, motherkin, your friends!   55
Cheer up, all safe at home! Warm inside makes amends
For outside cold, — sup quick! Don't look as we were bears!
What is it startles you? What strange adventure stares
Up at us in your face? You know friends — which is which?
I'm Vàssili, he's Sergeì, Ivàn Ivànovitch...'   60

At the word, the woman's eyes, slow-wandering till they neared
The blue eyes o'er the bush of honey-coloured beard,
Took in full light and sense and — torn to rags, some dream
Which hid the naked truth — O loud and long the scream
She gave, as if all power of voice within her throat   65
Poured itself wild away to waste in one dread note!
Then followed gasps and sobs, and then the steady flow
Of kindly tears: the brain was saved, a man might know.
Down fell her face upon the good friend's propping knee;
His broad hands smoothed her head, as fain to brush it free   70
From fancies, swarms that stung like bees unhived. He soothed —
'Loukèria, Loùscha!' — still he, fondling, smoothed and smoothed.
At last her lips formed speech.
                'Ivàn, dear — you indeed!
You, just the same dear you! While I... O intercede,
Sweet Mother, with thy Son Almighty — let his might   75
Bring yesterday once more, undo all done last night!
But this time yesterday, Ivàn, I sat like you,
A child on either knee, and, dearer than the two,
A babe inside my arms, close to my heart — that's lost
In morsels o'er the snow! Father, Son, Holy Ghost,   80
Cannot you bring again my blessed yesterday?'

When no more tears would flow, she told her tale: this way.

'Maybe, a month ago, — was it not? — news came here,
They wanted, deeper down, good workmen fit to rear
A church and roof it in. "We'll go," my husband said: 85

"None understands like me to melt and mould their lead."
So, friends here helped us off — Ivàn, dear, you the first!
How gay we jingled forth, all five — (my heart will burst) —
While Dmìtri shook the reins, urged Droug upon his track!
'Well, soon the month ran out, we just were coming back,   90
When yesterday — behold, the village was on fire!
Fire ran from house to house. What help, as, nigh and nigher,
The flames came furious? "Haste," cried Dmìtri, "men must do
The little good man may: to sledge and in with you,
You and our three! We check the fire by laying flat   95
Each building in its path, — I needs must stay for that, —
But you... no time for talk! Wrap round you every rug,
Cover the couple close, — you'll have the babe to hug.
No care to guide old Droug, he knows his way, by guess,
Once start him on the road: but chirrup, none the less!   100
The snow lies glib as glass and hard as steel, and soon
You'll have rise, fine and full, a marvel of a moon.
Hold straight up, all the same, this lighted twist of pitch!
Once home and with our friend Ivàn Ivànovitch,
All's safe: I have my pay in pouch, all's right with me,   105
So I but find as safe you and our precious three!
Off, Droug!" — because the flames had reached us, and the men
Shouted "But lend a hand, Dmìtri — as good as ten!"
'So, in we bundled — I, and those God gave me once;
Old Droug, that's stiff at first, seemed youthful for the nonce: 110
He understood the case, galloping straight ahead.
Out came the moon: my twist soon dwindled, feebly red
In that unnatural day — yes, daylight, bred between
Moon-light and snow-light, lamped those grotto-depths which screen
Such devils from God's eye. Ah, pines, how straight you grow   115
Nor bend one pitying branch, true breed of brutal snow!
Some undergrowth had served to keep the devils blind
While we escaped outside their border!
                             'Was that — wind?
Anyhow, Droug starts, stops, back go his ears, he snuffs,
Snorts, — never such a snort! then plunges, knows the sough's   120
Only the wind: yet, no — our breath goes up too straight!
Still the low sound, — less low, loud, louder, at a rate
There's no mistaking more! Shall I lean out — look — learn
The truth whatever it be? Pad, pad! At last, I turn —
''Tis the regular pad of the wolves in pursuit of the life in the sledge!   125
An army they are: close packed they press like the thrust of a wedge:
They increase as they hunt: for I see, through the pine-trunks ranged each side,
Slip forth new fiend and fiend, make wider and still more wide
The four-footed steady advance. The foremost — none may pass:
They are elders and lead the line, eye and eye — green-glowing brass!   130
But a long way distant still. Droug, save us! He does his best:
Yet they gain on us, gain, till they reach, — one reaches... How utter the rest?
O that Satan-faced first of the band! How he lolls out the length of his tongue,
How he laughs and lets gleam his white teeth! He is on me, his paws pry among
The wraps and the rugs! O my pair, my twin-pigeons, lie still and seem dead!   135
Stepàn, he shall never have you for a meal, here's your mother instead!
No, he will not be counselled — must cry, poor Stiòpka, so foolish! though first
Of my boy-brood, he was not the best: nay, neighbours have called him the worst:
He was puny, an undersized slip, — a darling to me, all the same!

But little there was to be praised in the boy, and a plenty to blame.   140
I loved him with heart and soul, yes — but, deal him a blow for a fault,
He would sulk for whole days. "Foolish boy! lie still or the villain will vault,
Will snatch you from over my head!" No use! he cries, screams, — who can hold
Fast a boy in a frenzy of fear! It follows — as I foretold!
The Satan-face snatched and snapped: I tugged, I tore — and then   145
His brother too needs must shriek! If one must go, 'tis men
The Tsar needs, so we hear, not ailing boys! Perhaps
My hands relaxed their grasp, got tangled in the wraps:
God, he was gone! I looked: there tumbled the cursed crew,
Each fighting for a share: too busy to pursue!   150
That so far gain at least: Droug, gallop another verst
Or two, or three — God sends we beat them, arrive the first!
A mother who boasts two boys was ever accounted rich:
Some have not a boy: some have, but lose him, — God knows which
Is worse: how pitiful to see your weakling pine   155
And pale and pass away! Strong brats, this pair of mine!

'O misery! for while I settle to what near seems
Content, I am 'ware again of the tramp, and again there gleams —
Point and point — the line, eyes, levelled green brassy fire!
So soon is resumed your chase? Will nothing appease, nought tire   160
The furies? And yet I think — I am certain the race is slack,
And the numbers are nothing like. Not a quarter of the pack!
Feasters and those full-fed are staying behind... Ah why?
We'll sorrow for that too soon! Now, — gallop, reach home, and die,
Nor ever again leave house, to trust our life in the trap   165
For life — we call a sledge! Teriòscha, in my lap!
Yes, I'll lie down upon you, tight — tie you with the strings
Here — of my heart! No fear, this time, your mother flings...
Flings? I flung? Never! But think! — a woman, after all,
Contending with a wolf! Save you I must and shall,   170
Terentiì!
                    'How now? What, you still head the race,
Your eyes and tongue and teeth crave fresh food, Satan-face?
There and there! Plain I struck green fire out! Flash again?
All a poor fist can do to damage eyes proves vain!
My fist — why not crunch that? He is wanton for... O God,   175
Why give this wolf his taste? Common wolves scrape and prod
The earth till out they scratch some corpse — mere putrid flesh!
Why must this glutton leave the faded, choose the fresh?
Terentiì — God, feel! — his neck keeps fast thy bag
Of holy things, saints' bones, this Satan-face will drag   180
Forth, and devour along with him, our Pope declared
The relics were to save from danger!
                              'Spurned, not spared!
'Twas through my arms, crossed arms, he — nuzzling now with snout,
Now ripping, tooth and claw — plucked, pulled Terentiì out,
A prize indeed! I saw — how could I else but see? —   185
My precious one — I bit to hold back — pulled from me!
Up came the others, fell to dancing — did the imps! —
Skipped as they scampered round. There one is grey, and limps:
Who knows but old bad Màrpha, — she always owed me spite
And envied me my births, — skulks out of doors at night   190
And turns into a wolf, and joins the sisterhood,

And laps the youthful life, then slinks from out the wood,
Squats down at door by dawn, spins there demure as erst
— No strength, old crone, — not she! — to crawl forth half a verst!

'Well, I escaped with one: 'twixt one and none there lies   195
The space 'twixt heaven and hell. And see, a rose-light dyes
The endmost snow: 'tis dawn, 'tis day, 'tis safe at home!
We have outwitted you! Ay, monsters, snarl and foam,
Fight each the other fiend, disputing for a share,
Forgetful, in your greed, our finest off we bear,   200
Tough Droug and I, — my babe, my boy that shall be man,
My man that shall be more, do all a hunter can
To trace and follow and find and catch and crucify
Wolves, wolfkins, all your crew! A thousand deaths shall die
The whimperingest cub that ever squeezed the teat!   205
"Take that!" we'll stab you with, — "the tenderness we met
When, wretches, you danced round — not this, thank God — not this!
Hellhounds, we baulk you!"
                         'But — Ah, God above! — Bliss, bliss —
Not the band, no! And yet — yes, for Droug knows him! One —
This only of them all has said "She saves a son!"   210
His fellows disbelieve such luck: but he believes,
He lets them pick the bones, laugh at him in their sleeves:
He off and after us, — one speck, one spot, one ball
Grows bigger, bound on bound, — one wolf as good as all!
Oh but I know the trick! Have at the snaky tongue!   215
That's the right way with wolves! Go, tell your mates I wrung
The panting morsel out, left you to howl your worst!
Now for it — now! Ah me! I know him — thrice-accurst
Satan-face, — him to the end my foe!
                                 'All fight's in vain
This time the green brass points pierce to my very brain   220
I fall — fall as I ought — quite on the babe I guard:
I overspread with flesh the whole of him. Too hard
To die this way, torn piecemeal? Move hence? Not I — one inch!
Gnaw through me, through and through: flat thus I lie nor flinch!
O God, the feel of the fang furrowing my shoulder! — see!
                                                      225
It grinds — it grates the bone. O Kìrill under me,
Could I do more ? Beside he knew wolf's way to win:
I clung, closed round like wax: yet in he wedged and in,
Past my neck, past my breasts, my heart, until… how feels
The onion-bulb your knife parts, pushing through its peels,   230
Till out you scoop its clove wherein lie stalk and leaf
And bloom and seed unborn?
                         'That slew me: yes, in brief,
I died then, dead I lay doubtlessly till Droug stopped
Here, I suppose. I come to life, I find me propped
Thus — how or when or why, — I know not. Tell me, friends,   235
All was a dream: laugh quick and say the nightmare ends!
Soon I shall find my house: 'tis over there: in proof,
Save for that chimney heaped with snow, you'd see the roof
Which holds my three — my two — my one — not one?

                         'Life's mixed

With misery, yet we live — must live. The Satan fixed   240
His face on mine so fast, I took its print as pitch
Takes what it cools beneath. Ivàn Ivànovitch,
'Tis you unharden me, you thaw, disperse the thing!
Only keep looking kind, the horror will not cling.
Your face smooths fast away each print of Satan. Tears   245
— What good they do! Life sweet, and all its after-years,
Ivàn Ivànovitch, I owe you! Yours am I!
May God reward you, dear!'

                  Down she sank. Solemnly
Ivàn rose, raised his axe, — for fitly, as she knelt,
Her head lay: well-apart, each side, her arms hung, — dealt   250
Lightning-swift thunder-strong one blow — no need of more!
Headless she knelt on still: that pine was sound at core
(Neighbours were used to say) — cast-iron-kernelled — which
Taxed for a second stroke Ivàn Ivànovitch.

The man was scant of words as strokes. 'It had to be: 255
I could no other: God it was bade "Act for me!"'
Then stooping, peering round — what is it now he lacks?
A proper strip of bark wherewith to wipe his axe.
Which done, he turns, goes in, closes the door behind.
The others mute remain, watching the blood-snake wind   260
Into a hiding-place among the splinter-heaps.

At length, still mute, all move: one lifts, — from where it steeps
Redder each ruddy rag of pine, — the head: two more
Take up the dripping body: then, mute still as before,
Move in a sort of march, march on till marching ends   265
Opposite to the church; where halting, — who suspends,
By its long hair, the thing, deposits in its place
The piteous head: once more the body shows no trace
Of harm done: there lies whole the Loùscha, maid and wife
And mother, loved until this latest of her life.   270
Then all sit on the bank of snow which bounds a space
Kept free before the porch for judgment: just the place!

Presently all the souls, man, woman, child, which make
The village up, are found assembling for the sake
Of what is to be done. The very Jews are there: 275
A Gipsy troop, though bound with horses for the Fair,
Squats with the rest. Each heart with its conception seethes
And simmers, but no tongue speaks: one may say, — none breathes.
Anon from out the church totters the Pope — the priest —
Hardly alive, so old, a hundred years at least.   280
With him, the Commune's head, a hoary senior too,
Stàrosta, that's his style, — like Equity Judge with you, —
Natural Jurisconsult: then, fenced about with furs,
Pomeschìk, — Lord of the Land, who wields — and none demurs —
A power of life and death. They stoop, survey the corpse.   285

Then, straightened on his staff, the Stàrosta — the thorpe's
Sagaciousest old man — hears what you just have heard,
From Droug's first inrush, all, up to Ivàn's last word

'God bade me act for him: I dared not disobey!'
Silence — the Pomeschìk broke with 'A wild wrong way   290
Of righting wrong — if wrong there were, such wrath to rouse!
Why was not law observed? What article allows
Whoso may please to play the judge, and, judgment dealt,
Play executioner, as promptly as we pelt
To death, without appeal, the vermin whose sole fault   295
Has been — it dared to leave the darkness of its vault,
Intrude upon our day! Too sudden and too rash!
What was this woman's crime? Suppose the church should crash
Down where I stand, your lord: bound are my serfs to dare
Their utmost that I 'scape: yet, if the crashing scare   300
My children, — as you are, — if sons fly, one and all,
Leave father to his fate, — poor cowards though I call
The runaways, I pause before I claim their life
Because they prized it more than mine. I would each wife
Died for her husband's sake, each son to save his sire: 305
'Tis glory, I applaud — scarce duty, I require.
Ivàn Ivànovitch has done a deed that's named
Murder by law and me: who doubts, may speak unblamed!

All turned to the old Pope. 'Ay, children, I am old —
How old, myself have got to know no longer. Rolled   310
Quite round, my orb of life, from infancy to age,
Seems passing back again to youth. A certain stage
At least I reach, or dream I reach, where I discern
Truer truths, laws behold more lawlike than we learn
When first we set our foot to tread the course I trod   315
With man to guide my steps: who leads me now is God.
"Your young men shall see visions:" and in my youth I saw
And paid obedience to man's visionary law:
"Your old men shall dream dreams:" and, in my age, a hand
Conducts me through the cloud round law to where I stand   320
Firm on its base, — know cause, who, before, knew effect.

'The world lies under me: and nowhere I detect
So great a gift as this — God's own — of human life.
"Shall the dead praise thee?" No! "The whole live world is rife,
God, with thy glory," rather! Life then, God's best of gifts,   325
For what shall man exchange? For life — when so he shifts
The weight and turns the scale, lets life for life restore
God's balance, sacrifice the less to gain the more,
Substitute — for low life, another's or his own —
Life large and liker God's who gave it: thus alone   330
May life extinguish life that life may trulier be!
How low this law descends on earth, is not for me
To trace: complexed becomes the simple, intricate
The plain, when I pursue law's winding. 'Tis the straight
Outflow of law I know and name: to law, the fount   335
Fresh from God's footstool, friends, follow while I remount.

'A mother bears a child: perfection is complete
So far in such a birth. Enabled to repeat
The miracle of life, — herself was born so just
A type of womankind, that God sees fit to trust   340

Her with the holy task of giving life in turn.
Crowned by this crowning pride, — how say you, should she spurn
Regality — discrowned, unchilded, by her choice
Of barrenness exchanged for fruit which made rejoice
Creation, though life's self were lost in giving birth   345
To life more fresh and fit to glorify God's earth?
How say you, should the hand God trusted with life's torch
Kindled to light the world — aware of sparks that scorch,
Let fall the same? Forsooth, her flesh a fire-flake stings:
The mother drops the child! Among what monstrous things   350
Shall she be classed? Because of motherhood, each male
Yields to his partner place, sinks proudly in the scale:
His strength owned weakness, wit — folly, and courage — fear,
Beside the female proved male's mistress — only here.
The fox-dam, hunger-pined, will slay the felon sire   355
Who dares assault her whelp: the beaver, stretched on fire,
Will die without a groan: no pang avails to wrest
Her young from where they hide — her sanctuary breast.
What's here then? Answer me, thou dead one, as, I trow,
Standing at God's own bar, he bids thee answer now!   360
Thrice crowned wast thou — each crown of pride, a child — thy charge!
Where are they? Lost? Enough: no need that thou enlarge
On how or why the loss: life left to utter "lost"
Condemns itself beyond appeal. The soldier's post
Guards from the foe's attack the camp he sentinels: 365
That he no traitor proved, this and this only tells —
Over the corpse of him trod foe to foe's success.
Yet — one by one thy crowns torn from thee — thou no less
To scare the world, shame God, — livedst! I hold He saw
The unexampled sin, ordained the novel law,   370
Whereof first instrument was first intelligence
Found loyal here. I hold that, failing human sense,
The very earth had oped, sky fallen, to efface
Humanity's new wrong, motherhood's first disgrace.
Earth oped not, neither fell the sky, for prompt was found   375
A man and man enough, head-sober and heart-sound,
Ready to hear God's voice, resolute to obey.
Ivàn Ivànovitch, I hold, has done, this day,
No otherwise than did, in ages long ago,
Moses when he made known the purport of that flow   380
Of fire athwart the law's twain-tables! I proclaim
Ivàn Ivànovitch God's servant!'

                     At which name
Uprose that creepy whisper from out the crowd, is wont
To swell and surge and sink when fellow-men confront
A punishment that falls on fellow flesh and blood,   385
Appallingly beheld — shudderingly understood,
No less, to be the right, the just, the merciful.
'God's servant!' hissed the crowd.
                     When that Amen grew dull
And died away and left acquittal plain adjudged,
'Amen!' last sighed the lord. 'There's none shall say I grudged   390
Escape from punishment in such a novel case.
Deferring to old age and holy life, — be grace

Granted! say I. No less, scruples might shake a sense
Firmer than I boast mine. Law's law, and evidence
Of breach therein lies plain, — blood-red-bright, — all may see!   39:
Yet all absolve the deed: absolved the deed must be!

'And next — as mercy rules the hour — methinks 'twere well
You signify forthwith its sentence, and dispel
The doubts and fears, I judge, which busy now the head
Law puts a halter round — a halo — you, instead!   40
Ivàn Ivànovitch — what think you he expects
Will follow from his feat? Go, tell him — law protects
Murder, for once: no need he longer keep behind
The Sacred Pictures — where skulks Innocence enshrined,
Or I missay! Go, some! You others, haste and hide   40
The dismal object there: get done, whate'er betide!
So, while the youngers raised the corpse, the elders trooped
Silently to the house: where halting, someone stooped,
Listened beside the door; all there was silent too.
Then they held counsel; then pushed door and, passing through,   41
Stood in the murderer's presence.
                                        Ivàn Ivànovitch
Knelt, building on the floor that Kremlin rare and rich
He deftly cut and carved on lazy winter nights.
Some five young faces watched, breathlessly, as, to rights,
Piece upon piece, he reared the fabric nigh complete.   41
Stèscha, Ivàn's old mother, sat spinning by the heat
Of the oven where his wife Kàtia stood baking bread.
Ivàn's self, as he turned his honey-coloured head,
Was just in act to drop, 'twixt fir-cones, — each a dome, —
The scooped-out yellow gourd presumably the home   42
Of Kolokol the Big: the bell, therein to hitch,
— An acorn-cup — was ready: Ivàn Ivànovitch
Turned with it in his mouth.
                                        They told him he was free
As air to walk abroad. 'How otherwise?' asked he.

INDEX

Note: this Index includes all significant persons and literary works mentioned in the main body of the book, together with a few new or explanatory references to them in the notes section and elsewhere; it does not contain place-names, musical and artistic works, or titles of newspapers and journals.